AN ENTIRELY ORIGINAL, COMPREHENSIVE BOOK

Here's what the experts say about Kaplan's
WINNING CONTRACT BRIDGE COMPLETE:

"Captures what bridge players and students need and
presents it beautifully . . ."
From the Introduction by Samuel M. Stayman

"Kaplan has the rare combination required to produce a
bridge classic of the first magnitude. As a player, he has
won almost every honor in the game. As a writer,
he has been responsible for two major
books. . . . As a bridge teacher of vast experience, he has
acquired deep insights into the right way of presenting
technical ideas to players. . . ."
Alan Truscott, Bridge Editor
The New York Times

WINNING CONTRACT
♠ BRIDGE COMPLETE ♠
♥ BY EDGAR KAPLAN ♥

BANTAM BOOKS
TORONTO · NEW YORK · LONDON

*This low-priced Bantam Book
has been completely reset in a type face
designed for easy reading, and was printed
from new plates. It contains the complete
text of the original hard-cover edition,*
NOT ONE WORD HAS BEEN OMITTED.

WINNING CONTRACT BRIDGE COMPLETE

*A Bantam Book / originally published by
Fleet Publishing Corp.*

PRINTING HISTORY

Fleet edition published February 1964

Bantam edition / February 1965

2nd printing ... October 1966	5th printing ..... August 1971
3rd printing .. September 1968	6th printing ...... June 1972
4th printing .. December 1969	7th printing .... October 1973
	8th printing .... February 1978

Library of Congress Catalog Card Number: 64-15703

ISBN 0-553-11871-4

Published simultaneously in the United States and Canada

PRINTED IN THE UNITED STATES OF AMERICA

Contents

BOOK ONE
THE FUNDAMENTALS

PART 1: BIDDING

PART 2: THE PLAY OF THE CARDS

BOOK TWO
THE FINE POINTS

PART 3: THE PLAY OF THE CARDS

Introduction

By SAMUEL M. STAYMAN

Three-times World Champion and
author of the Stayman Convention

It has been well said that contract bridge is a multiple game, for there are several types of tournament bridge as well as rubber games. Thus, bridge tends to produce experts who stand out in particular departments of the game. Some players develop with outstanding bidding ability; some as superb dummy players or exceptional defenders; a small number are profound scholars, producing new bidding ideas and defenses against others' innovations; and there are also those with unusual teaching ability.

Edgar Kaplan is outstanding in all of these departments of contract bridge. His record of many years as a practical player in all kinds of competition speaks for itself. He is a fine teacher, a partner in the famous Card School in New York; co-author of one of the most popular experts' systems in use today; and his famous book on the Italian Systems has marked him as the outstanding analyst of the defense against the very successful Italian methods.

He was captain and technical coach of the team which represented the United States in the 1964 Bridge Olympiad. As a member of this team, I can tell you what a marvellous choice he was. But possibly his best work is the writing of this great book.

Far from writing "another" bridge book, Edgar Kaplan here captures what bridge players and students need and presents it beautifully. Here they will find a difficult subject made easy to understand and enjoyable to read about.

Kaplan recognizes that the 40,000,000 bridge players in this country are not all devotees of the game; many are only occasional players. When they turn to a book on bridge, they need the fundamentals of the game presented clearly and understandably; thoroughly but not tediously; accurately but not technically. They must be presented with a method they can play in comfort with their friends or even with strangers.

He does the job. Starting with the classic foundation of

Standard American Bidding, and making few and simple changes, he presents a clear and comprehensive point-count system. This, along with a section devoted to basic card play is Book One—The Fundamentals.

The "occasional players" may stop there. But for the devotees, Kaplan goes further. Book Two covers the fine points of this deep and wonderful game. Read in conjunction with the related early chapters, the second book is a cohesive exposition for those who want to become advanced players.

I am delighted and honored to have been given the opportunity to congratulate Mr. Kaplan on this book. With its publication, he places himself even more surely than before among the world's best bridge writers. There is no better book for bridgeurs below the expert class. I am sure that all who read and study it will find the surest road to the pleasures of contract bridge.

Foreword

This work actually consists of two separate books—each with its own sections on bidding and card play. Book One is concerned with fundamentals, with the basic language of bidding and the basic mechanics of play. Book Two deals with fine points—with advanced techniques for planning the play and defense, tactical and exceptional positions in the bidding.

Bridge is not the sort of game which has hard-and-fast rules for proper bidding or play. It abounds in exceptions, and the exceptions to the exceptions have exceptions. It is for this reason that I have written two books here—one to present an uncluttered view of the basics, the other to examine the positions in which you must depart from the normal procedures. Thus, in Book One I will treat how to finesse, while in Book Two I will try to show how to accomplish the same objective without risk. In Book One, long suits are bid ahead of short ones; while in Book Two you may bid the shorter first, or even bid a suit in which you have no great length at all.

Necessarily, there will be contradictions; do not be disturbed by this. A bid or play can be right with an average partner, yet wrong with an expert one. Remember that nothing I (or anyone else) will tell you about bridge is absolutely true.

EDGAR KAPLAN

BOOK ONE

THE FUNDAMENTALS

CHAPTER 1

The Nature of the Game

There are two great families of card games. In one, the objective is to form combinations of cards which have an arbitrary value. In the other family, to which contract bridge belongs, the objective is to win tricks.

Bridge is played by four contestants using a deck of 52 cards. The entire deck is dealt out, so that each player has a hand of 13 cards. A trick consists of four cards played in sequence, one from each of the four hands. The contestant who has played the highest-ranking of the four cards wins the trick.

The **ace** is the highest-ranking card, followed in order by the king, queen, jack, 10, 9, 8, 7, 6, 5, 4, 3, and 2—the lowest-ranking card. Thus, there are thirteen ranks. The deck has four suits—spades, hearts, diamonds, and clubs—each with a complete set of ranks from ace through 2.

• FOLLOWING SUIT

What if two or more cards of identical rank are played to one trick? The first rule of play provides for this: you must **follow suit**. That is, you must play a card of the same suit as the one first played (led) to a trick. If the player to your right leads a spade, you are next to play (tricks are played clockwise around the table) and you must follow suit with a spade. When you cannot follow suit, because you have no cards of the suit led, you may play any card in your hand. But it is the highest card in the first-led suit which wins the trick. For example, if the king of clubs is led to a trick and you, having no clubs, play the ace of hearts, the king wins the trick. Only the ace of clubs beats the king of clubs.

• TRUMPS

However, there is an exception to this. One of the four suits is usually designated as the **trump** suit. Any card in the trump suit ranks higher than even an ace in a plain suit. So if hearts are trump, the 2 of hearts will beat the ace of clubs even when clubs are led. But remember that your first obligation is to follow suit. You may beat a high card with a trump only when you have no card of the suit led.

Bridge is a partnership game. The players facing each other at the table are **partners,** and try together to win more tricks than the opposing partnership. It is just as good for your partner to win a trick as for you to win it—your tricks are kept together and counted together. The only difference it makes which partner wins the trick is that the particular player who wins a trick gains the privilege of leading to the subsequent trick.

• THE GAME OF WHIST

The rules given so far are sufficient to let you play the game of whist, the ancestor of bridge. In whist, one player **deals** out all 52 cards face down, turning up the last card to set the trump suit. The player to **dealer's** left leads to the first trick; whoever wins the first trick leads to the second; and this goes on until all 13 tricks have been played. The partnership winning the majority of tricks scores points— 1 point for each trick more than 6. Seven points wins the game.

• OLD-FASHIONED BRIDGE

In about 1880, the earliest form of bridge was played in London. It differs from whist in two major respects. After the opening lead is made, dealer's partner, known as the **dummy,** places his cards face up on the table and takes no part in the play. Dealer plays both his own hand and the dummy hand. (This greatly increases the accuracy possible in card play, since each player sees two hands instead of one.) The second innovation in bridge is that the dealer or his partner can *name* the trump suit, or may play without a trump suit at all —in **notrump.** Differing values are assigned for the four suits and notrump. Each trick more than 6 won by a partnership counts some number of points (according to the suit) toward winning a game. The partnership which first wins *two* games (wins the **rubber**) scores a considerable bonus.

• AUCTION BRIDGE

By about 1900, this game had developed further, into auction bridge. Here, no player has the sole right to name the trump suit; each player has the privilege of bidding to name it. A bid promises to take a certain number of tricks with a particular suit as trump. The dealer, who bids first, could say "1 heart," which means "I promise to win at least 7 (1 more than 6) tricks with hearts as trump." Any player can then, in turn, make a higher bid. This might be a bid of one in a higher-valued suit, the rank of suits being notrump (highest), spades, hearts, diamonds, clubs (lowest); or, it might be any bid of two—a promise to take 8 (6 plus 2) tricks.

The privilege of bidding passes from the dealer to his left-hand opponent, then to dealer's partner, and so on around and around the table. Each player in his turn can make a higher bid or can say "Pass"—that is, make no bid. A bid followed by passes from the other three contestants closes the auction.

The player who first names his side's eventual trump suit is known as the **declarer**, and his partner becomes the dummy. Declarer must take as many tricks as his bid has promised, or suffer heavy penalties. Should he win more tricks than he has contracted for, his side gets full credit for them.

• CONTRACT BRIDGE

Contract bridge developed from auction bridge in the 1920's, and has today virtually superseded all the earlier games. The rules of card play are the same as in whist; as in old-fashioned bridge, there is a dummy and differing values for notrump and the various suits; there is bidding as in auction bridge. But declarer gets full credit not for all the tricks he takes, *but only for the tricks he bids and then takes*. Thus, accuracy in bidding becomes the single most important element of the game.

• SCORING

In learning to play contract bridge, it is vital to understand how the game is scored, for this affects both bidding and play. Your objective is to score more points than do the opponents. Points are scored in three different ways: (1) by contracting to win tricks and then succeeding in taking them (bidding and **making** a contract), (2) by winning enough tricks to prevent an enemy declarer from making his contract (**setting** a contract), and (3) by earning bonus points.

If you have ever seen a contract bridge score pad, you will have noticed a heavy horizontal line drawn across the paper. Some points are written above this line, some **below the line.** When adding up the total score, all points count equally; but, as we will see shortly, points below the line are especially valuable because they count toward winning a heavy bonus. Let us examine all three methods of winning points, and see where these points are written.

POINTS FOR MAKING A CONTRACT

Whenever you bid and make a contract, you score a number of points depending on how many tricks over 6* you take and on the value of tricks in the trump suit you have selected. It is important to remember this table:

(NT)	Notrump	:	40 points for the first trick over 6
			30 points for each subsequent trick
(♠)	Spades or		
(♡)	Hearts	:	30 points for each trick over 6
(◇)	Diamonds or		
(♣)	Clubs	:	20 points for each trick over 6

Suppose you win the auction with a bid of 2 notrump (you promise to take 8 tricks without benefit of a trump suit); and you win 8 tricks in play. You score 70 points—40 for the first (seventh) trick, 30 for the second. Suppose you bid 4 hearts and take 10 tricks. You score 120 points—30 points for each trick over 6. Suppose you bid 5 diamonds and win 9 tricks. You do *not* score 60 points for taking 3 tricks more than your book. You have been set, since you took 2 tricks fewer than the 11 tricks you contracted for. You are **down two,** and your opponents, not you, score points.

Only points scored by winning the actual number of tricks you contract for are written below the line. And only points below the line count toward winning games and rubbers. A game is 100 points below the line. The partnership which first scores two games wins the rubber and earns a huge bonus.

You do score points for **overtricks**—tricks won in excess of the number you promised to take. But these points, computed on the same scale, are written **above the line** and do not count toward game and rubber. Suppose you bid 2 spades and take 10 tricks. You score 60 points below the line for the

---

* The first 6 tricks which you take as declarer are known as your *book.* It is tricks in excess of your *book* which count toward fulfilling your contract and scoring points.

tricks you bid, and another 60 points above the line for the 2 overtricks. It looks like this:

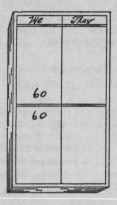

Clearly you would have been much better off to have bid 4 spades instead of 2 spades. Then all 120 points would be scored below the line, and you would have made a game. (As you can work out for yourself, to make game—100 points below the line—in one deal, you must bid 3 notrump, 4 hearts or spades, 5 clubs or diamonds.) In the example above, you have made a **part score** or **partial** instead of a game. Its advantage to you is that on the next hand you need only 40 points below the line (*1* notrump, *2* of any suit) to score a game.

When your side has made one game, you are **vulnerable**. This means that the enemy will score more points if they set you. However, you enjoy being vulnerable, since you need only one more game to win the rubber, and some of your bonuses are increased.

POINTS FOR SETTING A CONTRACT

Whenever your opponents fail to take the tricks they contracted for, your side scores a number of points for each trick they go down. Your score is not affected by the particular trump suit the opponents selected, but only by how many tricks they go down (**undertricks**) and by whether or not *they* are vulnerable. You win:

50 points for each undertrick nonvulnerable
100 points for each undertrick vulnerable

If, while the auction is going on, you are quite sure that the opponents cannot win as many tricks as they have bid, you can say "Double" when it is your turn to bid. When the opponents go down in a doubled contract, you score:

100 points for the first undertrick, 200 for each subsequent undertrick if they are *not vulnerable*
200 points for the first undertrick, 300 for each subsequent undertrick if they are *vulnerable*

However, you double not only their penalty if they go down but also their reward should they make their contract. Two spades doubled and made scores a game—60 doubled is 120. Also, the opponents score a bonus for making a doubled contract and a bonus for overtricks.

What is more, after you double, either opponent has the right to say "Redouble" at his turn to bid. A redoubled contract fulfilled scores *four* times the value of the tricks. However, if a redoubled contract is set the **penalties** are twice as great as those for a doubled contract.

All points for setting the opponents' contracts are written above the line

BONUS POINTS

The most important **bonus** is for winning a rubber, for being the first side to score two games. For this you earn:

700 points if the opponents are nonvulnerable
500 points if the opponents are vulnerable (have scored a game)

We have already mentioned the bonus points for making a contract which the opponents have doubled. You score:

50 points for making a doubled contract
100 points for each overtrick by nonvulnerable declarer
200 points for each overtrick by vulnerable declarer

A redouble multiplies by two the value of overtricks, but does not affect the bonus for making a doubled contract.

A bonus is given for holding in one hand all or almost all of the five highest trumps, known as the **honors**—the ace, king, queen, jack, and 10. You score:

100 points for four of the five trump honors in one hand
150 points for all five trump honors in one hand
150 points for all four aces in one hand—in notrump only

These bonuses, **100 honors** or **150 honors**, are scored regardless of whether the contract is made or set. Honors may be scored by Declarer, by dummy, or by either defender.

There is a substantial bonus for bidding and then making an extremely high contract. A contract of six (12 tricks) is known as a **small slam**; a contract of seven (all 13 tricks) is called a **grand slam**. Obviously, slams are difficult to make, and your enterprise in bidding them is handsomely rewarded (unless you go down):

Small Slam: 500 points (nonvulnerable declarer)
               750 points (vulnerable declarer)
Grand Slam: 1000 points (nonvulnerable declarer)
             1500 points (vulnerable declarer)

Note that it is not enough to *win* 12 or 13 tricks; you must *bid* and make your slam to earn the bonus.

All bonuses are written above the line

Do not be frightened away from contract bridge by its complicated scoring. You do not have to memorize it all, for slams and doubled or redoubled contracts are very rare, and there is usually a scoring table handy. You *do* have to remember the value of tricks bid and made in each suit. And it is well to keep in mind the *relative* value of the common scores—for making a contract, for setting the enemy 1 trick or so undoubled, for winning the rubber.

If you bid 3 diamonds and take 10 tricks, you score 80 points altogether. If you set the opponents 1 trick when they are vulnerable, you get 100 points. But if you win the rubber, you earn a far greater amount—500 or 700 points. The side which wins the rubber bonus almost always outscores its opponents heavily. Therefore, the main emphasis is on scoring below the line, bidding and making games whenever possible.

The huge penalties in doubled and redoubled contracts serve mainly to prevent a player who enjoys being declarer from bidding every time it is his turn. Slams are profitable and exciting, but they are very rare, and provide only some spice to the game. The meat of contract bridge is bidding games and winning rubbers.

• A SAMPLE RUBBER

Let us see how a typical rubber of bridge is played and scored. Four players gather at a bridge table on which are placed two decks of cards with different-colored backs. Each one draws a card, and the two with the highest cards sit as partners against the two with the lowest. Let us call the players **South**, **West**, **North**, and **East** according to their position at the table.

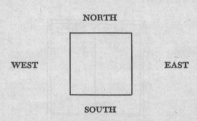

South and North are partners against West and East. South drew the highest card, so he is the dealer of the first hand.

West shuffles one deck of cards and hands them to East for the cut. South deals these cards face down, one at a time, clockwise around the table, starting with West, then to North, to East, to himself, again to West, etc. After all 52 cards are dealt, the players pick up their 13-card hands. South, as dealer, is first to bid.

He has few high cards and does not wish to bid; he says "Pass." West has the next turn; he also passes. Now North: he bids 1 heart. East bids 1 spade (since spades are higher ranking than hearts, he need bid only one to make a higher bid). It is South's turn again, and he bids 2 hearts (hearts are *lower* ranking than spades, so South must bid two). West passes once more. North bids 4 hearts. East passes, South passes, West passes. The auction is over, for a bid has been followed by three consecutive passes. North, who first bid hearts for his side, is declarer and the contract is 4 hearts.

East, the opponent to Declarer's left, is first to play—the

opening leader. He leads the ace of spades, playing it into the center of the table. Now South, Declarer's partner, places his cards, face up and arranged in suits, on the table in front of him. This is the dummy. Declarer reaches over and detaches a spade from the dummy, playing it into the center of the table. Next, West follows suit with a spade. Declarer, North, has no spades in his hand, so he plays the 2 of hearts (trumps) from his own hand, winning the trick. He gathers up the four cards in a neat bundle, and puts them face down in front of him so that he can keep count of the tricks he wins.

North plays first to the second trick, since his hand won the previous trick. Play goes on until all 13 tricks have been played. Declarer's side wins 11 of these, East and West—the **defenders**—only 2. If South is keeping score, he does it like this:

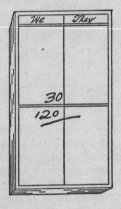

He writes 120 below the line, for 4 hearts bid and made; he writes 30 above the line for the extra (eleventh) trick. He draws a new horizontal line under the 120 to indicate that his side has scored a game (and is now vulnerable).

While South was dealing the first hand, North—dealer's partner—shuffled the second deck and placed it to his right, near West who will deal the next hand. Now West presents this deck to South for the cut, and deals out the second hand. West, as dealer, bids first. The final contract becomes 2 no-trump, with South as declarer. Therefore, West is the opening leader and North the dummy. South takes 9 tricks, one more than he bid, and the score pad now shows:

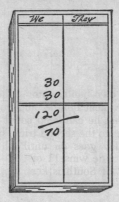

North deals the third hand (East has shuffled the first deck, and West cuts it). West becomes declarer at a contract of 3 notrump, so East is dummy, North the opening leader. Declarer wins 9 tricks, so South's score now shows:

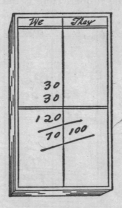

East-West have made a game, so a line is drawn underneath their score. Notice that North-South's part score of 70 is now above the line and no longer will count toward game. The East-West *game* wiped out the North-South *partial*.

West deals the fourth hand. South buys the contract with a bid of 4 spades, and takes 9 tricks to the defenders' 4. He is down one, for he promised to win 10 tricks. "They" score 100 points above the line, since "We" are vulnerable.

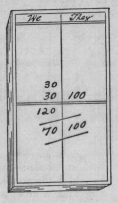

South deals the fifth hand, and East becomes declarer at a contract of 5 diamonds. Declarer takes 12 tricks and makes his side's second game, winning the rubber. "They" receive 100 below the line, 20 above the line, and the big bonus of 500 for winning the rubber. Here is the full score:

A double line is drawn under the **rubber game,** and the scores are totaled. All points—above or below the line—now count equally. "They" win the difference between the scores, 570 points. The players can now draw cards again and start a new rubber.

Have you noticed that "We" lost an opportunity to win the rubber? In the second hand, North-South bid 2 notrump and took 9 tricks, scoring 70 below the line and 30 above. Had the bid been 3 notrump, all 100 points would have gone below the line. "We" would have made the rubber game before "They" even became vulnerable; "We" would have earned a 700-point bonus, and won 950 points instead of losing 570 points. Quite a difference!

In this sample rubber, you can see clearly the overwhelming importance of bidding. North and South won 34 tricks to their opponents' 31; they had the better cards, but they lost because they bid less accurately. North-South bid too high on the fourth hand and too low on the second hand, while their opponents bid both their games. East-West could have done better too, for they *made* a small slam on the last hand but *bid* only game. Had they bid 6 diamonds, they would have earned a 750-point bonus and won a rubber worth 1320 points instead of 570 points.

There are two requisites for good bidding. First, you must know exactly how much your cards are worth. Second, you must learn the language in which you and your partner exchange information, telling each other the *combined* value of your two hands. Then you will be able to determine how high to bid.

Let us see how this is done.

CHAPTER 2

The Value of Your Hand

The deck is dealt out and you pick up your hand, arranging your 13 cards into the four suits so that you can readily see what you have. (You hold your hand well back from the table, for it is uncharitable to expose either opponent to the temptation of peeking at your cards.) Suppose you pick up the ace, king, 9, and 5 of spades; the queen, 7, and 2 of hearts; the 10, 8, and 3 of diamonds; the jack, 6, and 4 of clubs. For convenience, we write the cards down like this:

♠ A K 9 5   ♡ Q 7 2   ◇ 10 8 3   ♣ J 6 4

What should you feel about the strength of this hand? If you examine it very carefully, you will notice that it contains one card of every rank from ace through 2; it is an exactly average hand, and you should be neither pleased nor unhappy on inspecting it. When you have more high cards than low ones, you can be a little proud of your hand; when you have fewer high cards, you are entitled to grumble a bit.

• THE POINT COUNT

Actually, it is too much work to notice each time how many 9's and 7's and 3's you have been dealt. And, in any case, it is the really high cards—aces, kings, queens, jacks—which win most tricks. For all practical purposes, you can count only these **honor cards** in determining the value of your hand. This can be done quite accurately by means of a simple **point-count** method:

Ace	=	4 points
King	=	3 points
Queen	=	2 points
Jack	=	1 point

Each time you pick up your hand, count your points at once. Count 4 for each ace, 3 for each king, 2 for each queen, 1 for each jack; add the points up, and the total is the value of your high cards. If, after the game, you discuss some hand you held, you can refer to it not as "three aces, a king, and a jack" or "an ace and two queens," but as "a 16-point hand" or "an 8-point hand." Now you can sound like a bridge expert.

There are 10 points in each suit; 40 high-card points in the deck. The average hand we saw earlier is worth 10 points—one-quarter of the points in the deck. If each player has a 10-point hand, the high cards are so evenly divided that neither side will be able to make much more than half the tricks. (Actually, such a deal would be passed out—no player would bid, and a new hand would be dealt.) But suppose you pick up a hand like this one:

$$\overset{4}{\spadesuit}\,A\,7\,3 \quad \overset{3\,2}{\heartsuit}\,K\,Q\,10\,7 \quad \overset{4\,2}{\diamondsuit}\,A\,Q\,2 \quad \overset{3\,1}{\clubsuit}\,K\,J\,2$$

Here you have 19 points, 9 points more than average. If the 21 points remaining in the deck are split evenly among the other three players, 7 to each, your side will have a total of 26 points to 14 for the enemy. This will enable you to bid and make a very high contract. Of course, partner may have been dealt a hand worth only 2 or 3 points; then your side will have no substantial advantage. Thus you cannot become too enthusiastic right away. But you are entitled to a warm inner glow on looking at your exciting collection of aces, kings, queens, and jacks.

Next, assume that you are dealt this hand:

$$\overset{3}{\spadesuit}\,K\,10\,3 \quad \heartsuit\,8\,6\,4 \quad \overset{1}{\diamondsuit}\,J\,8\,4\,2 \quad \overset{2}{\clubsuit}\,Q\,9\,3$$

You have a meager total of 6 points, much less than an average count. The odds are that the opponents will be able to win many more tricks than your side, for, unless partner holds much more than his share of the remaining points, your side is outgunned. Your hand is not hopeless (you will hold many worse ones), but it *is* discouraging.

• COUNTING YOUR LONG SUITS

A simple count of the high cards in your hand gives you an immediate indication of your side's prospects for bidding and making a high contract. However, in determining the true value of your cards, there is one additional factor which you must consider—*the possession of long suits*. Compare these two hands:

(a) ♠ K Q 6 3   ♡ K J 4   ◇ A Q 8   ♣ 8 6 4
(b) ♠ K Q 8 6 4 3   ♡ K J 4   ◇ A Q 8   ♣ 6

Each has 15 high-card points, but hand (a) has an even, **balanced distribution** of cards into the four suits, while hand (b) contains a long suit. The 6-card spade suit in hand (b) will almost surely help you to win additional tricks. If you succeed in naming spades as the trump suit, you will be able to win many tricks with your small trumps. Even if the final contract is notrump, your long suit is valuable. After spades have been led two or three times, you will have several cards in that suit left in your hand while no other player will have any—now when you lead, say, the 4 of spades, no one can follow suit and your small card will win a trick.

Therefore, hand (b) is worth more than is hand (a); you must allow for this in valuing your cards. Do so this way:

Add 1 point for each card over four in any suit

Now hand (b) has a value of 17 points—15 for high cards, 1 point each for the fifth and the sixth spade. Hand (a) is worth only the original 15 points, all for high cards. This hand:

$$\spadesuit 1053 \quad \overset{4\ 2}{\heartsuit} \text{A Q} 643 \quad \overset{3\ 1}{\diamondsuit} \text{K J} 7 \quad \overset{2}{\clubsuit} \text{Q} 6$$

has a value of 13 points, including 1 point for the fifth heart. Try counting the points yourself in these examples:

(c) $\spadesuit$ Q J 4 $\heartsuit$ A 10 $\diamondsuit$ K 9 8 4 2 $\clubsuit$ J 6 2
(d) $\spadesuit$ 3 $\heartsuit$ K J 5 $\diamondsuit$ Q 9 $\clubsuit$ A 10 8 7 5 3 2
(e) $\spadesuit$ J 7 4 3 2 $\heartsuit$ K 8 $\diamondsuit$ 9 7 6 4 2 $\clubsuit$ 10

Hand (c) counts to 12 points—11 points in high cards, 1 point for the fifth diamond. Hand (d) has 13 points—10 for the high cards, 3 for the long clubs. Hand (e) is worth 6 points—4 in high cards, 1 point each for the fifth spade and the fifth diamond.

What is the value of a very *short* suit—a void (none of one suit), a **singleton** (only one card of a suit), or a **doubleton** (two cards)? When you first pick up your hand, a short suit is a danger, not an advantage. With alarming frequency, your partner will be long in the suit in which you are short and will want that suit to be trump. If the contract is notrump, the enemy will probably lead your short suit, and you may have to let them win tricks with low cards because you cannot follow suit. Still, if your side plays in a trump suit your shortness in **another** suit will help you win tricks with small trumps. Therefore, as we will see later, you may eventually count extra points for a void, singleton, or doubleton—but only after the bidding has proven it to be valuable.*

• POINTS NEEDED FOR GAME AND SLAM

Now you can count up the total value of your hand. How does this help you in bidding? Any bid you make promises to take at least a majority of the tricks, and, as we have seen, your point count tells you the probability of doing so. For example, if you hold a 7-point hand, 3 points under average, it is unlikely that your side can win more tricks than the enemy; so you will make no bid until your partner shows you considerable strength. In contrast, if you hold a 13-point hand, 3 points over average, the likelihood is that your side can win a majority of the tricks. Therefore, you will make a bid yourself even if partner has been silent.

Thus, your own point count will tell you *whether* or not to bid. But it will not tell you *how high* to bid; it will not answer the question which must always be uppermost in your mind: can your side bid and make a game contract? How many tricks your side can win is determined not by how many points *you* hold, but by the *total* number of points your partnership holds. Your points added to partner's—that is the crucial figure.

The number to remember is 26. If the total of your points and partner's points comes to 26, your side has enough strength to warrant a game bid. Actually, this is true only of the 9-trick game contract in notrump or of the 10-trick game contract in hearts and spades, the major suits. In clubs and diamonds, the minor suits, you must win 11 tricks for game, and this requires additional strength. But for just this reason, your usual game contracts will be 3 notrump, 4 hearts, or 4 spades (they all require the same point count, for it is as difficult to take 9 tricks in notrump as 10 tricks in a suit). Therefore, the figure 26 must be constantly in your mind.

If your hand has a value of 15 points, your prime task in the bidding is to find out whether partner has 11 points. If you hold a 9-point hand, you may contract for game as soon as you discover that partner has 17 points. Even if you hold

---

* Some bridge authorities recommend that you add for shortness instead of for length when valuing your hand initially. Actually, if you count a void 3, a singleton 2, a doubleton 1, and ignore length, you will usually come to the same total as by our method. (When you have a long suit, you must have compensating shortness elsewhere.) But this is a needlessly roundabout method of counting your real values—your long suits.

only 6 points, you do not despair of reaching game so long as it is possible that partner has 20 points. Remember to think in terms of the total of your points and partner's, seeking always to determine whether it can reach the magic number of 26.

There are other magic numbers as well. Here is a complete list:

26 points = Game in notrump or major suit
29 points = Game (11 tricks) in minor suit
33 points = Small Slam (12 tricks)
37 points = Grand Slam (13 tricks)

However, slams are rare and minor-suit games are even rarer. The figure 26 is far and away the most important number in bridge.

Obviously, there is a lot more to bidding than merely valuing your hand. You must learn how to tell partner what this value is; you must understand what partner tells you in return. And, equally important, you must conduct a search for the best trump suit at the same time as you exchange information about point count.

All this starts with the opening bid.

♣ RULES TO REMEMBER

1. Count your high-card points.
2. Add extra points for long suits.
3. Always think: have *we* the 26 points we need for game?

CHAPTER 3

The Opening Bid

To **open the bidding** is to make the first bid of an auction. The dealer has the first opportunity, but he is not compelled to bid—he may say "Pass" if his hand is undistinguished. On rare occasions, all four players will pass in turn; no one will open the bidding. Then the hands are thrown in and there is a new deal.

The player who makes the opening bid does so in the belief that his side can win more tricks than can the opponents, that his partnership has more points than the enemy have. The opening bidder cannot be *certain* of this unless he himself holds more than 20 points. But if bridge players were to wait for this sure thing, they would have to deal and redeal countless times before an auction started; it would be a dull game indeed.

• HOW MANY POINTS TO OPEN?

When your hand is worth considerably more than the average 10 points, the odds favor your side winning a majority of the tricks; and this means that you should open the bidding. The minimum count for an opening bid is 13 points, a king over average.

Almost invariably, you will open the bidding by saying "One" of some suit or notrump. This is true of hands with much more than the 13-point minimum—of 17-point and 20-point hands as well. Remember that even a 20-point powerhouse contains only half the deck's high cards; unless partner has some strength to contribute, you will be hard pressed to win the 7 tricks you need to make your contract of one. As we will see later on, it is *possible* to open with a bid of two or three, but you rarely will. The general rule is:

> Open any hand worth 13 points or more with a bid of one. Do not open any hand worth 12 points or less

Which of these hands qualify for an opening bid?

(1) ♠ A K 4   ♡ J 10 6   ◇ Q 8 3   ♣ K 9 7 5
(2) ♠ K 3   ♡ A 7   ◇ 10 9 4   ♣ A 10 8 7 6 3
(3) ♠ 8 6 3   ♡ 9 2   ◇ 7 4   ♣ A K Q J 10 8

Example (1) is worth 13 points, all in high cards; you should open the bidding. Example (2) has a value of 13 points also—11 points in high cards, 2 points for the long suit; it is worth an opening bid. Example (3) has only 12 points in all, despite the beautiful club suit; do *not* open the bidding with it.

Our minimum count for an opening bid, 13, is half of 26—the key number for bidding game. This is not a coincidence. If the minimum were set at 14 points, for example, you and partner might each fail to open 13-point hands, and thus pass out a deal in which you could make a game. But if you open all 13-point hands, you should never pass out a game. (And if it nonetheless happens, you can have the satisfaction of blaming the disaster on partner.)

• WHICH SUIT TO BID?

Once you determine to open the bidding, you must decide which **one-bid** to make. Let us look at two examples again:

(1) ♠ A K 4 ♡ J 10 6 ◇ Q 8 3 ♣ K 9 7 5
(2) ♠ K 3 ♡ A 7 ◇ 10 9 4 ♣ A 10 8 7 6 3

It is obvious that with hand (2) you should bid 1 club. This promises to take 7 tricks with clubs as trump. It tells partner that you have 13 points or more, and that you suggest clubs as the trump suit. (If clubs are trump, you are sure to win tricks with several low clubs, as well as with your high cards.)

Hand (1), however, does not present such a clear-cut choice of a trump suit. Your spade honors are impressive, but you have no reason to suggest spades as trumps—your ace and king there will almost surely win two tricks at any contract. It is the *number* of cards in a suit, not the quality of the cards, which recommend it as trump. What little preference you have for a trump suit is thus for clubs, your longest suit. So bid 1 club with hand (1), just as with hand (2).

If you are to open 1 club holding only the K 9 7 5, it is obvious that the opening bid must make merely a tentative suggestion as to a trump suit. Partner, at his turn to bid, will suggest a different trump suit unless he has length in yours, and you will never repeat your suggestion when you have only 4-card length. So there is no danger in bidding so short a suit. When your opening bid is made in a really long suit —5 cards, 6 cards, or more—you may indicate your *strong* desire to make this suit trump by bidding it again, by **rebidding** your suit.

The basic rule is to open the bidding in your longest suit. We will see that this principle runs all through bidding in bridge; when you have to choose a suit to bid first, you pick the one in which you have the *most*, not the *highest*, cards. This will not be a 3-card suit (for every hand has a suit longer than that), but there is no harm in bidding a suit of 4 cards.

Often you will have to choose between two suits of equal length. For example, suppose you hold:

♠ K 10 8 6 3   ♡ A Q J 7 3   ◇ K 4   ♣ 5

This 15-point hand must be opened; which suit should be suggested as trump? The fact that your hearts have more honors than your spades does not make hearts superior as a trump suit—it is the *number* of trumps that counts. The better suit will be the one in which partner holds more cards. To discover which suit partner prefers, you must plan to bid *both* hearts and spades—one at your first opportunity, the other at your next.

Convenience dictates which to bid first. If you open 1 heart, your next bid must be 2 spades; now partner would have to bid 3 hearts if he prefers your first suit. But if you open 1 spade, your next bid will be 2 hearts; now partner need not increase the bid with a poor hand—he can pass 2 hearts or return to 2 spades, according to his preference.

Notice how much more comfortable the auction is when you bid spades first. This leads to the second basic rule of bidding (which applies not only to the opening, but to almost all other bidding as well)—with two suits of equal length, bid the *higher-ranking* one first.

So:

1. Bid your longest suit first
2. With equal length, bid the higher-ranking suit first

Observe that there is no mention anywhere of your *strongest* suit. High cards do not determine *whether* or in *what order* you bid suits.

With this hand:

♠ A K Q   ♡ 8 7 4 3 2   ◇ K J 9 8 5   ♣ ——

you should not even consider opening 1 *spade*. The purpose of bidding is not at all to show *where* your points are. You want to tell partner *how many* points you have; and you want to tell partner *how long* your suits are. It is because of the 9 points in spades that you can open the bidding and promise 13 points or more. But you do not want spades to be trumps, so you do not bid them. You open 1 *heart,* bidding first the higher ranking of two equally long suits.

• CHOICE OF 4-CARD SUITS

When you must choose between two 4-card suits to make your opening bid, you can no longer automatically follow the principle of bidding the higher-ranking one first. With two 5-card suits, you are fairly sure that the one partner prefers will make a satisfactory trump; so the basic rule is designed to offer partner a convenient choice between them. But with two 4-card suits, you must worry that neither will be adequate as trump; so your first concern is to bid both suits as cheaply as possible, to keep the auction low.

You must open in a 4-card suit if you have no longer one, but here you are safely at the one-level, with plenty of room to find a different trump. By the time you bid your second suit, you may be much higher. Suppose you hold:

♠ A K 7 2   ♡ 3 2   ◇ 1 0 8 4   ♣ A K 5 3

You open 1 spade (incorrectly, as we will see). Partner bids 2 hearts, you bid 3 clubs. Now you are up at the three-level in your short suit, and this is perilous. How much better it would be to start with 1 *club!* Partner would bid *1* heart, you would bid *1* spade. You may not have found a good trump suit yet, but you are still contracting for only 7 tricks.

The proper technique of opening with two 4-card suits is based on trying to bid both of them at the one-level. This is possible when there is room in between your suits for a bid from partner. Then you start with the *lower* suit. For example, suppose you hold 4 clubs and 4 hearts—diamonds is in between. You start with 1 club, and if partner bids 1 diamond you can bid 1 heart.

However, if your suits are right next to each other in rank, with no suit in between for partner to bid, there is no chance whatever of showing both suits at the one-level. Obey the general rule and open in the higher-ranking suit. For example, with 4 diamonds and 4 hearts, open 1 *heart.* If you were to start with 1 diamond, no response partner can make would allow you to bid *1* heart at your second turn.

Open the *higher* of two 4-card suits *touching in rank*
Open the *lower* of two 4-card suits *separate in rank*

Spades and hearts, hearts and diamonds, diamonds and clubs touch in rank, so you open the higher suit. Spades and clubs, spades and diamonds, hearts and clubs are separate in rank, so you start with the lower suit.

What if you hold *three* 4-card suits? For example:

♠ K J 7 4   ♡ A Q 6 3   ◇ 6   ♣ K 10 8 4

Consideration of the touching suits (spades-hearts) suggests a 1 spade opening; but your separate suits argue for 1 club. So another rule is needed to cover this distribution.

This rule is predicated on the suspicion (usually well grounded, unfortunately) that partner is about to bid your singleton suit. If he should, instead, bid one of your 4-card suits, half your bidding chore is done—you have found your trump. But when he bids your short suit you have a lot of work still to do, and need all the bidding room you can obtain. Therefore, waste no space at all, and start with the suit directly beneath your singleton, right under partner's expected response. In the example above, you open 1 club. If partner responds 1 heart or 1 spade, that is a pleasant surprise. And when partner bids 1 diamond, as you fear he will, you are low as you possibly can be.

With three 4-card suits, open in the one which ranks directly beneath your singleton

If your singleton is in clubs, go around the circle and treat spades as the next suit beneath.

What is your opening bid with these hands?

(a) ♠ 10 6 5   ♡ A K J 7   ◇ K 3   ♣ Q 8 7 2
(b) ♠ A K J   ♡ K 3   ◇ Q J 10 4   ♣ A J 9 2
(c) ♠ Q J 9 3   ♡ A   ◇ Q 10 7 2   ♣ A Q 7 4
(d) ♠ A 9 2   ♡ K 10 7 5 3   ◇ 4   ♣ A K Q 7
(e) ♠ K J 7 2   ♡ Q J 10 3   ◇ A 8 4 2   ♣ 5

(a) Open 1 club, the lower ranking of two separate 4-card suits. Note that the high-card content of the suit is immaterial.

(b) Open 1 diamond, the higher ranking of touching suits.

(c) Open 1 diamond, the suit which ranks beneath your singleton; you hold three 4-card suits.

(d) Open 1 heart. You start with the lower of two separate suits or the suit below the singleton only when choosing between 4-card suits. Bid a 5-card suit ahead of a 4-carder. With a fifth club, you would still start with 1 heart. Only with *four* hearts and *four* clubs do you open 1 club.

(e) If you were to open the bidding with this hand, you would start with 1 spade, the suit "beneath" clubs. However, 11 points is not enough strength for an opening bid—you must pass, for you do not have the required 13 points. Note that you may open with a great deal *more* than this minimum —hand (b), for example, is worth 19 points—but you may not open with less.

• OPENING WITH 1 NOTRUMP

The opening bid of one in a suit has, as we have seen, a very wide range. If you open 1 club, you may have 13 points or 20 points, 4 cards in clubs or 7; but the opening bid of 1 *notrump* is much more precise, both in point count and suit length (distribution).

You will never open 1 notrump when you have a very long suit, 6 cards or more, for then you are anxious to suggest your long suit as trump by bidding it. You will never open 1 notrump when you have a very short suit, a singleton or a void, for then the enemy may take too many tricks in your short suit before you gain the lead. (They lead first, and in *notrump* you cannot stop the run of their suit by trumping when you have no more.)

The ideal distribution for this opening bid is 4 cards of one suit and 3 of each of the others, 4–3–3–3. There are two other distributional patterns which are acceptable, one card away from the ideal (that is, one card is taken from a 3-card suit, leaving a doubleton, and added to another suit). These two patterns are 4–4–3–2 (two 4-card suits, one 3-card suit, one doubleton) and 5–3–3–2 (a 5-card suit, two 3-card suits, one doubleton). Thus, you are allowed to open 1 notrump with a doubleton, but here there is a further requirement: your doubleton must contain a high honor, queen or better. And you may never hold *two* doubletons, and never a *singleton.*

The fact that your distribution is evenly balanced does not mean that your opening bid should be 1 notrump; your strength must be within a narrow range. The point count for this opening is 16, 17, or 18—no more and no less. Neither a 15-point hand nor a 19-point hand may be opened 1 notrump even if the distribution is ideal. The perfect 1 notrump opening bid has 17 points and 4–3–3–3 distribution. You may be only 1 point away from this strength, and only 1 card away from this pattern.

Which of these hands should be opened with 1 notrump?

(1) ♠ K 10 4   ♡ A Q J   ◇ A K J   ♣ Q 9 8 3
(2) ♠ A 7   ♡ K J 6   ◇ Q 10 2   ♣ A Q J 8 4
(3) ♠ A K 7   ♡ K Q 10 5   ◇ 8 3   ♣ A 6 4 3
(4) ♠ A Q   ♡ J 7 6 3 2   ◇ K J   ♣ A J 8 3
(5) ♠ Q J 8 2   ♡ K 3   ◇ Q 9 4   ♣ A K J 4
(6) ♠ 7 4 3 2   ♡ A Q 8   ◇ A Q 7   ♣ K Q 10

(1) You have 20 points, too many for 1 notrump. Open 1 club.

(2) You have 18 points and almost even distribution. Open 1 notrump despite your strong suit.

(3) You have the right strength and pattern, but dare not open 1 notrump with a weak doubleton. Open 1 club, the lower ranking of separate suits.

(4) You have 17 points, but *two* doubletons. Open 1 heart, your longest suit.

(5) You have acceptable count and distribution, with a *strong* doubleton. Open 1 notrump.

(6) You have ideal strength and pattern. Open 1 notrump even though you have no spade honor. It is only in a *doubleton* suit that you require a high honor.

It is never *necessary* to open 1 notrump. If your hand contains a flaw—too many or too few points, improper pattern, a weak doubleton—you can always open in a suit. However, if your hand meets all the requirements you should prefer the 1 notrump opening to any other, for it gives partner a most accurate description of your strength and distribution.

After an opening of 1 notrump, the battle to find your proper contract is half over. But an opening of one in a suit is only the first shot in what may be, as we shall see, a long campaign.

♣ RULES TO REMEMBER

1. Open with 13 points or more. Pass with less.
2. Bid your longest suit first, and the higher ranking first of equally long suits.
3. With two 4-card suits, bid the lower-ranking one first if suits are separated, the higher first if they touch.
4. With three 4-card suits, bid first the one under your singleton.
5. Open 1 notrump with 16 to 18 points, even distribution, and no weak doubleton.

CHAPTER 4

Responding to Partner's Opening Bid

Partner opens the auction with a bid of 1 club. Your right-hand opponent passes, and it is your turn to bid. You hold:

♠ K 8 6 3 ♡ K 9 4 3 ◇ 10 7 5 ♣ 6 5

Should you pass with this weak hand and leave partner in his low contract, or should you "respond" to the opening with a bid of your own? You must respond for two compelling reasons. First, clubs may not be the proper trump suit—partner could easily have only a 4-card club suit, with a 4-card heart or spade suit on the side. Second, and more important, your side may be able to bid and make a game contract—partner could have 20 points to add to your 6 points, and if you pass he will not get the chance to bid again and show you his strength.

We see in the example above the two prime objectives of bidding. You must keep your eye firmly on them at every stage of the auction:

Where to Play? (finding your best trump suit or deciding to play in notrump)

How High to Play? (determining whether the partnership hands contain together enough points for game)

A good trump suit is one with at least 8 cards between the partnership hands; then the opponents have five trumps or fewer, and your side has a pronounced advantage. If you play with a good suit as trump, you will almost always be able to win at least one more trick than you would if you played in notrump. Therefore, you should prefer a 10-trick game contract in spades or hearts to the 9-trick game contract in notrump. However, rather than play in the 11-trick game contracts of 5 diamonds and 5 clubs, you should prefer to play in 3 notrump whenever possible (that is, whenever your side has high cards in the enemy's long suits). Note that it is the rank of a suit and the combined *number* of cards in a suit (not the *quality* of those cards) which determines a good trump. The high cards you hold—in *all* suits—determine not *where* you play but *how high* a contract you reach.

For the favored game contracts—3 notrump or 4 in a major suit—your partnership needs 26 points. Remember to concentrate on the *total* number of points you and partner have together. If partner opens the bidding and you hold 8 points, game is unlikely; but you must make one bid to find out whether partner has 18 points. If you hold 11 points, your prospects are rosy; but you may not bid a game until you are sure that partner has more than 13 or 14 points. If you hold 13 points, game is sure no matter what sort of opening bid partner has; the total must come to 26 points, since he cannot open with less than 13.

The two major objectives of all bidding can be restated simply in two questions:

1. Do your partnership hands contain a total of 8 cards in spades or hearts?
2. Do your two hands contain a total of 26 points?

• RESPONDING TO 1 NOTRUMP

The process of answering these two questions can be seen in its simplest form after partner opens with a bid of 1 notrump. He shows, you will remember, 16 to 18 points with even distribution. Add your assets to his, and you will be able to answer both key questions.

Suppose partner opens 1 notrump and you hold this hand:

    ♠ K 3   ♡ 8 3 2   ◇ 10 8 5 3   ♣ A Q J 9

Where to Play?	The only suits in which you have length are clubs and diamonds—the minors. Since there is little prospect of finding a total of 8 cards in either major suit, you will play at notrump.
How High to Play:	You have 10 points, partner has 16 to 18. Together you have 26 to 28 points. Therefore, you want to be in a game contract.
What to Bid?	Bid 3 notrump. Note that you do *not* bid clubs. There is no reason to show partner where your high cards are—he will see your club honors when you put down your dummy. You must indicate *where* and *how high* to play.

Now, partner opens 1 notrump and you hold:

♠ 10 8 4 ♡ J 3 ◇ A J 7 5 4 ♣ 9 8 5

Your hand is worth 7 points, so the partnership total is 23 to 25 points, not quite enough for a game contract. You will play in a part-score contract. Where? There is no assurance of a good trump suit (for partner may have only two diamonds) and you have nearly balanced distribution; therefore, play in notrump. You should *pass*.

However, the fact that your side cannot have 26 points does not mean that you must automatically pass. You should play your partial contract in a suit if you are sure that you have eight trumps. For example, with:

♠ 8 4 2 ♡ J 8 7 4 3 2 ◇ Q 9 4 ♣ 8

bid 2 hearts over partner's 1 notrump opening. You have 5 points, so there is no chance for game. But you should not want to play in notrump: (1) because you have a singleton, an asset in a suit contract but a serious liability in notrump; (2) because hearts must be a good trump suit, as you have six and partner must have at least two. Partner has no option but to *pass* your 2 heart response. He has already told you all about his hand, and you have added up the *total* partnership values and placed the contract.

If you hold the same distribution with greater strength:

♠ A 4 2 ♡ J 8 7 4 3 2 ◇ K 9 4 ♣ 8

you should bid 4 hearts over 1 notrump. Why? You have 10 points to add to partner's 16 to 18, so together you have enough power for game. You have six hearts to add to partner's two or more, so together you have at least the 8 trumps you require. You know right away both *how high* and *where* to play. Partner must not interpret your 4 heart bid as a powerhouse, and should pass.

As we have seen, partner's 1 notrump opening usually gives you enough information about his strength and distribution to allow you to place the contract immediately. But occasionally you may be in some doubt where or how high to play. For example, if you hold:

♠ K 7 ♡ A Q 8 4 2 ◇ 10 7 ♣ J 9 6 3

you know that the combined point count is sufficient for game, but where? You could bid 3 notrump, but if partner holds 3 or 4 cards in hearts you will have eight trumps, and should play in the preferable major-suit game. Only if he has two hearts should you play in notrump.

With this hand, you skip a level of bidding and jump to 3 hearts. This promises a 5-card suit and is a forcing bid, compelling partner to choose between game in your suit and game in notrump. Remember that you can bid neither 2 hearts (which says "We do not have enough points for game, and I am bidding only because my distribution is unsuited to notrump") nor 4 hearts (which says "We have enough points and surely enough trumps for this suit game but no higher").

In the previous example, you know *how high* but not *where* to place the contract. In the next one, you know *where* but are in doubt as to *how high*.

♠ K 8 4   ♡ Q 9   ◇ K 10 7 4 3   ♣ 10 6 5

After partner's 1 notrump opening, you know that the final contract must be in notrump—there is little prospect of finding a *major*-suit trump fit, and you much prefer to play game in notrump rather than in a *minor* suit. However, are there enough points for game? Adding your 9 points to partner's 16, 17, or 18, you discover that it is possible but not certain that the total comes to 26. You may not pass, since opener could have 18 points; you may not bid 3 notrump, for opener could have 16 points. So you compromise and bid 2 notrump. Partner will go on to game unless he has the bare minimum of 16 points.

The last two auctions we have treated (1 notrump—3 hearts; 1 notrump—2 notrump) are examples of responses that are very common in *all* bidding—the jump and the raise. Whenever partner opens the bidding and you *jump* (bid one more than you have to), you promise enough points for game. Whenever partner opens and you raise (bid two of partner's declaration), you agree on *where* to play and ask partner *how high*.

Let us summarize the responses to 1 notrump in the form of a table of rules (see facing page).

Remember that responder is in control after a 1 notrump opening. If the response is 2 diamonds, for example, opener must pass. He has a magnificent collection of high cards, but responder knows all about them and has nonetheless decided to play a partial. Likewise, if the response is a jump to game, opener must not go adventuring after a slam; responder has bid the full *combined* value of the two hands.

When you want to play in notrump
(You have even distribution)

Pass 1 Notrump: with 0 to 7 points
Bid 2 Notrump: with 8 to 9 points
Bid 3 Notrump: with 10 or more points

When you want to play in a suit
(You have a void or singleton, or a
long major suit)

Bid Two:	with no chance for game (0 to 7 points)
Bid Three:	to let opener choose between suit and notrump game
Bid game in Suit:	if you are sure that you have enough points and trumps

• RESPONDING TO A SUIT BID

When the opening bid is one of a suit instead of 1 notrump, the objectives of bidding—Where to play? How high to play?—are the same. But the search for the answers to these key questions is more difficult. It is impossible for responder to take charge and name the final contract right away, for now he knows much less about opener's strength and distribution. Opener must have at least 13 points, but he could just as well have 20. He must have at least 4-card length in his suit, but he could have 7 cards.

Therefore, responder can no longer bid a game with 10 points (opener might have fewer than 16 points) or pass with 7 points (opener could easily have 19 points or more). A 6-card spade suit in responder's hand could be unsatisfactory as trump, for partner might have a void or singleton; a 2-card heart holding might provide a good trump suit, for opener could have six hearts.

True, when responder has 4 cards in opener's suit he may know immediately where to play, for a good trump suit has been found. But this may be in clubs or diamonds, and then the search for a major suit or notrump must go on. And even when responder has 13 points or more, so that a total of 26 is assured, he cannot know *how high* to play. Opener could have 20 points, and the combined value of 33 points would then indicate a slam, not a game, contract. Clearly responder can never place the contract right over a suit opening bid—more information must be exchanged before the crucial questions can be answered.

When partner opens, your first decision is whether to respond at all. With a nearly worthless hand—0 to 5 points—you must pass, even when you dislike opener's suit. There is virtually no chance for a total of 26 points, and the danger of getting to a higher contract far outweighs the prospect of improving the trump suit. When you have 6 points or more (as you will have most of the time), keep the auction alive by making a bid. Partner may have the 20 points you need for game, and he can show his strength only if you respond and give him a second chance to bid.

> **Never respond to a suit opening with fewer than 6 points**
> **Never pass a suit opening with 6 points or more**

Your first response should indicate your best guess at *where* to play. Most often, you bid your longest suit, suggesting it as trump. With two suits of equal length, bid the higher-ranking one first. Suppose that partner's opening bid is 1 club. What is your response with these hands?

(a) ♠ 7 6 2   ♡ A K Q   ◇ Q 8 6 2   ♣ 7 5 3
(b) ♠ J 6 5 3 2   ♡ 10 4   ◇ K Q 9 8   ♣ 5 2
(c) ♠ A   ♡ Q 8 7 5 3   ◇ A K J 9 4   ♣ 7 3
(d) ♠ J 4 2   ♡ 9 6 3   ◇ Q 10 7 5 3 2   ♣ 8

(a) Bid 1 diamond. Your response does not *insist* that your suit be trumps, it is only a mild suggestion. Often, you will have to suggest a 4-card suit when you have no longer one. But you never have to bid a 3-card suit.

(b) Bid 1 spade, your *longest* suit. In suggesting a trump suit, consider length, not strength.

(c) Bid 1 heart, the higher ranking of equally long suits.

(d) Pass. This hand is worth only 5 points, and so is too weak for any response.

NEW SUITS FORCING

Notice that your first response says very little about *how high* to play. Hands (a), (b), and (c) are worth 11, 7, and

16 points respectively, yet you respond by bidding one of a suit with all three. First, you must search for a trump suit; you will indicate your strength later. You will surely get a chance to show your point count with your second bid, for *opener will not pass your response.* If he has length in your suit, he will raise it; otherwise, he will bid a second suit of his own, or rebid his first suit if it is very long, or bid notrump with even distribution. But he will not pass—he is not allowed to. Whenever you suggest a *new suit* as responder (as distinguished from raising opener's own suit or bidding notrump) *opener must keep the auction alive by making another bid.*

This rule, that responder's change of suit forces opener to bid again, is what allows you to search for a trump suit with safety. You can suggest a 4-card suit as trump without risk, since partner cannot leave you in your response; your suit will become trump only if partner has length there and raises. You can bid *one* of your longest suit even when you know that the partnership has 26 points or more; opener cannot pass. You can make a high bid at your *second* turn, after you learn *where* to play the hand; since partner cannot pass your response (when it is a new suit), there is no danger of staying in too low a contract.

However, this same rule can sharply increase the danger of getting *too high.* Before you respond in a new suit and force opener to bid again, you must consider the *level* to which you are forcing him. Notice the difference between these two auctions:

OPENER	RESPONDER
♠ K 3	♠ Q 8 7 6
♡ A 7 4 2	♡ 8 6
◇ K 8	◇ A 10 7 5 2
♣ Q J 9 5 3	♣ 10 6

1 club	1 diamond
1 heart	1 spade
1 notrump	pass

Opener and responder each bid their two suits—longer first, shorter second. The search for a trump suit is unsuccessful, for neither partner can support the other. Therefore, the partnership plays in notrump.

OPENER	RESPONDER
♠ K 3	♠ Q 8 7 6
♡ Q J 9 5 3	♡ 8 6
◇ K 8	◇ A 10 7 5 2
♣ A 7 4 2	♣ 10 6

1 heart	2 diamonds
3 clubs	3 spades
3 notrump	pass

The description of the first auction applies exactly to this second one. But now the partnership, with a total of 21 points, has reached 3 notrump instead of 1 notrump. What has gone wrong?

The trouble started with the response of 2 *diamonds*. When responder bids a new suit at the two-level, he gives the auction a vigorous push, and the resultant momentum often carries the partnership to a high contract. Remember, opener is not allowed to pass a new-suit response; even if he has length in responder's suit, he must raise to the three-level:

OPENER	RESPONDER
1 spade	2 hearts
3 hearts	

"Three" sounds like an innocuously small number, but it is a contract to take 9 tricks. Therefore, responder must not make this forcing change of suit at the two-level unless he has an average hand or better—10 points or more. This assures a partnership total of 23 or 24 points, enough for safety at the three-level. But with 9 points or fewer, responder *must not bid a new suit at the level of two*. With the previous example hand:

♠ Q 8 7 6   ♡ 8 6   ◇ A 10 7 5 2   ♣ 10 6

responder must not bid 2 diamonds over a 1 heart opening bid, for he does not have the required 10 points. Instead, he should bid 1 spade; to bid a new suit at the *one*-level, the usual 6 points is sufficient. Responder *wants* to suggest diamonds as trumps, but he dares not get so high with such a scrawny hand; so he suggests the only suit which he *is* allowed to bid.

Now, let us change responder's hand to:

♠ 8 6   ♡ 10 6   ◇ A 10 7 5 2   ♣ Q 8 7 6

What is he to do if partner opens the bidding, with 1 heart? Neither suit can be bid at the one-level, and there are too few points to bid two. Yet responder is not allowed to pass the opening bid with his 7 points. He must make the only response possible—1 notrump.

THE 1 NOTRUMP RESPONSE

This bid of 1 notrump is a very common response to a suit opening. Responder should always *prefer* to show a suit (remember, the search for a trump suit is the first order of business). However, he is unable to do so when he has no suit higher in rank than opener's, and has less than 10 points. Then responder is caught between two rules: never *pass* with 6 points or more; never go to the *two*-level in a new suit with 9 points or less. The 1 notrump response is the only escape from this trap.

Here are three hands with which you must respond 1 notrump to partner's opening bid of 1 heart:

(a) ♠ 10 4 2   ♡ 6   ◇ A J 7 4   ♣ J 8 4 3 2
(b) ♠ A Q 7   ♡ 8 6 3   ◇ J 10 6   ♣ Q 8 7 5
(c) ♠ 7 4   ♡ 6 2   ◇ K Q 10 8 7 4   ♣ J 3 2

Observe that two of these examples—(a) and (c)—have the wrong distribution for a notrump bid. Hand (a) has a singleton; hand (c) has a long suit. But the 1 notrump response does *not* indicate a burning desire to play in notrump. You bid it because no other response is possible. For instance, you may not bid 2 diamonds with hand (c) (although you would dearly like to suggest diamonds as trumps), since this would promise 10 points or more and you have a hand worth only 8. Thus, you bid notrump as a substitute for going to the two-level when your hand is weak.

Now let us change the three examples slightly, so that no one of them is a proper 1 notrump response to 1 heart:

(a) ♠ A J 7 4   ♡ 6   ◇ 10 4 2   ♣ J 8 4 3 2
(b) ♠ A Q 7   ♡ 8 6 3   ◇ K 10 6   ♣ Q 8 7 5
(c) ♠ 7 4   ♡ 6 2   ◇ K Q 10 8 7 4   ♣ K 3 2

Hand (a) still has 7 points, but now you need not bid 1 notrump, for you have a spade suit to bid at the one-level.

Hand (b) now has 11 points, so you can go to the two-level and bid 2 clubs. Hand (c) is worth 10 points, and therefore you may now suggest your long diamond suit as trump.

You should always hate to respond 1 notrump, for this bid does not help your partnership to find its best trump suit. Therefore, when you do respond in notrump, you will never have a 4-card suit higher in rank than partner's (for then you could bid a *suit* at the one-level); and you will never have 10 points or more (for then you could bid your suit even at the two-level).

What point count does your 1 notrump response promise? At least 6 points, since otherwise you would pass; not 10 points or more, for then you would certainly be able to bid a suit regardless of level. Therefore, 6 to 9 points. Commit this point range—6 to 9—to memory, for it will crop up again and again in countless bidding situations.

With 6 to 9 points, you have a **minimum response**. Game is possible, but only if opener shows considerable additional strength by making an enthusiastic second bid. With 10 to 12 points, you have a **strong response**. You may bid a new suit at any level, for game is likely (although not certain). Even if partner shows no great extra strength with his second bid, you will make an effort to reach game.

RAISING OPENER'S SUIT

Occasionally, partner will be obligingly enough to open the bidding in a suit in which you have 4 or more cards. For example, suppose partner opens with 1 heart and you hold:

♠ K J 8 2   ♡ 7 5 3 2   ◇ J 9 4   ♣ K 3

A very bad bridge player might respond 1 notrump, to show that he has 6 to 9 points, but it is more important to suggest a trump suit than to show your point count. Therefore, a 1 spade response is preferable to 1 notrump, but just barely. Why suggest *spades* as the trump suit when a good trump suit—hearts—has already been found? There are at least eight hearts in the partnership hands, so the search for a trump suit is over. The proper response is 2 *hearts*, the raise of partner's suit.

This raise is a minimum response, promising the same 6 to 9 points as a 1 notrump response. With fewer than 6 points you can pass; with 10 points or more you must find a stronger bid (such as bidding a new suit and raising at your *second* turn). However, when you are within the prescribed limits the raise is a highly desirable response. It goes a long way toward answering both key questions: Where? How high? If you raise a major suit, opener knows the proper trump suit at once; and he can add his points to your 6-to-9 to determine whether the total comes to 26.

In counting your points for a raise, you must consider a third factor in addition to your high cards and long cards. Now your short side suits—voids, singletons, even doubletons—are valuable. Once you have found a fit in a trump suit, any short side suits will allow you to win extra tricks by trumping. Therefore, *after finding an 8-card trump fit,* add to the previous value of your hand:

1 Point —for each doubleton
2 Points—for each singleton
3 Points—for each void

Suppose you are dealt this hand:

♠ 3   ♡ Q 6 4 2   ◇ 9 7 3   ♣ Q 10 7 5 3

It has a value of 5 points, 4 in high cards and 1 for the fifth club. If partner opens 1 spade, you will pass. But if partner opens 1 *heart,* your hand improves; the singleton spade, which before was a liability, is now an asset worth 2 points. Your total comes to 7 points, so you can raise to 2 hearts. This hand:

♠ Q J 8 7 2   ♡ 6   ◇ K J 9 5 3   ♣ 7 4

is worth 9 points when you pick it up. If partner opens 1 heart or 1 club, it is still worth 9 points. But the instant partner bids spades or diamonds, your strength increases by 3 points—2 for the singleton, 1 for the doubleton. You have 12 points (and your game prospects are bright) where before you had only a minimum responding hand.

To raise partner's suit, then, you must have 6 to 9 points after adding for high cards, length, and shortness. What must you have in the trump suit itself? Any 4 cards constitute magnificent support; here, you do not need honors in the trump suit in order to raise. You are allowed to raise a major suit with only *three* trumps—the major-suit raise makes the auction so simple that you go out of your way to use it. When you raise with 3-card support, you are gambling that partner has 5 cards or more in his first bid suit (as he usually has).

However, to protect yourself against being in a very risky contract when opener has only 4-card length, you must never raise with three *small* trumps. You should have a high honor (ace, king, or queen) for the 3-card raise.

When partner opens 1 spade, raise to 2 spades with either of these hands:

♠ 7 5 3 2   ♡ 9 4   ◇ 8 5   ♣ A J 10 9 6

♠ K 8 4   ♡ 7 3   ◇ 9 4 2   ♣ A 10 8 5 3

Do *not* raise spades with:

♠ 10 7 5   ♡ 8 4   ◇ 7 5 3   ♣ A Q 10 9 6

Bid 1 notrump instead. (You dare not raise with three trumps headed by the *10*; you dare not bid a new suit at the *two*-level with only 7 points.)

While a major-suit raise is highly desirable, since if you find a heart or spade fit you know at once where to play, a raise in clubs or diamonds has a lower priority. A fit found in a minor suit leaves the question of where to play unanswered; you still will want to search for a major suit, or to discover whether to play notrump. Therefore, you do not raise in a minor suit with only three trumps. And sometimes you do not raise immediately even with four trumps or more and a minimum response:

♠ Q 10 6 3   ♡ 8 4   ◇ Q J 9 3   ♣ K 7 5

If partner opens 1 club, do not even consider raising to 2 clubs. And if partner opens 1 diamond, respond *1 spade*, not *2 diamonds*. You have the requirements for a raise, but you should prefer to suggest the major suit as trump before agreeing to play in diamonds. Raise a minor suit only (1) with four trumps or more, and (2) with no major suit to suggest.

TABLE OF MINIMUM RESPONSES

Here is a table listing the possible responses with a minimum (6-to-9-point) hand, in descending order of preference.

1. **Raise spades or hearts**
   (requires any four trumps, or three including a high honor)
2. **Bid a four-card or longer suit at the one-level**
   (longest suit first, higher ranking of equally long suits)

3. **Raise diamonds or clubs**
   (requires four trumps at least)
4. **Bid one notrump**
   (only if none of the first three bids is possible)

Consider this responding hand:

♠ K 7   ♡ K 10 5 2   ◇ 10 8 7 6 4   ♣ 8 3

What would be your response to an opening bid of 1 club? Of 1 diamond? Of 1 heart? Of 1 spade? How many points is your hand worth in each case?

Partner opens 1 club: Respond *1 diamond,* the longer of your two suits. Your 7 points suffice for a new suit bid at the one-level.

Partner opens 1 diamond: Respond *1 heart.* A diamond raise is permissible, but you should prefer to suggest a major suit as trump. Your hand is worth 9 points.

Partner opens 1 heart: Respond *2 hearts.* Here again you have found a fit and can add for your two doubletons to total 9 points. The major-suit raise is your most desirable minimum response.

Partner opens 1 spade: Respond *1 notrump.* You cannot raise spades with only two trumps or bid a new suit at the two-level with only 7 points. No other bid is possible, so you are forced to make the undesirable 1 notrump response.

• JUMP RESPONSES

So far, the responding hands shown have almost all been drab 6-to-9-point minimums, with an occasional strong (10-to-12-point) response. That is what you will have most of the time, but you must be prepared for a glorious surprise once in a while. Partner may open the bidding when you have an opening bid or better (13 points or more) in your own hand. Game is assured (there must be a total of 26 points at least) and even slam is possible. How do you let partner know the good news?

One way is by making a jump response—that is, by skipping a level and bidding one more than is necessary. For example, if partner opens 1 spade and you respond 3 spades, you have made a jump raise. If you respond, instead, 2 notrump, you have jumped in notrump. And if your response is 3 diamonds, you have jumped in a new suit (this is called a jump shift). These are the three different kinds of jump response: jump raise, jump in notrump, jump shift. Each has its own message to partner and its own specific requirements.

Before describing them, however, let me make one point clear. When partner opens, **the fact that you have 13 points or more does not automatically mean that you should jump.** Remember that a simple change of suit (a 1 heart response to 1 club, a 2 diamond response to 1 spade) is enough to force opener to bid again. You can always make sure of reaching game with your *second* bid, after first obtaining more information about opener's strength and distribution. An *immediate* jump bid by responder says more than "We have enough points for game." It says "I think I know the answers to *both* key questions—*where* as well as *how high* to play."

THE JUMP IN NOTRUMP

For example, suppose partner opens the bidding 1 spade and your hand is:

     ♠ K 4   ♡ A Q 6   ◇ K 10 8 4   ♣ Q 9 4 2

You can answer both questions. How high? Game, for you have 14 points to add to partner's 13 points or more. (Slam is possible but unlikely, since partner would have to be unusually strong; and then he can bid slam himself.) Where? *Notrump,* for you have even distribution with protection in all unbid suits. Therefore, make a jump response—2 notrump.

When you jump to 2 notrump over partner's opening bid, you express the opinion that the final contract should be 3 notrump. Therefore, you must have at least 13 points (so that the partnership total must come to 26). In addition, you must have the proper distribution for notrump—preferably 4-3-3-3, possibly 4-4-3-2 or 5-3-3-2, just as for the notrump opening bid. And to guard against an enemy long suit, you must have some strength in all three unbid suits (partner, presumably, has protection in his own suit). Here are two more hands with which you should jump to 2 notrump over partner's 1 spade opening:

    (1)   ♠ J 5 3   ♡ K J 7   ◇ A Q 6 4   ♣ Q 10 8
    (2)   ♠ 8 3   ♡ K Q 4   ◇ A J 10 7 2   ♣ A 9 4

Note that these hands meet all three requirements: 13 points or a little more, even distribution, honors in the three unbid suits. These next examples do *not* qualify for a 2 notrump response when partner opens 1 spade.

(3) ♠K72 ♡A84 ◇Q1083 ♣Q85
(4) ♠AJ4 ♡42 ◇Q97 ♣AQJ82
(5) ♠7 ♡KQ5 ◇J7432 ♣AK108

Hand (3) has the right distribution but the wrong strength (you know "where" but not "how high"). If partner has 13 or 14 points, your 11 points will not produce game. Respond 2 *diamonds*.

Hands (4) and (5) have the proper strength to allow you to answer "Game" to the question "How high?" But in neither example can you answer the question "Where?" with any assurance. Hand (4) has no protection in an unbid suit; hand (5) is unbalanced, containing a singleton. Either might well have to play in a trump suit, so go slow. Respond 2 *clubs* with hand (4); respond 2 *diamonds* with hand (5).

On rare occasions, you may hold a hand too strong for the jump to 2 notrump. Partner opens 1 spade and you hold:

♠853 ♡AQ10 ◇KJ83 ♣AK9

Notrump is quite likely to be your final declaration, but how high? Obviously, game is sure, but now *slam* is likely. You have 17 points, and partner will not be particularly proud of his opening bid even if he holds the 16 points needed to total 33—slam. When you have even distribution, protection in all unbid suits, and close to 17 points (a 1 notrump opening bid of your own) jump to 3 notrump, instead of to 2 notrump, over partner's opening bid.

THE JUMP RAISE

The *jump raise* of partner's suit is similar to the jump to 2 notrump in that it answers the question "How high?" by stating "Game." However, the question "Where?" is now answered "In your suit, partner." For example, suppose partner opens 1 heart and your hand is:

♠K5 ♡K853 ◇KJ94 ♣K42

You have 14 points (adding for the doubleton, now that you have found a trump suit), so there are more than enough points for game, but probably not enough for slam. You and partner must have at least eight hearts together, a good trump suit. Therefore, jump-raise to 3 *hearts*. Note that this hand meets the requirements for a jump in notrump also. However, you should always prefer to play in a major suit.

This jump to 3 hearts expresses your strong opinion that the final contract should be 4 hearts. You promise 13 to 16 points (13 to be sure of a total of 26, no more than 16 so that a total of 33 is unlikely). And you unconditionally guarantee to hold at least four trumps, to assure a total of eight. We saw earlier that you can occasionally raise a major suit from one to *two* with 3 cards headed by a high honor. But the *jump* raise, from one to *three,* must always contain 4-card support or longer.

Bid 3 hearts over partner's 1 heart opening if you hold:

♠ 7 2   ♡ A 6 4 3   ◇ 9 5   ♣ K Q J 10 4

Your hand is worth 13 points—10 in high cards, 1 for the fifth club, 1 for each doubleton now that a fit has been found. Why not bid clubs? Because *the sole purpose of bidding suits is to suggest them as trump*. You surely do not want to suggest that a minor suit be trump when you have already found a good major suit to play in. But with this hand:

♠ 7 2   ♡ A 6 4   ◇ 9 5 3   ♣ A K J 6 4

respond 2 *clubs* if partner opens one heart. Again you have 13 points (counting high cards and length, but not your doubleton since a good trump suit has not yet been assured). Now, however, you must not jump-raise, for you lack 4-card support. You must suggest clubs as trumps and wait to see whether partner can bid his heart suit again, showing a 5-card suit.

Even with four trumps, you should not be at all anxious to jump-raise partner's suit when it is a minor—clubs or diamonds. If partner opens 1 diamond, and you hold:

♠ K J 7 2   ♡ 9 3   ◇ A Q 10 4   ♣ K 8 5

respond 1 *spade*. Just as with a minimum response, you suggest a major suit as trump before agreeing to play in a minor. And if partner opens 1 club when you have:

♠ A Q 7   ♡ K J 4   ◇ Q 10 5   ♣ Q J 10 6

respond 2 *notrump*, not 3 clubs. It is the 9-trick game at notrump that you should suggest, not the 11-trick game at clubs. Only with a hand like:

♠ K 8 2   ♡ 5 3   ◇ A 6 4   ♣ A Q 10 7 3

should you jump-raise to *3 clubs* over a 1 club opening. You have no major suit to suggest; you dare not jump in notrump with the hearts unprotected. Therefore, the jump in clubs is your only possible response.

THE JUMP SHIFT

When you have the distributional requirements for a jump raise, but 17 or more points (so that a slam is likely), you do *not* skip two levels as you would in notrump. The *double* jump in partner's suit (4 spades in response to 1 spade) is a rare, gambling bid. It is based on great length in trumps and wild distribution, with few high cards. For example, double-jump to *4 hearts* over partner's 1 heart opening bid if you hold:

♠ 2   ♡ J 10 8 6 5 3   ◇ K 9 8 5 3   ♣ 8

Note that this hand is *too weak* for a jump raise. What should you bid with a hand *too strong* for a jump raise?

♠ 5   ♡ A Q 9 3   ◇ K Q J 4 2   ♣ K 10 5

If partner opens 1 heart, this hand will be worth 18 points, far too much for the 13-to-16-point 3 heart response. Here, you use your most powerful response, the jump shift. You jump to *3 diamonds*. At your next turn, you will support hearts. This jump in a new suit (followed by a bid in partner's suit) states that you are interested in more than game; you have your eye on a slam.

The jump shift always suggests a slam. However, you may be interested in a slam contract played with your own suit as trumps instead of partner's. Then you will bid your own suit again at your second turn. For example, if partner opens 1 heart and you hold:

♠ A K Q J 5 3   ♡ 6 4   ◇ A Q 8   ♣ 10 5

jump-shift to 2 spades, intending to repeat your spade bid at your next opportunity. This shows a magnificent suit and at least 17 points. You want the final contract to be 6 spades if partner has a little more than a bare minimum opening bid.

Remember that the jump shift is unnecessary when *game* is all you have in mind, for partner is not allowed to pass a simple *nonjump* bid in a new suit. If partner opens 1 heart and you hold:

♠ A K Q J 5 3   ♡ 6 4   ◇ Q 8 2   ♣ 10 5

respond *1* spade. Your 14 points assure game but do not suggest slam, so a simple change of suit is sufficient. As we will see later, you can show your full strength by jumping with your *second* bid.

To review the jump responses to partner's opening suit bid, consider your action if you hold this hand:

    ♠ 7 5   ♡ K J 8 2   ◇ A Q 7 3   ♣ K 8 7

What would be your response if partner opens 1 club? If he opens 1 diamond? If he opens 1 heart? If he opens 1 spade?

When partner opens 1 club: Respond *1 heart.* You may not jump-raise with 3-card support; you may not jump in notrump lacking protection in an unbid suit.

When partner opens 1 diamond: Respond *1 heart.* You could jump-raise, but you should prefer to suggest your major suit first, reserving the jump in diamonds for your second turn to bid.

When partner opens 1 heart: Respond *3 hearts.* The jump raise in a major suit is always your first choice when you have the required 13 to 16 points and 4-card support.

When partner opens 1 spade: Respond *2 notrump.* You have even distribution, 13 points, and protection in all *unbid* suits.

Note that you do not *jump-shift* when you bid a new suit in answer to 1 club or 1 diamond. It is not mandatory to jump merely because you have 13 points or more. The simple change of suit by responder may be made with many strong hands which do not meet the exact requirements for one of the three types of jump response.

♚ RULES TO REMEMBER

To sum up this chapter, here is a table of all the common responses to your partner's opening bid of one in a suit:

You respond—	
One in a New Suit	: 6 points or more (no upper limit). At least 4 cards in your suit.
Two in a New Suit (nonjump)	: 10 points or more (no upper limit). At least 4 cards in your suit.
1 Notrump	: 6 to 9 points. No suit to bid at the one-level.
Two in Partner's Suit	: 6 to 9 points. At least 4 cards in partner's suit or 3 to a high honor in a major suit.
2 Notrump	: 13 to 15 points. Even distribution, protection in all unbid suits. With 16 to 18 points, bid 3 notrump.
Three of Partner's Suit	: 13 to 16 points. At least 4 cards in partner's suit.
Jump in New Suit	: 17 points or more (no upper limit). Strong support for partner or solid suit of your own.

Two of these responses—1 notrump and 2 in partner's suit —have an upper limit of 9 points. Partner may pass either response, for he is in a position to know that your side cannot hold 26 points. But opener *may not pass* any of the other responses. Either he does not know your upper limit (if you have bid a new suit) or your lower limit is 13 points (if you jump). Therefore, he cannot possibly be sure that the partnership lacks 26 points—he must bid again. *What* he bids, we will see in the next chapter.

CHAPTER 5

Opening Bidder's Rebid

When you open the bidding with one in a suit, you may have a point count of anywhere from 13 to 20 or more, and you may have virtually any distribution. With your second bid, your **rebid**, you must tell partner approximately how many points you hold, so that the partnership can determine *how high* to play. And you must further describe your distribution in order to learn *where* to play. Great care must be exercised in selecting your rebid, for this is usually the key bid of the auction.

• AFTER A RAISE

When partner's response has been a raise of your suit—

YOU	OPPONENT	PARTNER	OPPONENT
1 heart	pass	2 hearts	pass

your rebid problems are usually simple. Most often, you will have already learned *where* to play the hand; your only worry is *how high*. Suppose you open 1 heart, holding:

♠ A 5   ♡ A Q 9 6 2   ◇ 2   ♣ K Q 10 8 5

Partner raises to 2 hearts. What is your rebid? You have found a good trump suit, and how high you go depends on your prospects of making game, of totaling 26 points between the partnership hands. Your hand was worth 17 points when you picked it up, counting high cards and length; now that you have found a good trump suit, you add for shortness as well—2 points for the singleton, 1 point for the doubleton. *You* have 20 points in all, and *partner* promises 6 to 9 points for his raise; the partnership total comes to 26–29. Therefore, bid 4 hearts, since you must have the 26 points needed for game, and cannot hold the 33 points needed for slam. Observe that you never consider bidding your clubs; once a good major suit is found there is no need to continue the search for trump.

Now, suppose you open 1 diamond, holding:

♠ K 9 3   ♡ Q 10 4   ◇ A Q 6 2   ♣ A 10 3

Partner raises to 2 diamonds. What is your rebid? Well, what are the total points of the partnership? You have 15 points; partner has 6 to 9 points; between you there are 21 to 24. Game is out of the question, so you *pass* and settle for a part score. If partner has a maximum raise (9 points), you may be able to make 2 notrump or 3 diamonds. *But you never keep on bidding just in order to increase the size of your part score.* A partial of 40 is practically as valuable as one of 60 or 70. If you keep on bidding (raise 2 diamonds to 3, or bid 2 notrump) it must be because game is still possible. When your partnership cannot have 26 points, you end the auction as soon as you can.

Finally, suppose you open 1 spade, holding:

♠ Q 8 6 4 2   ♡ K 5   ◊ A Q J 9   ♣ K 2

What is your rebid after partner raises to 2 spades? Your hand, worth 16 points initially, now improves to 18 points, since you can add 1 point each for the doubletons. Partner has 6 to 9, the total is 24 to 27. You do not want to pass, for game might be made, yet you dare not bid *4 spades*, since the partnership may have only 24 points. Therefore, you bid *3 spades*. This tells partner that game is possible (since you kept on bidding) but not certain (otherwise you would bid game yourself). You ask partner to go on to game with a top-notch raise—8 to 9 points, but to pass with a skinny raise—6 to 7 points.

• MINIMUM, STRONG, OR MAXIMUM OPENING?

Notice that the wide point range of the opening bid has been broken down into three narrow subdivisions, according to whether your hand *cannot*, *might*, or *must* add to 26 points opposite a 6-to-9-point response. That is, a hand of 13 to 16 points cannot possibly yield a 26-point total when partner has 9 points at most—it is a *minimum* opening bid. A hand of 17 to 19 points can produce a 26-point game when partner has 9 points, but not when he has 6 points—it is a *strong* opening bid. A hand worth 20 points or more adds up to 26 even when partner has only 6 points—it is a *maximum* opening bid.

As we will see throughout this chapter, the type of opening bid you hold will determine how high a rebid you make in all situations—no matter what response partner has made. Therefore, before selecting your second bid always ask yourself what category of opening you have: **minimum** (13 to 16), **strong** (17 to 19), or **maximum** (20 or more). The figure of 20 points for the maximum opening is easy to remember; the instant partner shows you 6 points by responding with any bid, you can add to 26. To distinguish between a strong and a minimum opening, you may be helped by this device: cover up an ace in your hand; if you still have an opening bid (13 points) with the remaining cards, you have a *strong* bid, while if you would not open with the remaining cards you have a *minimum*. A strong opening bid is a *minimum plus an extra ace* (4 points).

With each of the example hands following, you open the bidding in your long suit, and partner responds by raising to two of your suit. What category of opening bid do you have? What is your rebid?

(a) ♠ K J 8 4 2   ♡ A Q 5   ◇ 7 4   ♣ K Q J

(b) ♠ 3   ♡ J 8 6 4 3 2   ◇ A K 5   ♣ A K J

(c) ♠ K 8   ♡ A K J 10 9 5   ◇ 7 5 3   ♣ 5 2

(d) ♠ A Q 8   ♡ K 4   ◇ A Q 10 8 2   ♣ A 10 6

(a) You have a *strong* opening (18 points) once partner raises spades, for now you add 1 point for your doubleton to your original 17 points. Raise to 3 *spades*, inviting game.

(b) You have a *maximum* opening (20 points) once hearts are supported; so jump to 4 hearts. Do not worry about the lack of honors in the trump suit—you need only length in trumps; high cards are just as good in side suits.

(c) You have a *minimum* opening (15 points) despite your powerful suit. (Cover up the heart ace and see what you have left.) *Pass* partner's raise, since there cannot be enough combined strength for game.

(d) You have a *maximum* opening, worth 21 points for play in diamonds. However, you may not bid 5 diamonds, as this 11-trick minor-suit game requires 29 points, and partner may have only 6 or 7. Instead, jump to 3 *notrump*, a game contract which requires only 26 points. For notrump, your hand is worth 20 points (never add for short suits if you intend to play in notrump) and partner will provide at least 6 points. When a minor suit is raised and you have hope for game, always think of notrump (unless you have a singleton or void in a side suit). With a *strong* opening, try for game by bidding 2 notrump. With a *maximum* opening, bid the most likely game yourself: 3 notrump.

• AFTER A 1 NOTRUMP RESPONSE

When partner responds to your opening by bidding 1 no-trump, your proper rebid may be more difficult to determine. Just as after a raise, you are likely to know at once *how high* to bid, for partner promises the same 6 to 9 points. With a minimum opening, you give up all thought of game; with a strong opening, you can try for game; with a maximum opening, you are sure of game. However, you often do not know *where* to play, since a trump suit has not yet been found. Your rebid must show the quality of your opening (minimum, strong, or maximum) and must continue the search for a trump suit.

Of course, if your distribution is evenly balanced (no sin-gleton or void, at most one doubleton—the pattern for a no-trump bid of your own), you are not at all anxious to search for a suit; you are willing to play in notrump. Consider these three example hands:

(1) ♠ A Q 6 4 2   ♡ J 5   ◇ Q 8 4   ♣ A 10 5
(2) ♠ A Q 6 4 2   ♡ J 5   ◇ A Q 8   ♣ A 10 5
(3) ♠ A Q 6 4 2   ♡ K 5   ◇ A Q 8   ♣ A 10 5

With all three, you open 1 spade, and when partner responds 1 notrump, you will indicate your even distribution by stay-ing in notrump. Hand (1) is a minimum opening—game is impossible opposite 6 to 9 points, so *pass*. Hand (2) is a strong opening—game is possible but not certain, so raise to 2 *notrump*. Hand (3) is a maximum opening—game is sure, so bid 3 *notrump*.

When your opening bid is made in a very long suit (6 cards or more), you should be unwilling to play in notrump. You have a strong desire to make your long suit trump, and you indicate this by bidding it again, by rebidding your suit.

(4) ♠ 3   ♡ K J 10 8 4 2   ◇ A Q 5   ♣ Q 7 4
(5) ♠ 3   ♡ A K J 10 8 4   ◇ A Q 5   ♣ Q 7 4
(6) ♠ 3   ♡ A K J 10 8 4 2   ◇ A Q 5   ♣ K 4

With all three hands above, open 1 heart and rebid hearts over partner's 1 notrump response. How high do you bid? With hand (4), a 14-point minimum, rebid 2 hearts. This tells partner that game is impossible, and that you want to play a part score in hearts. With hand (5), a strong opening because of the surplus ace, jump to 3 hearts. This urges partner to go on to game with 8 or 9 points and two or three trumps, but allows him to pass. With hand (6), a 20-point maximum, go right to 4 hearts yourself. Partner has already shown the 6 points you need for game, and even a singleton heart in his hand will give you the required total of eight trumps.

There are many hands with which you are unwilling to play in notrump even though your first suit is *not* very long—you may have a singleton or two doubletons, unbalanced distribution which is good for suit play and poor for notrump. Then you will make your second bid in a *new* suit. For example, suppose you open 1 heart, holding:

♠ 4   ♡ K J 8 4 2   ◇ A K 3 2   ♣ Q 8 5

Partner responds 1 notrump. Bid 2 *diamonds*. There is no chance for game when you have this minimum opening; but you should turn pale at the very thought of playing notrump with an unbid singleton. You must continue to search for a trump suit, and it is best to suggest your second suit, offering partner a choice. You have a slight preference for hearts over diamonds, but you have already expressed this by bidding hearts first. *Partner* may have more diamonds than hearts; and if he has equal length in the two suits, he will take you back to hearts, your first bid suit.

This rebid in a new suit may also be made with a strong opening.

♠ A K J 4 2   ♡ 5 3   ◇ 6 2   ♣ A K J 7

Open 1 spade and, over a 1 notrump response, rebid 2 clubs. Partner will pass your rebid only if he has more clubs than spades and a bare 6 to 7 points. When he has the 8 or 9 points you need to total 26, he will bid again. Now, after finding out *where* to play, you can show your extra ace by moving toward game.

In order to jump to 3 clubs over partner's 1 notrump response, you need a *maximum* opening, not merely a strong one. This jump in a new suit, the jump shift, is always opener's most powerful rebid. It guarantees that the partnership has the 26 points needed for game. Therefore, you must have 20 points for a jump in a new suit, since partner has promised only 6 points. You may jump-shift with this hand:

♠ A 4   ♡ A Q 10 6 3   ◇ 4   ♣ A K Q 5 2

Open 1 heart and, over a 1 notrump response, jump to 3 clubs. This rebid forces both partners to keep bidding until game is reached. You already know *how high* to play, and the jump shift allows you to discover *where* to play without risking an abrupt end to the auction.

You will have noticed that in none of the examples have you rebid your first suit when it is only 5 cards long. This is because you usually prefer to offer partner a choice of suits when you have two to bid; and when you have no second suit and only 5 cards in your first, your distribution is balanced—you are willing to play in notrump. However, you are *allowed* to rebid a 5-card suit—you should not *want* to, but on rare occasions it may be your best action. Consider this hand:

♠ 4   ♡ Q 7 4 3   ◇ A Q J 9 2   ♣ K 10 4

You open 1 diamond; partner responds 1 notrump. You dare not stay in notrump, and your obvious rebid seems to be 2 hearts. However, this bid is both dangerous and futile. It is *dangerous* because it may force partner to the *three*-level (if he prefers diamonds to hearts). It is *futile* because partner cannot have the 4-card heart length you need, for he would then have preferred to respond 1 *heart*, not 1 notrump. Therefore, take advantage of the fact that you are *allowed* to rebid a 5-card suit—bid 2 diamonds. Be very wary of bidding your second suit at the two-level when it is higher in rank than your first. (This is called, for no good reason, **reversing**.) You are unlikely to find a good trump suit, and you can be forced dangerously high unless you have a strong opening bid.

• AFTER A NEW SUIT RESPONSE

When partner responds to your opening bid by suggesting a suit, you do not know his point count as you would had he responded by raising your suit or bidding 1 notrump. He must have 6 points to respond at all (or 10 points if he responds two in a new suit), but the sky is his upper limit. Therefore, you can never know immediately how high to play.

Suppose you open 1 diamond, holding:

(a) ♠ K 8 4   ♡ J 7 2   ◇ A Q 7 3   ♣ K 10 5

Partner responds 1 heart. *You must not pass,* despite your minimum values, because partner may have the 13 points needed for game (he could even have much more). When partner bids a new suit, you choose your rebid to tell him more about your opening bid: how strong you are, what sort of distribution you have. Then *he* will pick the final contract.

With example (a) above, you will show your even distribution by rebidding in notrump, and your minimum strength by bidding as cheaply as possible—*1 notrump.* With balanced pattern and protection in unbid suits, but greater strength:

(b) ♠ A Q 4   ♡ 7 2   ◊ A Q 7 3   ♣ A Q 10 5
(c) ♠ A K J   ♡ 7 2   ◊ A J 10 7 3   ♣ A Q 5

you make a *jump* rebid in notrump. With hand (b), an 18-point strong opening, bid 2 notrump over partner's 1 heart response. Hand (c) is a 20-point maximum opening—rebid 3 notrump.

If you have, instead of even distribution, a long first suit, rebid your suit just as you would have over a 1 notrump response. Consider these examples:

(d) ♠ 8 2   ♡ Q J 10 8 6 4   ◊ A 10 5   ♣ A 8
(e) ♠ A 2   ♡ Q J 10 8 6 4   ◊ A 10 5   ♣ A 8
(f) ♠ A   ♡ K Q J 10 8 6 4   ◊ K 10 5   ♣ A 8

With each hand, you open 1 heart; partner responds 1 spade. Example (d) is a 13-point minimum—rebid *2 hearts.* Example (e) has an extra ace, it is a 17-point strong opening—rebid *3 hearts.* Example (f) is a 20-point maximum—rebid *4 hearts.*

When you have 4 cards in *partner's* suit, your support for partner's suit is by far the most important distributional feature to show with your rebid. For example, suppose you open 1 club, holding:

(g) ♠ Q 7 5 3   ♡ A 4   ◊ 6   ♣ A Q J 10 8 3

Partner responds 1 spade. Do not even consider bidding clubs again. *You* have six clubs, but *we* have eight spades (partner has four at least to add to your four). Therefore a trump suit has been found, and you will raise spades.

How many spades do you bid with example (g)? That is

determined, as usual, by whether your opening is minimum, strong, or maximum. This hand was worth 15 points originally, but it improves after a fit is found—it is now worth 3 points more, 18 points in all. With this strong opening, jump to 3 spades, inviting game. Now consider these hands:

(h) ♠ K Q 5 3   ♡ A 4   ◇ 6   ♣ A Q J 10 8 3
(i) ♠ K Q 5 3   ♡ K 4   ◇ 6 3 2   ♣ A J 6 2

You bid 1 club, and partner answers 1 spade. Example (h) is now a maximum opening—jump to 4 *spades*. Example (i) is still a minimum opening—raise to 2 *spades*.

This minimum raise can (like *responder's* raise) occasionally be made with only three trumps if they include a high honor. For example, you open 1 diamond, holding:

♠ 8 3   ♡ A 9 4   ◇ A Q 8 4 3   ♣ K 5 2

Partner responds 1 heart. You have a choice of three minimum rebids: *1 notrump,* dangerous because of the small unbid doubleton; *2 diamonds,* unpleasant because you have only a 5-card suit; *2 hearts,* unattractive because you have 3-card support. Two hearts is the best of a bad lot. However, never *jump*-raise partner's suit without 4-card support. Any time you jump in partner's suit, you guarantee absolutely that the partnership has the required eight trumps.

The rebids we have treated so far—in notrump, in your first suit, in partner's suit—are the most desirable ones, for they suggest specifically *where* to play and state within a narrow range how strong you are. Occasionally, however, your rebid over partner's change of suit will be in still another new suit:

	YOU	PARTNER			YOU	PARTNER
(1)	1 diamond	1 spade		(2)	1 diamond	1 heart
	2 clubs					1 spade	

When your rebid is in a third suit, as above, you may have either a minimum or a strong opening bid. Partner will bid again when he has a little more than the bare 6 points he has promised; then you can try for game with a strong opening (or pass with a minimum) after you have found out where to play. You must employ the rebid in a third suit when you have unbalanced distribution, no very long first suit, and no support for partner. Again, beware of an auction like:

	YOU	PARTNER
(3)	1 club	1 spade
	2 diamonds	

Partner will have to bid three to return to your first suit, so you had better have a strong opening bid. With a minimum, rebid your 5-card club suit. (Note that in auction (2) above you have bid a higher-ranking suit second, but you may still have a minimum opening since you stay at the one-level.)

When you have a *maximum* opening, you must not merely bid a third suit. You know that game can be made somewhere (you have 20 points, partner has 6 at least), so you cannot give partner the chance to pass you out in a part-score contract. Remember, although *responder's* change of suit forces opener to bid again, opener's change of suit may (on rare occasions) be passed by responder. Therefore, with a hand like:

♠ A K J 7   ♡ 5 3   ◇ A Q J 9 4   ♣ A 4

open 1 diamond and, over a 1 heart response, jump to 2 spades. This jump shift shows your maximum opening—20 points or more—and is forcing to game, since both partners now know that their side has 26 points at least.

• AFTER A JUMP RESPONSE

When partner's response has been a jump in notrump (you open 1 spade; partner bids 2 notrump) or a jump raise (you open 1 heart, partner bids 3 hearts), you can usually decide immediately both *where* and *how high* to play.

"How high?" is a simple question to answer. Partner has 13 points at least, 15 to 16 points at most. When you have a minimum opening, the partnership total must be 26 or more, but cannot reach 33 (slam); therefore, you will play in a game contract. When you have a *strong* opening, the total may possibly come to 33 points, therefore, you will try for slam. When you have a *maximum* opening, the total must be 33 or more; you will usually bid a slam. How to try for and bid these slams will be discussed more fully in Chapter 7, but here is a preview:

OPENER	RESPONDER
♠ K 3	♠ A Q 8 7
♡ A Q 8 4 2	♡ K J 9 3
◇ A J 9 3	◇ 6 5
♣ A 7	♣ K 8 2

| 1 heart | 3 hearts |
| *6 hearts* | pass |

Your hand was worth 19 points originally, and improves to 21 points after partner's jump raise. Partner's response promises 13 to 16 points; therefore, there are at least 34 points in the two hands combined. This total is more than enough to enable you to bid the slam.

However, let us weaken your hand by removing the diamond honors:

♠ K 3   ♡ A Q 8 4 2   ◇ 10 8 4 3   ♣ A 7

Now if partner jumps to 3 hearts after you open with 1 heart, the total cannot reach 33 points. (You have 16 points; partner has 16 at most.) Since slam is impossible, your rebid will be *4* hearts.

"Where to play?" may occasionally be a more difficult question to answer after a jump response. Of course, if partner has jump-raised in hearts or spades, the question is answered immediately; you will play in the major suit. However, after a jump raise in *clubs* or *diamonds,* you must always consider playing in 3 notrump (where 26 points suffice for game) rather than in a contract of five in a minor suit (where 29 points are needed). When partner jumps in your minor suit, rebid 3 notrump with any minimum opening that has balanced distribution; and even with a long suit, rebid 3 notrump when you have a likely trick, a **stopper**, in each unbid suit. You should open 1 diamond with either of these hands:

(1) ♠ K 5   ♡ K 6   ◇ K 10 9 7 5 2   ♣ Q J 8
(2) ♠ Q 10 8 4   ♡ K J 5   ◇ A Q 8 6   ♣ J 2

Suppose partner responds 3 diamonds. Bid 3 notrump with example (1). You have protection in all suits, so your long diamonds will surely enable you to win 9 tricks. Bid 3 notrump with example (2) also. Here you are worried about clubs. However, your flat minimum opening is most unlikely to produce eleven winners in diamonds; therefore, bid the only game which seems possible.

When partner responds 2 notrump to your opening bid, raise to 3 notrump with any minimum opening unless there is a chance to find a major-suit fit—8 cards between the two hands in spades or hearts. Consider these two examples:

(3) ♠ K 5   ♡ 8 2   ◇ A Q 9 4 3   ♣ K 10 7 2
(4) ♠ A Q 9 4 3   ♡ K 10 7 2   ◇ 8 2   ♣ K 5

Suppose you open hand (3) with 1 diamond, and partner responds 2 notrump: bid 3 notrump. The only suit games possible are 11-trick contracts in clubs or diamonds, so play in notrump instead. Contrast this with hand (4). You open 1 spade and again partner jumps to 2 notrump: bid 3 hearts. If partner has 4-card length in hearts, he will raise to 4 hearts; if he has 3 cards in spades, he will support your first suit. In either case, you will reach the superior major-suit game contract. And if partner has only three hearts and two spades, he will bid 3 notrump himself.

Remember, 4 hearts and 4 spades are your first choice among game contracts. When you have no major-suit fit, but can add to 26 points, you usually play in 3 notrump. Five club and 5 diamond contracts are reached only when you cannot play in a major suit and dare not play in notrump: because you have a void or singleton in an unbid suit, or because you cannot win a trick in a suit which the enemy have bid.

• REVIEW QUIZ

Let us review all of opener's rebids by means of a quiz. You are the opening bidder in the following five bidding situations. What is your rebid with each of the three hands listed beneath its auction?

1. You open 1 spade; partner responds 2 spades:

(a) ♠ A K Q 5   ♡ K 9 4   ◇ K 7 2   ♣ 8 6 3
(b) ♠ K J 7 4 2   ♡ A K Q J 5   ◇ K 8   ♣ 3
(c) ♠ J 8 5 3 2   ♡ 8 4   ◇ A K J 9   ♣ A K

2. You open 1 heart; partner responds 1 notrump:

(a) ♠ K 2   ♡ A Q J 6 3   ◇ Q J 8   ♣ 10 4 2
(b) ♠ A 5   ♡ A K J 8 4   ◇ A Q 10 6 3   ♣ 7
(c) ♠ 7 4   ♡ K Q J 8 4 2   ◇ K 5   ♣ A K 2

3. You open 1 club; partner responds 1 heart:

  (a) ♠K74   ♡AK   ◇J53   ♣K10754
  (b) ♠94   ♡J632   ◇A5   ♣AKQJ7
  (c) ♠76   ♡AKQ6   ◇Q42   ♣K853

4. You open 1 diamond; partner responds 1 spade:

  (a) ♠5   ♡AJ6   ◇KQ1042   ♣AQ53
  (b) ♠K1054   ♡K6   ◇AQJ8   ♣AQ7
  (c) ♠4   ♡K7   ◇AKJ1053   ♣KQ84

5. You open 1 heart; partner responds 2 notrump:

  (a) ♠54   ♡AQ63   ◇AQ106   ♣K84
  (b) ♠A8   ♡1086532   ◇AKJ4   ♣5
  (c) ♠KJ3   ♡AKJ5   ◇Q106   ♣AK4

ANSWERS

1 (a) *pass*, (b) *4 spades*, (c) *3 spades*
When partner raises a major suit, you have found *where* to play. *How high* to bid is determined by whether you have a minimum (a), strong (c), or maximum (b) opening. Remember to add for short suits after a fit is found.

2 (a) *pass*, (b) *3 diamonds*, (c) *3 hearts*
When partner responds 1 notrump, you must decide both where and how high to play. You pass only with a minimum opening which, like (a), has even distribution. With a maximum opening, (b), you may jump-shift. With a strong opening, (c), you may jump in a very long first suit.

3 (a) *1 notrump*, (b) *3 hearts*, (c) *2 hearts*
When partner responds in a new suit, *whether* you raise is determined by the number of cards you have in support; *how high* you raise is decided according to the strength of your opening. You may never raise with two trumps (a), instead you show a minimum opening with even pattern. You *must* raise with four trumps (b), (c), a jump raise with the strong opening (b) and a single raise with the minimum opening (c).

4 (a) *2 clubs*, (b) *4 spades*, (c) *3 diamonds*
Do not rebid in notrump with hand (a); you have unbalanced distribution. Prefer to suggest a second suit rather than repeat a 5-carder; but do not jump-*shift* with

merely a strong opening. Hand (c) is also a strong opening with a second suit, but your first suit is very long, so
prefer to bid it again. Hand (b) is a maximum opening,
so you may jump to game; choose the major-suit game
when you know that your side has at least eight trumps.

5 (a) *3 notrump,* (b) *4 hearts,* (c) *6 notrump*

With a minimum opening (a) you have no chance for
slam. Bid your game in notrump since your side cannot
have 8 cards in either major suit. With a 6-card major
(b), you know that your side has eight trumps, for partner has even distribution; bid game in your suit. With a
maximum opening (c), you know both *how high to play*
—slam, since 33 points are assured—and *where to play*—
notrump, since both hands have even distribution. End
this chapter with a bang by leaping to your proper contract.

❧ RULES TO REMEMBER

13 to 16 points: A minimum opening. Pass a minimum
response. Rebid your suit, raise partner,
bid notrump or a new suit without
jumping.

17 to 19 points: A strong opening. Try for game over a
minimum response. Jump in your first
suit, jump in notrump or jump-raise
partner's suit.

20 to 21 points: A maximum opening. Bid a game or
jump in a new suit.

CHAPTER 6

Placing the Final Contract

Have you noticed that finding the proper contract is getting to be more and more complex the further you go in this book? It was delightfully simple back in the first part of Chapter 4, when the opening bid was 1 notrump. Responder could look at his hand and tell right away both where and how high to play. Suit opening bids, however, introduce many difficulties, for responder can no longer add up the partnership assets at once.

• WHERE AND HOW HIGH?

Now responder has two jobs: to search for a trump suit, and to indicate his point count. When his response is a raise, the auction becomes simple again—here, opener can take over the captaincy and determine *where* and *how high* to play. When the response is in notrump, opener can tell at least *how high* to play, if not *where* as well. But when the response is in a new suit, neither partner is in a position to name the final contract; both are still in the dark about the other's strength and pattern. It then becomes opener's turn to continue the search for a trump suit, and to show the strength of his opening, so that *responder* can make a decision at his second turn.

You will be relieved to know that after these first three bids of the auction—opening bid, response, opener's rebid—the partnership is usually out of the woods. At this point, responder should know as much about opener's point count and distribution as he would had the opening been 1 notrump. Therefore, responder can once again become the captain of the partnership. He can add his points to opener's to determine how high to play; he can add his suit length to opener's and tell where to play.

• EXAMPLE AUCTIONS

Let us see how this works in a few example auctions:

OPENER	RESPONDER
♠ K J 5	♠ 7 3
♡ 7 2	♡ Q J 8 3
♢ A Q 8 6 3	♢ K 9 5
♣ K 9 5	♣ A Q J 4

1 diamond	1 heart
1 notrump	3 notrump

Opener, with his rebid, describes a minimum opening bid with balanced distribution. Responder now knows *how high* to play: adding his 13 points to opener's minimum range, 13 to 16, he totals 26 to 29; game is sure and slam is impossible. Responder now knows *where* to play the game contract: no fit has been found in a major suit, so notrump is the best declaration available. Therefore, responder places the final contract.

OPENER	RESPONDER
♠ 8 4	♠ A 10 7 6 3
♡ A Q J 7 4 2	♡ 8 5 3
♢ A 9 3	♢ K 6
♣ A 5	♣ 9 4 2

1 heart	1 spade
3 hearts	4 hearts

With his jump rebid, opener announces a strong opening (note that he has an ace more than a bare minimum) containing a long heart suit. Responder knows *where* to play, since he can add to nine trumps in a major suit; he knows *how high* to play, since his 9 points (7 in high cards, 1 for length, 1 for shortness after finding the fit) assure 26 points when added to opener's 17-to-19.

OPENER	RESPONDER
♠ A J 7 6	♠ Q 8 5 2
♡ 5 3	♡ A 9 4
♢ K Q 5 2	♢ 8 7 4
♣ K 10 4	♣ Q J 2

1 diamond	1 spade
2 spades	pass

A fit is found in a major suit, but responder knows that there is no chance for game. How? He adds his 9 points to opener's

13-to-16 (minimum opening bid), and gets a total of 22-to-25. The partnership cannot have the 26 points required for game, so responder passes, playing in the cheapest part-score contract possible.

As we have seen in these three sample auctions, opener's rebid usually gives responder all the information necessary to determine the final contract. However, responder is not compelled to choose immediately between bidding game and passing at a part score. If he is still in doubt about *where* and *how high* to play, responder may make a further bid under game. Such a bid will ask opener either of two questions: (1) "Are you at the *upper* or the *lower* end of the point range you have announced?" or (2) "Where shall we play our game contract?" Here is an example of the first question:

OPENER	RESPONDER
♠ K 8 3	♠ Q J 5
♡ A 9 2	♡ K 10 4 3
◇ A J 6 5	◇ K Q 8 2
♣ K 10 8	♣ 5 3
1 diamond	1 heart
1 notrump	2 notrump
3 notrump	

After opener's rebid, responder knows *where* to play—no major-suit fit exists, so if there is a game possible it will be in notrump (not diamonds). But responder's problem is *how high* to play. He has 11 points; opener promises 13 to 16 points; the total is 24 to 27. The combined hands contain 26 points if opener has 15 or 16, but not if opener has only 13 or 14. Therefore, responder *raises* notrump, neither bidding game nor passing. Opener is expected to pass 2 notrump if he has a *bare* minimum (13 or 14 points); with the hand above, he goes on to game because he has close to a "maximum" minimum.

Responder can ask this same sort of question about a suit game, as in these two auctions:

OPENER	RESPONDER	OPENER	RESPONDER
1 club	1 spade	1 heart	1 spade
2 spades	3 *spades*	2 hearts	3 *hearts*

In each case, responder asks opener to go on to game in the suit responder has raised, but only if opener has a top-notch (15- or 16-point) minimum, not a skinny (13- or 14-point) minimum. How many points has *responder* for the auctions above? Try to work it out for yourself—it is good exercise.°

The second question responder can ask is *where* to play a game contract. Here is an example:

OPENER	RESPONDER
♠ K 9 4	♠ 5 3
♡ 2	♡ A K 10 6 4 3
◇ Q 8 4	◇ K 6
♣ A K J 9 6 3	♣ Q 8 5

1 club	1 heart
2 clubs	3 hearts
3 notrump	pass

Responder's jump to 3 hearts is (like all of *responder's* jump bids) forcing to game. Its message to partner is this: "I have an opening bid of my own, so we can add up to 26 points even if you have only 13 points; I have a long suit, so bid game in hearts if you have some little support; look for game elsewhere (notrump, clubs) if you have no tolerance for hearts." Above, opener bids the game in notrump since he has protection in the unbid suits and no desire to play with hearts as trumps.

OPENER	RESPONDER
♠ 7 5	♠ K J 6 4 2
♡ A Q 8 4 3	♡ J 7 5
◇ A Q 6	◇ K 8 7 3
♣ A J 8	♣ 5

1 heart	1 spade
2 notrump	3 *hearts*
4 hearts	pass

After opener's strong rebid, responder can add up enough points for game. But should the game contract be in hearts, spades, or notrump? Responder's second bid shows 3-card heart support (with *four* hearts, he would have raised immediately) and asks opener to bid the game in this suit if he has 5-card length. Opener, with only a 4-card heart suit, would show 3-card support for responder's suit, or, failing that,

---

° He cannot have 6 to 9 points, for a *minimum response* will never make game facing a *minimum opening;* he would pass. Responder cannot have 13 points or more, for then he would bid game himself. He must have a *strong response* (10 to 12 points), which may or may not produce 26 points opposite a minimum opening bid.

would bid 3 notrump. Note that neither partner will agree to play in notrump so long as there is a possibility of an eight-card fit in hearts or spades. The delayed support of partner's major suit shows 3 cards, not 4 (since you did not raise at once); it asks partner to play in his suit if he has 5 cards (you know that he does not have 6, because he did not bid his suit again).

When you are responder, it is largely *your* job to pick the final contract after opener's rebid. Ask yourself first, "Have we a total of 26 points?" If the answer is "No," pass in any reasonable part-score contract. If the answer is "Yes" or "Maybe," ask yourself a second question, "Have we 8 cards together in a major suit?"

♥ RULES TO REMEMBER

Here, in outline form, are your actions as responder after opening bidder's rebid:

After Opener Makes a Minimum Rebid

Your points:

6-9 With a minimum response, you have no chance for game. Pass.

10-12 With a strong response, you may have game. Bid again, but do not jump.

13-16 With a minimum opening of your own, you *must* have game (but not slam). Bid a game or make a jump bid.

After Opener Makes a Strong Rebid

6-7 With just barely enough for your first response, pass.

8-12 With a little extra, bid game if you know *where* to play. Otherwise, make any bid to suggest a trump suit. You need not *jump*, since *all* bids accept opener's invitation to go to game.

13-16 With an opening bid of your own, you have a chance for slam. Now you may *jump*. We will explore slam auctions further in the next chapter.

CHAPTER 7

Slam Bidding

There is very little difference between bidding for slam and the more common bidding for game. Once you know *where* to play, the question "How high?" is answered according to the total number of points in the partnership hands: *part score* if your total is under 26, *game* with a total of 26 to 32, *small slam* with 33 to 36, *grand slam* with 37 or more. To illustrate this in its simplest form, suppose that your partner opens 1 notrump (so that you can tell immediately both where and how high to play). What should be your response with these hands?:

(a) ♠K84 ♡Q73 ◇Q975 ♣852
(b) ♠K84 ♡Q73 ◇AQJ5 ♣J52
(c) ♠KQ8 ♡Q73 ◇AQJ5 ♣K52
(d) ♠KQ8 ♡Q73 ◇AQJ5 ♣AKJ

Where to play? Notrump! How high to play? With hand (a), you add your 7 points to partner's 16 to 18 and total 23 to 25—part score. With hand (b) the total comes to 29 to 31 —game. With hand (c) you add up to 33 to 35 points— small slam. With hand (d) you have 38 to 40 points—grand slam. Therefore, *pass* with (a), bid 3 *notrump* with (b), 6 *notrump* with (c), and 7 *notrump* with (d).

● SLAM INVITATIONS

In previous chapters, we have seen many occasions when your addition of partnership points tells you that there *might* be enough for game, but only if partner has maximum values. For example, suppose partner opens 1 notrump and you hold:

(e) ♠K84 ♡Q73 ◇K975 ♣J52

The total is 25 to 27, so you can compromise between part score and game, bidding 2 notrump; partner goes on with 17 or 18 and passes with 16. This same type of problem can arise in *slam* bidding, and is solved in similar fashion. When partner opens 1 notrump and you hold:

♠ K Q 8   ♡ Q 7 3   ◇ A Q J 5   ♣ Q 5 2

your total is 32 to 34 points. Therefore, you compromise between game and slam, bidding 4 notrump. Again, opener will bid on with maximum values, or pass with minimum strength.

This bid of *one more than game* is always used to invite partner to go on to slam. There is no advantage whatever in playing contracts of 4 notrumps or 5 hearts or 5 spades—they are harder to fulfill than game contracts are, and there is no extra reward for making them. If you bid one more than game, it must be because you can add up nearly enough points to bid slam yourself, and you want partner to bid the slam if he has a little more than the minimum values he has promised. For example, in this auction:

OPENER	RESPONDER
1 heart	3 hearts
5 hearts	?

opener has bid over game. He says to responder, "I know that you have 13 to 16 points. If all you have is 13, we do not have quite the 33 points we need for slam, so pass—but if you have close to 16, bid 6 hearts." Opener must have a strong bid—17 to 19 points. With 16 or fewer he could not add to 33 even if responder had 16, so opener would bid 4 hearts. With 20 or more, opener would add to 33 even if responder had 13, so he would bid the slam all by himself.

Unfortunately, it is not strictly true that opener can bid a slam with 20 points when responder jump raises, showing 13. In bidding slams, there is another question to be answered along with "Have we at least 33 points?" This question is "Have we at least three aces?"

Consider this auction:

OPENER	RESPONDER
♠ A Q 8 7 5 2	♠ K 10 6 3
♡ K Q J 10	♡ 7
◇ K 4	◇ A 10 8 7 2
♣ 6	♣ K Q 4
1 spade	3 spades
6 *spades*	pass

Responder's hand is worth 15 points (12 in high cards, 1 for the fifth diamond, 2 for the singleton, once a fit is found); opener's hand is worth 20 points after the jump raise (15 in high cards, 2 for length, 2 for the singleton, 1 for the doubleton). The combined count is 35, more than enough for slam. Yet the 6 spade contract reached above will probably go down, for the opponents can win the ace of hearts and the ace of clubs.

What is wrong with the point-count method? Nothing! The combined total of 33 points or more means that the partnership hands contain enough power to win 12 tricks. And they do. Declarer can take 6 spade tricks, 3 heart tricks (after losing to the heart ace), 2 diamond tricks, and 1 club trick (after losing to the club ace)—a total of 12. But since the enemy tricks are *aces*, they win theirs first, and no bridge player in the world is good enough to win 12 tricks after the opponents have taken two.

Therefore, you must not bid a slam, even with 33 points, until you are sure that the opponents do not have two aces. You can check up on aces by using the **Blackwood Convention.**[*]

• THE BLACKWOOD CONVENTION

This is a device to find out how many aces partner holds. After finding your trump suit and determining that your side has 33 points, you bid *4 notrump*. This is the Blackwood bid, and orders partner, "Tell me how many aces you hold!" Partner answers:

    5 Clubs—with no aces
    5 Diamonds—with one ace
    5 Hearts—with two aces
    5 Spades—with three aces

Note that the *lowest*-ranking suit—clubs—shows no aces, and each higher suit shows one more ace.

After learning how many aces partner holds, you can bid your slam when the partnership total is at least three aces, or sign off at five of your suit when your side has only *two* aces. The earlier example should be bid like this:

[*] A *Convention* is a bid with an artificial meaning. This one was invented by Mr. Easley Blackwood.

OPENER	RESPONDER
♠ A Q 8 7 5 2	♠ K 10 6 3
♡ K Q J 10	♡ 7
◇ K 4	◇ A 10 8 7 2
♣ 6	♣ K Q 4

1 spade	3 spades
4 notrump	5 diamonds
5 spades	pass

Opener knows, after the raise, that a good trump suit has been found and that a total of 33 points is sure. However, before jumping to slam he bids 4 notrump, Blackwood. The 5 diamond reply shows one ace; opener has one himself; the enemy have two. So opener stops safely at 5 spades, which responder is obliged to pass. (The partner who bids 4 no-trump is the boss; if he says there is no slam, then no slam is bid.)

Now, change responder's hand slightly to:

♠ K 10 6 3   ♡ 7   ◇ A 10 8 7 2   ♣ A 5 4

Here, responder would show *two* aces by answering 5 hearts to partner's 4 notrump. Opener would then bid 6 spades, knowing that his side has *three* aces, the enemy only one.

The Blackwood Convention can be extended one step further, to ask for *kings* after finding out about aces. Suppose you have bid 4 notrump; partner answers five of the appropriate suit. Now you bid 5 *notrump*. This tells partner to announce how many kings he holds, by the same type of bid one level higher:

6 Clubs—with no kings
6 Diamonds—with one king
6 Hearts—with two kings
6 Spades—with three kings
6 Notrump—with four kings

This extension of Blackwood is very rare, for it should be used only when a *grand* slam is in prospect. Obviously, when you bid 5 notrump you are committed to a small slam at least, for partner's response is at the six-level. Unless you have enough points for a grand slam, you are wasting breath in asking about kings; you should bid six of your suit directly. However, if your side has all the aces and 37 points or more, you are interested in a grand slam, and should check to be sure that you are not missing a key king. (You must never bid a grand slam if there is the slightest danger of losing a trick, and a missing king usually presents such a danger.) Here is a sample auction:

OPENER	RESPONDER
♠ K 8 3 2	♠ A Q 10 7 6 5
♡ A 7	♡ K 8
◇ A 5	◇ K 7 2
♣ A K 8 6 4	♣ Q 9
1 club	1 spade
4 spades	4 notrump
5 spades	5 notrump
6 hearts	7 spades

Opener's maximum rebid shows 20 points or more (actually, he has 21, counting his doubletons after finding a fit). Responder, therefore, can add up to 38 points—his hand is worth 18 points after opener's raise—and can diagnose the possibility of a grand slam. First, he bids *4 notrump* to check aces. (If by some strange chance, the enemy have *two* aces, he will stop at 5 spades; if they have one ace, he will bid 6 spades.) When opener shows the missing three aces, the grand slam is still possible; responder bids 5 *notrump* to check kings. If either missing king is held by the opponents, a trick might be lost; but opener's response shows that he holds both. Now responder can confidently bid the grand slam.

You will have noticed that the bid of 4 notrump has been given two different meanings in this chapter: (1) a bid of one more than game, to invite slam in notrump; (2) the Blackwood Convention, to ask partner how many aces he holds. When you are headed for a *notrump* contract (both partners have even distribution; no good trump suit has been found), 4 notrump is "one more than game," and asks about *points*, not about aces. But when you are headed for a *suit* contract (a fit has been found; *4* notrump is *not* a raise in notrump) then 4 notrump is Blackwood, asking about aces.

OPENER	RESPONDER
1 club	1 heart
3 hearts	4 notrump

This is Blackwood. You are intending to play in a suit contract.

OPENER	RESPONDER
1 notrump	4 notrump

This is the invitation to bid 6 notrump; both hands have even distribution and no fit has been found.

What if opener bids 6 notrump on the auction above, and the opponents have two aces? Impossible! If the partnership is bidding properly, it will have 33 points in *high cards* alone; neither partner has added for long suits or short suits, since both have evenly balanced hands. There are 40 high-card points in the deck, and when you have 33, the enemy have 7 at most. Two aces count 8 points, so the opponents cannot have them.

This line of reasoning does not apply to *suit* contracts, where each partner is likely to be counting extra points for long suits, voids, singletons, etc. Your side can easily have 33 points when the opponents hold 8 or even 10 high-card points. So you need the Blackwood Convention to make sure that the enemy points are not in aces.

Never use the Blackwood Convention until you are *certain* that your side has the 33-point total needed for slam. This device is used not to *bid* slams but to *stay out* of them. You certainly do not want to bid six if the opponents can win 2 tricks—Blackwood is used to make sure that *they* do not have two aces. But *you* can have all four aces and be unable to make even a part score, much less a slam. Slams are *beaten* by aces, but not made by them. They are made by 33 points.

There are quite a few auctions in which you can know, after the first or second round of bidding, that you and partner total 33 points. For example: you have a strong opening (17–19) and partner makes a jump-shift response (17–up). You have a maximum opening (20–up) and partner makes a jump response in notrump or your suit (13–16). Or partner opens and makes a strong rebid (17–19) when you have 16 points; partner opens and makes a maximum rebid (20–up) when you have 13 points. If you know where to play, jump right to slam when you have at least three aces yourself, use Blackwood if you have not.

When the auction suggests that a total of 33 points is possible but not certain, you must check up on partner's points, not his aces. And if you can tell that your side has fewer than 33 points, forget all about slam bidding—no matter how many aces you and partner hold, your limit is game. Slams are fun, but only when they are made.

♣ RULES TO REMEMBER

1. With an assured total of 33 points, jump to slam in notrump (or in a suit if you hold three aces).
2. Use Blackwood to check on aces for a suit slam, but only if sure of 33 points.
3. If unsure of 33 points, invite slam by bidding one more than game.

CHAPTER 8

High Opening Bids

The vast majority of auctions begin with an opening bid of one, but it is possible to start with a higher bid: two, three, or even four or five. These openings are rare, but very useful when you hold the specific sort of hands which call for them. In brief, hands are opened with **two-bids** if they are *too strong* for one-bids; hands are opened with bids of **three** or higher when they are *too weak* for one-bids, but contain an extraordinarily long suit.

• OPENING TWO-BIDS

Partner will pass your opening bid of *one* in a suit when he has fewer than 6 points. Therefore, if you are lucky enough to pick up a hand like this one:

♠ A K Q J 10 5   ♡ K Q J   ◇ A 6   ♣ A 4

you would be foolish to open *1* spade and risk being passed out under game. You hold in your own hand the 26 points needed; to put it another way, you can win ten tricks all by yourself. This is the sort of hand with which you should open two—here, 2 spades.

Actually, you need not hold in your hand the full 26 points (or ten winners) needed for game in order to open two. You should have enough points to give your side a fighting chance for game even when partner has fewer than 6. If your hand is worth 22 points, it is usually most unwise to open with one—partner will pass with 4 points, and then a game contract will be missed. Therefore, if you hold a long, strong suit in a hand worth 22 points or more, open with a bid of two in your suit. Consider these examples:

(a) ♠ A K Q J 10 7   ♡ A K J   ◇ 84   ♣ 62
(b) ♠ A K 10 8 4 2   ♡ 3   ◇ A K J 7   ♣ A Q
(c) ♠ 5   ♡ A K J 4 2   ◇ A K Q 8 3   ♣ K 8
(d) ♠ 4   ♡ A   ◇ A Q J 10 7   ♣ A K J 9 4 3

Open *1* spade, not 2 spades with hand (a). It has 20 points, and if partner has the 6 points you need for game, he will respond to a one-bid. Open two-bids with the next three examples: 2 spades with (b), 2 hearts with (c) (higher ranking of two equally long suits), 2 clubs with (d) (longer suit first).

What if you have 22 points or more, but no long suit? For example:

   (e) ♠ K 8 ♡ A Q J 5 ◊ K Q 6 4 ♣ A K J
   (f) ♠ A J 3 ♡ K Q J 2 ◊ A K Q ♣ A Q 7

With hand (e), open 2 *notrump*. This shows balanced distribution, with 22 points to 24 points. Hand (f) is even stronger—26 points. Open 3 notrump. This promises 25 to 27 high-card points, without a long suit.

RESPONDING TO TWO-BIDS

When partner opens with a bid of two in a suit, the cardinal rule is: **Never allow the auction to die below game.** No matter how miserable a collection of worthless cards you have been dealt, you must respond, and you must keep on responding until a game contract is reached. Suppose partner opens 2 hearts, and you hold:

   ♠ Q 6 3 2 ♡ 8 5 3 ◊ 6 4 3 ♣ 1 0 9 2

Clearly you would have passed had partner opened 1 heart, but now you are forced to bid. Respond 2 *notrump*. The response of 2 notrump to partner's two-bid is *negative*, corresponding to the pass of a one-bid. It says, "Partner, I am delighted to hear that you have a strong hand, but do not count on me for anything much. I am bidding only because you have a gun to my back." This negative response does not finish your job, however. If you have the preceding hand and the auction goes:

PARTNER	YOU
2 hearts	2 notrump
3 hearts	?

Bid 4 hearts! *You may not pass under game,* so you raise partner. Remember, he opened with a two-bid just because he wanted to be in game when you hold this horrible hand. Partner's 3 heart rebid was intended *not* to let you pass, but to permit you to express an opinion on *where* to play the game contract. You might have a long suit in your weak hand, for example:

♠ Q 10 8 6 3 2   ♡ 8 5   ◇ 6 4   ♣ J 9 2

Now you would suggest your suit as trump at your second turn to bid:

PARTNER	YOU
2 diamonds	2 notrump
3 diamonds	3 spades

Notice that your *first* bid is the negative 2 notrump response, telling partner that you would have passed a one-bid.

If you *would* have responded to a one-bid, then you may make a *positive* response to a two-bid. Any bid other than 2 notrump—either a raise of partner's suit or a change of suit—is positive, showing 6 points or more. With this hand:

♠ K Q 8 7 3   ♡ Q 8 5   ◇ 7 4 2   ♣ 9 6

bid 2 spades in answer to a 2 club or 2 diamond opening. However, if partner opens 2 *hearts*, raise to 3 hearts. (Your first choice of a positive response should be the raise of partner's suit, if you can support it.) Raise a 2 spade opening to 3 spades.

The attitude of both partners should be that a two-bid faced by a positive response is likely to produce a slam (a two-bid will produce *game* opposite a *negative* response). After a fit is found, opener will usually use Blackwood to check on aces, and then go on to some very high contract. Here is a typical auction:

OPENER	RESPONDER
♠ A K Q 10 7 4	♠ 6 5 3
♡ A K J 5	♡ 9 2
◇ A 2	◇ K Q J 7 5
♣ 8	♣ K 6 4
2 spades	3 diamonds
3 hearts	3 spades
4 notrump	5 clubs
6 spades	pass

Notice that no jump bid was made in the early auction, even though both partners knew that a slam was in view. There is never any need for a jump after an opening two-bid; *how high* to play is already settled, so *where* to play is the first order of business. Responder makes a positive response, suggesting diamonds as trumps; opener shows his second suit (he has no need to rebid his first suit; the opening bid indicated long, strong spades). Next, responder shows his preference for spades (with a high honor and two other spades, he would have raised directly). Now that a fit is located, opener launches into Blackwood, finds that the enemy have an ace, and settles for a small slam.

RESPONDING TO 2 NOTRUMP

When partner opens 2 *notrump,* instead of 2 in a suit, you are not forced to respond. This does not mean that you are encouraged to pass with all poor hands. For example, you should respond to a 2 notrump opening with either of these sad specimens:

(1) ♠ Q 5 2   ♡ 9 6 3   ◇ Q 8 7 4   ♣ 8 5 2
(2) ♠ Q 10 7 6 3   ♡ 7 2   ◇ J 7 3 2   ♣ 7 4

A 4-point hand is sufficient for game, since partner has 22. With hand (1) raise to 3 notrump. With hand (2), bid 3 spades, and offer partner his choice of game contracts. However, if you have an even weaker hand:

(3) ♠ J 8 4   ♡ 7 3 2   ◇ 10 7 5 3   ♣ 9 6 5

pass partner's 2 notrump. He would have opened 3 notrump if he could make game opposite your rubbish. Remember, though, that you must not pass a forcing two-bid in a *suit* even with the hand above. Bridge players have been shot by their partners with less excuse than this, and passing a forcing two-bid may well be deemed justification for homicide in your home state.

If you hold a fairly strong responding hand when partner opens 2 notrump, you may think of slam. Add your assets to partner's, and compare the total with 33.

OPENER	RESPONDER
♠ A Q 5	♠ K 8 4
♡ K J 7	♡ A Q 6 5
◇ A K J 4	◇ Q 9 2
♣ A 9 2	♣ 8 6 3
2 notrump	6 notrump
pass	

The 2 notrump opening promises 22 to 24 points, so responder, with 11 points, can add up to a sure 33 or more. Observe that he need not check on aces; with 33 points in *high cards*, the partnership cannot be missing two aces. In fact, if responder bids 4 notrump over 2 notrump, this is *not* Blackwood. It is a raise over game in notrump, requesting opener to go on to slam with 24 points, but to pass with 22 points. If, in the example above, responder's hand were:

♠ K 8 4   ♡ A Q 6 5   ◊ 9 6 2   ♣ 8 6 3

he should raise to 4 notrump with his 9 points, and opener, with a minimum, would pass. (Or, at any rate, he *should* pass. Some players find it impossible to believe that they have a minimum when they are looking at 22 fat points. Still, the 2 notrump opener has already shown his tremendous high-card strength, and must leave almost the entire burden of determining how high to play on partner's shoulders.)

• OPENING BIDS OF THREE OR MORE

When you open the bidding with *three* in a suit, you are not announcing a hand too strong for two (nothing is stronger than a two-bid). In fact, you should not have enough points even to open one. Why bid at all, then? Because you urgently, desperately, want your suit to be the trump. Consider this hand:

♠ A Q J 9 7 4 3   ♡ 3   ◊ 9 5 2   ♣ 8 4

If spades are trumps, this hand can win 6 or 7 tricks; if any other suit is trump, it will win 1 trick. Therefore, you want to bid, to suggest your long suit as trump. However, you have only 10 points, not nearly enough for a one-bid. With such a hand you open 3 spades.

Obviously, you will not be able to make your contract when partner is weak; but if partner does not have the high cards to permit you to take 9 tricks, he does not have enough to stop the enemy from making game. That is when your three-bid will show its biggest profit. If the opponents allow you to play with spades as trumps, they will earn a paltry little score, yet they have too little bidding room to determine accurately where or how high to play their own contract. Here you see clearly the principal purpose of a high **preemptive** opening bid: not to find out what *your* side can make, but to prevent the enemy from discovering what *they* can make.

Opening with a preemptive bid is like turning out the lights and forcing everyone to bid in the dark.

REQUIREMENTS FOR A THREE-BID

What are the requirements for an opening bid of three? First a hand *weak* enough to tempt you to "turn off the lights." **Never open with three if you are strong enough to open with one.** Second, a very long, very strong suit: 7 cards or longer, with at least three of the top five honors. You want to be able to win 6 tricks yourself (mostly with trumps), so that it is not too expensive a set when partner has a poor hand. Here, by the way, you must worry about being *vulnerable* (having already scored a game, so that your penalties are increased). So far in this book, you have expected to make every contract you bid; but when you open with a three-bid, you expect to go down. Therefore, avoid opening with three if you have made one game and are vulnerable. Assuming you are nonvulnerable, which of these hands would you open with three?

(a) ♠5 ♡A84 ◇K1076532 ♣Q9
(b) ♠A4 ♡KQJ9863 ◇J52 ♣6
(c) ♠7 ♡84 ◇653 ♣KQJ10842

Do *not* open 3 diamonds with example (a). You do not have three honors in your long suit; you must pass. Do *not* open 3 hearts with example (b). Your hand has a value of 14 points, far too much for a preemptive opening; bid 1 heart. With example (c) you *should* open 3 clubs. Do not worry about having too few points; the strength requirement for a three-bid is a *maximum*, not a minimum. You have a 7-card suit with sufficient honors, in a hand that can win 6 tricks: and you have *few enough* points.

RESPONDING TO THREE-BIDS

When your partner opens with a three-bid, you should almost always pass. Remember, partner is not strong enough to open one, so game is unlikely; also, he has a magnificent suit and no interest in any suit of yours. Suppose partner opens 3 hearts, and you hold:

♠K108752 ♡4 ◇KQ6 ♣QJ4

Pass! Your hand is worth 13 points, but partner has *less* than 13, so the total cannot reach 26. Partner's hearts are much longer and stronger than your spades; so no purpose can be served in bidding. Your high cards may be barely enough to allow partner to make his contract; he expected, you will recall, to go down.

Of course, it is possible to hold a hand strong enough to make game opposite a three-bid. This will usually require 15 or 16 points, since partner's hand is unlikely to be worth more than 10 or 11. Suppose partner opens 3 spades, and you hold:

(a) ♠ 8 5 3   ♡ A 7   ◇ A K Q 10 8 4   ♣ 7 4
(b) ♠ 4   ♡ A K 8 6 3   ◇ A K 6   ♣ Q 10 5 2

With either hand raise to *4 spades*. Observe that you do not bid diamonds with hand (a); never bid a new suit over partner's preemptive opening. Notice the raise on a singleton with hand (b); partner has seven spades, so your singleton guarantees a good trump suit (8 cards between the two hands).

If partner's three-bid is in a *minor* suit, you should think about game in notrump. This requires the same minimum of 15 to 16 points, protection in the three unbid suits, and 3 cards in partner's suit (2 is enough if they include the ace or king). This last requirement is to be sure that you can use partner's long suit to win tricks in notrump. If partner opens 3 diamonds, what is your action with these hands?

(c) ♠ A Q 4   ♡ A 8 5   ◇ A 2   ♣ J 10 8 4 3
(d) ♠ K Q 7 2   ♡ Q J 9 5   ◇ 8   ♣ A K 5 3

Bid 3 notrump with example (c); you have protection in all unbid suits, a fit for diamonds, and 16 points. However, do *not* bid 3 notrump with example (d), for you have no fit in partner's suit—you would have to try to take 9 tricks all in your own hand, and you would fail miserably. What do you bid? You pass. Even 15 points is not sufficient to produce game in a *minor* suit opposite a three-bid. Since no game is possible, you settle for a part score.

FOUR-BIDS AND FIVE-BIDS

Almost always, you will open three when you have a long, strong suit in a weak hand. However, on rare freak hands, you may wish to open *4* hearts or *4* spades. These are still preemptive openings, made in the expectation of going down (if you could take 10 tricks in your own hand you would open *two*, not four). Now, however, you have at least an 8-card suit, and you expect to win 7 or 8 tricks unaided. For example, open 4 hearts with this hand:

♠ —— ♡ K Q J 9 8 6 5 2 ♢ J 10 9 6 ♣ 4

Notice that you still do not have enough points to open *1* heart. Still, you have such powerful distribution that you might easily make game even if partner has too little to bid over 3 hearts.

Avoid opening four-bids in minor suits. If partner happens to hold a very strong hand, your most likely game is 3 notrump. Thus, if you have opened 4 clubs or 4 diamonds, you may have preempted your own side out of its own best contract. With a gigantic freak hand in a *minor* suit—a 9-card suit, for example—you can open *five*. However, I would not recommend that you overdo this; once every nine years is about right.

♥ RULES TO REMEMBER

1. With a long suit, open two with 22 points or more.
2. Partner's two-bid in a suit is forcing to game. Respond 2 notrump if you would have passed a one-bid. Any other response suggests slam.
3. With even distribution, open 2 notrump with 22–24 points, 3 notrump with 25–27.
4. Open three or more in a 7-card or longer powerful suit when you are not strong enough to open with one.
5. When partner opens three or more, you usually pass.

CHAPTER 9

When the Opponents Open the Bidding

So far, you and your partner have been doing all the bidding. We have examined in detail how to develop the auction after your side makes the opening bid, but how do you proceed when an opponent opens?

The first answer to this question is to proceed *with caution*. It is very dangerous to enter the auction after an enemy opening bid. Suppose that you are dealt this hand:

♠ 8 5   ♡ Q 9 2   ◇ A K J 4   ♣ J 8 7 3

If *partner* opens the bidding with 1 spade you are perfectly safe in responding 2 diamonds; partner has 13 points or more, and the combined total of at least 24 points is assurance that your side can make an 8- or 9-trick contract even though no trump fit has yet been found. In contrast, if your *opponent* opens 1 spade, no such safety exists, since opener's points count against you, not for you. Now when you bid 2 diamonds you may find partner with only 3 or 4 points and no trump fit. Then you will be able to win only 2 or 3 tricks instead of the 8 you have contracted for, and this can lead to a disastrous penalty. How can you expect to win a substantial majority of the tricks when all you know is that one opponent has a stronger hand than you have?

OVERCALLS AND DOUBLES

With the preceding 11-point example hand you cannot expect to win many tricks, so you must pass. However, you may be dealt an 11-point hand that looks like this one:

♠ 4   ♡ Q J 7   ◇ K Q J 10 6 3   ♣ 9 5 2

Now it is safe to bid 2 diamonds when your opponent opens 1 spade. Why? Because *with your long suit as trump* you expect to win more tricks than will the opening bidder. You can take about 6 tricks with your own cards if diamonds are trumps, so the set will be small even if partner contributes nothing. And in that case the enemy could surely score more points by playing with their own suit as trump.

This 2-diamond bid, the bid in a suit of your own after an opponent's opening, is called an **overcall**. The basic ingredient of an overcall is *not* a high point count, but a long, strong suit. With such a suit, you may safely overcall even when your hand is too weak for an opening bid; without such a suit, you may *not* overcall, regardless of the strength of your *hand*.

This raises the problem of what to do after an enemy opening when you have a powerful hand that contains no long suit. For example, suppose your opponent opens 1 spade and you hold:

♠ 7 5   ♡ A Q 6   ◇ K J 4 2   ♣ A J 9 6

You cannot overcall, for none of your suits is nearly long enough. Yet there is every prospect that your side can win more tricks than can the enemy. After all, you have 15 points —probably as much strength as the opening bidder holds, and quite possibly more.

With such a hand, you say "Double." As we will see later, this is called a **takeout double**. It is your principal means of telling your partner, "Do not be intimidated by our opponent's opening bid, for I have at least as many points as he has."

We see, then, that you enter the auction after an enemy opening bid in two entirely different fashions, corresponding to the two different reasons you can have for bidding:

1. You think that you can win a great many tricks, but only if your long suit is trump, in which case you *overcall*.
2. You think that you have as many points as opener has (or more), in which case you *double*.

• THE OVERCALL

In determining whether or not to overcall after an opponent's opening bid, you must ask yourself first, "How long and strong is my *suit?*" Only after answering the first question satisfactorily should you bother to think, "How strong is my hand?"

SUIT REQUIREMENTS

The minimum requirements for length and strength of your suit vary with the level at which you are forced to bid. (You will always overcall as cheaply as possible. If you have a diamond suit, you will bid *1* diamond over a 1 club opening; but you are forced to bid 2 diamonds over a 1 heart opening —and here the requirements are stricter.)

If you can overcall at the one-level, you require at least:
a 5-card suit headed by two honors, or a 6-card suit headed by one honor
If you must overcall at the two-level, you require at least:
a 5-card suit headed by three honors, or a 6-card suit headed by two honors
Never overcall in a 4-card suit, however strong

Consider these heart suits:

(a) ♡ A 8 6 4 3 2   (d) ♡ K Q J 9 4
(b) ♡ K Q 9 7 4 2   (e) ♡ A J 6 3
(c) ♡ A 10 7 6 3   (f) ♡ A K J 2

With which could you overcall 1 heart after a 1 diamond opening bid? With which could you overcall 2 hearts after a 1 spade opening bid?

Suit (a) qualifies for 1 heart, but *not* for 2 hearts.

Suit (b) qualifies for either overcall.

Suit (c) barely qualifies for 1 heart, certainly *not* for 2 hearts.

Suit (d) qualifies for either overcall.

Suits (e) and (f) are not long enough for any overcall at any level.

POINT-COUNT REQUIREMENTS

Once your suit qualifies for an overcall, you may look to see whether your *hand* is strong enough. You may overcall at the one-level with as little as 8 points. However, if your overcall must be made at the two-level, the minimum requirement is 10 points. Clearly, you will seldom have any difficulty in meeting these requirements—any long, strong suit counts almost enough by itself. Remember, the overcall describes a strong *suit*, not a strong *hand*. The one-level overcall may be as weak as a minimum response to an opening bid, so long as the suit is a good one. The two-level overcall has the same lower limit (10 points) as a two-level *response* to partner's opening; the difference is that the suit must be very long and powerful.

The range of the overcall extends from these low requirements (8 to 10 points) up as high as a minimum opening bid, 13 to 16 points. However, 16 points is almost too much strength for an overcall, and is the absolute top limit. A hand that would be a strong opening bid (17 points or more) is *never* an overcall, regardless of suit quality—we will see that alternative actions are available. The normal strength for an overcall is 10 to 12 points (a strong *responding* hand). You may have a point or two less if you can bid at the one-level; you can have as much as an ace more, on rare occasions. But if you can take an ace out of your hand and still have an opening bid remaining, you *must not overcall*.

Your right-hand opponent opens the bidding 1 heart. What is your action with these hands?

(1) ♠ Q 8 4 ♡ 7 2 ◇ K J 9 7 4 3 ♣ 6 4
(2) ♠ J 8 6 4 3 ♡ A Q 5 ◇ K 9 4 ♣ 8 2
(3) ♠ A Q 7 4 ♡ 2 ◇ 9 4 ♣ Q J 10 8 5 3
(4) ♠ K J 6 3 2 ♡ 7 4 ◇ A Q 10 8 5 ♣ 6
(5) ♠ A K Q J 8 4 ♡ 6 2 ◇ A Q 2 ♣ 9 3

(1) *Pass.* Your suit is strong enough for an overcall, but your hand is not—you must not bid at the *two*-level with only 8 points. However, had the opening bid been 1 *club*, you could overcall *1* diamond.

(2) *Pass.* Your suit is too weak for an overcall, so the fact that you have 11 points is meaningless.

(3) Bid 2 *clubs*. In overcalling, you still bid your longer suit first. Both the club suit and the point count are satisfactory.

(4) Bid *1 spade*. With two equally long · suits, bid the higher-ranking one first. Your spades qualify for a one-level overcall.

(5) Do *not* bid 1 spade! Your suit is magnificent, but your hand is worth 18 points, too much for an overcall. (We will see later that this hand qualifies for a jump to *2 spades*.)

WHEN PARTNER OVERCALLS

How do you respond when your partner overcalls? Most of the time, the answer is simple: *you pass*. With a minimum responding hand (6 to 9 points), you have enough to keep the auction alive when partner *opens the· bidding*, but not when partner *overcalls*.

After all, if partner *opens*, your 6 to 9 points might well produce game. And since partner may have opened in a 4-card suit, you may wish to search for a different trump. In contrast, if partner *overcalls*, he cannot have a strong (17-to-19-point) or a maximum (20-point) hand; therefore, even 9 points cannot yield game. What is more, you know that partner's overcall is in a strong suit, so there is no need to suggest a different trump. Thus, if the auction goes:

OPPONENT	PARTNER	OPPONENT	YOU
1 diamond	1 spade	pass	?

and your hand is:

♠ 8 4   ♡ K J 7 2   ◇ 9 6 3   ♣ A 10 5 2

you should pass. Had partner opened 1 spade, you would have responded 1 notrump for two reasons: (1) game would be possible (partner could easily have 18 points facing your 8); (2) a better trump suit might be found. But when partner *overcalls*, neither reason applies: he cannot have the 18 points you need to total 26: his spade suit is long and strong, so you need not search for a different trump.

You do not *always* have to pass partner's overcall. With 10 points or more, you have some slight chance for game (since partner may possibly have 15 or 16 points), so you should try to find a response. Most often, your action will be a raise of partner's suit. The overcall promises at least a 5-card, and usually a 6-card, suit; therefore, three small trumps in your hand constitute good support. Suppose that you hold:

♠ 9 6 3   ♡ K 8 3   ◇ Q 10 9 5 4   ♣ A 7

Your left-hand opponent opens 1 club and partner overcalls 1 spade. Raise to 2 *spades*. If the opening bid is, instead, 1 spade, and partner overcalls 2 hearts, raise to 3 *hearts*. Notice that you do not bid diamonds on either auction. Partner is unlikely to be interested in *your* suit when he overcalls, and, in any event, you have found a fit in *his* suit, so why look for another?

Nonetheless, you are allowed to bid a new suit if you have a long, strong one (the requirements are the same as for an independent overcall of your own). You should do this primarily when your suit is a major, and partner has overcalled in a minor. However, when partner overcalls in clubs or diamonds and you have enough strength for a response, think of bidding *notrump* if you have some protection in opener's suit. Notrump is always the most promising game contract when partner has a long minor suit.

Once in a while, you will have enough strength to give you a *lively* interest in game even opposite an overcall. If you have a minimum opening bid of your own, *jump* in partner's suit (if you can support it) or *jump* in notrump (if you have a stopper in the enemy suit). These jump bids are limited, inviting partner to go to game, but allowing him to pass with a minimum overcall. *None* of the responses we have discussed so far is forcing (not these jump bids, not even a change of suit). Therefore, if you should hold a strong opening bid when partner overcalls, you must make a different bid which partner may not pass. This is the jump shift, the jump in a new suit, which is forcing to game.

The bidding goes:

OPPONENT	PARTNER	OPPONENT	YOU
1 club	1 spade	pass	?

What action do you take with these hands?

    (a) ♠ J 4 ♡ K Q 8 6 4 3 ◇ 7 2 ♣ 10 8 3
    (b) ♠ Q 5 4 ♡ 8 3 ◇ A Q 10 7 4 ♣ 7 5 2
    (c) ♠ 6 3 ♡ K Q 9 4 ◇ Q 8 2 ♣ A 10 8 4
    (d) ♠ 5 ♡ A Q 10 9 6 3 ◇ K 5 4 ♣ 9 8 4
    (e) ♠ J 8 4 ♡ K 3 ◇ A K J 5 2 ♣ 6 5 3
    (f) ♠ K 4 ♡ A Q J 7 3 ◇ K 6 5 ♣ A 4 2

    (a) Pass. You should not respond to partner's overcall with an 8-point hand.

    (b) Bid *2 spades*. Your hand is worth 10 points, adding for the fifth diamond and the doubleton heart. *Two diamonds* is a foolish response, for you have found a good major suit for trump.

    (c) Bid *1 notrump*. There is a slight chance for game even though you cannot support partner. Your heart suit is not long enough to bid, but your club strength allows you to bid notrump.

    (d) Bid *2 hearts*. This is the rare hand with which you suggest a new suit after an overcall. Note that you would have overcalled yourself even if partner had passed. When you bid a new suit, you are not really "responding" to partner, you are bidding independently.

    (e) Bid *3 spades*. Your 14 points and 3-card support (partner must have five spades at least) suffice for this jump raise. Partner will pass with a minimum overcall, or go to game with a maximum.

(f) Bid *3 hearts*. With 18 points, you must insist on game, not merely invite it. Your jump shift is forcing, and allows you to find out where to play your game contract without risking a pass from partner.

• THE TAKEOUT DOUBLE

PENALTY AND TAKEOUT DOUBLES

The bid "double" has this primary meaning: "I do not believe that the opponents can make the contract they have just bid. Therefore, at the risk of doubling their score should they fulfill their contract, I am going to double (or more) the size of their penalty when they go down." For example, suppose that you hold this hand:

♠ 5　♡ K Q 10 8 4　♢ A J 7 3　♣ Q 8 4

Your opponents, no doubt unwisely, reach a contract of 4 hearts. How can they win 10 tricks when you will probably take three or four trump tricks plus your ace? Since you expect the opponents to go down, you say "Double."

Now, suppose that you hold the same hand above and the bidding goes:

PARTNER	OPPONENT	YOU	OPPONENT
1 spade	2 hearts	?	

Once again, the enemy are out beyond their depth. Your side has many more high cards than theirs; and they will not make up the difference by winning a great number of trump tricks, for *you* are long and strong in their suit. Therefore, they will not come close to making their contract. You say "Double," expecting to collect a huge penalty.

These are examples of the normal **penalty** or **business double**. Observe that in each case you are certain that the opponents will go down. In the first instance, they reached a high contract which you could defeat with your own cards. In the second example, they were in a low contract which you could not defeat on your own, but partner had opened the bidding and you knew *he* could take high-card tricks as well—your combined strength was much greater than theirs.

However, consider your position when an opponent opens the bidding with one of a suit, and you are next to speak. You know nothing about partner's hand, so even if you hold

16 or 18 points you cannot be sure that your *side* has more points than have the enemy. And you are most unlikely to hold enough tricks *in your own hand* to guarantee the defeat of such a low contract. Therefore, *you cannot want to make a penalty double*. The conditions which make a penalty double impossible are these:

(1) **Your partner has never entered the auction, and**
(2) **The enemy bid is low (under game)**

Under these circumstances, the bid "double" is given an entirely different meaning. You say "I have a strong hand, partner, so bid your best suit." This is called a takeout double because partner must "take out" the double by bidding a new suit.

Obviously, you will make this takeout double at your first opportunity to do so; you are forcing partner to bid, and you want him to be able to respond as cheaply as possible. In fact, if you double at your second turn instead of your first, as in this auction:

OPPONENT	YOU	OPPONENT	PARTNER
1 spade	pass	1 notrump	pass
2 spades	*double*		

your double is for penalties. Had you wanted partner to bid, you would have doubled right over *1* spade; since you did not, you must hold some extraordinary hand that can defeat 2 spades unaided.

Thus, there are really *three* conditions which must be met before a double is for takeout: partner must never have bid; you must double an under-game contract; you must not have passed up an earlier chance to double. In effect, the takeout double must be made right over an enemy opening bid, or right over the first response to this opening bid.

	OPPONENT	YOU	OPPONENT	PARTNER
(a)	1 diamond	double		

or

	OPPONENT	PARTNER	OPPONENT	YOU
(b)	1 heart	pass	2 hearts	double

Note that in both of these auctions you are doubling a *partial* contract at your *first turn, before partner has bid*. If any one of these conditions is *not* met (for example, if partner had made an overcall instead of passing in auction (b) above), your double is for penalties.

REQUIREMENTS FOR A TAKEOUT DOUBLE

The minimum requirement for a takeout double is 13 points—the same as for an opening bid. With fewer than 13 points you may overcall (if your suit is strong enough), but you may not double. When you employ the takeout double, your basic message to partner is, "I have an opening bid of my own, so do not assume that the enemy have more points than we do, simply because they opened."

Like an opening bid, the takeout double has a wide range of strength. It can be made with a 13-to-16-point minimum hand, with a 17-to-19-point strong hand, or with a 20-to-21-point maximum hand. *Unlike* an opening bid, the takeout double must meet rather strict distributional requirements. After all, you are asking partner to bid his best suit and you must be prepared to like what you hear. For example, suppose that your right-hand opponent opens 1 heart and you are next to speak with one of these hands:

(a) ♠ 10 7 4 3 ♡ Q J 8 6 4 2 ◇ A ♣ A 5
(b) ♠ A Q 9 4 ♡ 5 ◇ A J 6 2 ♣ Q 8 7 4

If you double with hand (a), partner will answer by bidding 2 clubs or 2 diamonds (he is most likely to be long in your short suits); you are then in the unenviable position of hating the contract your side is in, but having no place to go. Therefore, you would be wiser to pass over 1 heart and hope to score points by setting the opponents. Contrast this with your position if you double with hand (b), which has the perfect distribution for a takeout double. Partner will bid 1 spade or 2 clubs or 2 diamonds, and you have excellent support for whichever suit he picks.

Actually, you will seldom be dealt this ideal pattern—three 4-card suits with a singleton in the opponent's suit. Often, however, you will have distribution which is reasonably close, as in these examples:

(c) ♠ K Q 8 4 ♡ A 2 ◇ K 7 5 4 ♣ Q 10 3
(d) ♠ A Q 7 5 ♡ 4 ◇ K Q J 7 2 ♣ Q 9 4
(e) ♠ K 10 4 ♡ J 9 3 ◇ A K J 2 ♣ K 10 2

With all three, you may double a 1 heart opening bid. The patterns are not perfect, but they are acceptable. You have at least 3-card support for any of the three unbid suits and, after all, partner may be gracious enough to pick a suit in which you hold 4 or 5 cards.

However, when you have 2 cards or fewer in any unbid suit, your distribution is *poor* for a takeout double. Do *not* double with poor distribution if you hold a minimum (13-to-16-point) hand. For example, consider your action with the three hands above if the opening bid on your right is 1 *spade*, instead of 1 heart.

Hand (c): *Pass*. You have a minimum doubling hand which lacks support for hearts. Therefore, if you double and partner answers 2 hearts, you are in serious trouble.

Hand (d): Bid *2 diamonds*. Again, you must not double for fear of a heart response. Now, however, you need not pass, since your suit qualifies for an overcall. Remember, the overcall range extends up as high as a minimum double.

Hand (e): *Double*. You still have at least 3 cards in each unbid suit.

Observe that in examples (c) (14 points) and (d) (15 points) you dare not double even though you have the strength of a minimum opening bid. However, if you hold a "strong" (17-to-19) or "maximum" (20-to-21) hand, you need never fear to double. For instance, with:

♠ A J 8 4   ♡ A K J 7 2   ◇ K 5   ♣ J 3

You may double *any* enemy opening bid, regardless of your poor pattern. You are much too strong either to pass or to overcall. Thus, the minimum point count for a takeout double is 13 with ideal or acceptable distribution (at least 3 cards in each unbid suit), and 17 with poor distribution.

Let us illustrate this with a few more examples. What would be your action with each of the following hands when your right-hand opponent opens the bidding 1 heart? And what would you bid if, instead, he opens 1 diamond?

(1) ♠ Q J 8 6 4   ♡ 7   ◇ K J 7   ♣ A K 9 3
(2) ♠ A Q 7 2   ♡ A 10 8 4   ◇ 5   ♣ K 10 7 2
(3) ♠ K J 5   ♡ K 8 4   ◇ 7   ♣ A K Q J 9 3
(4) ♠ K 9 5 2   ♡ K J 10 6 5   ◇ 3   ♣ Q 10 4

(1) Over 1 heart, *double*. Over 1 diamond, overcall *1 spade;* you may not make a minimum double when short in an unbid suit, but your spades are long and strong enough for an overcall.

(2) Over 1 heart, *pass;* you may not double short in diamonds, and you have no suit which qualifies for an overcall. Over 1 diamond, you have an ideal *double*.

(3) *Double* over either opening; with a 19-point strong hand, you need not have acceptable distribution.

(4) Over 1 heart, *pass.* Over 1 diamond, overcall *1 heart;* your distribution is entirely acceptable for a double of 1 diamond, but your point count of 10 is insufficient.

RESPONDING TO PARTNER'S TAKEOUT DOUBLE

The basic rule of responding to partner's takeout double is a simple one: **You are not allowed to pass.** Never forget this, for all auctions following a takeout double are founded on it: no matter how poor a hand you hold, you must not pass. This means that if the auction should go:

OPPONENT	PARTNER	OPPONENT	YOU
1 heart	double	pass	?

and your hand is:

♠ Q 6 5 2   ♡ 8 4 3   ◊ 7 5 4   ♣ 9 6 2

you must bid *1 spade!* In fact, you would have to make the same bid without your queen—with a completely worthless hand.

If partner had *opened the bidding,* you would pass; why bid when he doubles? Because when you pass partner's opening bid, he is playing the contract and, at worst, will go down and lose 100 points or so; but when you pass partner's double, the *enemy* is left playing a *doubled* contract. The less strength you have, the more tricks they will take; and the opponents can score an astronomical number of points by making overtricks in a doubled contract. Therefore, the less strength you have, the *more certainly* you must respond to partner's double.

This does not apply when your right-hand opponent acts:

OPPONENT	PARTNER	OPPONENT	YOU
1 heart	double	1 spade	?

Now you may pass with a poor hand, for the opponents are no longer in a doubled contract (and your partner gets another chance to bid; so you may pass even if your opponent *redoubles*). Actually, when your hand is valueless, your opponent will usually make some bid, and this takes you off the spot. However, if he passes, you have no choice but to respond.

In choosing your response to partner's double, you follow the familiar general principles: longer suit first, and of two equally long suits, the higher ranking first. Thus, if partner doubles an opening bid of 1 spade, and you hold:

♠ 8 3   ♡ 7 3   ◇ K 10 9 4   ♣ J 8 5 3 2

you answer 2 *clubs*, bidding your longer suit. And if, on the same auction, you hold:

♠ 9 2   ♡ Q 6 4 2   ◇ 8 5 3   ♣ K Q J 6

you respond 2 *hearts,* bidding your higher-ranking suit. Note that it shows no particular strength to respond at the two-level. Partner has forced you to bid, and you merely obey orders. Actually, no one can expect you to have a strong hand when both opener and partner have 13 points or more. There are usually only 10 or 12 high-card points left in the deck, to be split between you and opener's partner.

This means that it is not particularly surprising if your hand is worth only 3 or 4 or 5 points (although it is depressing). If your hand is worth 6 to 9 points, a normal minimum responding hand, you have more than your share of the remainder, and should be quite cheerful. When your hand is worth 10 points or more, a strong responding hand, you should be bursting with enthusiasm.

How do you burst with enthusiasm? By *jumping* in your longest (or higher-ranking) suit, instead of making the cheapest response. That is, if partner doubles an opening bid of 1 diamond, and you hold:

(a) ♠ A Q 8 4 2   ♡ K 7 4   ◇ 8 5 3   ♣ 9 2

you should respond 2 spades, not 1 spade. Remember, you would have been forced to answer *1* spade with:

(b) ♠ Q 6 5 2   ♡ 8 4 3   ◇ 7 5 4   ♣ 9 6 2

Hand (a) is so much stronger than hand (b) that you must *jump* to show the difference. If you hold a hand of moderate strength in between (a) and (b), such as:

(c) ♠ K 10 8 4   ♡ A 9 5 3   ◇ 8 5 2   ♣ 7 4

you respond only *1* spade. However, you plan to indicate that you have a fair number of honors by bidding *again* if you have the chance. And with hand (c) you would respond even if you did not have to (even if your right-hand opponent intervened over partner's double). In contrast, with hand (b) you would respond only if forced, and then you would never bid again.

It is possible to respond to partner's double by bidding *1 notrump*. This is seldom done, for, as we have seen, partner can probably support any suit you bid. However, if you have a hand in the 6-to-9-point range, with protection in the enemy suit, and with no desire to suggest a *major* suit as trump, then you may respond 1 notrump. This is a moderately encouraging bid, and should never be made with a hopeless hand. If partner doubles an opening bid of 1 club, respond *1 notrump* holding:

♠ Q 5   ♡ J 6 2   ◇ K J 8 2   ♣ Q 10 8 4

Your side may have enough points for game, and, if so, the likely spot is notrump. However, on the same auction you must respond *1 diamond* holding:

♠ 8 2   ♡ Q 5 4   ◇ J 8 6 2   ♣ J 10 7 3

There is no real chance for game, so why play in notrump, the hardest declaration of all? Likewise, if you hold:

♠ K J 8 2   ♡ Q 5   ◇ J 6 2   ♣ Q 10 8 4

you should prefer to bid *1 spade* instead of 1 notrump. Major-suit games are the easiest of all to make; therefore you must always tend to respond to partner's double by suggesting any 4-card or longer unbid *major* suit in your hand.

Consider these two auctions:

	OPPONENT	PARTNER	OPPONENT	YOU
(a)	1 heart	double	pass	?
(b)	1 heart	double	2 clubs	?

What would be your response with the following hands on auction (a), and on auction (b)?

(1) ♠ 10 8 6 4 3   ♡ 7 4   ◇ A Q 9 6   ♣ 9 2
(2) ♠ 8 5 2   ♡ Q 7 4   ◇ 7 4 3   ♣ Q 10 5 2
(3) ♠ 9 4   ♡ 8 3 2   ◇ A K Q 10 5   ♣ 7 6 4
(4) ♠ 6 4 3   ♡ K J 8   ◇ K J 10 7 2   ♣ 9 2

(1) On auction (a), respond *1 spade*. On auction (b) you no longer are forced to bid, but should *want* to respond with 7 points. Bid *2 spades*.

(2) Bid *2 clubs* on auction (a). You *must* respond, and are too weak to bid 1 notrump. On auction (b) *pass*. When your opponent intervenes, you are no longer compelled to respond.

(3) Jump to *3 diamonds* on either auction. With 10 points, you must urge partner to go game. A response of *2 diamonds* on auction (b) would show 6 to 9 points, not 10 or more.

(4) On auction (a), bid 1 notrump, suggesting the most likely game contract. On auction (b), respond *2 diamonds*. You dare not bid notrump without protection in *all* suits bid by the enemy.

Responses to partner's takeout double can be tabulated like this:

Your points:	You bid:
0 to 5	You must respond in your longest unbid suit. Never bid notrump. If your right-hand opponent acts, pass.
6 to 9	Respond in your longest suit or notrump. Plan to bid again. Respond even if your opponent intervenes.
10 or more	Jump in your longest suit (or notrump). Jump even if your opponent bids.

REBIDDING AFTER YOU HAVE DOUBLED

Your right-hand opponent opens the bidding; you double, partner responds to your double. Now, how do you proceed with the auction? You must bear in mind the two basic objectives of all bidding: Where to play? How high to play?

"How high?" is likely to be answered immediately. When you have a minimum double and partner has made a forced, nonjump response, your side will play a part-score contract at most (or let the enemy play the hand). You have 13 to 16 points; partner has fewer than 10 points; there cannot be the required total of 26 points for game. Thus, if you double an opening bid of 1 heart, holding:

♠ A Q 8 4   ♡ 7 2   ◇ K J 5 3   ♣ K 10 4

and partner responds 1 spade, or 2 clubs, or 2 diamonds, *you must pass*. There is no chance that partner has the 12 points or so which will produce game (he would then have made a *jump* response). However, there is a considerable danger that partner has a nearly worthless hand, and that you will be exposed to a disastrous penalty if you bid again.

In contrast, there *is* a fighting chance for game opposite a forced response when you have a strong double (17 to 19 points). Partner will not jump when he holds only 7 or 8 or 9 points; you may have a 26-point total and therefore must keep the auction alive. Do this either by raising partner's suit (usually with 4-card or longer support) or by bidding a new suit of your own. Partner, at his second turn, will pass with a hopeless hand, or move toward game with the required points. Suppose you double a 1 heart opening bid with this hand:

♠ K Q 7 3 ♡ 6 5 ♢ A Q J 8 2 ♣ K J

If partner responds 1 spade, raise to 2 *spades*. If partner, instead, answers 2 diamonds, raise to 3 *diamonds*. And if partner, as is more likely, should respond 2 clubs, you rebid 2 *diamonds*. All these actions promise a 17-to-19-point strong double, for you doubled and then *bid again*.

Notice that you are in a most difficult position if you have doubled a 1 heart opening bid, holding:

♠ K Q 5 ♡ 7 4 ♢ A Q 10 8 5 3 ♣ 9 2

Partner responds 2 clubs; what do you do now? Your side cannot have a total of 26 points, so you are supposed to pass. However, you must consider "Where?" as well as "How high?"; diamonds figures to be your best trump suit, since partner may have only four clubs. Yet if you bid 2 diamonds here, you have doubled and bid again, showing 17 to 19 points instead of the 13 you hold.

The way out of this dilemma is to *overcall* originally instead of doubling. In this example, you can see exactly why you must not double with a minimum hand that has a doubleton in an unbid suit: because you have to pass partner's response, and hate to do it. When you have a long, strong suit of your own, you double for takeout only if you have enough points to warrant a second bid—17 or more. Thus you should overcall with the example above, but *double* 1 heart with this hand:

♠ K Q 5 ♡ 7 4 ♢ A Q 10 8 5 3 ♣ A 9

Now you have an extra ace, and are too strong for an immediate overcall. Therefore, you are strong enough to double and bid again.

Even when you hold a maximum double (20 or 21 points), you cannot be sure of game opposite a nonjump response, for, remember, partner is forced to answer with a worthless hand. However, you must do more than merely bid again —you must issue a strong invitation to game. You do this by jumping at your second turn: a jump raise if you have 4-card support for partner's suit, or a jump shift if you have not. Partner will bid again over your jump rebid when he has any values at all (about 6 points); if he passes, he responded originally only because he had no choice (it is high treason for him to pass at his first turn).

You double a 1 heart opening bid, holding this hand:

♠ A Q 7 3   ♡ 8 4   ◇ A K Q 10 7 5   ♣ 3

If partner responds 1 spade, your hand is worth 20 points— 17 for high cards and length, 3 more for shortness after finding a fit. Therefore, your rebid is *3 spades*, showing a maximum double and begging partner to go to game with any high cards at all. (Why not bid your diamond suit? Because you want spades, not diamonds, to be trumps.)

What if your partner responds, instead, 2 clubs? Now your hand is worth only the original 17 points, since no fit has been found. This is not enough for the jump to 3 diamonds; you rebid 2 *diamonds* to show a strong but not a maximum double.

Let us review the material covered so far in this section by considering the proper rebid with these example hands:

(a) ♠ K Q 7   ♡ A J 10 6 4   ◇ Q 9 2   ♣ 5 3
(b) ♠ K Q 8 2   ♡ A J 10 8 3   ◇ A 4   ♣ Q 5
(c) ♠ A K Q J 4   ♡ A 9 3   ◇ A J 5   ♣ 8 6

Your right-hand opponent opens 1 club, and you quite correctly double. What is your action with each hand after partner responds 1 diamond?—when he responds 1 heart?—when he responds 1 spade?

(a) *Pass* over any response, since you have a minimum double. Do not bid 1 heart over a 1 diamond response; if you feel that you just *have* to bid your hearts, overcall originally. Do not raise a 1 heart response; it is pleasant to have

5-card support, but it does not make up for a minimum point count.

(b) Over a 1 diamond response, bid *1 heart*. Over a 1 heart or 1 spade response, raise to *2 hearts* or *2 spades*. With this strong double, you may bid again.

(c) Over a 1 diamond or 1 heart response, jump to *2 spades*. Over an unexpected 1 spade response, jump to *3 spades*. All jump rebids show a maximum double.

Note that in each case in which you have support for partner, your rebid is one level lower than it would be if you *open* the bidding and raise partner's response. That is, with a minimum hand you *pass* instead of raising to two; with a strong hand you *raise to two* instead of jumping to three; with a maximum hand you *jump to three* instead of jumping to game.

The conservatism comes from the fear that partner has some horrible hand like our earlier example:

♠ Q 6 5 2   ♡ 8 4 3   ◇ 7 5 4   ♣ 9 6 2

If you open, partner will not respond with this little monster; but he may hold it when he responds to your *double*. However, there are two sequences in which your rebidding can be more liberal, for you know that partner cannot have a "little monster." One goes like this:

OPPONENT	YOU	OPPONENT	PARTNER
1 club	double	1 heart	1 spade

Here partner was *not* forced to respond; after the intervening 1 heart bid, he would have passed with a worthless hand. Therefore, you may now rebid normally (as if you had opened, not doubled). When you have 4-card support, raise with a minimum double, jump-raise with a strong double, jump to game with a maximum double.

The second sequence in which you loosen up your rebid occurs when partner *jumps* in response to your double.

OPPONENT	YOU	OPPONENT	PARTNER
1 heart	double	pass	2 spades

Since partner's jump response promises 10 points or more, you may go right to game even with a minimum double if you are near the upper (16 points) limit. With a bare 13 to 14 points, you can raise—partner will pass under game if he also has nothing extra. And when you have a strong or maxi-

mum double, game is obviously assured. Jump to game with
4-card support, or force by bidding a new suit of your own.

EXAMPLE AUCTIONS

Here are three sample auctions, to demonstrate how the
double, response, and rebid work out:

(1) YOUR HAND   PARTNER'S HAND
     ♠ K Q 8 6   ♠ 7 4
     ♡ A 9 2   ♡ K 8 6 5 3
     ◇ A 7 5 2   ◇ K 8 4
     ♣ 4 3   ♣ J 6 2

OPPONENT	YOU	OPPONENT	PARTNER
1 club	double	pass	1 heart
2 clubs	pass	pass	2 hearts
pass	pass	pass	

Your Bidding: You *double* at your first turn with a minimum
hand that has support for all unbid suits.
You *pass* at your second turn because you do
not have a strong double, and partner was
forced to respond. You *pass* partner's 2 heart
rebid, knowing that a 26-point total is impossible (partner did not jump originally).

Partner's Bidding: Since partner did not have 10 points, he responded without jumping. He bid again at
his second turn to show that he had a normal
minimum response, not a "little monster."
Had *you* rebid 2 hearts over opener's 2 club
bid, partner would have jumped to game, expecting you to have 17 to 19 points.

(2) YOUR HAND   PARTNER'S HAND
     ♠ A 5   ♠ K 9 8 2
     ♡ 7 3   ♡ K 10 6
     ◇ A K J 9 8 5   ◇ Q 7 2
     ♣ A 6 3   ♣ 8 4 2

OPPONENT	YOU	OPPONENT	PARTNER
1 heart	double	pass	1 spade
pass	2 diamonds	pass	2 notrump
pass	3 notrump	pass	pass

Your Bidding: You *double* since, with 18 points, you are too strong to overcall. When partner responds, you rebid 2 *diamonds*—by doubling and bidding again, you show a strong *hand* as well as a strong *suit*. You raise partner's rebid to 3 *notrump* because no other 26-point game is possible, and because your long minor suit is excellent for notrump—partner must have some protection in hearts and moderate strength.

Partner's Bidding: Partner, with 8 points, could respond 1 notrump but prefers to suggest his major suit. When you bid again, showing 17 to 19 points, game becomes odds-on; partner tries for the notrump game because he has a heart stopper, and because you have not raised spades. Note that partner would have passed had you overcalled 2 diamonds originally instead of doubling first (you *would* have overcalled without one of your side aces).

(3) | YOUR HAND | PARTNER'S HAND |
|---|---|
| ♠ A K 7 | ♠ 8 3 2 |
| ♡ K Q 10 6 | ♡ J 5 4 3 |
| ◇ A 4 | ◇ J 7 6 2 |
| ♣ A 9 4 3 | ♣ 8 6 |

OPPONENT	YOU	OPPONENT	PARTNER
1 diamond	double	pass	1 heart
pass	3 hearts	pass	pass
pass			

Your Bidding: You have a maximum *double,* but you cannot go to game even when partner responds in hearts. Your jump rebid of 3 *hearts* is the strongest possible invitation to game; you must give partner the opportunity to pass.

Partner's Bidding: Partner is forced to respond once, since he may not leave the opponents in a doubled contract (which they would make). However, when you give him the chance to pass under game, he accepts it gratefully.

• OTHER DEFENSIVE BIDS

In the vast majority of cases in which you enter the bidding over an enemy opening, you will do so with a double or an overcall. However, there are four other methods of contesting the auction: the jump overcall, the double jump overcall, the 1 notrump overcall, and the cue bid. All these are rare, but you must know what they mean, and how to respond to them.

JUMP OVERCALLS

When you have a long, strong suit and 17 to 19 points, you will usually double first and then bid your suit. However, you have available an alternative—the **jump overcall:**

OPPONENT	YOU
1 heart	2 spades (or 3 *clubs* or 3 *diamonds*)

This shows the same strong hand as this more common sequence:

OPPONENT	YOU	OPPONENT	PARTNER
1 heart	*double*	pass	2 clubs
pass	*2 spades*		

The difference is that the direct jump overcall shows a colossal suit—a 6- or 7-card solid suit that needs no support from partner. If you double, you have some slight interest in *partner's* long suit even if you prefer your own; but when you jump overcall in a major suit, you announce that the hand must be played *only in your suit*. Consider these two examples:

(a) ♠ K J 8 6 5 3   ♡ A 9 2   ◊ 5   ♣ A K 7
(b) ♠ A K J 10 9 6 4   ♡ 7 4   ◊ 4   ♣ A Q 5

Both are 17-point hands with long spade suits. Over a 1 diamond opening bid, you should *double* with hand (a), intending to bid spades later; if partner persistently bids and rebids hearts, you are willing to play in that suit. In contrast, with hand (b) you want spades as the trump suit if partner has only a singleton; therefore, you jump-overcall to 2 *spades*.

How do you respond when your partner uses the jump overcall? You are not forced to bid; if you would have passed an opening bid, pass over the jump. However, keep the auction alive with even a minimum responding hand, for there is likely to be a game. Usually, you will raise partner's suit, particularly if it is a major. When partner jumps in a minor suit, bid notrump if you can stop the enemy suit. Suppose you hold:

♠ J 3   ♡ A 10 4   ◇ 8 6 3   ♣ J 10 8 7 2

Your left-hand opponent opens 1 heart, and partner jumps to 2 spades. Raise to 3 *spades*. Two-card support is excellent when you know that partner has six or seven trumps himself. However, if partner jumps to 3 diamonds over the one heart opening, respond 3 *notrump*. You could raise diamonds, but when partner has a long solid minor, you should always try for the 9-trick notrump game if you can stop the enemy suit. Note that you never consider bidding your club suit on either auction. If partner were at all interested in hearing your suit, he would have *doubled*.

DOUBLE JUMP OVERCALLS

The jump overcall skips one level of bidding (2 hearts instead of *1* heart, over 1 diamond.) The **double jump over-call:**

OPPONENT	YOU
1 diamond	*3 hearts*

skips *two* levels. This is a very much *weaker* bid than the single jump. The double jump overcall describes a powerful 7- or 8-card suit in a hand not worth an opening bid.

♠ 8 3   ♡ K Q J 10 7 6 5   ◇ Q 9 4   ♣ 3

With the hand above, jump to 3 *hearts* over an enemy 1 club or 1 diamond opening bid. However, if the opening bid is 1 *spade*, do not bid 3 hearts—this is now the strong *single* jump, not the preemptive *double* jump. You could, of course, double-jump to *4* hearts, but you should have at least an 8-card suit to bid at the four-level with a weak hand. Therefore, over the 1 spade opening content yourself with the sim-ple overcall of 2 *hearts*.

Observe that the double jump overcall is made with the identical hand with which you would open a three-bid. However, an *overcall* to the three-level describes a weak hand only when it skips *two* levels of bidding.

Treat partner's double jump overcalls the way you do his

opening three-bids. That is, almost always pass. If you have unusual strength—15 points at least—raise his suit.

1 NOTRUMP OVERCALLS

Another alternative to the takeout double is the overcall of 1 notrump:

OPPONENT	YOU
1 heart	*1 notrump*

This describes a hand which you would have opened with 1 notrump—16 to 18 points, and even distribution. The only difference between the *opening* and the *overcall* of 1 notrump arises because the opponents have bid a suit. You must have a sure trick in the enemy suit for the overcall. With this hand:

♠ J 8 4   ♡ K J 7   ◇ A Q 6 2   ♣ A Q 5

you would *open the bidding* 1 notrump. If the bidding is opened ahead of you with 1 club, 1 diamond, or 1 heart, you should *overcall* 1 notrump. However, if the opening bid is *1 spade,* you dare not bid notrump—the enemy might win too many spade tricks before you gain the lead. There is no need to pass over 1 spade though; you may *double.*

Actually, it is never necessary to overcall 1 notrump; you can always double instead. However, when you meet all the requirements (16 to 18 points, even distribution, protection in opener's suit), you should prefer to bid 1 notrump. This overcall gives partner a full picture of your strength and distribution in one bid.

It follows, therefore, that after your *partner* overcalls 1 notrump, *you* must add up the partnership assets and place the contract. You jump to 3 notrump with 10 points or more, bid 2 notrump with 8 or 9 points. Your response of two in a suit must be passed; your jump to three in a suit shows 10 points or more, and offers partner his choice of game contract. If you are sure of a suit game, you jump right to it. All this is exactly as if partner had *opened* 1 notrump.

THE CUE BID

The rarest action over an opponent's opening bid is the **cue bid,** the overcall in the enemy's own suit:

OPPONENT	YOU
1 heart	*2 hearts*

This auction does *not* mean that you want to play in hearts. You could not want your opponent's longest suit as *your* trump suit; if you were long in hearts, you would pass and let the enemy go down. This overcall is a "cue" bid, that is, an artificial bid which must not be passed out by partner. In fact, partner is not allowed to let the bidding die out until your side has reached game.

The cue bid is your strongest possible action over an enemy opening; it is the equivalent of an opening bid of two. You can use this bid either as a gigantic takeout double when you want to play in partner's best suit, or as a means of getting to game or slam when you have one or two magnificent suits of your own. For example, cue-bid 2 diamonds over an opponent's 1 diamond opening with all three of these hands:

(a) ♠ K Q J 5   ♡ A Q J 8   ◇ ——   ♣ A K J 10 3
(b) ♠ A Q J 10 8 4   ♡ K Q J 10 7   ◇ 4   ♣ A
(c) ♠ A K J 9 8 5 2   ♡ A Q 10   ◇ ——   ♣ K Q 5

Hand (a) is much stronger than a maximum (20-or-21-point) take-out double. It is worth 25 points in support of any unbid suit, so you will raise partner's response to game. Hand (b) can win 10 tricks all by itself; the cue bid allows you to find the proper trump suit without the risk of missing the sure game. (Partner must answer—probably by bidding 3 clubs; now you bid 3 *spades* and partner must bid again, for game has not been reached. If he has not raised spades, you can show your heart suit at your third turn.) With hand (c), you would have opened 2 spades if you were the dealer, but you must not bid 2 spades when an opponent opens. This, remember, would be a jump overcall, showing 17 to 19, not 22, points; partner could pass. Your cue bid makes sure of getting to game and even allows you to investigate your chance for slam.

When your *partner* cue-bids, respond initially just as if he had doubled, by bidding your best suit. You may pass only if there is an intervening bid:

OPPONENT	PARTNER	OPPONENT	YOU
1 heart	2 hearts	3 hearts	*pass*

Here you are not ending the auction; partner gets another chance to bid. However, your responsibilities are not over. If, on the auction above, partner next bids 3 spades, you would then be forced to bid, since game has not yet been reached. You must not *end the auction* with a pass until your side is in a game contract.

When partner cue-bids, just as when he opens with a two-bid, you should start thinking of slam if you have as much as a 6-to-9-point normal minimum responding hand.

♥ RULES TO REMEMBER

Below, in outline form, is a review of all the basic bids, responses, and rebids covered in this chapter.

You Enter the Bidding Yourself

Your Point Count:	Your Action:
6–9	You may act only with a long strong suit that can be bid at the one-level. Then, *overcall* (8 or 9 points).
10–12	(1) With a long, strong suit, overcall as cheaply as possible, either at the one-level or the two-level. (2) With a 7- or 8-card suit, you may *double-jump-overcall*.
13–16	(1) *Double* if you have at least 3 cards in all unbid suits. Pass partner's non-jump response. (2) *Overcall* if you have a long suit, and poor support for one or more unbid suits.
17–19	(1) *Double* and bid again over partner's response. (2) *Jump-overcall* with a self-sufficient suit. (3) *Bid 1 notrump* (16 to 18 points) with even distribution and protection in the enemy suit.
20–21	*Double*, and then jump over partner's response.
22–up	Cue-bid the enemy suit.

Partner Enters the Bidding

Your Point Count:	Your Response:
0–5	*Pass* unless partner doubles or cue-bids. Then bid your longest unbid suit. However, if opponent intervenes, *pass*.

6–9	(1) If partner overcalls, *pass*.
	(2) If partner doubles, bid your longest suit or notrump—even in competition. Bid a second time if you can.
	(3) Respond to a jump overcall—usually by raising or by bidding notrump.
10–12	(1) Respond to an overcall—usually by raising or by bidding notrump.
	(2) If partner doubles, jump in your longest suit.
	(3) Bid game over a jump or notrump overcall.
13–up	(1) If partner overcalls, jump-raise (13 to 16 points) or jump-shift (17 or more).
	(2) Jump-shift after any of partner's stronger actions. Check to see that you are not using a pinochle deck by mistake.

In conclusion, let me repeat my initial warning; it is very dangerous to enter the auction when the opponents open. If your point count and distribution do not warrant a double, a notrump overcall, a jump overcall, or a cue bid, if your length and strength of suit do not warrant a single overcall or a double jump overcall—do not despair. There is available to you the most common, most useful and, in the long run, most profitable action of all—the pass.

CHAPTER 10

Competitive Auctions

In this chapter, we shall examine in detail how to conduct auctions when *your* side opens the bidding and the opponents intervene—either with an overcall or with a takeout double.

• AFTER AN ENEMY OVERCALL

How does an opponent's overcall change your bidding? When partner opens, your response can be affected in three different ways:

1. You may no longer be *able* to make your normal response (partner opens 1 diamond; you intend to answer 1 heart, but you no longer can when an opponent intervenes with an overcall of 1 spade).

2. You are no longer *forced* to bid in order to keep the auction alive (partner opens 1 diamond; you intend to answer 1 spade with a 6-point hand, just to let partner rebid in case he holds 20 points, but you no longer have to when an opponent intervenes with an overcall of 1 heart—partner will have his chance to rebid even if you pass).

3. You may no longer *want* to make your normal response because the overcall gives you additional information (partner opens 1 diamond; you intend to respond 1 notrump, but you no longer want to after an opponent overcalls with 1 spade, for you have no stopper in spades. Or, you intend to respond 2 clubs, but an opponent overcalls in clubs—you no longer want to suggest this suit as your trump).

When you are unable to make your normal response, the key question is whether you are strong enough to bid your suit *at the level now necessary*. Suppose partner opens 1 club and you hold:

♠952 ♡AQJ86 ◇763 ♣64

Clearly, you would like to suggest your long, strong heart suit as trump. However, if your right-hand opponent overcalls 1 spade, you would have to bid 2 hearts. And, you will recall, it requires 10 points at least, not the 8 points you hold, to bid a new suit at the *two*-level. (It is not that you are afraid to be at the two-level, but that your change of suit forces opener to bid again—you will almost surely wind up at the three-level at least.) Therefore, you may not bid hearts after this overcall; you must *pass*. Contrast this with the situation when you hold:

♠ 9 5 2 ♡ A Q J 8 6 ◇ 7 6 3 ♣ K 4

Now, if partner opens 1 club and there is an overcall of 1 spade, you should bid 2 hearts. With 11 points, you need not fear to bid your suit at the necessary level.

Remember that the requirement of 10 points to bid a new suit over an enemy overcall applies *only when you must bid at the two-level*. In the preceding two examples, if your opponent's overcall were 1 *diamond*, you should respond 1 heart with either hand. There is no need to allow an overcall to stop you from bidding a strong suit at the *one*-level.

However, you may take advantage of an enemy overcall to avoid making a response for which you had little enthusiasm in the first place. Suppose that partner opens 1 club and you hold:

♠ Q 8 5 ♡ Q 7 6 4 ◇ Q 6 2 ♣ 9 5 3

If your right-hand opponent passes, you will respond 1 heart. True, you have no great desire to make hearts trump, and have little interest in game. Still, you must respond with 6 points, to give partner a chance to rebid in case he has 20 points; and so long as you are forced to bid, you may as well mention your suit, just in case partner has 4-card support.

All this is changed when your opponent overcalls with 1 diamond. You still *can* bid 1 heart, but you are no longer *forced* to. Why not? Because when the auction goes:

PARTNER	OPPONENT	YOU	OPPONENT
1 club	1 diamond	pass	pass

partner has his opportunity to rebid anyway—there have not been three consecutive passes. Therefore, you can now pass with the example hand above—you would have bid only to keep the auction alive, and your opponent has already performed this service for you.

THE FREE RESPONSE

Any response after an enemy overcall is known as a **free bid** (since you are no longer forced to answer with 6 points).

A free response does not necessarily promise great strength, but it does suggest that responder actively desires to call attention to some feature of his hand. That is, you may free-bid in a new suit at the one-level with a minimum responding hand (6 to 9 points)—but you will then have a strong *suit*, for you could otherwise pass. You may raise partner freely with 6 to 9 points—but you will then have strong support, or close to 9 points. You may make a free 1 notrump response with a minimum hand—but you will then have solid protection in the opponent's suit. Let us see some examples:

1. Partner opens 1 diamond; your opponent overcalls 1 heart. You hold:

   (a) ♠ K 8 4 2 ♡ Q 7 3 ◇ 7 3 ♣ J 6 5 4
   (b) ♠ K Q 10 9 6 3 ♡ 6 4 ◇ 8 2 ♣ 5 3 2

Were there no overcall, you would respond 1 spade with either hand. Now, pass with hand (a), since neither your suit nor your point count is exciting. However, bid *1 spade* with hand (b). With such a strong suit, you *want* to bid even though you are not forced to respond.

2. Partner opens 1 heart; your opponent overcalls 1 spade. You hold:

   (c) ♠ 8 3 ♡ Q 5 2 ◇ K 9 4 2 ♣ J 7 6 3
   (d) ♠ 7 4 ♡ K Q J 3 ◇ Q 10 8 2 ♣ 6 5 3

Here, you would have raised to 2 hearts with either hand had your opponent passed. Now, raise only with hand (d). Example (c) has the barest minimum both in point count and trump support, so *pass*.

3. Partner opens 1 diamond; your opponent overcalls 1 spade. You hold:

   (e) ♠ 5 2 ♡ Q 7 4 ◇ 8 4 3 ♣ A Q 10 6 4
   (f) ♠ K J 4 ♡ Q 8 3 ◇ 7 5 2 ♣ K 10 9 3

In each case, your intended response was 1 notrump. After the overcall, however, you must *pass* with hand (e)—you may not bid notrump without protection in the enemy suit, and you lack the 10 points to respond 2 clubs. With hand (f), make the free bid of 1 notrump, since you have ample stoppers in spades.

4. Partner opens 1 spade; your opponent overcalls 2 clubs. You hold:

(g) ♠ 9 5 2   ♡ A 8 4   ◇ A Q 4 2   ♣ 8 7 3
(h) ♠ 7 4   ♡ K 9 3   ◇ K Q J 10 4   ♣ 6 5 2

You intended to respond 2 diamonds with either hand. Do so anyway! An enemy overcall should never stop you from bidding when you have 10 points or more, a strong, not merely a minimum, responding hand.

THE PENALTY DOUBLE

When you hold a strong responding hand (10 points or more), an opponent's overcall presents you with the opportunity for an entirely different free action—the penalty double.

PARTNER	OPPONENT	YOU	OPPONENT
1 heart	2 diamonds	*double*	

To double on the auction above, you might have:

♠ A J 7 2   ♡ 4   ◇ Q J 8 3   ♣ K 10 7 4

Note that you have more than a minimum response; therefore, you and partner together have many more high cards than have the enemy. And you yourself have a biddable holding in diamonds, so declarer cannot win large numbers of trump tricks.

If you have 10 points or more when partner opens, your side **owns the hand**—that is, you are entitled to score points either by making your own contract or by setting the opponents. Almost always, your side can earn a greater number of points by doubling the enemy—but only if they will not win all the trump tricks. Therefore, double any two-level overcall when you might have bid the enemy suit yourself— you have 4-card length and at least one honor.

This is a penalty, not a *takeout*, double, since partner has already bid. You expect opener to pass your double; to **leave your double in.** He should **take it out,** by rebidding his first suit or suggesting a new one, only if he has wildly unbalanced distribution with a singleton or void in the enemy trump suit.

THE FREE REBID

An overcall can present new problems and opportunities to the *opening bidder* as well as to responder: Suppose *you* open the bidding, partner responds, and *your* right-hand opponent intervenes:

YOU	OPPONENT	PARTNER	OPPONENT
1 diamond	pass	1 heart	1 spade

You are no longer forced to bid again, even though partner has responded in a new suit. True, partner may have a hand strong enough to produce game opposite a minimum opening bid; but the enemy overcall gives him his chance to bid again and show his point count—you, therefore, may pass.

Obviously, this does not mean that you *must* pass. If you have a strong opening bid, you make your normal jump rebid. And with a minimum opening, you may make a minimum free rebid—but only if you want to, not because you have to. Consider these examples:

(1) ♠ 9 6   ♡ A Q 4 2   ◇ K 7 4   ♣ K J 7 3
(2) ♠ 7 2   ♡ K 8   ◇ 9 4 3   ♣ A K Q 10 6 2
(3) ♠ Q 5   ♡ K 7 4   ◇ Q J 2   ♣ A J 8 4 3

With each hand, you open the bidding 1 club. Partner responds 1 heart; your right-hand opponent overcalls 1 spade. What do you bid now?

(1) Rebid *2 hearts*. With 4-card support for partner's suit, you should be itching for the chance to raise. The fact that you are not *forced* to bid is immaterial—you *want* to bid.

(2) Rebid *2 clubs*. Again, there is a feature of your hand which you are anxious to show—here, your magnificent suit.

(3) *Pass*. Had there been no overcall, you would have been forced to find a minimum rebid—preferably 1 notrump to show your even distribution, although either 2 hearts or 2 clubs would be acceptable. However, you are not happy about bidding notrump with so little spade protection; you are not anxious to support partner with three trumps (although you are allowed to); you are not excited about your club suit, which is barely long enough to rebid. Since there is no particular message you wish to give partner, you avail yourself of the opportunity to pass afforded by the overcall.

A somewhat different problem is created for opener by an overcall at his *left*:

YOU	OPPONENT	PARTNER	OPPONENT
1 heart	1 spade	pass	pass

Here, you will certainly bid again if you have a strong or maximum opening bid, for your side can still have a total of 26 points (partner, by failing to bid freely, did not deny holding 6 points—he denied holding *10* points). However, if you have a minimum opening there is virtually no chance for game, so you are not compelled to rebid.

If you pass, though, the auction is over—the opponents have bought the contract. Partner might well have a minimum response of 6 to 9 points and be unable to make a free bid; then you may have let the enemy steal "your" hand if you pass. Therefore, bid again in this position, even with a minimum opening, when you have the least excuse. This excuse could be a long first suit:

♠ 84   ♡ A Q J 9 6 4   ◇ A J 5   ♣ 7 4

(You open 1 heart and left-hand opponent overcalls 1 spade. After two passes, rebid *2 hearts*.) Your excuse could be, instead, the possession of a second suit:

♠ A 3   ♡ A J 7 6 2   ◇ 5   ♣ K 10 9 7 2

(You open 1 heart and your opponent overcalls 1 spade. After two passes, rebid 2 clubs.) You should pass and end the auction only if you hold a bare minimum with no distributional assets, a hand like:

♠ J 84   ♡ A 10 6 5 3   ◇ A 84   ♣ K 2

(You open 1 heart, opponent overcalls 1 spade. After two passes, you pass also.)

To illustrate how all this works, here is a typical auction:

	OPENER		RESPONDER
♠	A 5	♠	J 4 2
♡	A J 7 5 3	♡	7
◇	K 7	◇	A Q 10 8 5 2
♣	A J 9 4	♣	8 5 3

OPENER	OPPONENT	RESPONDER	OPPONENT
1 heart	1 spade	pass	pass
2 clubs	pass	2 diamonds	pass
2 notrump	pass	3 notrump	

Observe all three of responder's bids carefully. At his first turn, responder *passed* because he lacked the 10 points needed for a new suit bid at the two-level. At his second turn, responder bid his suit, showing that he had enough strength to keep the auction alive—a 6-to-9-point hand that did not qualify for a free bid. When opener tried for game by bidding 2 notrump (showing a strong opening; opener would have passed 2 diamonds if he had already bid a second time with a minimum hand), responder bid the only game contract possible—in notrump. A long minor suit makes a fine dummy for a notrump game when partner can stop the enemy suit.

● AFTER AN ENEMY TAKEOUT DOUBLE

Your responses are considerably affected when an opponent doubles partner's opening bid for takeout:

PARTNER	OPPONENT	YOU	OPPONENT
1 diamond	double	?	

Any bid you make here is free. That is, you are not forced to keep the auction alive—partner will have his opportunity to rebid anyway. The double occupies no bidding room, so you still *could* make any intended response; but if there is no bid which you are anxious to make, you can safely pass.

THE REDOUBLE

However, the main alteration in your bidding comes from the addition of a new response—the redouble.

PARTNER	OPPONENT	YOU	OPPONENT
1 spade	double	redouble	

This is the action you must take whenever you have more than a minimum responding hand. It is your only strong response over an enemy double. *You must redouble any time you have 10 points or more, and you may not redouble with less strength.*

On the auction above, redouble with all three of these hands:

(1) ♠ K 5   ♡ A K 9 7 5   ◇ 9 4 2   ♣ 10 6 3
(2) ♠ K J 8 3   ♡ 9 2   ◇ A J 7 4   ♣ 6 5 2
(3) ♠ 4   ♡ A J 8 6   ◇ Q 7 5 3   ♣ K 10 7 6

Your redouble tells partner, "Do not let the enemy double intimidate you; this hand surely belongs to our side." Observe that you do not promise support for partner's suit. You may have a fit, as in example (2) (here it is the fit which allows you to add for your doubleton and count to 10 points). You may have a suit of your own, as in example (1); or you may have all three missing suits, as in example (3). Do not worry about having the auction go:

PARTNER	OPPONENT	YOU	OPPONENT
1 spade	double	redouble	pass
pass	pass		

Even when you have a singleton in partner's suit, the combined point count will be sufficient to fulfill the redoubled 7-trick contract. And since your score for making a redoubled contract can be fantastically high (one spade redoubled is game, and overtricks count 200 or 400 points each) the whole question is academic. The opponent who doubled for takeout cannot possibly dare to pass, no matter how much strength he holds; he must rescue into a suit:

PARTNER	OPPONENT	YOU	OPPONENT
1 spade	double	redouble	pass
pass	2 clubs	?	

At this stage of the auction, you will tell partner what sort of redoubling hand you hold. With the first example:

♠ K 5   ♡ A K 9 7 5   ◇ 9 4 2   ♣ 10 6 3

you now bid 2 *hearts*. This is a forcing bid, just as if you had responded 2 hearts directly over partner's 1 spade opening were there no interference. With example (2) above:

♠ K J 8 3   ♡ 9 2   ◇ A J 7 4   ♣ 6 5 2

you now bid 2 *spades*. This shows support for partner's suit with 10 to 12 points (at least 10 because you redoubled; no more than 12 because you did not *jump*-raise at your second turn). Partner may conceivably pass this raise (but only with a bare 13-point opening), so you would jump to 3 spades here if you held another king—13 points instead of 10. This is equivalent to the *direct* jump raise in an uncontested auction. Finally, if you held example (3) above:

♠ 4   ♡ A J 8 6   ◇ Q 7 5 3   ♣ K 10 7 6

your action over 2 clubs would be to *double* for penalties. With a strong responding hand facing partner's opening, and a trump holding which you might have bid yourself, you should feel confident that the enemy cannot come close to winning 8 tricks. Actually, whenever you are strong enough to redouble you should be alert to the possibility of doubling the opponents. They have stepped into the auction on a hand that clearly belongs to your side; if they cannot find a good trump suit, they are up to their necks in trouble. The opponent who doubled was gambling on finding his partner with some high cards; instead, *you* hold almost all the missing strength. So he has lost his gamble—but only if you double him.

MINIMUM RESPONSES

Most of the time, unfortunately, you will not be strong enough to redouble. There are only 40 high-card points in the deck; partner has an opening bid, your opponent has a double—there is only a slim chance that you will have a hand worth 10 points with so few high cards remaining. Often, though, you will hold a minimum responding hand of 6 to 9 points. What do you do then, over an enemy double?

If you have a good-looking 5-card or longer suit, bid it. For example, suppose the auction goes:

PARTNER	OPPONENT	YOU	OPPONENT
1 diamond	double	?	

Consider your proper action with these hands:

(a) ♠ K 7 4 2   ♡ Q 9 4 3   ◇ 7 4   ♣ Q 5 2
(b) ♠ K J 10 8 4   ♡ 7 2   ◇ 9 2   ♣ Q 10 7 5
(c) ♠ 6 3   ♡ A 5   ◇ 9 8 6   ♣ Q J 10 7 6 4

(a) *Pass.* You would have kept the auction alive by bidding one of your weak 4-card suits had there been no interference; now you no longer have to. Your left-hand opponent must respond to the double, and may be forced to bid one of your suits. Do not take him out of his misery by bidding and allowing *him* to pass.

(b) Bid *1 spade.* You have a lively interest in suggesting spades as trumps; do so even though you no longer have to. Do not let the double stop you from making a response you wanted to make.

(c) Bid *2 clubs.* Here, the enemy double actually helps you. Without it, you would have been forced to respond 1 notrump—to bid your suit at the two-level would promise 10 points at least. Now, however, your 2 club bid *denies* 10 points, since you did not redouble. Therefore, you can afford to suggest your fine suit as trump and, incidentally, make it harder for the opponents to get together in a major suit. Your change of suit as responder in examples (b) and (c) is no longer forcing on partner. Why not? Because you have denied holding 10 points. If partner has a minimum opening bid with no fit for your suit, he will pass. With a fit, he will raise. And with a strong opening, he will make his normal jump rebid.

When you have 6 to 9 points and support for partner's suit, raise right over the double:

PARTNER	OPPONENT	YOU	OPPONENT
1 spade	double	2 spades	

On the above auction, bid 2 spades with both of these hands:

(d) ♠ K 8 3   ♡ 2   ◇ Q 9 6 4   ♣ J 10 8 6 4
(e) ♠ Q 9 8 4   ♡ 7 3   ◇ K J 8 3   ♣ 10 4 3

With either hand, you would have raised had there been no competition. You have excellent values for play in spades—a side singleton in (d), four trumps in (e)—so the bid is one you actually *want* to make. What is more, your raise helps your side buy the contract when partner has a minimum opening, for your left-hand opponent can no longer make a cheap response to the double. So important is this preemptive feature of a raise that you will occasionally *jump*-raise over an enemy double with a weak hand—a weak hand that has magnificent values for play in partner's suit. Bid:

PARTNER	OPPONENT	YOU	OPPONENT
1 heart	double	3 hearts	

with these hands:

(f) ♠ 5   ♡ K Q 10 7   ◇ J 10 9 6 3   ♣ 8 6 5
(g) ♠ 7 4   ♡ A Q 10 6 3   ◇ 10 9 7 6   ♣ 6 2

You have such a good fit with partner that you go right to the three-level in an attempt to inhibit the enemy from bidding. (When *you* have such a fine fit, *they* have a fit also, in some other suit—but they have not found their fit yet.) How does partner know that you have a minimum hand for your *jump* raise, instead of the usual 13 to 16 points? He knows because you would have *redoubled* before raising with any hand worth 10 points or more. Remember, the *only strong response* after an intervening double is the *redouble*.

QUIZ

Partner opens 1 club and your right-hand opponent doubles. What is your action with these hands?

  (1) ♠ 85   ♡ 962   ◇ Q 1043   ♣ K Q 94
  (2) ♠ A Q J 106   ♡ Q 103   ◇ 1094   ♣ 92
  (3) ♠ 72   ♡ Q 10973   ◇ A J 86   ♣ 53
  (4) ♠ 4   ♡ 83   ◇ K 10874   ♣ J 10952
  (5) ♠ Q 983   ♡ A 105   ◇ 864   ♣ Q 92

(1) Raise to 2 *clubs.* You want to show your support and, at the same time, make it hard for the opponents to bid. To respond 1 diamond accomplishes neither objective.

(2) *Redouble.* Show your 10 points first. Then, at your next turn, bid your strong suit.

(3) Bid 1 *heart.* The fact that the opponents are in the auction makes it even more important to bid a long suit in a minimum hand, for you may have to compete to see which side makes a part score.

(4) Raise to 3 *clubs.* Here, you should be terrified of an enemy major-suit contract, and strong measures are called for to shut them out. *Two* clubs is a boy sent to do a man's job.

(5) *Pass.* You have no long suit of your own to suggest, and should have no desire to raise partner's minor suit with 3-card support. You are no longer forced to respond, since partner will bid again by himself if he has either a strong opening or good distribution. And if he has neither, your best chance for a profit is to allow the opponents to struggle and go down.

COMPETITIVE BIDDING

In conclusion, let me give you some advice which applies to many competitive bidding situations. Often, the high cards will be split fairly evenly between your side and the opponents'. This will be the case when you have a minimum responding hand, and partner has a minimum opening; or when partner overcalls and your hand is worth 10 or 11 points; or when you double with a 13-point hand and partner responds freely. When you and partner have found a fit, do not sell this sort of hand to the enemy too cheap. Frequently, both sides can make a small part score—remember, if you have a fit, so have they. So bid up as high as three of your suit. Even if you go down, it will be less expensive than letting the opponent make *their* contract. And they may well be pushed up to a high part-score contract which you can defeat.

In contrast, if your side has *not* found a fit, do not be nearly so aggressive in competitive auctions. The opponents may well have no fit either, and so will go down fairly often. When your side has only half the high cards, do not make penalty doubles of enemy part-score contracts; but be willing to sell out at the two- or three-level when you have not found a trump suit, expecting a small profit from setting the opponents. Here is an example hand to illustrate both points:

♠ J 8 4　♡ K J 10 7 3　◇ J 10 7 2　♣ 5

Suppose that partner opens 1 club. The auction proceeds:

PARTNER	OPPONENT	YOU	OPPONENT
1 club	double	1 heart	1 spade
2 hearts	pass	pass	2 spades
pass	pass	?	

Bid 3 *hearts*. You passed partner's minimum rebid of 2 hearts, since your side had no prospect of a 26-point total. However, you should not allow the enemy to play a low part-score contract when you have found a fit. Therefore, you compete further over 2 spades.

In contrast, if you hold the same hand when the auction goes:

PARTNER	OPPONENT	YOU	OPPONENT
1 club	double	1 heart	2 diamonds
pass	2 spades	?	

Pass! You have no fit for clubs, partner has not supported hearts. Probably, the opponents have no fit either. On a misfit hand like this one, with the cards evenly split between the two partnerships, the side which buys the contract usually goes down. Be generous—let it be your opponents.

♥ RULES TO REMEMBER

After an Enemy Overcall

With 6 to 9 points:	Raise partner's suit with strong support.
	Bid a long suit at the one-level.
	Bid 1 notrump with the enemy suit well stopped.
	Otherwise, pass.
With 10 Points or More:	Make your normal response.
	Double for penalties if you could have bid the enemy suit.

After an Enemy Takeout Double

With 6 to 9 Points:	Raise or jump-raise with good or magnificent support.
	Bid a long suit at one- or two-level.
With 10 Points or More:	Redouble first, describe your hand next.

CHAPTER 11

How to Win Tricks

The auction is over, and you have become declarer and will play the hand in a contract of 4 spades. Your left-hand opponent leads, and partner lays down his hand which becomes your dummy. What now?

The first thing you might do is to follow a courtly old custom and say, "Thank you, partner." (The modern tendency is, instead, to favor partner with a curl of your lip.) Let us suppose that dummy contains its full complement of points:

YOUR HAND	DUMMY
♠ A K 7 6 2	♠ Q 9 8
♡ K 9 3	♡ 8 2
◇ 4 2	◇ K 8 5
♣ K 8 3	♣ A J 7 4 2

Your hand is worth 15 points; dummy is worth 12 points; you were right to reach 4 spades with 27 points. However, the points are of no further use—now you need tricks. You cannot expect your opponents to surrender and let you score up the game. In the bidding, you have *estimated* that you can take 10 tricks, and now you must try to win them.

There are only four ways to win tricks:

1. With honors that the enemy cannot beat, that are **high.** (For example, your ace and king of spades, your king of clubs, dummy's queen of spades and ace of clubs. The opponents have no higher cards in the same suits.)

2. With honors that are almost high. (For example, your king of hearts, dummy's king of diamonds and jack of clubs. The opponents have only one card to beat them.)

3. By trumping. (For example, the third time that hearts are led, dummy can take the trick with a small trump. Your hand can do the same in diamonds.)

4. With **long cards.** (For example, after spades have been led three times, you will have two little spades left in your

hand—the chances are that no other hand will contain any spades, and yours will be high. The same is true of dummy's fourth and fifth clubs. These remaining small cards are your long cards.)

Therefore, you, as declarer, are fairly sure of winning 5 tricks with high honors and two more with your long trumps. You can try to win 3 additional tricks with honors that are nearly high, one additional by trumping in dummy, two more with dummy's long clubs. Obviously, you will not succeed in winning all 13 of these tricks, but this is your potential. We will get back to the proper play of the example hand—the *order* in which you should try to win tricks—near the end of this Part, in Book One, Chapter 16. Meanwhile, let us examine in detail each of the four *methods* of winning tricks.

CHAPTER 12

High-Card Tricks

The easiest way to win tricks is to lead cards which are high. It is probably more satisfactory, esthetically, to win a trick with a 3 rather than with an ace; and, as we will see, leading out all your high cards is usually the worst method of producing *extra* tricks. However, there are hands in which this is all you have to do in order to make your contract. Let us see one:

YOUR HAND	DUMMY
♠ K Q 5	♠ A J 4 2
♡ A Q 10 7 3	♡ K J 8
♢ A 4	♢ 9 6 3
♣ 10 8 2	♣ 7 5 4

You are in 4 hearts. The opening lead is the diamond king. What are your prospects?

You should have no trouble making your contract, for you have 10 tricks in high cards—five top hearts, four top spades, the ace of diamonds. However, there are two dangers to be guarded against: the enemy may trump one of your high cards; you may not be able to lead one of your high cards because the previous trick was won in the wrong hand. To illustrate the first danger, suppose you win the opening trick with your diamond ace. Next, you lead your spade 5 and win dummy's ace; you lead the spade 2 from dummy and win your king; then you lead your spade queen. By now, one of your opponents will probably be out of spades and will win this trick with a small trump.

• DRAWING TRUMPS

Always draw the opponents' trumps before cashing your high cards in plain suits! You lead trumps, and keep leading them until the enemy has no small trumps with which to beat your high cards. When they have no more, you stop leading trumps and save your remaining ones to beat *their* high cards. You must **count trumps** in order to determine how many times to lead them.

The simplest method is to count the opponents' trumps only. That is, in the example hand your side has eight hearts, so the enemy has five. You lead to dummy's heart king and both opponents follow suit—now they have three trumps. You lead dummy's heart jack and again both opponents follow—now they have one trump. You lead dummy's heart 8 and win your ace; one opponent follows, the other discards a small diamond—now they are out of trump, so you can stop playing hearts.

• WHICH HONORS FIRST?

Notice the order in which you cashed your heart honors.

YOU: ♡ A Q 10 7 3   DUMMY: ♡ K J 8

If you were to lead your ace first, and then win dummy's jack, and third win dummy's king, you would be unable to lead a fourth round of trumps in case it proved necessary. Why? Because you won the third trick in *dummy*, and dummy's hand has no more hearts to lead. When your honors are **equals**—that is, in sequence, so that one is as good as another —first play the honors from the hand that has fewest cards. Then, you will win the late tricks in the long hand and can keep on leading the suit if you wish to.

This principle of play can be very important in side suits as well. After drawing the enemy trumps in our example hand, your remaining cards are these:

YOUR HAND   DUMMY
♠ K Q 5   ♠ A J 4 2
♡ Q 10   ♡ ——
◇ 4   ◇ 9 6
♣ 10 8 2   ♣ 7 5 4

Now you want to win your four spade tricks. If you lead your spade 5 to dummy's ace, then lead dummy's 2 to your king, and then lead your spade queen, you will win *three* spade tricks. The high jack of spades is still in dummy, but the lead is in *your* hand. And you will never be able to lead dummy's last spade since dummy can never win a trick and gain the right to lead.

Of course, what you must do is to lead *your* spade honors first, since in spades your hand is **short** and dummy is **long**.

Your king wins the first trick, your queen the second, dummy's ace wins the third trick; and the lead is now in dummy so that you can cash the spade jack also.

Thus, there are two principles to follow in winning tricks with high cards:

1. **Win the honors in the short hand first**
2. **Draw the enemy trumps before cashing honors in side suits**

• HONORS THAT ARE NOT QUITE HIGH

Most often, you will not have enough sure winners in the two hands to fulfill your contract. However, there will be a scattering of honors that are almost high, and which may win tricks with proper play. Suppose that you are declarer in a contract of 2 spades:

YOUR HAND	DUMMY
♠ K Q J 8 4	♠ 9 7 6 3
♡ K 2	♡ 8 5
◇ J 10 6 5	◇ K Q 4
♣ K 7	♣ J 8 4 3

Here, the opponents have all four aces, so no card in either hand is high. However, you have many kings, queens, and jacks to make up your point count; they can win tricks, but you must work to produce them.

This work is easiest when you have three or more honors in sequence, like your K Q J of spades, or the combined K Q J 10 in diamonds. You can lead either of these kings, which will lose to the enemy ace. Then your lower honors become high. (Observe that it will do you no good to lead your king of *hearts* or *clubs;* the opponents will win their ace, and now *their* lower honors are high.)

The opening lead, made by your left-hand opponent, is a small heart; your right-hand opponent wins the ace, and leads another heart won by your king. What do you lead now? You lead your king of spades, establishing your lower spade honors as winners, and starting to draw the enemy trump. (Here, you have nine trumps—they have *four;* after both opponents follow suit, they have *two* left.) Your left-hand opponent wins the trump ace, and leads a small trump; all hands follow suit and you win with the spade jack. The position is now:

YOUR HAND   DUMMY
♠ Q 8 4   ♠ 9 7
♡ ——   ♡ ——
◇ J 10 6 5   ◇ K Q 4
♣ K 7   ♣ J 8 4 3

The opponents have no more trumps, so you start to work establishing your diamond winners. You can use an honor to force out the enemy ace, and have three high honors remaining. Since you have already won 2 tricks, your three trumps and three diamond tricks assure that you will fulfill your 8-trick contract.

How would you go about winning a trick with your club king and making an overtrick? You cannot *lead* this king, for the opponents hold the queen as well as the ace. Here, you must use a different technique.

♧ RULE TO REMEMBER

Lead an honor to force out an enemy high card only when it is in sequence with two others.

CHAPTER 13

Finessing

It is easy to win tricks with honors which are high, or which are in sequence. However, it takes more skill, and quite a little luck as well, to win tricks with isolated kings, queens, and jacks.

Actually, we have already seen one instance of this. In the last example of Book One, Chapter 12, this was your heart suit:

YOU: ♡ K 2   DUMMY: ♡ 8 5

In this suit you won your king even though the enemy held all the other honors. How? Your left-hand opponent led a low heart; you played small from dummy; your right-hand opponent held the ace, and when he played it you followed suit with the 2. Had he played a smaller heart instead, you could have won your king directly, but either way you were sure to win it eventually. The way to take a trick with a king, then, is to play to a trick *after* the opponent who holds the ace. You must not *lead* your king; you must have the lead come toward it.

In the same example hand, you wanted to win a trick with your king of clubs:

(1) YOU: ♣ K 7   DUMMY: ♣ J 8 4 3

You must hope that your right-hand opponent holds the club ace, and arrange to play to a club trick *after he does*. When you win a trick in dummy's hand, lead the 3 of clubs *toward* your king. If your opponent plays the ace, you play small and win your king later; if *he* plays small, you play your king and win it immediately. (Of course, this play will fail if your left-hand opponent, who plays *after you do*, holds the ace, but then you could never have won your king in any case.)

This type of play—leading *toward* an honor that is *nearly* high in the hope that the enemy honor which *is* high is in the hand which plays before it—is called a **finesse**. We are about to examine many varieties of finesses, but *the basic principle in all finesses is to force an opponent with a missing honor* *to commit himself before you do,* to play his honor or not and give *you* the option of playing or not playing yours according to what *he* has done.

Of course, all finesses are chancy—the missing enemy honor may lie in the hand that plays *after* you do, **behind** instead of **in front of** your honor. Then your finesse will fail. However, leading toward an honor gives you at least a hope of winning a trick with it, while leading the honor itself does not.

Actually, there are three different types of finesse which we will examine here. These are (1) leading toward an honor, (2) leading toward two separated honors, (3) leading an un-needed honor toward a higher one.

• LEADING TOWARD AN HONOR

The examples we have seen of leading up to a king are the most basic instances of a finesse. Here is another simple card combination.

(2)   YOU: Q 7 4   DUMMY: A 6 3

How can you win your queen? By leading dummy's 3-spot toward the queen, and finding the enemy king on your right. You first cash dummy's ace, just in case the king should drop under it; then you lead up to your honor.

Similarly, with:

(3)   YOU: A K 3   DUMMY: J 7 6 2

you can attempt to win a trick with the jack by leading toward it, hoping that the missing queen lies to your left, in front of the jack. Here, too, you should win your ace and king first, hoping that the queen will fall.

This type of finesse has a variation in which you may finesse *twice* against a missing honor.

(4)   YOU: 8 4 2   DUMMY: K Q 6

You must lose to the ace, but you can prevent it from capturing either of dummy's honors if it must play *before* them. You lead your 2 toward dummy's queen. If the queen takes the trick, play some other suit in order to regain the lead in your own hand. Then, repeat the finesse by leading your 4 toward dummy's king.

In another variation, you may finesse against *two* missing honors. For example:

(5)   YOU: Q J 5   DUMMY: 8 3 2

Here, you must lead twice from dummy toward the honors in your hand. If either enemy honor is to your right, in front of your Q J, you will win a trick.

Notice that in these first five examples, you are willing to lose a trick to the missing enemy honors. Your finesse is an attempt to prevent the high enemy honor from capturing your lower one; then you will win a trick with your honor too. Suppose that the whole suit in our fifth example is divided like this:

LEFT-HAND OPPONENT

K 10 7 4

YOU	DUMMY
Q J 5	8 3 2

RIGHT-HAND OPPONENT

A 9 6

You lead the 2 from dummy; the 6 is played, and your jack is captured by the king on your left. This finesse has lost. However, when dummy next gains the lead, you play the 3 toward your queen. If the ace wins, you follow with the 5 and win your queen later; otherwise, you win your queen directly. The ace cannot capture your queen (if you play properly) because it must play before it—this finesse will win. The enemy will take tricks with their high honors, but you will take a trick too.

Now let us consider a different type of finesse, in which your object will be to *prevent* a missing honor from winning a trick.

● **LEADING TOWARD SEPARATED HONORS**

The simplest example of this finesse is:

(6) YOU: 7 3   DUMMY: A Q

Here, dummy has what is called a **tenace,** a term which describes two separated honors. You lead *toward* a tenace, and play the lower honor when your opponent follows with a small card. In the example above, lead your 3 and play dummy's queen (unless, of course, the king is played on your left). Whenever the king lies *in front* of the A Q, the queen will win the trick; the only card which could beat dummy's queen is in a hand that has already played low to the trick.

Here is the same play in a different form:

(7) YOU: K J 5   DUMMY: A 7 2

Now the tenace is in your hand—the K J. If the queen is in the enemy hand to your right, the one that plays before you, you can win three tricks. Cash dummy's ace, to see if the queen falls; when it does not, lead dummy's 2 and finesse your jack (unless the queen is played). Half the time your jack will win this trick, and you will have bypassed the missing queen. Similarly, you can finesse against a jack:

(8) YOU: K 7 3   DUMMY: Q 10 5

The tenace here is dummy's Q 10. You plan to lead your 3 and play dummy's 10 unless the jack appears. Before you do this, however, lead dummy's 5 toward your king. Notice that in every instance, before leading up to a tenace (or up to a single honor like a queen), you play any high card in the same suit which is not involved in the finesse. This is to give yourself the slim extra chance of **dropping** the missing honor under your "unnecessary" one, in case it is a singleton.

Do you see what is different about these finesses? In examples (1) through (5), the missing enemy honor is high; you must lose a trick to it, but you try to prevent it from capturing your lower honor, which will then win a trick also. In the second type of finesse, examples (6), (7), and (8), the missing enemy honor is (if you are lucky) surrounded by two of your honors; when your tenace lies *behind* the missing honor, you can avoid losing to it—you can bypass the missing honor completely. (In example (6), you need not lose to the king; or to the queen in example (7), or to the jack in example (8). That is, you need not if the missing honor is in *front* of your tenace and you play properly.)

This type also has the slightly more complicated forms in which you must finesse *twice*. For example:

(9) YOU: 6 5 2   DUMMY: A J 10

Here is a finesse against two honors, a **double finesse**, using dummy's tenace. Lead your 2, and play dummy's 10 (unless the king or queen is played first). If this loses to an honor, regain the lead in your hand and play toward dummy's A J. If one of the two missing honors is in front of the tenace (or onside), you will bypass it and win 2 tricks. The same is true of this combination:

(10) YOU: 8 4 3 DUMMY: A Q 10

Lead your 3 to dummy's 10, finessing against the jack. If the jack wins behind the 10, lead up to dummy's A Q and finesse against the king. Here, you will win all 3 tricks if both missing honors are onside, and you will win 2 tricks if either is onside.

In the next example, you can take two finesses against *one* missing honor.

(11) YOU: A Q J DUMMY: 7 5 4

Here, you can bypass the missing king twice if it lies in front of your tenace. Lead dummy's 4 toward your jack. When the jack wins, play some other suit to put dummy back in the lead. Then play dummy's five to repeat the finesse toward your A Q. Notice that you have to go to some trouble to finesse a second time, for you must regain the lead in dummy. Is there any way to *hold the lead* in dummy after winning the finesse? There is in this next example:

(12) YOU: A Q 10 DUMMY: J 6 3

Lead dummy's jack, and, if your opponent plays small, follow suit with the 10. When the missing king is on your right, dummy's jack will win the trick, and you can immediately finesse again by leading the 6 toward your A Q. Actually, when the king is on your right, it will usually be played over dummy's jack, **covering** the honor. (As we will see in Book One, Chapter 18, your opponent should stop the jack from winning a trick by playing his king on it—by covering it.) However, you will then smother the king with your ace, and your queen and 10 are high. Notice, though, that if your holding were:

(13) YOU: A Q 5 DUMMY: J 6 3

it would do you no good to lead the jack. It would be covered by the king, and, when you won your ace you would have only *one* more winner left. Your proper play here is to lead dummy's 3 to your queen, and, if the queen wins, cash your ace in the hope that the king will fall; then dummy's jack will win the third trick. You cannot *lead* the jack because you need it for later. *You can lead an honor in taking a finesse only*

when you surround the missing enemy card by four honors.
Then, if two of your honors go on one trick (like dummy's
jack, covered by the enemy king, and won by your ace), you
have two honors left to win the next 2 tricks.

• FINESSING BY LEADING AN HONOR

Notice that we have come across a third type of finesse. In
example (12) above, you were not trying to bypass the
enemy king, but to capture it by leading an honor and having
it covered. Here is a similar position:

(14) YOU: Q J 10   DUMMY: A 6 3

Lead your queen, hoping to trap the enemy king between
your queen and dummy's ace. If the king covers, win the ace;
your jack and 10 are now high. If the king does not cover,
play dummy's 3—your queen will take the trick (if the king
is in the proper hand for your purposes); now you lead the
jack and repeat the same finesse. Observe that you can start
this finesse by leading an honor, because you surround the
missing king with *four* honors of your own.

(15) YOU: A K 5   DUMMY: J 10 6

This is the same type of finesse, since if the queen is in front
of your A K, it is surrounded by four honors. Lead dummy's
jack toward your king.

Here is a third example of this sort of finesse:

(16) YOU: J 10 9 6   DUMMY: K 8 4 2

Again, lead your jack toward dummy's king. If it is covered
by the queen, play the king. Should all four top honors be
played to the first trick, your 10 and 9 become high. Notice
that you surround the missing queen with 4 cards—a sequence of 3 below, and 1 above.

You should take this same type of finesse when you are
missing *two* honors, as in this instance:

(17) YOU: A 7 4   DUMMY: J 10 9

Lead dummy's jack. If it is not covered, play your 4; presumably this trick will be lost to the king or queen. Next,
regain the lead in dummy and lead the 10, repeating the
finesse. If one of the two missing honors is in front of your

ace, you will capture it. Again, you can lead honors in finessing because you are **four deep.**

Let us see how these finesses work in an example hand:

DUMMY

♠ A 8 6 5
♡ A 5 2
♢ K J 6 3
♣ 8 4

OPPONENT

♠ K 9 2
♡ K
♢ Q 10 7 4
♣ Q J 10 5 3

OPPONENT

♠ 7 4
♡ J 10 9 5 2
♢ 9 2
♣ K 9 6 2

YOU

♠ Q J 10 3
♡ Q 8 7 4
♢ A 8 5
♣ A 7

You are declarer in a 4 spade contract. The opening lead is the club queen, and you win your ace. How do you proceed?

First, draw trumps. Lead your spade queen for a finesse. When the king covers, capture it with dummy's ace, and win the following two tricks with your 10 and jack. (If the king does *not* cover, play low from dummy; your queen wins the trick, and now you repeat the finesse by leading your jack.)

Next, tackle the diamond suit. Cash your ace (in case the queen is singleton) and then lead low toward the tenace in dummy. When your opponent plays the 7, play dummy's jack. This wins the trick, so cash the king (if both opponents follow, the 6 of diamonds in dummy will be high; however, your right-hand opponent shows out).

Finally, go after hearts. You plan to lead toward your queen, but first you cash the **idle ace.** Your precaution is rewarded, as the king falls, making the finesse (which would have lost) unnecessary. Notice that only in spades could you finesse by leading an honor. Had you led your queen of hearts, you would not have won a trick with it; the same is true of your jack of diamonds. Your spade queen, which you led, did not win a trick, either, but in this suit you had three *other* honors to win the tricks, so you could afford to **throw away** your queen by leading it.

♥ RULES TO REMEMBER

1. Lead toward single honors, or twice toward two honors in sequence.
2. Lead toward two separated honors, and play the lower.
3. Finesse by leading an honor only when you surround the missing honor or honors with 4 cards.

CHAPTER 14

Winning Tricks with Trumps (Ruffing)

So far, we have been winning tricks with honors, but small cards can win tricks too—particularly small trumps. Let us see how this is done.

YOUR HAND	DUMMY
♠ A K Q J 6	♠ 10 9 7 3
♡ A 10 8 4	♡ 2
◊ A Q	◊ 8 6 5 2
♣ K 6	♣ 9 8 4 3

You are declarer in a 4 spade contract. The opening lead is the heart queen. Where are your 10 tricks coming from?

You have 7 cards that are high (five spades, the diamond ace, and the heart ace) and 2 more that are nearly high (the diamond queen, the club king) with which you can finesse. However, finesses are chancy—you have three additional *sure* tricks. These are tricks which can be won by dummy's little trumps on the second, third, and fourth rounds of hearts.

Win your ace of hearts, and lead the heart 4; since dummy cannot follow suit you win the trick with dummy's spade 3. Now you must try to regain the lead in your hand to lead another heart; lead a small diamond from dummy and finesse your queen—it wins. Lead another heart and ruff in dummy; return to your hand with the ace of diamonds; lead your last heart and trump (ruff) in dummy. You have already won 6 tricks (the ace of hearts, the ace and queen of diamonds, three heart ruffs in dummy), and the remaining cards are:

YOUR HAND	DUMMY
♠ A K Q J 6	♠ 10
♡ ——	♡ ——
◊ ——	◊ 8 6
♣ K 6	♣ 9 8 4 3

You are sure of 5 more tricks, with a chance for a sixth in clubs. Cash dummy's remaining spade 10, and since this is the last time dummy will have the lead, play a small club toward your king. Here, the finesse loses, for the ace is *behind* your king; but you make your contract with an overtrick, losing only 2 tricks in clubs.

One finesse won and one lost, but the trumping tricks—the ruffs—were certain. In order to ruff, however, you had to postpone drawing the enemy trumps. Had you played trumps first, there would not have been enough spades left in dummy to ruff your losing hearts.

Note that in the preceding position, you do *not* lead a diamond from dummy and ruff it in your own hand. You have 5 sure tricks with *your* trumps just by leading them out; there is no need to trump with them. By ruffing three times in *dummy*, you won *eight* spade tricks—five of your own plus three of dummy's. Ruffing in your own hand does not win extra tricks; it is merely another way of cashing your *original* 5 tricks.

Here is another example, to underline this point:

YOUR HAND	DUMMY
♠ A K Q 10 9	♠ J 6 3
♡ A 5 2	♡ Q 4
◇ 7	◇ A J 8
♣ Q 8 7 3	♣ A 10 6 4 2

Once again, your contract is 4 spades. The opening lead is a small heart. Where are your 10 tricks?

You have 8 cards that are high (five top spades, three outside aces), and two queens which are almost high. To try to make your club queen, you will lead toward it; to try to make your heart queen, you must play it to the first trick—this is your only chance to play it to a trick *after* your left-hand opponent has played a small card. Can you win any tricks by ruffing? Yes, you can trump diamonds twice in your hand; however, these are not *extra* tricks—you still will have only five spade tricks this way. Or you can trump hearts once in dummy—and this is an extra trick, for you will win all five trumps in your hand *plus* one in dummy. In addition, you may win tricks with low clubs. You have a total of nine clubs; the enemy have only four. After clubs have been played two or three times, your little ones will be high.

In what order do you go about winning your high trumps and your aces, taking your finesses, ruffing in dummy, cashing long clubs? Let us work it out. You dare not play clubs until you have drawn trumps, for fear that the enemy will ruff your club honors. You must not draw trumps until you have ruffed in dummy, for you need a trump there to do this work. Therefore: first play hearts, next draw trumps, finally attack clubs.

Play the queen of hearts from dummy to the first trick. It is covered by the king and you win the ace. Lead back a low heart, giving the opponents the second trick, so that dummy will have no more of this suit. The opponents lead spades; you win in your own hand and lead the third heart, ruffing in dummy. (Trump with dummy's *jack* of spades; you do not need this honor to draw trumps, so you can make sure that your right-hand opponent cannot **overruff** with a higher spade if he also started with a doubleton heart.)

Now take out the enemy trumps. They started with five, and have already played two. A spade lead to your ace draws two more trumps; your king of spades extracts their last trump. The position now is this:

YOUR HAND	DUMMY
♠ Q 10	♠ ——
♡ ——	♡ ——
◊ 7	◊ A J
♣ Q 8 7 3	♣ A 10 6 4 2

Lead your club 3 to dummy's ace, and play dummy's 2 toward your queen. Both opponents follow to the first lead. On the club lead from dummy, your right-hand opponent plays the king; you therefore follow with the 7 and your left-hand opponent discards a diamond. The club jack is missing, but it must drop under your queen—the rest of the tricks are yours. Note that if you had trumped diamonds twice in your hand, the position at the end would have been:

YOUR HAND	DUMMY
♠ ——	♠ ——
♡ ——	♡ ——
◊ ——	◊ ——
♣ Q 8 7 3	♣ A 10 6 4

Now, when the opponents win their king of clubs the rest of the tricks are *theirs*. You have no trumps left in your hand, so you will have to discard long clubs on their long hearts and diamonds. The trump length in your *own hand* is precious—it prevents the enemy from winning tricks with long suits, while allowing *you* to do so. Thus, you cannot gain by ruffing with your own trumps and can often lose. You want to ruff with dummy's trumps; the *opponents* want you to ruff with your own.

♣ RULES TO REMEMBER

These are the general principles for winning extra tricks by ruffing:

1. Ruff with dummy's trumps, not your own.
2. Do not draw trumps until you have taken your ruffs in dummy.
3. Ruff with *high* cards in dummy if you do not need the honors to draw the enemy trumps.

CHAPTER 15

Long-Card Tricks

The power of a long suit is that after it has been led several times the enemy will have no more; all the remaining cards are high. This is one of the surest ways of winning tricks with small cards; a 5-card or longer side suit either in your own hand or in dummy should always tempt you to play it early and often.

YOUR HAND	DUMMY
♠ K 8 6 4 3	♠ J 5
♡ K Q 9 7 4	♡ J 10 2
◇ K 2	◇ A 9 4
♣ 6	♣ K 10 7 5 3

Your contract is 4 hearts. The opening lead is the jack of diamonds. What is your plan? Work on the long spade suit in your hand!

Win the diamond lead with dummy's ace, so that you can finesse in spades. Lead the 5 toward your king. Your right-hand opponent plays low and you play the spade king, which wins the trick. Now lead your 3 of spades, conceding this trick to the enemy. A second diamond is played, won by your king. Now lead a third spade and trump it in dummy with the heart 10. Both opponents follow suit, so your remaining two spades are high.

Next lead the trump jack from dummy (high card from the short hand first) and force out the ace. Regain the lead by trumping in your hand when the opponents play diamonds again, and draw all the enemy trump. Finally, cash your two long spades and long trumps. You win 2 tricks with high diamonds, 4 tricks with high trumps, 1 trick with a high spade, 1 trick by ruffing in dummy, 2 tricks with long spades —10 in all, to make your contract.

Notice these points about the play: (1) You did not draw trumps until *after* ruffing your spade in dummy; had the opponents' spades split less evenly, you might have had to ruff *two* spades in dummy, and you need to leave trumps there to ruff with. (2) You trumped with a *high* heart, for fear of an overruff; you are willing to have the enemy overtrump with the *ace*, which must make anyway. (3) You won the first trick in dummy, to lead *up to* your king; you saved your own high diamond for later, to regain the lead in your hand for a spade lead after dummy had no more.

• WHICH SUIT TO SET UP

How did you decide to tackle your own long suit instead of dummy's? First, the opponents had fewer cards in spades than in clubs, so your suit was easier to set up. Second, when you trumped spades to establish the suit, you ruffed in *dummy* and won extra tricks. To set up clubs, you would have had to ruff in your *own hand*, gaining nothing. In the example above, you *could* have played to set up dummy's clubs (you would then win the first trick in your hand, to lead toward dummy's clubs, and save dummy's high diamond for gaining the lead later). However, this is a much more difficult and complicated line of attack; it is usually much easier to work on a long side suit in your own hand. Most often, though, only dummy will have such a suit.

YOUR HAND	DUMMY
♠ A K Q 10 9 4	♠ J 2
♡ A 5	♡ K 9 8 4 3
◊ Q 8 3	◊ A 7 4
♣ 9 6	♣ 8 5 2

You are declarer in a 4 spade contract. The opening lead is the club queen, which wins the trick. A small club is led, won by the king to your right; the ace of clubs is then played. You must trump in your hand, to stop the enemy from winning their third trick, and you ruff with the 9 since you can spare this high trump. (Your left-hand opponent shows out also, and you feel virtuous, for had you ruffed low he would have overruffed.)

There is still work to be done, however. You will win six trump tricks and three high cards on the side. Your tenth trick could possibly be made by leading toward your diamond queen, but a surer trick is available. You can set up a long heart in dummy, even if one opponent holds 4 cards in that suit.

Cash your heart ace, lead to dummy's king, and play a third round of hearts trumping (high) in your hand. The enemy started with six hearts altogether, so if each one follows suit three times, the remaining hearts in dummy are high. However, your right-hand opponent follows only twice, discarding on the third round, so one high heart is outstanding. Lead to dummy's spade jack, and play a fourth round of hearts, trumping in your hand. Finally, draw the opponents' trumps, go to dummy with the ace of diamonds, and cash that hard-earned tenth trick—the fifth heart.

Observe that in order to play hearts so often, you needed cards with which to put dummy on lead—entries to dummy. The heart king was the entry to play the third heart, the spade jack was the entry for the fourth round, the diamond ace served as the entry to lead the high fifth round. *When you wish to set up a long suit, be very jealous of your entries*. This often means, as it did in this example, delaying the drawing of trumps in order to use dummy's trump honors as entries, enabling you to lead dummy's suit often enough to exhaust the opponents.

♣ RULES TO REMEMBER

The general principles to follow in setting up tricks with long cards are these:

1. In a trump contract, prefer to work on a long side suit in your own hand rather than one in dummy.
2. When working on dummy's suit, be sure that you make use of all available entries.
3. The easiest suit to set up will usually be the one in which the enemy have the fewest cards.
4. Keep count of the enemy cards in your long suit so that you will know when they have no more.

CHAPTER 16

Planning Your Play in Suit Contracts

One telltale sign of an inexperienced bridge player is the tendency to lead out all his high cards as soon as he can. This type of declarer then surveys the wreck of his own hand and dummy after he has cashed all of his winners, and, with a baffled expression on his face, wonders where the rest of his tricks are coming from. Usually, he goes down; for his high cards were needed to help along the other three methods of winning tricks: to let him take finesses, to serve as entries back to his hand so that he could ruff in dummy, or as entries to dummy in setting up a long side suit.

Of course, you should not be too proud to draw trumps and cash all your high cards, if there are enough of them to fulfill your contract. This simple line of play is suited to an occasional simple hand. Most often, however, you will be one or two winners short for this sort of play, and you must stop to ask yourself which of the three additional methods you will use to make up the difference—finessing, ruffing, or establishing long cards. The most vexing problems you will have as declarer will be in choosing which of these lines of attack to adopt.

• LONG-CARD OR RUFFING TRICKS?

One of the most common choices you must make as declarer is whether to go after long-suit tricks or ruffing tricks. When dummy has uneven distribution, it frequently contains both a long side suit and a short suit. You must decide which to use in order to produce the extra winners which you need. For example:

YOUR HAND	DUMMY
♠ A 10 8 7 4	♠ K Q 3
♡ 5	♡ Q J 8 6 4 2
◇ J 6 2	◇ A K 5
♣ A 9 5 2	♣ 8

Your contract is 4 spades. The king of clubs is the opening lead, and you win your ace.

If you draw trumps and cash your winners, you will take 8 tricks—five trumps (the A K Q will probably drop all the enemy spades) and three high cards on the side. You need two extra tricks. Should you use dummy's *shortness* or dummy's *length* to produce them?

The trouble with using dummy's singleton to win ruffing tricks is that too many of your side's high cards are in dummy. If you trump a club, how do you get back to your hand to do it again, and then a third time to draw the enemy trumps? In addition, you will have to trump the third round of clubs with one of dummy's honors, which you cannot spare.

The fact that dummy is so strong makes it difficult to try for ruffing tricks, but it makes it easy to work on long-card tricks, since there are so many entries. Lead your heart at trick two. Dummy's jack loses to the king, and a diamond is returned; win in dummy and lead a low heart, ruffing in your hand. Get back to dummy with the queen of spades and lead another low heart, ruffing again. If all the enemy hearts have dropped, you can draw trumps and go back to dummy (with the diamond ace) to cash the long cards. If the suit has not split evenly, you have two entries left—the high spade, the high diamond—to let you play a fourth round of hearts, and get back to dummy after trumps are drawn to cash the remaining two long hearts.

Notice how you saved all of dummy's entries to help you set up the long suit. It was because dummy had so many entries (and your hand so few) that you decided to go after long-card, not ruffing tricks.

Contrast this deal with the following one, in which you have the same high cards and distribution:

YOUR HAND	DUMMY
♠ A Q 10 8 7	♠ K 4 3
♡ 5	♡ Q J 8 6 4 2
◇ A K 5	◇ J 6 2
♣ A 9 5 2	♣ 8

Again you are declarer in 4 spades. The opening lead is the king of clubs, won by your ace.

You have the same 8 top tricks, and this time should go after two ruffs in dummy to make your contract. Why? Because there are not enough entries in dummy to set up the hearts; because you *have* enough entries to your hand to lead clubs often enough; because you will not have to waste a vital trump honor in dummy by ruffing with it.

Lead a small club and ruff with dummy's 3. Return to your hand with a high diamond. Lead another club, ruffing with dummy's 4. Now, cash dummy's spade king, return to your hand with the other winning diamond, and draw the enemy trumps.

• WHEN TO DRAW TRUMPS

Observe that in neither of the last two examples could you afford to draw trumps immediately. When you set up dummy's long suit, you saved dummy's trumps for use as entries; when you ruffed in dummy, you needed trumps there to ruff with. A good rule of thumb is this: If there is a lot of work to do, delay drawing trumps; if the hand looks easy (that is, if you have enough top cards, and honors that are almost high, to make your contract), extract the opponents' trumps right away.

Finally, let us return, as promised, to the first example in Part 2:

YOUR HAND	DUMMY
♠ A K 7 6 2	♠ Q 9 8
♡ K 9 3	♡ 8 2
◊ 4 2	◊ K 8 5
♣ K 8 3	♣ A J 7 4 2

Your final contract is 4 spades. The opening lead is the heart queen. The ace of hearts wins on your right and a heart is led to the second trick, won by your king. Before you read any further, plan your play.

Your thinking should go like this: "I have 8 top tricks—five trumps, one heart, two clubs. Where can I get two more? I can ruff my low heart in dummy—that is one trick. I can try the club finesse for the second extra winner, and even if it loses, the *long* clubs in dummy should be high—the enemy clubs probably are divided three-two. I want to draw trumps before playing clubs, for fear that the opponents will ruff my winners; I want to ruff my heart in dummy before drawing trumps."

Therefore lead your heart to trick three, trumping in dummy. Next, lead dummy's queen of spades (playing the honor from the short hand first), and continue with a spade

to your king and the ace of spades. Both opponents follow to
the first two spade leads, so your third high spade draws the
last enemy trump. Now, cash your club king, and lead the
three. Left-hand opponent plays the 10; finesse dummy's
jack. It wins, as your right-hand opponent follows with the 9.
Dummy's club ace drops the queen, and the two long clubs
are good; you discard your two little diamonds on them. In
all, you win 12 tricks—your original 8 plus a ruff in dummy,
a successful finesse, and two long cards. Here is the complete
deal:

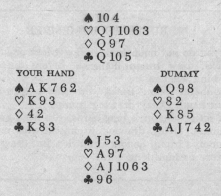

```
                        ♠ 10 4
                        ♡ Q J 10 6 3
                        ◇ Q 9 7
                        ♣ Q 10 5

YOUR HAND                               DUMMY
♠ A K 7 6 2                             ♠ Q 9 8
♡ K 9 3                                 ♡ 8 2
◇ 4 2                                   ◇ K 8 5
♣ K 8 3                                 ♣ A J 7 4 2

                        ♠ J 5 3
                        ♡ A 9 7
                        ◇ A J 10 6 3
                        ♣ 9 6
```

Do you see that if you had cashed all your winners to start
with, you would have won 8 tricks instead of 12? After you
cash three high spades, and two high clubs, the remaining
cards would be:

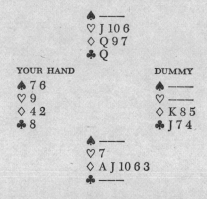

```
                        ♠ ——
                        ♡ J 10 6
                        ◇ Q 9 7
                        ♣ Q

YOUR HAND                               DUMMY
♠ 7 6                                   ♠ ——
♡ 9                                     ♡ ——
◇ 4 2                                   ◇ K 8 5
♣ 8                                     ♣ J 7 4

                        ♠ ——
                        ♡ 7
                        ◇ A J 10 6 3
                        ♣ ——
```

You have won 6 tricks already, and have two long trumps in
your hand. However, you can no longer ruff your heart in
dummy; you can no longer finesse with the club jack; you can
no longer use dummy's long clubs, since there is no entry to
them. No amount of thought will help you now—you are
down two.

You must do your thinking at the start of the hand. How
many high-card tricks have you? How will you plan to win
the extra tricks you need—by taking finesses, by ruffing in
dummy, or by establishing a long suit?

♣ RULES TO REMEMBER

1. If you do not need extra ruffing tricks or long-card
   tricks, draw trumps at once, before finessing or
   cashing winners.
2. To obtain ruffing tricks, you need entries to your
   own hand. Delay drawing trumps.
3. To set up dummy's long cards, you need entries to
   dummy. Delay drawing trumps if you must use
   dummy's trump honors as entries. But draw trumps
   before cashing long cards.

CHAPTER 17

Planning Your Play in Notrump

When you are playing in notrump, long-card tricks are of crucial importance (since ruffing tricks are unavailable); and they are a little easier to obtain (since you need not worry about enemy trumps while setting up your suit). Notrump contracts usually develop into a race between Declarer and his opponents to see who can take long-card tricks first. Consider this deal:

YOUR HAND	DUMMY
♠ A K	♠ 8 6 4
♡ A 9 6 2	♡ 7 5 4
◇ K 8 3	◇ A 9 6 4 2
♣ Q 7 6 4	♣ 9 3

You bid 1 notrump, and everyone passes. The opening lead is the spade 5, and you win your ace. Where are your 7 tricks? You have five sure winners in high cards, but no other prospect of tricks to win with honors. Your extra 2 tricks must be won with long cards, and dummy's 5-card diamond suit is clearly the one to provide them.

The opponents have 5 cards in diamonds; most likely one has three, the other two. Therefore, if you cash your king, lead to dummy's ace, and concede a third round of diamonds, there will be two winning long diamonds remaining in dummy. The position will look like this:

YOUR HAND	DUMMY
♠ K	♠ 8 6
♡ A 9 6 2	♡ 7 5 4
◇ ——	◇ 9 6
♣ Q 7 6 4	♣ 9 3

Do you see that dummy's diamonds, although high, are of no use to you? To cash them, you must first win a trick in dummy, but there is no entry. The only entry to dummy is the ace of diamonds, so you must not win this card until dummy's two long diamonds can be cashed. The way to do this is to take your king of diamonds, and then concede the *second* round of this suit to the opponents. The diamond suit is then:

YOU: ◇ 3   DUMMY: ◇ A 9 6

The opponents continue to lead spades, and you win in your hand. Now, lead your 3 to dummy's ace. You can cash two long diamonds, since you have won the previous trick in dummy. You used dummy's lone entry at the proper time.

• THE RACE TO SET UP SUITS

Of course, both sides can work to set up and cash long cards at notrump. Usually, the side which wins the race by taking its long-card tricks first is the one to score points in a notrump deal. Note that the defenders, East-West, in the following deal, have *eight* possible winners against your 3 notrump contract.

DUMMY
♠ 8 3
♡ 10 7 3
◇ A J 7 5 3
♣ 8 6 2

WEST
♠ K Q J 6 2
♡ J 8 4
◇ 9 4
♣ Q 10 9

EAST
♠ 9 7 5
♡ Q 9 6 2
◇ Q 10 6
♣ J 5 4

YOUR HAND
♠ A 10 4
♡ A K 5
◇ K 8 2
♣ A K 7 3

They might win 4 tricks in spades, 2 in hearts, 1 each in clubs and diamonds. What stops them from doing so at once is your high-card strength in their long suits—they cannot win long spades while you hold the ace, or long hearts until you play your A K. These are your stoppers. If you cash them right off, the enemy will win the race, but if you manage your stoppers carefully, you can take *your* long cards (dummy's diamonds) before they win theirs.

Their weapons are their stopper (the queen) in your long suit and the advantage of leading first. The opening lead is the spade king. If you win your ace and finesse in diamonds, you have lost the race—the enemy take one diamond and four spades before you get a chance to cash your long cards.

Here, you must **hold off** with your spade stopper. Allow the spade king to win the first trick, the spade queen to win the second trick; finally, take your ace on the third round, as late as possible. Now cash the diamond king and lead to dummy's jack for a finesse. It loses to East, but he has no spade left to lead, no entry to his partner's hand. So you can win whatever he leads, and play to dummy's diamond ace— your entry to cash your long cards and win the race.

• THE PERCENTAGES

In notrump, your only methods of winning extra tricks are finessing and setting up long cards. Occasionally, you must choose between them.

YOUR HAND	DUMMY
♠ A K	♠ 8 5
♡ J 9 5 2	♡ K 7 3
◇ 9 8 6	◇ A K 5 2
♣ A K Q J	♣ 10 8 6 3

Your contract is 3 notrump. The queen of spades is led, and you win your ace.

You have 8 top tricks, and must work for the ninth. (If you cash your top cards immediately, the opponents will surely win the remainder.) You have two choices: (1) lead up to dummy's heart king—if the ace is in front of the king, the successful finesse will produce the extra trick; (2) give the enemy a trick in diamonds, saving a high diamond in dummy as an entry—if the six missing diamonds are split evenly (three and three) between the opponents, dummy's fourth diamond will win the extra trick. You cannot try *both* plays, for the moment you surrender the lead in either hearts or diamonds, the enemy will force out your last high spade; if you give up the lead again, they will cash enough long-card tricks to defeat your contract. You must either finesse or try to set up a long card. Which is more likely to succeed?

The answer, it will turn out, is the finesse—this will work half the time. The chance of an **even split** in your long suit depends on how many cards the opponents hold in it. When they have six, as in this deal, the odds are approximately two to one *against* a three-three split (more often, one opponent will hold four, the other two). Therefore, the 50-50 chance of a finesse is superior. However, if the enemy holds only 5 cards in your long suit (that is, when you and partner have 8 cards) the odds are approximately 2 to 1 *in favor* of a three-two division. Thus, if the deal were:

YOUR HAND	DUMMY
♠ A K	♠ 8 4
♡ J 9 5 2	♡ K 7
◇ 9 8 6	◇ A K 5 3 2
♣ A K Q J	♣ 10 8 6 3

you should concede an early diamond trick and play for an even division in the long suit, rather than finesse in hearts. (Actually, it is a good idea in either deal to cash all four high clubs before finessing or playing diamonds; the opponents will have to make some discards, and perhaps they will discard foolishly.)

You do not have to be a mathematician to play bridge, but you do have to be aware of a few simple percentages. Six missing cards are more likely to divide four-two than three-three; five missing cards are far more likely to divide three-two than four-one.

Another **percentage play** you have to remember is in choosing whether to finesse against a missing queen or to cash your ace and king in the hope that the queen will fall. Suppose that this is your suit:

YOU: ♡ A J 8 7 6   DUMMY: ♡ K 9 5 3

You should cash your king and ace, trying to drop the queen. When you have 9 cards in a suit, this is slightly superior to the finesse (leading toward your A J). However, if you have only 8 cards:

YOU: ♡ A J 7 2   DUMMY: ♡ K 6 5 3

your best chance to win all the tricks is to cash dummy's king and lead the 3 toward your A J tenace, finessing unless the queen appears. Finesse against a queen when you have 8 cards; play to drop a queen when you have 9 cards. Be sure to remember that this rule of eight and nine applies only to a

missing *queen*. If it is the *jack* that is missing, you should almost always cash your A K Q, hoping that it will fall. And if
the king is missing, you should finesse even with 10 cards:

YOU: ♡ A J 8 7 3   DUMMY: ♡ Q 10 6 5 2

Lead the queen from dummy, and play low unless the king
covers. When you have *11* cards in a suit, you may play to
drop the king rather than finesse; and unless you can figure
out for yourself what to do with 12 cards (missing the king),
you will never make a bridge player.

♥ RULES TO REMEMBER

1. In notrump, race to set up your longest suit.
2. When entries to dummy are scarce, save a winning
   card in its long suit for an entry.
3. Hoard your stoppers in the enemy's long suit. Win
   your stopper at the last possible moment.
4. A finesse against a missing honor works half the
   time. This is a better chance than finding 6 enemy
   cards divided three-three, not so good as finding 5
   cards divided three-two.
5. *Finesse* against a missing queen when you are missing 5 (or more) cards; play to *drop* it missing 4
   cards or less.
6. Almost always play to *drop* a missing jack when
   you hold A K Q. Almost always *finesse* against a
   missing king.

CHAPTER 18

Defending Against an Enemy Contract

When an opponent is declarer and your side is on defense, your methods of winning tricks are unchanged. You can win tricks with *honors* (1) by cashing cards which are high, (2) by leading honors in sequence to promote cards which are nearly high (3) by finessing—leading toward honors and tenaces, or trapping an enemy honor surrounded by four of yours. In addition, you can win tricks with *small cards* by ruffing or by establishing a long suit. However, defensive play is more difficult than declarer play, for two reasons.

First, small-card tricks are not so readily available to the defense. When the opponents have named *their* long suit as trump, your side can almost never win tricks with its *long cards*—Declarer or dummy will have extra trumps, and will ruff them. Defensive *ruffing* tricks are possible, but they are hard to produce, since Declarer is usually in a position to draw your trumps early. Consider this deal:

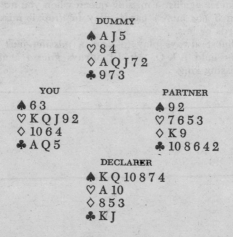

DUMMY
♠ A J 5
♡ 8 4
♢ A Q J 7 2
♣ 9 7 3

YOU
♠ 6 3
♡ K Q J 9 2
♢ 10 6 4
♣ A Q 5

PARTNER
♠ 9 2
♡ 7 6 5 3
♢ K 9
♣ 10 8 6 4 2

DECLARER
♠ K Q 10 8 7 4
♡ A 10
♢ 8 5 3
♣ K J

The enemy have reached a contract of 4 spades. Your long hearts and partner's long clubs are useless here, for they will be trumped. Partner can ruff the third round of diamonds, but he will surely not get the chance to do so, for Declarer will draw his trumps long before diamonds are played three times. You cannot win tricks with small cards. To defeat this contract, you must win four tricks with *honors*.

What is more, you must win your honors quickly. *Declarer* is in no hurry to win his honors, since his trump length guarantees that he will always take them; but the *defenders* are likely to lose their tricks if they wait too long to cash them. (In the hand above, Declarer can throw away losing hearts or clubs on dummy's long diamonds, if given time to do so, and then he can ruff your honors.)

Proper defense will defeat the contract above. Your opening lead is the heart king. Declarer wins his ace, draws trumps, and leads a low diamond, finessing dummy's jack. Partner takes his king, and leads back a club toward your tenace. Now you can win two club tricks, one heart trick, and partner's diamond trick—four in all, so Declarer takes only 9, and is down one. You started with one high card—the club ace—and produced 3 more tricks: the queen of hearts was set up by leading a sequence, the queen of clubs and king of diamonds were finessed successfully.

• THROUGH STRENGTH—UP TO WEAKNESS

This defense looks easy when you see all four hands, but remember that in practice you see only two—your hand and dummy. Just looking at your own hand, you could tell you should lead hearts (since you had a sequence of honors) and should not lead clubs (since you had a tenace); but how did partner know to lead clubs? When he won his diamond king, what he saw was:

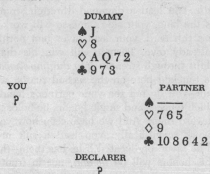

```
                    DUMMY
                    ♠ J
                    ♡ 8
                    ◇ A Q 7 2
                    ♣ 9 7 3

     YOU                          PARTNER
      ?                           ♠ ———
                                  ♡ 7 6 5
                                  ◇ 9
                                  ♣ 10 8 6 4 2

                   DECLARER
                      ?
```

He had no way to tell that you had the A Q of clubs. However, he *did* know that whatever club honors you had were *behind Declarer's honors*, since dummy had only little clubs. Therefore, this was a good suit to lead, for *your* finesses must work, Declarer's finesses must lose. This is called **leading through Declarer's strength into the dummy's weakness.**

To illustrate this further, suppose Declarer had led the heart 10 after drawing trumps. You would win your jack, and see:

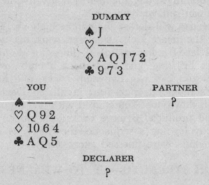

DUMMY

♠ J
♡ ——
♢ A Q J 7 2
♣ 9 7 3

YOU

♠ ——
♡ Q 9 2
♢ 10 6 4
♣ A Q 5

PARTNER

?

DECLARER

?

What should *you* lead? Not hearts, surely, since dummy can trump (you are perfectly willing, on defense, to force Declarer to ruff in his *own* hand, but you do not want to play a suit which *dummy* can ruff—your policy is exactly the opposite of Declarer's, who wants to ruff in dummy but not in his hand). Not clubs, for you would be leading through *weakness* into *strength*. You lead a diamond, through strength. When partner has the king, your side's finesse will work, and when Declarer has this card, your lead gives him nothing that he does not already own. Partner will win his diamond king and lead clubs through strength *into dummy's weakness*.

We have touched here on the second reason why defense is so difficult—you do not see your partner's hand; you have to guess which tenaces and single honors he holds, so that you can lead toward them. And we have seen how you go about this guesswork scientifically: you lead a suit in which his honors will be favorably located if he has them—that is, a suit in which his honors will be *behind*, not in front of, enemy honors.

Let us defend against a different contract, this time without seeing all the hands. You hold:

♠ 7 4   ♡ 9 8 3   ◇ A Q 10   ♣ A K J 6 4

The opponent to your right deals, and opens 1 spade; you double; your left-hand opponent bids 2 spades. Partner passes, Declarer passes, you pass—the auction is over. You must select your opening lead.

Your proper lead is the club king. This will win the trick (since you have the ace) and will allow you to see dummy while retaining the lead. For this reason, the king from an A K sequence will always be your first choice as an opening lead against a suit contract. Dummy goes down, and you see:

DUMMY

♠ 10 9 5 2
♡ A Q 7
◇ 7 5 3
♣ Q 8 2

YOU   PARTNER
♠ 7 4   ?
♡ 9 8 3
◇ A Q 10
♣ A K J 6 4

DECLARER

?

Dummy plays the 2, partner plays the 5, Declarer the 3. What do you lead next? Well, in which suits are your side's honors favorably located? Not in clubs, for dummy's queen is behind your ace—you must stop playing this suit. Not in spades, for Declarer's honors are behind whatever strength partner has—you will not lead trumps. In diamonds your honors are well placed, behind any enemy honors—but to finesse successfully, the lead must come *toward* your tenace, so you will not lead this suit. In hearts, any honors partner has are behind dummy's strength—this is the suit to attack. You lead the heart 9, for when you lead a suit in which you have no honors, you play your highest spot-card. (When you lead a suit in which you *have* an honor, you play a low spot-card.) Dummy plays the 7, partner the jack, Declarer the 5. Partner leads the diamond 8; Declarer plays the jack; you win with your queen.

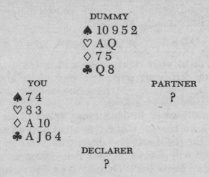

DUMMY
♠ 10 9 5 2
♡ A Q
◇ 7 5
♣ Q 8

YOU   PARTNER
♠ 7 4   ?
♡ 8 3
◇ A 10
♣ A J 6 4

DECLARER
?

What now? Lead another heart through dummy's strength to partner's king. Partner will return another diamond through Declarer's strength to your tenace. And your side will defeat the contract, winning two hearts, three diamonds, and one club. Here is the whole deal:

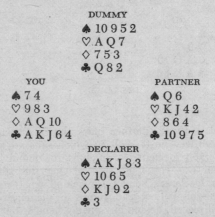

DUMMY
♠ 10 9 5 2
♡ A Q 7
◇ 7 5 3
♣ Q 8 2

YOU   PARTNER
♠ 7 4   ♠ Q 6
♡ 9 8 3   ♡ K J 4 2
◇ A Q 10   ◇ 8 6 4
♣ A K J 6 4   ♣ 10 9 7 5

DECLARER
♠ A K J 8 3
♡ 10 6 5
◇ K J 9 2
♣ 3

Let us examine partner's play. When you led the club king, he played the 5—this, as we will see shortly, was a signal that he did not want clubs continued. When you **shifted** to the heart 9 and dummy played low, he finessed his jack. (One of the *advantages* of being on defense is that you can see whether your finesses will work. If the queen of hearts had *not* been in dummy, partner would know that the finesse of the jack would lose; then he would win his king.) Partner led the diamond 8 for much the same reason as yours for leading hearts—any honors your side had were *behind* enemy honors. Notice how each of you led suits in which your finesses, if any, would work, and avoided the suits (spades, clubs) in which your finesses, if any, would fail because enemy honors were behind yours.

• LEADING TO A TRICK

The two problems of first-hand play are which *suit* to lead, and which *card* to lead in the suit you select.

Sequences of honors (three cards in a row, like K Q J) make excellent leads, since a sequence presents your best chance to promote honors. A suit with *two* touching honors (like Q J) is often a good lead, since partner may well hold the third honor (the 10 or the king, in our example). A suit with one honor or two honors not in sequence is less inviting to lead; you would rather have partner lead to you. A suit with no honors is often a reasonable one to lead, for you may be leading *toward* partner's honors; and if you are short in this suit, holding only one or two little cards, you have the chance for a ruff as well. Of course, all this is affected by the look of dummy; as we have seen, you try to lead through strength and up to weakness. However, if your right-hand opponent is declarer, you must make a lead before you see the dummy. Here is a table of opening leads against suit contracts; you should choose the one available closest to the head of the list:

OPENING LEADS AGAINST SUIT
CONTRACTS

---

1. An A K combination.
2. A singleton (not, of course, in trump).
3. A 3-card sequence headed by an honor. (If the lowest card is one rank away—K Q *10*, Q J *9*— consider it a 3-card sequence.)
4. A 2-card sequence headed by an honor.
5. A suit with no honors, preferably a doubleton suit (but not in trumps).
6. A suit with honors other than the ace, but not in sequence.
7. The trump suit.
8. A suit in which you hold the ace but not the king.

However, if partner has overcalled, lead his suit in preference to any other. And if he has opened the bidding, lead his suit unless you have one of the three best leads.

**WHICH CARD YOU LEAD IN THE SUIT
YOU SELECT**

---

1. From an A K, lead the king.
2. From any other sequence of honors, lead the highest honor.
3. From any other long suit (4 or more cards) lead the fourth highest card.
4. From any doubleton, lead the higher card.
5. From a 3-card suit, lead the highest if you have no honor, the lowest if you have one.
6. From *any* holding including the ace and not the king, lead the ace notwithstanding any rules above (but remember that this is a very poor suit to lead).

The auction, all by the enemy, goes: 1 spade—3 spades—4 spades. What is your opening lead from these hands?

(a) ♠ Q J 10   ♡ 8 6   ◇ Q J 9 5 2   ♣ A K J
(b) ♠ 8 4 2   ♡ Q J 5   ◇ K J 9 7 2   ♣ 7 5
(c) ♠ J 6 4   ♡ A 10 8 6 3   ◇ Q 10 2   ♣ A 2

(a) Lead the club king, for an A K combination is the best opening lead of all.

(b) Lead the heart queen, the top of a 2-card sequence. This is preferable to leading clubs where you have no honor, or diamonds where your honors are not in sequence.

(c) Lead the diamond 2. Spades are trumps, and in hearts and clubs you hold the ace, so you decide to open diamonds by elimination. Since your honors are not in sequence, you lead low.

OPENING LEADS AGAINST NOTRUMP

Against a notrump contract, your opening lead should almost always be in your longest suit, regardless of high-card combinations. If this suit is headed by a 3-card sequence of honors (either three in a row or with the lowest one just barely out of sequence), lead the top card. Lacking a 3-card sequence in your long suit, lead the fourth-highest card. Thus, with the three examples just given, against notrump, open the diamond queen from (a), the diamond 7 from (b), the heart 6 from (c). Note that there is no prohibition against leading a suit in which you hold the ace when the contract is notrump.

Here, too, you must tend to lead partner's suit if he has bid one strongly. In leading partner's suit, open the same card that you would against a suit contract. (If partner has bid spades, lead the queen from (a), the 8 from (b), the 4 from (c).

• WHEN PARTNER LEADS

When *partner* leads to a trick, you are the third hand to play. This is often an unfavorable position, for an opponent plays after you do; if he has honors, he can determine *his* play after seeing yours. For example, suppose that partner leads the 2 of spades, and this is the setup:

DUMMY
♠ 7 5 3

PARTNER   YOU
♠ Q 10 6 2   ♠ K 9 4

DECLARER
♠ A J 8

Dummy plays the 3 on partner's 2. If you play the king, Declarer takes his ace; if you play the 9. Declarer wins the jack; and if you follow with your 4, Declarer will win with the 8. Of course, your proper play is the king—third hand high. This seems to sacrifice a valuable honor, but your king is not wasted even though it loses to Declarer's ace—by forcing Declarer to use a high card to win the trick, you have set up two future tricks for partner. His Q 10 now lie in wait behind Declarer's jack.

FINESSING AGAINST DUMMY

The general principle, then, is to put up your highest card in third seat, trying either to win the trick yourself or to prevent Declarer from winning it cheaply. The chief exception occurs when there is an honor in dummy which you can finesse against. Obviously, with

DUMMY

♠ K 5 3

PARTNER   YOU

♠ A Q 4

when partner leads the 2 and dummy plays the 3, you finesse your queen. It is less obvious, but just as correct, to finesse if you hold the ace-*jack*.

(1)   ♠ K 5 3

♠ Q 10 6 2   ♠ A J 4

♠ 9 8 7

(2)   ♠ K 5 3

♠ 10 8 6 3   ♠ A J 4

♠ Q 9 7

In both (1) and (2), you must play the jack when partner leads the 2 and dummy follows with the 3 (you would, of course, take the *king* with the ace). In (1), you prevent the enemy from winning any tricks in the suit; in (2), you hold them to one trick. Playing your ace would lose a trick in either example, for you can capture dummy's king with your ace if you wait for it. Here is another instance of waiting to kill dummy's honors:

DUMMY

♠ J 7 5

YOU

♠ K 10 9

Partner leads the 2, and dummy plays the 5; you must finesse your 9, saving your king for dummy's jack. If the full position is:

♠ J 7 5

♠ 8 4 3 2   ♠ K 10 9

♠ A Q 6

Declarer will win all three of his honors when you play your king on dummy's 5, but can win only his queen and ace if you finesse the 9. And if *partner* holds the queen:

♠ J 7 5

♠ Q 4 3 2   ♠ K 10 9

♠ A 8 6

your 9 will force out Declarer's ace. If instead you play your king, dummy's jack will win a trick later.

SIGNALING TO PARTNER

Note, by the way, that you play the 9, not the 10. When following suit (as opposed to *leading*) with a sequence of honors, always follow with the lowest card in sequence. It is easy to see why in the preceding example. When your 9 forces out Declarer's ace, partner knows that you must have the 10 also (otherwise Declarer would have won the trick with it). However, if your *10* forced out the ace, partner could not know that you hold the 9. Likewise:

♠ 8 5 3

♠ K 9 6 4   ♠ Q J 10

♠ A 7 2

when partner leads the four, play your 10. This forces Declarer's ace, so partner knows that you hold the queen and jack as well. Therefore he can tell to play the suit again when he regains the lead.

Another method of telling partner whether to continue playing the suit he has led is by **signaling** in third seat. A common occasion for this is when you cannot beat the enemy card played in *second* seat. For example:

DUMMY

♠ A 6 5

YOU

♠ K 8 2

Partner leads the 3, and dummy plays the ace. Obviously, you must save your king for later use, but it seems to make no difference whether you follow suit with the 8 or the 2. However, either card is a signal. The 8, a high spot-card, asks partner to continue playing the same suit; the 2, a low spot-card, warns partner that you have no desire to have the suit played again. In the instance above, you would signal enthusiasm for spades with your eight. In this example:

DUMMY

♠ A 6 5

YOU

♠ 10 8 2

you would discourage with your 2. Note that you signal only if you cannot try to win the trick; that is, if dummy played the 5 instead of the ace in either example, you would play third hand high—your king in the first instance, your 10 in the second.

Another occasion for a signal occurs when partner's lead is an honor. Suppose partner leads the spade queen, and you see:

DUMMY

♠ 10 6 4

YOU

♠ K 7 3

Dummy plays the 4, and you signal "Come ahead" with your 7. If you held 8 7 3, you would signal "Stop" with your 3.

You may signal with a high spot-card even when you yourself have no honor in the suit led, if you want to ruff a later round. Suppose partner leads the king of spades against a heart contract:

DUMMY

♠ Q 8 4

PARTNER   YOU

♠ A K 10 6 2   ♠ 9 3

DECLARER

♠ J 7 5

you should follow with your 9, signaling "Come ahead." Partner will then continue with his ace, and your 3 falls—completing the high-low signal (called an **echo**) which is an emphatic demand for a continuation. Therefore, partner plays a third spade and you obtain a ruff. If instead, the cards were:

DUMMY

♠ Q 8 4

PARTNER   YOU

♠ A K 10 6 2   ♠ J 9 7 3

DECLARER

♠ 5

you would signal with the three on partner's king, warning him to switch to some other suit. Observe that partner has no way of knowing whether to continue or to switch—you must tell him. Some players do this by beaming approval when they like partner's suit and scowling when they do not, but they soon run out of opponents willing to play against them. It is better to do your signaling properly with otherwise meaningless high and low spot-cards.

How high or low must a card be to be a signal? Anything above a 5 looks high, and cards below it look low, but this is no real answer. If partner leads the queen when you hold K 4 3 2, you must encourage with the 4; and if you hold 9 8 7, you must discourage with the 7—your lowest card. To urge a continuation, signal with the highest card that you can afford. Thus, if partner leads the king and you see:

DUMMY

♠ J 8 2

YOU

♠ Q 9 7 6

you cannot afford the *queen,* obviously, but you can spare the 9—so that is your correct play.

• WHEN THE OPPONENTS LEAD

You will have fewer problems playing to tricks when the opponents lead. In fourth seat, after all three hands have already played, win the trick if you can as cheaply as possible; if you cannot win it, follow suit with your smallest card. It is almost never proper to signal when the enemy have led to the trick. For instance:

DUMMY
♠ A 7 4

YOU
♠ K 9 2

Declarer leads the spade 5; partner plays the 3, dummy the ace. Follow with your 2, not your 9. If *partner* had led the spades, you would signal to give him the good news that you have a high honor; but when *Declarer* leads the suit, this information is important to *him* and must be withheld. The whole suit might be:

DUMMY
♠ A 7 4

PARTNER
♠ J 8 3

YOU
♠ K 9 2

DECLARER
♠ Q 10 6 5

Notice that Declarer is going to lead from dummy toward his Q 10; he will have to guess whether to finesse his 10 or his queen. If you play the 2 and then the 9, he is likely to misguess, but if you signal with your 9 and tell him where the king is, his problem is solved.

Observe, too, that you must play your 9, not your king, when spades are led a second time from dummy. Here, you are in second seat, and your normal policy is to play low. If partner holds the queen, there is no need for you to take your king; and if Declarer holds the queen, he must win a trick with it later if you go up with your king, while he may not guess to play it immediately if you properly play second hand low.

If you do not dash up with a *winning* honor in second seat, you obviously will not play a lower honor. That is, with:

DUMMY
♠ 8 6 4

YOU
♠ K 9 2

when the 4 is led from dummy, you follow with the 2. You are relying on partner, in fourth position, to win the trick or to force Declarer to win it with a high honor. The whole difference between *second*-hand play and *third*-hand play is simply that partner has not yet followed to the trick—there is no need for you to do anything violent when partner is still a factor. *He* is in the favorable position, behind the enemy, while you are in poor position to win a trick cheaply.

SPLITTING YOUR HONORS

There are two common exceptions to this policy of second-hand low. One occurs when you have a sequence of honors. For example:

DUMMY
♠ 8 6 4

YOU
♠ Q J 10 2

If the 4 is led from dummy, **split your honors** by playing the 10. This guarantees you a trick in the suit, and may help you to capture Declarer's king if partner holds the ace. You might split even a 2-card sequence if this ensures a trick:

DUMMY
♠ A 6 4

YOU
♠ Q J 2

When the 4 is led from dummy, play your jack. This will force Declarer's king, and now your queen must win behind dummy's ace. However, if dummy held three *small* spades, you should play second hand low, for splitting your honors would not guarantee a trick.

COVERING HONORS

The most frequent occasion for playing an honor in second seat is to cover an honor led by first hand. Consider this suit:

DUMMY
♠ J 6

PARTNER   YOU
♠ 10 9 3   ♠ K 8 7

DECLARER
♠ A Q 5 4 2

If dummy leads the six, you play your 7—second hand low. However, if the *jack* is led from dummy, you must play your king. This is called **covering an honor.** Your object is not to win your king, but to spoil the enemy jack. If you do not cover it, the jack holds the trick, and Declarer now leads low to his queen and ace—winning all the tricks. In contrast, if you cover the jack with your king, Declarer wins his ace and queen, but must then surrender a trick to partner's ten. The purpose of covering is to set up a lower honor either in your or in partner's hand, by forcing Declarer to waste *two* honors on one trick. If an honor is led by first hand, you should almost always cover it, if you can, in second seat.

Of course, you should not cover if there is no hope of establishing a lower honor for yourself or partner. For example:

DUMMY
♠ Q J 10 9 2

YOU
♠ K 7 4

When the queen is led from dummy, it is pointless for you to cover, since all the lower honors are in dummy. Play low, hoping that Declarer has only a *doubleton* ace and cannot repeat the finesse. Likewise, if you *see* a doubleton ace in dummy:

DUMMY
♠ A 3

YOU
♠ K 7 4

and Declarer leads the queen, it is often right to play low, since your king cannot then be captured.

Another instance in which it is wrong to cover is when you hold the queen—guarded by small cards—in a suit in which the enemy are very long. For example, if you have three trumps including the queen, it is seldom right to cover. Partner is very short, and so can have no lower honor to set up; and if you do *not* cover, Declarer may refuse to finesse, playing for the missing queen to drop. Suppose this is the trump suit:

DUMMY
♠ A 10 6 2

YOU   PARTNER
♠ Q 7 4   ♠ 8

DECLARER
♠ K J 9 5 3

With nine trumps, Declarer plans to cash ace and king, hoping to drop the queen. However, it costs him nothing to lead his jack, coaxing you to cover. You should not cover, of course, for you have no lower honor to establish, and partner must be too short to have one.

A final occasion when you should *not* cover an honor is when dummy has *two* honors in sequence. For instance:

DUMMY

♠ Q J 4

YOU

♠ K 5 2

If the queen is led, play low; however, if the jack is led next, cover it. It is because there is a second honor for you to spoil that you can afford not to cover the first one. For a variety of reasons, it is more effective to cover the *second* honor instead of the first.

Somehow, I have devoted far more space to the rare positions in which you should *not* cover honors than to the common positions in which you should. Do not let me confuse you. It is important to recognize the exceptional situations, but if you cover with a higher honor whenever you are in second seat and first hand leads an honor, you will be right 90 per cent of the time.

♥ RULES TO REMEMBER

In fact, all the old bromides for defensive play, some of which date from the days of whist, are surprisingly sound:

> Lead through dummy's strength
> Lead up to dummy's weakness
> Third hand high
> Second hand low
> Cover an honor with an honor

These are policies, not rules, and they all have exceptions. Still, you should have a good reason before you violate one of these precepts. You will not go far wrong following them.

BOOK TWO
THE FINE POINTS

Foreword

Here in Book Two, we will examine from a new standpoint much of the ground which we have already covered. In order to avoid repetition, I have omitted almost all reference to the basic rules and policies stated in Book One. Therefore, the sections on bidding will treat only rare situations in which you must violate the normal rules, bid tactically, or employ some fancy convention. The great majority of hands can be handled perfectly well with the methods presented in Book One, but you must be prepared to cope with the exceptions also.

My suggestion for using the bidding sections is this: before reading a chapter, review its equivalent in Book One. This way, you will get a clear picture of the fundamentals before going on to the fine points. It is much more fun to violate the basic rules if you know what they are.

E. K.

CHAPTER 1

The Value of Your Hand

(See Book One, Chapter 2)

• THE STANDARD SYSTEM

Nowadays, the majority of bridge players throughout the world value their hands in terms of points on the 4–3–2–1 scale for aces, kings, queens, and jacks. It is well to remember that this point count is not a "system" of bidding—that is, it has nothing to do with the message your bids convey to partner. For example, if you open the bidding 1 heart, partner responds 1 spade, and you rebid 1 notrump, you might hold:

♠ 8 4   ♡ Q 9 8 6 2   ◇ K Q 2   ♣ A Q 4

Twenty years ago, when almost no one used the point count, this hand was bid identically. Today, you say to yourself that you have 14 points; then, you said to yourself that you had 2½+ honor tricks. However, what you say to partner in either case is "I have a minimum opening with even distribution; hearts is my longest suit, and I have no great support for spades." Your *bidding system* has not changed; you simply are valuing your hand in different terms.

In contrast, one school of Italian bidders would open 1 heart and rebid 1 notrump over a 1 spade response holding:

♠ Q 9 8 6 2   ♡ A J 6 3   ◇ A 4   ♣ K 8

In their system, the 1 notrump rebid promises *five spades* with a minimum opening.

These Italians do value their hands in points, but they play a *different system*—their bids have a different meaning to partner.

The basic bidding system described in this book has been used for years, and still is used, by almost all American players. You can use it successfully with a partner who counts points differently, or with a partner who still uses honor tricks, or with a partner who just gets a feeling about what his hand is worth without counting anything. *How* you and partner value your hands is unimportant, so long as you value them accurately and understand the vocabulary and grammar of the language you are speaking—Standard American Bidding.

• COUNTING FOR DISTRIBUTION

The 4–3–2–1 point count (the Milton Work count) deserves its popularity, for it is a very simple and reasonably accurate method of valuing a hand. However, it is necessary to correct high-card count by adding for *distributional* strength. The method I recommend is to count extra for long suits, adding 1 point for each card over four in any suit, to determine the *original* value of your hand. Then, after a trump fit has been found, each partner revalues his hand by adding extra points for short side suits—3 for a void, 2 for a singleton, 1 for a doubleton. Counting your distribution this way has two advantages: (1) it is logical, since you count your long suits (which always are valuable) initially, and count short suits (which are worthless until a fit is found) only after their value becomes manifest; (2) it is not complicated by a multiplicity of rules, since opener and responder count points in identical fashion.

However, if you are comfortable with a different method of valuing distribution (counting shortness first, revaluing honors as responder, counting more for shortness as responder than as opener, adding extra for long trumps as opener after being supported, etc.), stick with it. We will still be speaking the same language, so long as your counting method caters to these two basic truths: any hand with even pattern is worth less than a hand with unbalanced pattern; both partners' hands are worth a little more for suit play after a trump fit has been found.

• QUICK TRICKS

The point count, even corrected for distribution, does not take into account all the features which make a hand valuable. For example, honors are more valuable when in combination with other honors—obviously, a king is worth more when you have the ace of the same suit, a queen is worth more when combined with the king or ace. If you learned bridge in the 1940's or earlier, you have an advantage, for you probably remember **honor-trick** or **quick-trick** valuation. Here is a simple table of quick tricks:

AK = 2	A = 1	K = ½
AQ = 1½	KQ = 1	

These two hands have the same point count:

(a) ♠ Q J 8 4 2   ♡ K 5 3   ◇ A 6   ♣ Q 4 2
(b) ♠ A Q J 8 2   ♡ K Q 3   ◇ 6 4   ♣ 4 3 2

However, hand (b) is stronger because all its honors are in combination. It has 2½ quick tricks, while hand (a) has only 1½ quick tricks. Quick tricks are particularly important in deciding to open the bidding. I myself rarely open with fewer than 2 quick tricks, and then certainly not with only 13 points. I would pass hand (a), but open hand (b). In contrast, I am old-fashioned enough never to pass a hand that contains 3 quick tricks:

(c) ♠ A K 5   ♡ A 9 4   ◇ 6 4 2   ♣ J 10 8 4

Hand (c) above counts to only 12 points, but it looks to me like a sound opening bid. To illustrate my point, let me give partner this hand:

(d) ♠ 7 6   ♡ J 10 7 6 2   ◇ K 3   ♣ A K 7 5

If you hold hand (a) facing hand (d) you would be lucky to make 3 hearts; hand (b) facing hand (d) has a fighting chance to produce 4 hearts; and hand (c) opposite hand (d) will make a heart game most of the time. The high-card combinations give you control—the opponents have to dig for tricks instead of being able to cash them off the top. Another advantage of hands with quick tricks is that they will stop high enemy contracts even when partner holds very little strength. That is, if partner holds:

(e) ♠ 7 6 4   ♡ J 10   ◇ 9 7 5 3   ♣ K 8 6 5

the opponents can surely make 4 hearts if you hold hand (a); they will probably make only 3 hearts if you hold hand (b); they are unlikely to make more than 2 hearts if you hold hand (c). Thus, you do not fear that you are opening the auction for the enemy when you have quick-trick strength.

I do not suggest that you count quick tricks *instead* of points, only that you be aware of them in addition, for they are the high-card "skeleton" of your hand. Be reluctant to open the bidding with fewer than 2 quick tricks; do so only with 14 points or more, and even then do not be surprised if you get a poor result. Be equally reluctant to pass with 3 quick tricks—open even with 12 points, and blame me if it goes wrong. In the later auction, strain to bid suit games if you have good quick-trick structure, but underbid slightly when you have not.

• HONORS IN LONG OR SHORT SUITS

Another factor which the point count ignores is the *location* of your honors. When your high cards are in your *long* suits, both the honors and the suits themselves are more valuable. Consider these two hands:

(f) ♠ A K 10 8 3   ♡ K Q 6 4   ◇ 9 2   ♣ 8 5
(g) ♠ 9 8 6 5 2   ♡ 10 8 6 4   ◇ A K   ♣ K Q

They contain exactly the same rank of cards, and have identical distribution. However, hand (f) is considerably more valuable than hand (g)—it will win more tricks in play, and it is safer and easier to handle in the auction. Each hand counts to 13 points and 3 quick tricks, and I would open either with a bid of 1 spade. Still, I would be ashamed of hand (g), and would firmly decline any subsequent game or slam invitations no matter how strongly partner had bid. In contrast, I would rather like hand (f) and would cheerfully cooperate with any effort partner made to reach a high contract. For example, if the auction were to go:

OPENER	RESPONDER
1 spade	2 diamonds
2 hearts	3 hearts

I would go on to 4 hearts holding hand (f), but would pass in a flash with hand (g).

An allied problem is the value of unguarded honors—doubleton jacks or queens, singleton kings or lower honors. My own policy is not to value a singleton jack or queen at all unless partner has bid the suit; and to count a doubleton Q J as only 2 points. The other holdings can be counted at face value, but you should realize that they constitute a flaw, and that you must take a conservative view in any close decision subsequently. For example, I would open 1 heart with either:

(h) ♠ 4   ♡ A K J 8 6   ◇ K J 10 7 3   ♣ K 7
(i) ♠ K   ♡ A K J 8 6   ◇ K 10 7 4 3   ♣ J 7

If partner raises to 2 hearts, I would jump to 4 hearts with hand (h). (My value is 20 points—15 in high cards, 2 for length, 3 for shortness after a fit is found.) However, I would bid only 3 hearts with hand (i), since I do not like either my singleton king or my doubleton jack.

• POSITIONAL VALUE

Another factor in the total worth of your hand is the **positional value** of your cards after an enemy bid. Obviously, an ace-queen or a king in an opponent's suit is worth much more if it is *behind* the bidder than if it is in front of him. Queens, kings, and tenaces increase in value when behind enemy strength, for your finesses will almost surely succeed. Likewise, they diminish in value when in front of the strength, since your finesses will fail. A hand like this one:

♠ A Q 10   ♡ K 5   ◇ A Q J 9 4   ♣ Q 10 7

is worth a great deal more if your *right*-hand opponent opens 1 spade than if your *left*-hand opponent makes the same bid. In the first instance, 4 or 5 points in partner's hand could easily produce game; in the second case, partner will need 8 or 9 points at least to take the same number of tricks.

• TRUE VALUE OF THE HONORS

Finally, the 4–3–2–1 point count itself has a built-in flaw. It would be too much to expect that such a neat and orderly scale would happen to be completely accurate. The truth is that the relative values of the four honors are slightly distorted—particularly those of the queen and ace. One ace is worth a lot more than two queens, no matter what anyone's point count says. Hands with three or four aces have more value than their points indicate, while hands with three or four queens have a good deal less. Jacks are slightly overvalued, and kings are slightly undervalued in the Milton

Work count, but here the distortion is not great. My own conception of an accurate count would look like this:

Ace = 4.3   Queen = 1.7
King = 3.1   Jack = .9

However, the count above is completely unusable, for the principal merit of any point count is not accuracy but simplicity. By all means, use the 4–3–2–1 valuation. Do not clutter it up with additions and subtractions and corrections. But use it with sense.

• POINT COUNT WITH SENSE

This means allowing the other factors I have mentioned—quick-trick structure, honors in long or short suits, positional values, the true worth of aces and queens—to color your judgment. In many auctions you will have close decisions to make: Shall you go on to game when the partnership may have only 25 points? Shall you try for a doubtful slam? Shall you step into the bidding with a vulnerable overcall? Here, you allow the other considerations to influence your answer. Be aggressive if your points are in combinations of high honors located in your long suits; be conservative if you have too many queens or if your honors are in short suits. For example, suppose that your right-hand opponent opens the bidding with 1 diamond. You hold one of these hands:

(j) ♠ A Q 8 6 4   ♡ A J 7 5   ◊ K 6   ♣ 8 3
(k) ♠ K Q 8 6 4   ♡ K J 7 5   ◊ Q J   ♣ Q 3

Neither hand is ideal for either a double or a 1 spade overcall. If you overcall, you might miss a heart game, but if you double you may be in trouble after a club response. Make the aggressive double with hand (j)—you should like your quick-trick skeleton, the clustering of your honors in long suits, the positional value of your king and your tenaces behind the bidder, the fact that you have two aces and only one queen. Make the more conservative overcall with hand (k)—you should be slowed down by your lack of aces and your three queens, by your doubleton honors (the Q J in the enemy suit is practically worthless), and your poor quick-trick structure.

The point count, if properly used, is an extremely good guide to proper bidding. Its principal contribution is to provide the language of bidding with a sensitive vocabulary. We need no longer talk vaguely of a "sound opening bid," for we can call it a 15- or 16-point hand. Instead of saying that a "powerful opening" facing a "minimum response" may make game, we can talk of 18 points opposite 8 adding to 26. Actually, the chief advantage of point count lies in the fact that you can add your points to partner's. No one could ever tell with much accuracy how many honor tricks a partnership must have to bid a game or slam, while the point count has the figures of 26 and 33. If you understand partner's bids in terms of points, and then add your points to his, comparing the total with 26 or 33, you will have a good indication of your side's prospects.

Still, an *indication* is all that you will have. No calculating machine will ever bid well, for there are too many imponderables at the bridge table. A long huddle by an opponent might add considerably to the value of your hand, and a greedy look in his eye might subtract. If your partner is a magnificent card player, your hand is worth more when you are to be dummy; if the opponents are demon defenders, it is worth less. No cold table of values can ever replace the judgment of an experienced bridge player.

Therefore, if your intuition tells you to bid game even though the point count tells you not to, go ahead and bid. Of course, you had better be right, for when you depart from the rules and get a poor result, you have no defense against partner's withering glances. Success, however, washes away all sin.

CHAPTER 2

Opening Bid and Opener's Rebid

(See Book One, Chapters 3 and 5)

There are two kinds of rules for bidding. One type is concerned with the actual language of bridge—the meaning of your bids. (For example, the rule that an opening suit bid promises 13 points or more; the rule that you should bid your longest suit first; the rule that you need at least three trumps headed by an honor to raise partner, etc.) A different type of rule is a kind of "traffic regulation" to make sure that the auction can proceed smoothly without reaching too high a level before a trump suit is found (for example, the rule that the higher ranking of equally long suits is bid first; the special rules for opening in 4-card suits; the rules which require extra strength for bidding new suits at a higher level).

• STAYING LOW WITH A MINIMUM

In this chapter, we shall examine many new traffic regulations which affect your choice of an opening bid. As opener, you must allow for the fact that you will have to bid a second time if partner changes suits. The science of opening the bidding is largely one of anticipation: What will you bid next if partner responds in your short suit? We have seen this type of thinking in your choice of opening bid with a hand like:

♠ A K 7 4   ♡ 5 3   ◇ 8 6 4   ♣ A Q 5 2

Here, you open *1 club*, so that you can rebid 1 spade if partner responds in one of the suits in between your separated 4-card suits. If you open *1 spade* and partner responds 2 hearts or 2 diamonds, you would have to go to the three-level with your minimum hand, in order to show your club suit. In contrast, when your suits are touching in rank:

♠ A K 7 4   ♡ A Q 5 2   ◇ 8 6 4   ♣ 5 3

you open *1 spade*, since now you can rebid 2 hearts over any change of suit. The critical level in opener's second bid is *two of his first suit.* If opener's rebid is at this level or lower, the partnership can easily stop at a low contract. However, when opener's second bid goes beyond two of his first suit, a high contract is often unavoidable.

(1)

OPENER	RESPONDER
♠ 8 5 2	♠ K Q 4
♡ A J 7 6 2	♡ 8 3
◇ 6	◇ A J 9 7 2
♣ A K J 7	♣ 10 9 2
1 heart	2 diamonds
3 clubs	3 notrump

(2)

OPENER	RESPONDER
♠ Q 6 4	♠ 8 5 2
♡ K Q 8 6 3	♡ J 5
◇ K 10 3	◇ Q 6 4
♣ K 2	♣ A Q 8 6 3
1 heart	2 clubs
2 notrump	3 notrump

In each example, the partnership reached a quite unmakable game contract, having only 22 or 23 points between the two hands. The fault lies in opener's rebid. Even though he did not *jump* in either auction, merely showing a second suit in (1) and making a minimum notrump rebid in (2), opener *went beyond two of his first suit*. The resulting momentum carried the partnership to game almost inevitably; therefore opener must expect to make game before he employs either rebid. That is, opener must have at least 15 or 16 points, so that he can add up to nearly 26 points the instant he hears that responder has at least 10 points (for his new suit takeout at the two-level). Opener must not go beyond two of his suit with a bare minimum opening.

Opener's proper rebid with each hand above is *2 hearts.* In example (1), responder would then rebid 2 notrump and opener would pass. In example (2), responder would pass the 2 heart rebid. Note that there is no longer any danger of reaching a foolish game contract on either auction.

Be sure to remember that opener's object in rebidding his suit is to slow the auction down, *not* to show that he has a 5-card suit. After opening either hand with 1 heart:

(1) ♠ 8 4 2　♡ A J 7 6 2　◇ 6　♣ A K J 7
(2) ♠ Q 6 4　♡ K Q 8 6 3　◇ K 10 3　♣ K 2

opener should *not* rebid 2 hearts over a *1 spade* response. With hand (1), opener should rebid 2 *clubs;* with hand (2) opener should rebid *1 notrump.* Observe that each recommended rebid is now cheaper than 2 hearts, so that *responder* can bid 2 hearts if that is the correct contract. Opener does not *want* to rebid a 5-card suit; he much prefers to bid a secondary 4-card suit, or rebid in notrump with even distribution. However, he can afford the luxury of describing his distribution accurately only when his intended second bid does not go beyond the critical level—two of his first suit.

Of course, opener *can* afford any rebid when he holds the few extra points which will guarantee a sound play for game. That is, after bidding 1 spade with either of these hands:

(3) ♠ A Q J 6 2　♡ K 8 4　◇ 6　♣ K Q 10 3
(4) ♠ K Q J 7 4　♡ A Q 2　◇ 10 3　♣ K 10 5

you should *not* rebid 2 spades over a response of 2 diamonds. You should bid 3 clubs with example (3) and 2 notrump with example (4). There is no need to stay at or below the level of two of your first suit when you can add up to the 26 points you need for game. However, transform the club king into the deuce, and 2 spades would then be the proper rebid with either hand, for you must not go galloping up to a game contract with a bare minimum opening.

• RAISING PARTNER'S SUIT

Whenever opener raises responder, he has gone beyond two of his own suit.

(5)	OPENER	RESPONSER
	1 club	1 heart
	2 hearts	
(6)	1 heart	2 diamonds
	3 diamonds	

Therefore, the auctions above are both encouraging, indicating more than a bare minimum opening. However, you need never hesitate to raise partner *when you have 4-card support,* merely because you opened with a minimum point count. Your hand grows stronger the minute partner responds in your side 4-card suit. For example, suppose that you open 1 club, holding:

    ♠ K 4   ♡ K 10 5 3   ◇ K 2   ♣ K 10 7 6 3

Since you have a minimum opening, you must not rebid 2 hearts if partner responds 1 spade, but must stay "at or below two of your suit" by rebidding 2 clubs or 1 notrump. However, if partner responds *1 heart* your point count is greater because a fit has been found (and partner's point count is likewise augmented). Therefore, you raise to 2 hearts.

In contrast, you must be very cautious in raising partner's suit when you have only *3-card* support. You are allowed to raise partner's first suit with a 3-card holding headed by a high honor, but here there is no assurance that a fit has been found, for partner may have responded in a 4-card suit. Your hand has *not* been improved by the response, so the moderate encouragement which you offer with a raise must be based on a point count which *originally* was greater than the bare minimum 13 or 14. Consider these two examples:

  (7) ♠ K 8 4 ♡ A J 7 3 ◇ K 4 ♣ Q 10 7 2
  (8) ♠ K 8 4 ♡ A K 7 3 ◇ 8 2 ♣ A Q 7 2

With either hand, you open 1 club; suppose partner responds 1 spade. Example (7) has a bare minimum 13 points, and so you must not encourage partner by raising: rebid 1 notrump. Example (8), however, is a maximum "minimum opening," and you raise to 2 spades. (If the response were, instead, 1 *heart*, you would raise to 2 hearts with hand (7), since you have 4-card support. With hand (8), you could jump-raise to 3 hearts, for once a sure fit is found this is a strong opening bid.)

Your policy toward 3-card raises is the same when partner's response is at the two-level. You would open 1 spade holding either:

  (9) ♠ A Q 10 6 2 ♡ 8 2 ◇ A Q 3 ♣ 6 4 2
  (10) ♠ A Q 10 6 2 ♡ 8 2 ◇ A Q 3 ♣ K 4 2

Partner responds 2 diamonds. Rebid 2 *spades* with hand (9), to slow the auction down when you have such a lean opening bid. Raise to 3 *diamonds* with hand (10). You are willing to go past two of your suit, since your side surely has enough points to warrant a game contract. Observe that it is neither the quality of your support nor the quality of your own suit that determines whether to raise partner with 3-card support. The critical factor is your point count.

• THE "SHORT CLUB"

The principles of rebidding which we have discussed so far may well affect your choice of an opening bid. Suppose that you deal yourself this hand:

♠ A K 10 3   ♡ 9 5 2   ◇ J 6 4   ♣ A Q 5

You open 1 spade; partner responds 2 diamonds. What is your rebid? Not 2 spades, for you have only a 4-card suit; not 2 notrump or 3 diamonds, for you dare not go beyond two of your suit; no rebid is possible. Yet you are not allowed to pass—your side could conceivably make even a slam, as partner's hand is unlimited. About the only solution is to put your cards on the table, excuse yourself for a minute, and go home.

To avoid breaking up the game, you open the example hand not 1 spade, but *1 club*. After opening 1 club, you are sure to have a good rebid. If partner responds 1 diamond or 1 heart, you can bid 1 spade. If partner responds 1 spade, you raise. And if partner responds 1 notrump or 2 clubs, you pass. Notice that it is never necessary to go beyond two of your first suit.

Notice also that partner is allowed to raise clubs. There is nothing special or mysterious about the opening bid of 1 club. If partner holds:

♠ 8 2   ♡ A 10 3   ◇ 8 6 3 2   ♣ K J 8 4

he will respond 2 clubs to your 1 club opening, just exactly as he would respond 2 hearts to 1 heart or 2 diamonds to 1 diamond. He should expect you to have a 4-card or longer suit, and you *will* have most of the time. When you have bid a short club, a 3-card club suit, you have told partner a lie, but you are not in serious trouble when he raises you. After all, you have seven trumps in the combined hands, the same number there are when you open in a 4-card major suit and partner raises with three. There are worse things in bridge than playing at the two-level in a three-four fit.

However, the short-club opening can lead to a major disaster if you get panicky when raised, and, instead of passing, bid again. You should open 1 club holding:

♠ 9 6 2   ♡ K Q J 8   ◇ A Q 4   ♣ Q 6 2

When partner responds 2 clubs, you must *not* bid 2 hearts. This would promise a strong (17-points-or-more) opening, and indicate that your side can make game if partner has a maximum (8- or 9-point) raise. Thus, you may arrive at a 22-point game contract, get doubled, and lose a small fortune. You must *pass* when partner raises; 2 clubs is probably as good a contract as is available, and, even if it is not, no great harm can come to you in a low-level, undoubled part score.

Likewise, partner should not panic when you open 1 club. If he holds:

♠ J742　♡ Q84　◇ 10763　♣ 32

he must pass your 1 club opening. Certainly, you will go down if you have bid a short club, but then the opponents could have scored a lot more points playing their own contract (for you have a minimum opening). And if partner bids, promising you 6 points at least, you may jump to game with a 20-point hand and suffer a major loss. Yet I have seen experienced players respond with a hand like the one above, bidding 1 spade or 1 diamond and suffering a huge loss because partner expected them to hold some high cards. Then came the plaintive explanations: "I bid 1 spade because I thought a club opening asked me to bid a major suit," or "I play that a 1 diamond response to 1 club means that I have nothing," or some such nonsense. If partner bases his bidding on the fear that you are lying with your opening, and you must fear that partner has nothing for his response, the auction becomes a guessing game instead of an orderly exchange of information.

When you lie by opening in a 3-card club suit, you must behave as if you had told the truth, and partner must behave as if he had never heard of such a beast as the short club. Your protection comes from the fact that partner hates to raise a minor suit, in which game is so difficult to make. Partner, holding:

♠ QJ83　♡ 82　◇ A104　♣ J963

will respond 1 spade to a 1 club opening, but not for fear that you have only three clubs. He wants to investigate the major suit before settling to play in the unattractive minor. And with:

♠ KJ4　♡ AQ2　◇ A104　♣ J963

partner jumps in notrump, not in clubs, over your 1 club
opening, but only because game is so much more easily made
in notrump. Partner must not be suspicious of your 1 club
openings, but he should hate to play a hand with clubs as
trump even if you have nine or 10 clubs in the combined
hands.

We have seen that you will occasionally open in a 3-card
club suit in order to prepare a rebid. Try never to do this
unless it is necessary. Consider these three hands:

(1) ♠ 10 6 3   ♡ K Q 10 2   ◇ A 87   ♣ A J 2
(2) ♠ 10 6   ♡ K Q 10 2   ◇ A 8 7 2   ♣ A J 2
(3) ♠ 10 6   ♡ Q 10 8 3 2   ◇ A 7 2   ♣ A K 4

Hand (1) must be opened 1 club, for what could you rebid
if, instead, you opened 1 heart, and partner responded 2 diamonds or 2 clubs? However, hand (2) *need not* be opened
1 club. You should open 1 heart, intending to rebid 1 notrump over a 1 spade response, or 2 diamonds over a 2 club
response, or 3 diamonds over a 2 diamond response. Likewise, you need not lie about hand (3). Open 1 heart, and
rebid hearts over a two-level response. The typical short club
has no 5-card suit and only one 4-card suit, so that no convenient rebid is available.

There is, however, one common type of hand containing
two 4-card suits which is best opened with a short club.
This has two *touching* suits, so that normally you would open
in the higher-ranking; but the higher-ranking suit is a spade
or heart suit weak in high cards. For example:

(4) ♠ J 8 4 3   ♡ A K 9 5   ◇ K 2   ♣ Q 10 3
(5) ♠ 8 3   ♡ Q 7 4 2   ◇ K Q 10 5   ♣ A Q 4

If you open 1 spade with hand (4), or 1 heart with hand
(5), you will have no problem *rebidding*, since you have a
lower-ranking 4-card suit in reserve. The danger is that partner will raise your first suit with 3-card support, as he is entitled to do when you open in a major suit. Trying to handle
a trump suit like four to the jack opposite three to the queen
has given many a declarer ulcers. Yet, it is no solution to open
1 heart with hand (4), or 1 diamond with hand (5), for
then you have no rebid over a new suit response at the two-
level. The answer, of course, is to open 1 club.

The general principle involved here is that you must *never open the bidding in a 4-card major suit unless it contains at least two of the four top honors.* This is one of the very few positions in bridge in which you consider your strength of suit in determining which suit to bid first. Normally, length and rank of suit are all that matter, since you do not need high honors in the trump suit when you have a sufficient *number* of trumps (eight) in the combined hands. However, when you stray into a trump suit with only 7 cards in the partnership hands, you desperately need at least three top honors so that you can draw the enemy trumps. And the opening bid in a 4-card major suit risks a raise with 3-card support. You are protected by two rules: you will have two honors yourself, to open; partner will have at least one honor to raise with three trumps. Thus, your side will always have three honors in its 7-card trump suit.

Note that it is only when you lack the normal 8-card trump length that your partnership needs high honors. You must have no compunction about bidding a 5-card major suit which has no honors at all; if partner raises, you will have eight trumps. You are free to open in a weak 4-card *minor* suit, since partner will not raise in clubs or diamonds without the required four trumps. And you may cheerfully bid even a weak 4-card major suit at your *second* turn, your rebid, for partner will never raise your *second* suit unless he has 4-card support, assuring the partnership of eight trumps.

Which of the following hands should be opened with a short club?

(a) ♠ K Q 10 4 ♡ Q 8 7 3 ◇ A 4 ♣ K 7 2

(b) ♠ J 9 4 ♡ A K J 6 ◇ J 4 2 ♣ A 10 3

(c) ♠ K 8 6 3 ♡ A Q ◇ K J 4 2 ♣ Q 8 2

(d) ♠ J 7 4 2 ♡ K 10 4 ◇ A J 2 ♣ A K 3

(e) ♠ K 9 8 4 ♡ K J 10 3 ◇ 8 4 ♣ A Q 5

Only examples (b) and (e) should be opened 1 club. The short club opening is a lie, and a successful liar at bridge follows these principles:

1. Never lie unless absolutely necessary.
2. If necessary, lie about the length of a suit, but never about your point count.
3. Prefer to lie about a minor suit rather than about a major suit.

Let us apply this liar's code to the five examples just given:

(a) ♠ K Q 10 4   ♡ Q 8 7 3   ◇ A 4   ♣ K 7 2

With hand (a), a lie is unnecessary. You can open 1 spade truthfully, since you have two high honors. And you have a satisfactory rebid, 2 hearts, available in case partner responds at the two-level. Observe that your *second* bid can be in a weak 4-card major since partner may not raise with 3-card support. With hand (b):

(b) ♠ J 9 4   ♡ A K J 6   ◇ J 4 2   ♣ A 10 3

you could look partner straight in the eye when you open 1 heart. However, suppose he responds 2 diamonds—then you must lie about a major suit by rebidding your hearts, or lie about your point count by going past two of your first suit. Therefore, you lie about a minor suit and open 1 club. With hand (c):

(c) ♠ K 8 6 3   ♡ A Q   ◇ K J 4 2   ♣ Q 8 2

it would be a shocking lie to open 1 spade or 1 notrump, but 1 diamond is both truthful and satisfactory. You can rebid 1 spade over a 1 heart response, or 2 notrump over 2 clubs (since your 15 points virtually guarantee game after a two-over-one response). With hand (d):

(d) ♠ J 7 4 2   ♡ K 10 4   ◇ A J 2   ♣ A K 3

there is no need to lie about either spades or clubs—you have 16 points and should open 1 notrump. Finally, with hand (e):

(e) ♠ K 9 8 4   ♡ K J 10 3   ◇ 8 4   ♣ A Q 5

you cannot bid truthfully. One spade would lie about a major suit, 1 heart might force you to lie about your point count with your rebid. And either 1 notrump or pass lies about your strength. Therefore, you lie about a minor suit and open 1 club.

• THE REVERSE

There is another rebid by opener which goes beyond two of his first suit: a new suit, higher ranking than his first, bid at the two-level. For example:

OPENER	RESPONDER		OPENER	RESPONDER
1 heart	1 notrump		1 club	1 spade
2 *spades*			2 *hearts*	

This type of rebid is called a **reverse** and, like all second bids which get the auction up high, shows extra strength. Note that an auction like:

OPENER	RESPONDER
1 club	1 diamond
1 heart	

is *not* a reverse, although opener has "reversed" the normal order by bidding his higher-ranking suit second. Opener has *not* gone beyond two of his first suit, and therefore has not promised more than a minimum opening. For the auction above, opener might hold:

♠ 3　♡ K 8 6 5　◇ K 8 2　♣ A Q 10 6 4

Suppose, however, that you open 1 club with this hand and partner responds 1 spade. Now you must rebid clubs, for to bid hearts at the two-level would get the auction up perilously high:

YOU	PARTNER
♠ 3	♠ Q 9 6 5 2
♡ K 8 6 5	♡ J 3
◇ K 8 2	◇ Q 6 4
♣ A Q 10 6 4	♣ J 8 3
1 club	1 spade
2 hearts	3 clubs

Observe that partner is forced to go to the three-level (he cannot pass 2 hearts with a doubleton, knowing that you probably have a 4-card suit), not because he has extra strength but because you have gone beyond two of your first suit. Partner's rebid, a preference back to your first suit, is his weakest possible action. When this preference must be given at the *three*-level, *you* had better have the extra strength needed for a 9-trick contract—a strong 17-point or better opening, not the minimum of the preceding example.

The reverse is, in effect, a jump rebid. These two sequences:

	OPENER	RESPONDER
(a)	1 diamond	1 spade
	2 *hearts*	

	OPENER	RESPONDER
(b)	1 diamond	1 spade
	3 diamonds	

promise the same strength, since responder, in auction (a), may be forced to bid 3 diamonds himself without any extra values. What is more, opener, in auction (a), has promised a rebiddable diamond suit, since with *four* diamonds and four hearts he would bid the higher suit first if at all. The only difference between the auctions above is that, in (a), opener promises a secondary heart suit along with his strong point count and long diamonds. He stops off on his way to 3 diamonds to suggest hearts as trump. For the sequences above, opener might hold:

(a) ♠3 ♡K832 ◇AKQ84 ♣A75
(b) ♠3 ♡K82 ◇AKQ843 ♣A75

Each of these example hands would still be worth an opening bid if the ace of clubs were the deuce. It is this *extra* ace which allows you to reverse with (a) or jump with (b). Without it, you would rebid only 2 diamonds with either hand. That is, with:

♠3 ♡K832 ◇AKQ84 ♣752

you must open 1 diamond and, over a 1 spade response, rebid 2 *diamonds*. It is not that you want to rebid your 5-card suit; actually, you would prefer to suggest your second suit as trump, relying on partner to take you back to your first suit unless he is longer in your second. However, you dare not go beyond two of your first suit by reversing with a minimum opening.

The necessity of avoiding a reverse rebid can affect your choice of opening bid. A typical hand in which this could occur is:

♠AKJ5 ♡J8532 ◇2 ♣A73

Your natural opening seems to be 1 heart, bidding your longer suit first. But what will your rebid be? If partner responds 1 notrump and you rebid 2 spades, you have reversed and will surely get too high. You *could* rebid 2 hearts, but this is distasteful with such a weak 5-card suit—when partner holds a singleton or doubleton heart, you will be unable to draw trumps. Your best opening is *1 spade*. Now you can bid hearts at your second turn, and you have promised neither a strong hand nor a strong suit.

Of course, when you bid a 4-card spade suit before a 5-card heart suit you have not told partner the strict truth. However, you have conformed to the liar's code: *Never lie about your point count, lie about suit length instead.* And since you are too weak to bid your suits honestly (hearts first, spades second), it comes closer to the truth to pretend that you are equally long (by bidding spades first) than it is to announce that you have a burning desire to make hearts trumps (by bidding and then rebidding hearts).

When you have a minimum opening bid which contains two touching suits (spades-hearts, hearts-diamonds, diamonds-clubs), with the lower-ranking suit the longer, so that you cannot bid both in normal order without reversing—then you must make a decision. Is your long suit powerful enough to rebid? If so, bid it first and then rebid it. Is your short suit powerful enough to open in? If so, consider bidding it first. What would be your opening bid and rebid with the following examples? (Partner will respond 1 notrump.)

(1) ♠ K J 7 4   ♡ K Q J 9 6   ◊ 3   ♣ K 10 2

(2) ♠ 8 3   ♡ K J 10 5   ◊ Q 8 6 4 2   ♣ A K

(3) ♠ Q 4 2   ♡ 3   ◊ A 7 4 2   ♣ A Q J 7 4

(4) ♠ K Q 10 6   ♡ Q 10 6 5 2   ◊ A   ♣ A Q 4

(5) ♠ A 3   ♡ K 7 5 2   ◊ J 9 7 5 2   ♣ A Q

(1) Open *1 heart;* rebid *2 hearts.* Your 4-card suit is strong enough to bid first, but there is no need to lie when your 5-card suit has three honors.

(2) Open *1 heart;* rebid *2 diamonds.* Here your long suit is too anemic to allow you to draw trumps when partner is short. Start with your biddable 4-card major suit.

(3) Open *1 club;* rebid *2 clubs.* Do not bid a weak 4-card suit ahead of a strong 5-carder.

(4) Open *1 heart;* rebid *2 spades.* You have a strong opening bid, and so can afford the luxury of bidding nor-

mally and reversing. With an ace less, you would open 1 spade and then bid hearts.

(5) Open *1 diamond; pass* 1 notrump. You may not open in a weak 4-card major, and you hate to rebid a weak 5-carder. If partner had responded 1 spade, you would have rebid 1 notrump. Only if partner responded 2 clubs would you rebid 2 diamonds (you dare not go beyond two of your first suit).

Before I leave the subject of reverses, let me make two points clear. First, do not be the sort of player who opens 1 club with a hand like:

♠ Q 4 2   ♡ A K J 3   ◇ J 8 4   ♣ Q J 8

and, when partner responds 1 spade, rebids 2 hearts. The usual explanation (after the smoke clears and the enemy have collected 500 points by doubling some ridiculous game contract) goes: "I play the short club, partner, so my reverses mean nothing." This is like jumping out of a window twenty stories up and explaining that you do not believe in the law of gravity. Reverses show great strength not because some conclave of graybearded bridge experts decided that they should, but simply because they get the auction up high. Opener needs extra strength to charge up to the three-level opposite a minimum response.

Second, do not invent a reverse merely in order to show that you have a strong opening. I have seen players open 1 heart with such a hand as:

♠ A K J 8 4   ♡ A Q 10 2   ◇ A J 6   ♣ 2

in order to reverse by bidding spades second. The proper opening is, of course, 1 spade, followed by a jump in hearts to show the great strength. The likely result of opening 1 heart with the hand above is to play in the wrong trump suit. Whenever you reverse, you promise unconditionally that you have *more cards in your first suit than in your second*. With this auction:

OPENER	RESPONDER
1 diamond	1 spade
2 hearts	2 notrump
3 hearts	

opener promises 17 points or more because he reversed, five
hearts or more because he rebid them, six diamonds at least
because he must have more diamonds than hearts to bid them
first. Of these three hands:

(6) ♠ 2　♡ A Q J 4 2　◇ A K Q J 4　♣ K 5
(7) ♠ 2　♡ A 10 7 4 2　◇ A Q J 6 5 3　♣ 5
(8) ♠ 2　♡ A K Q 10 2　◇ A Q 10 8 5 3　♣ 5

only example (8) justifies the auction above. Example (6)
is strong enough for a reverse but has the wrong distribution—you must open 1 heart and jump in diamonds next.
Example (7) has the right distribution but too few points—
you should open 1 heart, and rebid in diamonds, lying about
your suit length, not about your strength.

• THIRD- AND FOURTH-HAND OPENING BIDS

We have seen that you must constantly consider, as opener,
what will be your rebid. Partner's response in a new suit is
unlimited and therefore forcing; still, it does not guarantee
great strength, so you must have a rebid in reserve which will
not push the auction too high. This is the reasoning which
lies behind a 1 club opening bid with a hand such as:

♠ K Q J 4　♡ 8 5 3　◇ 7 6 4　♣ A K 5

However, if you hold this hand in third or fourth position—
that is, after two or three passes—you can afford to bid honestly and open 1 spade. Why? Because if partner responds
two of a new suit you now have a completely satisfactory
rebid—you will *pass*. Partner has refused to open the bidding
originally, so his hand is no longer unlimited. He cannot hold
13 points or more; your side cannot make game. There is no
earthly reason to continue bidding.

Similarly, you no longer need open a short club with:

♠ J 7 5 2　♡ A Q 8 4　◇ K 2　♣ K 10 3

in third or fourth seat. You will still avoid the spade bid, for
fear of a 3-card raise. Now, however, you may open 1 *heart*,
since you are prepared to pass any response.

Note that you will open 1 club with this hand:

♠ A K J 3　♡ K 3　◇ K 8 3　♣ J 7 5 3

whether in first or third seat. It is true that you could open
1 *spade* in third position, intending to pass any response.
However, with a 15-point or better opening, you should not
give up on game even though partner has passed originally.
You are *allowed* to pass a new suit response, but you do not
necessarily *want* to. In contrast, change the example to:

♠ A K J 3   ♡ K 3   ◇ J 8 3   ♣ J 7 5 3

Now you should open 1 club in first or second position (so
that you can rebid cheaply over a diamond or heart response), but open 1 spade in third or fourth seat (since you
no longer need prepare any rebid—you intend to pass).

The fact that you are permitted to pass partner's response
once he has failed to open the bidding allows you a little
more latitude in opening the bidding in third seat. For example, you should always be tempted to open a hand like:

♠ A Q 10 8 3   ♡ 10 6 4   ◇ 9 6 2   ♣ A 5

A 1 spade bid will make it harder for the enemy to bid
accurately; it may well steal a small part score if they stay
out, and will tell partner what to lead if they do compete—an
impressive list of virtues. Nonetheless, you dare not open in
first or second seat, since partner, expecting greater strength,
will force you to too many losing games and slams. Once
partner has passed, though, you can safely open—he cannot
force you to a high contract, since you will pass his response.

You may even be so frisky as to open 1 diamond with:

♠ 8 4 2   ♡ J 7 4   ◇ A K Q 6   ♣ 10 5 3

after two passes. Your purpose, of course, is to direct partner's opening lead against an eventual enemy contract. With
this poor playing hand, you should probably not open if vulnerable. And, naturally, you would never open in *fourth* seat
—you would merely pass the hand out.

It is winning tactics, then, to open the bidding in *third*
position with certain 12-, 11-, or even 10-point hands. But
you do not automatically open because you are in third seat
and have a fair hand. The purpose of the light opening is to
interfere with the enemy and direct a lead; this may be done
safely if you are prepared to pass any response. Do not open
light hands which do not fulfill this purpose, or which do not
have this safety. Consider these two examples:

(1) ♠ A Q 10 7 3   ♡ Q 7 4 2   ◇ Q 7 3   ♣ 2
(2) ♠ A K 5   ♡ Q 10 2   ◇ Q 6 2   ♣ J 6 4 2

Neither should be opened in third seat. Example (1) is unsuitable for a light opening because you are *not* prepared to pass partner's most likely response. If you open 1 spade and rebid 2 hearts when partner responds 2 clubs, you announce a normal, sound, 13-point-or-better opening bid. Partner will now push to the three-level or may even jump to game. When you open light, you are safe only if you pass the response; if there is a response you hate to pass, do not open.

Example (2) is a foolish third-hand opening because it is purposeless. A 1 club opening hardly interferes with the enemy at all, and you certainly do not want partner to lead clubs against an opponent's contract. If someone had a gun to my back, and threatened to shoot if I passed hand (2), I would open 1 spade (but only if I were sure the gun was loaded). This opening, although terribly dangerous, could do me some good by directing the lead I want, or by keeping my left-hand opponent from bidding at the one-level.

What is your action with these hands after partner, who dealt, and right-hand opponent both pass?

(a) ♠ A K 10 2   ♡ A 2   ◇ J 8 6 4 2   ♣ Q 3
(b) ♠ A 8 4   ♡ K J 10 4   ◇ 8 5 3   ♣ A J 2
(c) ♠ A Q J 6   ♡ J 7 2   ◇ Q 6 4   ♣ Q 5 2
(d) ♠ A K   ♡ 8 3   ◇ Q J 10 8 6 4 2   ♣ 7 2
(e) ♠ K Q J 2   ♡ 3   ◇ K 10 4   ♣ J 10 6 4 3

(a) Bid 1 diamond. This is not the hand with which you bid the suit you want led (spades) and then pass any response. You are opening not for a *lead*, but for a possible *game;* therefore, you bid normally.

(b) Bid 1 heart. You would open 1 club in first or second seat to prepare a rebid. In third seat, you bid your strong 4-card major suit and pass partner's response.

(c) Bid 1 spade. This is a perfect light third-hand opening. You desire a spade lead, and you can pass happily to any response.

(d) Bid 3 diamonds. You would be too strong to preempt before partner had passed, but now your 13 points cannot produce game. Therefore, you can try to choke off enemy competition with a high opening. You would take this action in *fourth* seat as well.

(e) Pass. It makes no sense to open light with 1 *club* when you want a spade or diamond lead. It is too dangerous to open 1 *spade,* for what is your rebid when partner responds 2 hearts? If you pass and put down your singleton trump, there is likely to be a nasty edge to the tone of the "Thank you, partner," with which your dummy will be greeted. Remember, the opponents are entitled to score penalties even though you opened in third seat.

CHAPTER 3

Responses and Responder's Rebid

(See Book One, Chapters 4 and 6)

In responding to partner's opening bid of one in a suit, it is not nearly so important to plan your second bid as it is when *you* are the opener. This is because you will have a great deal of information by the time you must bid again (you will usually be able to place the final contract with your rebid), and because you are not forced to rebid at all if you have a minimum responding hand.

• CHOICE OF 4-CARD SUITS

The basic rules given in Book One, Chapter 4, cover most situations. Still, there are a few exceptions. One of these comes in responding with two or three 4-card suits. Here it is often the best policy to *make the cheapest response*. That is, if you hold:

(a) ♠ 8 3   ♡ K Q 7 2   ◇ A 6 4   ♣ Q 10 7 3

respond 1 heart if partner opens 1 diamond, but respond 2 clubs if partner opens 1 spade. If you hold:

(b) ♠ K J 10 3   ♡ Q J 8 4   ◇ 10 5 2   ♣ 6 4

when partner opens 1 club or 1 diamond, respond 1 *heart*.

The reason for this policy is to make it as easy as possible for partner to bid your other suit. Consider the auction with these hands if the response is improper:

OPENER	RESPONDER
♠ Q 5	♠ K J 10 3
♡ A K 6 3	♡ Q J 8 4
◇ A 9 4	◇ 10 5 2
♣ J 8 3 2	♣ 6 4
1 club	1 spade
1 notrump	pass

Opener is not nearly strong enough to show his second suit by reversing at the two-level; responder must pass 1 notrump with his minimum. So the fit in hearts is never found. If, instead, the response had been 1 *heart*, opener would have raised, and a far superior contract would be reached.

Still, what if opener's second 4-card suit were spades, not hearts? Would it not cost then to respond in hearts? No, for then the auction would go:

OPENER	RESPONDER
♠ Q 8 7 5	♠ K J 10 3
♡ A K	♡ Q J 8 4
◇ A 9 4	◇ 10 5 2
♣ J 8 3 2	♣ 6 4
1 club	1 heart
1 spade	2 spades

The fit is found anyway, since opener can afford to bid his second suit so long as he has the opportunity to do so *cheaply*. Notice that responder will find *either* fit by bidding his cheaper suit, leaving room for opener to bid the other. Here is an extreme example of this. You hold:

♠ K J 10 6   ♡ Q J 7 3   ◇ Q 10 8 5   ♣ 3

Partner opens 1 club. Respond *1 diamond*, for this will enable you to find any fit immediately. Opener will rebid at the one-level in a 4-card major if he holds one, or will raise diamonds if that is his second suit. And what if, instead, partner rebids 2 clubs or 1 notrump? Then *pass*, for no fit exists and game is impossible. Similarly, suppose you hold:

♠ 7   ♡ A K 8 3   ◇ Q J 9 4   ♣ K J 8 3

Partner opens 1 spade. Respond *2 clubs*. If partner has a 4-card suit in diamonds or hearts, he can now bid it at the two-level without reversing (while had you responded 2 *hearts*, he would have to go to the three-level to bid a new suit, and might be too weak to do so). If you find a suit fit, you can play game or, conceivably slam, there. And if partner rebids 2 spades or 2 notrump, so that no suit fit exists, you can bid 3 notrump confident that this is the best contract.

• RESPONDER'S REVERSE

Observe that when you respond in a low-ranking 4-card suit, you do *not* bid a higher-ranking suit next:

OPENER	RESPONDER
1 diamond	1 heart
2 diamonds	2 *spades*

The sequence above describes *five* hearts and four spades, with a very strong response since you have reversed. (A reverse by responder, like a jump, is forcing to game.) Remember that opener would have bid 1 spade if he held a 4-card suit; since he did not, it is not important for responder to bid a 4-card spade suit. Thus, with

♠ K Q 8 3   ♡ Q 10 6 4   ◇ 8 3   ♣ K 10 4

you should respond 1 heart to 1 diamond, and, over a 2 diamond rebid, bid 2 *notrump*, not 2 spades. Likewise, with:

♠ K Q 8 3   ♡ Q 10 6 4 3   ◇ 8 3   ♣ K 4

you respond 1 heart and rebid 2 notrump. Here, a rebid of 2 spades would describe your distribution accurately, for you have five hearts. However, you are not strong enough to *force* to game with a reverse; you must *invite* game instead. It would be proper to reverse holding:

♠ K Q 8 3   ♡ Q 10 6 4 3   ◇ A 3   ♣ K 4

Respond 1 heart and rebid 2 spades. Since you are going to game, regardless, you can afford to bid your suits in the natural order even though it gets the auction up very high.

Do not make the mistake of responding in the lower suit when you have two 5-carders. That is, if you hold:

♠ Q 10 8 4 3   ♡ K Q 10 7 4   ◇ Q 2   ♣ 3

respond 1 *spade*, not 1 heart, to a 1 diamond opening. Why? Because a 5-card suit can provide a good trump suit even when partner has 3 cards, and cannot bid it himself. Thus, if you respond 1 *heart* with the example above and partner rebids 2 diamonds or 1 notrump, spades could still be your best trump. Yet if you bid spades yourself at your second turn, you have reversed. This lies about your point count, and also about your distribution (you should have *four* spades and five hearts). When you have two long suits you must bid them both, so you start with the higher ranking.

There is also a rare type of hand with two very strong 4-card suits which you should treat in the same fashion. If partner opens 1 club and you hold:

♠ 8 4   ♡ K Q 10 3   ◇ K Q J 6   ♣ 7 4 2

it is shortsighted to respond 1 diamond. Suppose partner rebids 2 clubs—what do you do now? To reverse with 2 hearts forces to a game that might not be there, and promises a long diamond suit which you cannot deliver. You cannot bid notrump without spade protection, and a raise in clubs may result in a missed notrump game when partner has no heart stopper. Thus, it is better to respond 1 heart, reserving a rebid of 2 diamonds. The general rule is to bid the higher-ranking suit first *when you must bid both suits.*

• FORCING WITH NEW SUITS

The rule that opener must keep on bidding whenever responder bids a new suit can be a great convenience to responder in many different awkward situations. For example, suppose that partner opens 1 spade and you hold:

♠ K J 8 4   ♡ A 8 3   ◇ 6 4 2   ♣ K 6 5

You are too strong for the minimum raise to 2 spades, yet not really strong enough for the jump raise to 3 spades. Therefore, your proper response is 2 clubs! Partner must bid again, since you have bid a new suit; at your next turn you will bid a minimum number of spades. This will complete the description of an "in-between" hand—10 points or more for your two-level response, fewer than 13 points since you have not forced to game with either your first or second action. Note that this response in a "false" suit conforms to our liar's code in the previous chapter: you lie about a suit, not about your point count; you lie about a minor suit, not a major. If you prefer never to admit that you tell a lie, you can call this response by its more polite name: a **temporizing bid.**

It may look very daring to bid a 3-card suit, but you are actually completely safe. Partner's suit is higher ranking than yours, so no matter how violently he raises you, you will be

able to return to the proper trump. You are protected, in
addition, by the fact that your response is in a *minor* suit;
partner should never be enthusiastic about finding a fit in
clubs or diamonds. This becomes important in the case of the
one temporizing bid which is commonly made in a suit *higher*
than partner's:

OPENER	RESPONDER
1 club	1 diamond

To respond in a 3-card diamond suit here you might have
either of these hands:

   (1) ♠ A J 2 ♡ Q J 4 ◇ Q 8 4 ♣ J 10 6 3
   (2) ♠ 8 6 4 3 ♡ K 8 4 ◇ K 7 4 ♣ 8 7 5

With example (1), you are "in between" 2 and 3 clubs, 1
and 2 notrump, and must not lie about your strength. With
example (2), you prefer to lie about a minor suit rather than
bid a 4-card major which contains no honor. (As *responder,*
you can bid a 4-card major with *one* honor, since opener will
rarely raise without 4-card support. But it is usually a poor
idea to bid on four small—partner will bid the suit himself if
it is the proper trump.)

Responder may occasionally have to bid a 3-card suit at
his *second* turn. This occurs when he must make a forcing
bid but has no convenient jump available. Consider this auction:

OPENER	RESPONDER
♠ A Q 9 6 4 3	♠ 7 2
♡ 6 2	♡ A K 10 5 3
◇ A J 9	◇ K Q 8
♣ 7 2	♣ J 5 4
1 spade	2 hearts
2 spades	3 *diamonds*
3 spades	4 spades

Notice responder's 3 diamond rebid. He knows that a game
must be reached, so he cannot bid 2 notrump or 3 hearts or
3 spades—these bids are not forcing, since they are neither
new suits nor jumps. Yet he cannot jump to game, since he

has no idea which of three contracts is best. Therefore, he makes a forcing bid in a new false suit: he will pass 3 no-trump or raise 3 hearts to 4. Here, when opener promises at least a 6-card suit by repeating spades again, responder finds the best contract.

Another example:

OPENER	RESPONDER
♠ K J 7 3	♠ 8 4
♡ J 3	♡ A K 6 4 2
◇ Q 4	◇ A 5 3
♣ A Q 10 8 4	♣ J 4 3

1 club	1 heart
1 spade	2 *diamonds*
2 notrump	3 notrump

Once again, responder has no really satisfactory second bid. Two hearts, 2 clubs, and 1 notrump could (and would) be passed. *Three* hearts is forcing, but overstates the heart suit; opener would raise, expecting 6-card length. Two notrump is possible, but poor because it *makes the wrong hand declarer.* That is, responder does not want the opening lead to come through opener's honors into his bare hand, but *through* his hand up to partner's intermediates. Remember that a hand without queens, unsupported kings, or tenaces makes a better dummy than declarer—and this is true even though you undoubtedly play better than your partner. In the example above, the opening lead will almost surely give opener his ninth trick if *he* is declarer, while it may set the contract immediately if responder is declarer.

Thus, responder temporizes with 2 diamonds; he will bid game in hearts if supported or in notrump if not. This bid of the *fourth suit* is often false—opener will practically never raise it, since he would have bid it himself earlier with 4-card length. Usually responder bids the fourth suit for convenience, to obtain more information about where to play without risking a pass under game.

In this section, responder has indulged in an orgy of 3-card suit bids. I have said that they are relatively safe, but any false bid can conceivably prove embarrassing. Never forget the first proviso of the liar's code—never lie unless necessary. If you have a satisfactory honest bid, make it. Only if there is no action which properly describes your strength and distribution should you force with a devious 3-card suit.

• RESPONDING AS A PASSED HAND

When you have passed, as dealer or second hand, and partner opens the bidding in third or fourth seat, your choice of responses may be altered in several different situations. The underlying reason is that *partner knows the upper limit of your hand.* You cannot have 13 points or more, since then you would have opened yourself.

Thus, a change of suit by responder is no longer forcing. Consider these auctions:

	OPENER	RESPONDER
(1)	1 spade	2 clubs
(2)		pass
	1 spade	2 clubs

In (1), opener must rebid even with a bare 13 points, because responder might have as many as 18 points—his hand is *unlimited,* so the partnership could have more than enough power for game. In contrast, in (2), opener can (and likely will) pass with a minimum or subminimum hand, since responder cannot hold enough points to produce game when he passed originally.

Another result of the known upper limit of responder's point count is a change in the meaning of his jump bids. Obviously, the jump raise (1 spade—3 spades) and the jump in notrump (1 diamond—2 notrump) can no longer promise 13 to 15 points, for with so much power responder would have opened himself. These jumps now show a maximum *pass*—a strong responding hand of 12, 11, or occasionally 10 husky points. Likewise, the jump *shift* (1 heart—2 spades) can promise no more than 12 points with a fine suit once it is limited by an original pass. Opener may pass any of these jump responses.

The fact that a change of suit is no longer forcing means that you must be wary of responding in 4-card suits at the two-level (when opener has no room for a cheap rebid) and that you must *never* bid 3-card suits. However, the fact that your jump responses show limited hands makes it unnecessary to temporize by bidding weak suits. For instance, suppose you hold our earlier example:

♠ K J 8 4 ♡ A 8 3 ◇ 6 4 2 ♣ K 6 5

You pass, and partner opens 1 spade. You no longer dare answer 2 clubs, since partner can pass. But you no longer have to lie—now, 3 spades is an honest, straightforward, and perfectly satisfactory response. Likewise, if partner opens 1 spade after you have passed these cards:

♠ 8 3 ♡ K 10 9 4 ◇ A Q 10 ♣ Q 9 7 4

2 clubs is not a reasonable response, for partner may pass with a doubleton. However, there is no need to bid a weak suit—you can jump to 2 notrump to show your maximum passed hand. If you hold:

♠ 7 2 ♡ 8 6 3 ◇ 4 2 ♣ A K Q J 9 5

you should jump to 3 clubs over any suit opening once you have passed. You cannot conceivably have a better hand than this, and you must urge partner to try 3 notrump even with a minimum opening. If you bid only 2 clubs after passing, opener may settle for a part score.

Since jump responses by a passed hand promise only 10 to 12 points, we must consider what to do with 13 points or more. Why should you pass such a hand? Because it became worth so much only because of your fit for partner's suit. That is, you would pass originally with:

♠ A 7 3 ♡ K 10 8 3 ◇ K J 10 6 3 ♣ 2

If partner opens 1 heart, your hand is worth a full 14 points. Thus, a jump to 3 hearts no longer does justice to your strength—partner will pass with a 12- or 13-point opening, and a game will be missed. Therefore, you jump right to 4 hearts. The double jump in a major suit is the strongest action a passed hand can take. It is not preemptive, as it would be by a nonpassed hand. Because the jump raise is nonforcing, the double jump is needed to show great strength; because both opponents have passed, a preemptive jump is not needed. An auction like

OPPONENT	YOU	OPPONENT	PARTNER
pass	pass	pass	1 spade
pass	4 spades		

cannot be intended to shut out the enemy, who have shown no disposition to compete. And it should not be intended to shut out partner who, after all, is supposed to be on your side. It is your only means of surely reaching game, and a slam may well be made if partner has a near-maximum opening.

• THE STAYMAN CONVENTION

The basic theory of auctions which start with a 1 notrump opening is that responder is in control. He knows almost all about opener's hand, so *he* places the contract—usually with his first bid. The typical auction has two bids—1 notrump by opener, final contract by responder.

If responder is not quite sure where or how high to play, he may obtain more information by asking any of three questions. Question 1 is "Have you a maximum or a minimum count?" This is asked by the response of 2 notrump, looking for game; or 4 notrump, looking for slam. Question 2 is "Have you three cards or more in my long suit?" This is asked by a jump to three in a suit, almost always in hearts or spades. Responder prefers a major suit game to 3 notrump; with a 5-card suit, he should check to be sure that opener has 3-card support.

However, suppose responder has one or two 4-card major suits? If opener has a matching 4-card suit, an 8-card fit exists, and the suit game will be superior to notrump. Here is where you need Question 3—"Have you a 4-card major suit?" This is asked by the artificial response of 2 clubs, the **Stayman Convention**.

OPENER	RESPONDER
1 notrump	2 clubs

For the 2 club bid above, responder might hold:

♠ 3 2   ♡ K J 6 4   ◇ A Q 7 6 5   ♣ 10 7

Had the Stayman Convention never been invented, you would jump to 3 notrump with this hand. You *could* bid 3 diamonds, but this is futile since you do not want diamonds for trump even if partner has 3- or 4-card support. However, if partner has 4-card support for hearts, the major suit will provide your best contract. Therefore, it is advisable to stop off on your way to 3 notrump to ask partner whether he has a 4-card major suit. Partner answers "Yes" by bidding the suit he has:

PARTNER	YOU
1 notrump	2 clubs?
2 *hearts* or 2 *spades*	

If, by chance, he has both hearts and spades, he bids spades first. And when partner has 4 cards in neither major suit, he answers "No" by bidding 2 diamonds.

PARTNER	YOU
1 notrump	2 clubs?
2 *diamonds*	

Let us look at a few example auctions:

PARTNER	YOU
♠ A J 6	♠ 3 2
♡ Q 10 8 7	♡ K J 6 4
◇ K 10 4	◇ A Q 7 6 5
♣ A Q 2	♣ 10 7

| 1 notrump | 2 clubs |
| 2 hearts | 4 hearts |

Had you bid 3 notrump, you would have reached a reasonable, although dangerous, contract. Since you take the trouble to stop off to check on the major suit, you arrive at the superior suit game. What if you had not found the heart fit?

PARTNER	YOU
♠ A J 6	♠ 3 2
♡ Q 8 7	♡ K J 6 4
◇ K 10 4	◇ A Q 7 6 5
♣ A Q 4 2	♣ 10 7

| 1 notrump | 2 clubs |
| 2 diamonds | 3 notrump |

Partner's 2 diamond reply tells you that you do not have an 8-card major-suit fit, so you bid 3 notrump. No better game contract is available. Your action would be the same if partner responded in spades, the "wrong" major suit. What, then, if partner holds *both* suits?

PARTNER	YOU
♠ A J 6 2	♠ 3 2
♡ Q 10 8 7	♡ K J 6 4
◇ K 10 4	◇ A Q 7 6 5
♣ A Q	♣ 10 7

1 notrump	2 clubs
2 spades	3 notrump
4 hearts	

You stop off on your way to 3 notrump to check on hearts; when partner bids the "wrong" major, you make the bid that you would have made *right over 1 notrump* had you never heard of the Stayman Convention. However, partner knows that you must have at least one 4-card major suit in order to use this gadget. Clearly it is not spades; therefore, there is a fit in hearts.

It is possible to stop off on your way to contracts other than 3 notrump in order to ask about major suits. Suppose you hold:

♠ A K 8 6 4   ♡ Q 8 7 3   ◇ 4 2   ♣ 8 5

It is reasonable to respond 3 spades to partner's 1 notrump opening. (Partner will rebid 4 spades with 3- or 4-card support, and 3 notrump with only two spades.) However, it is better to bid 2 clubs first. If partner answers 2 hearts, you jump to 4 hearts; naturally you will raise a 2 spade response to 4. If partner answers 2 diamonds, you *now* bid 3 spades— the bid you would make originally if you were not using Stayman.

Similarly, you can stop off on your way to 2 notrump to bid 2 clubs. That is, holding:

♠ K 10 8 4   ♡ 5 2   ◇ A J 6 3   ♣ 7 6 3

you *could* raise 1 notrump directly to 2. However, first bid 2 clubs to check for a spade fit. If partner answers 2 diamonds (no major suit) or 2 hearts (the wrong one), bid 2 notrump now. If partner obligingly answers 2 spades, raise only to 3 spades. In each auction, partner will go on to game with a maximum or pass with a minimum count.

You might even stop on your way to *slam* to ask about major suits—for instance, with:

♠ K Q 8 4   ♡ K Q 9 3   ♢ K 7 4   ♣ A 6

you bid 2 clubs in response to partner's unexpected 1 no-trump opening. If he answers in a major suit, you will raise his suit to slam. And if he answers 2 diamonds you have lost nothing; you now bid 6 notrump. Note that in every case in which you fail to find the major-suit fit that you were looking for, your second bid is the identical action that you would have taken *initially* if not for Stayman.

What, then, if your hand is:

♠ Q 10 6 4   ♡ J 8 7 3   ♢ K 6   ♣ 7 4 2

You use Stayman, and partner answers 2 diamonds. Ordinarily, you would have *passed* partner's opening; how do you get back to 1 notrump now? You cannot, and therefore you should not have bid 2 clubs—you must *still* pass 1 notrump. The Stayman Convention is used only when you are on your way to some possible game contract. And even if you have the 8 points or more that you need to think of game, do not use your shiny new gadget unless you have a 4-card major of your own and so are interested in the reply to your question. That is, neither of these hands is a proper 2 club response to 1 notrump:

  (a) ♠ K J 6   ♡ Q 10 5   ♢ A J 8 5 2   ♣ 8 7
  (b) ♠ A Q 10 7 4   ♡ 8 4   ♢ K J 3   ♣ 9 7 2

Bid 3 notrump with (a), for you will not play in either major even if partner has a 4-card suit. Bid 3 spades with (b), for you do not need 4-card support—three spades in partner's hand will be sufficient. To respond with the Stayman 2 clubs, you must meet these two conditions:

  1. **Eight points or more, so that game is possible**
  2. **At least one 4-card major suit of your own**

There are three exceptions to the rules above—one type of hand which meets the conditions but is unsuitable for Stayman, and two types which do not, yet which call for a 2 club bid. The exceptional hand with which you should *not* use

Stayman even though you have a 4-card major suit is one that has exactly even, 4–3–3–3 distribution. For example, with:

♠ K 10 7 4   ♡ Q J 3   ◇ K 8 4   ♣ Q 10 2

bid 3 notrump, not 2 clubs, over 1 notrump. The hand above is by no means ideal for notrump play (you should much prefer to have a long minor suit). However, it has horrible distribution for suit play, so you might as well try to make game with 9 tricks instead of 10.

There is one exceptional type of hand which is best handled with the 2 club response even though you hold a 5-card, not a 4-card, major suit. This has 8 or 9 points, the strength for a raise to 2 notrump:

♠ K J 8 6 3   ♡ 7 4   ◇ K J 2   ♣ 8 5 3

When partner opens 1 notrump, you are too strong for 2 spades, which gives up on game, but too weak for 3 spades, which forces to game. You could *invite* game by bidding 2 notrump, but now you might miss a suit fit. You can bid "2½ spades" by first using Stayman. When partner answers 2 diamonds or 2 hearts, you now bid 2 spades. Since you have not jumped, this is not forcing; but it shows an interest in game since with a poor hand you would have gone to 2 spades directly.

The final exception occurs when you hold a long string of clubs in a very weak hand. You have no wish to investigate game; all you want is to play a part-score contract in clubs. For example:

♠ 2   ♡ 6 2   ◇ J 10 7 4   ♣ Q 10 9 7 6 4

You dare not pass partner's 1 notrump opening, since your hand is worthless in notrump. Therefore, you bid 2 clubs. Partner, of course, responds 2 of a major or 2 diamonds; he expects you to have strength, and is on his way to game. Now, at your second turn, you rebid 3 *clubs*. This says, "Don't get excited, partner. My 2-club bid was *not* Stayman at all. Please leave me alone in this contract." On this auction, opener must pass.

You can see in the sequence above the one disadvantage of the Stayman Convention—you can no longer sign off at 2 clubs, but must go to 3. This is the price you pay for using the artificial 2 club response—not an exorbitant price at all for such a valuable device.

Incidentally, you can employ Stayman over an opening 2 notrump bid as well. Here you respond 3 clubs to check for a four-four major-suit fit. Now, of course, you need only 4 points to use the bid; and your side will always proceed at least to game.

CHAPTER 4

Slam Bidding

(See Book One, Chapter 7)

Bidding for game is a great deal easier than bidding for slam. This is because you are willing (if not delighted) to go down in game contracts fairly often—all you have lost is the part score (worth 150 to 250 points) which you could have made. In contrast, it is a tragedy when you go down in a slam, since you have lost a *game* (worth 350 to 500 points). Thus, in game bidding you are aiming at a broad target; any time you believe that you will have some sort of chance, you should take the plunge. But in slam bidding you aim at a narrow target; the odds do not favor slapdash gambling tactics, so much more precision is demanded.

Before you bid slam, you must have good reason to believe that your side has enough *power* and enough *controls*. That is, your partnership must have the high cards or long suits to win 12 tricks. And you must be able to prevent the enemy, who have the opening lead, from winning 2 tricks before you take your 12. Your worries about *power* usually can be stated, "Has our partnership the total of 33 points needed to win 12 tricks?" Your worries about *controls* are most often, "Can the opponents win the first 2 tricks with two aces, or with the ace and king of one suit?"

• SLAMS BID ON POWER

In notrump bidding, your problem is most typically power alone. If you and partner each have balanced hands (and so are not adding extra points for *distributional* values), a total of 33 points means that the enemy cannot hold two aces, and have only an infinitesimal chance of holding the A K of one suit. Suppose you open 1 club with:

♠ Q 8 5 4　♡ A K 6　◇ K Q 6　♣ A Q 2

Partner responds 2 notrump. You should bid 6 notrump directly, for your 20 points, added to partner's minimum of 13, guarantee sufficient power and therefore sufficient controls.

(If your partner sometimes cheats and bids 2 notrump with 12 points, you should bid 5 notrump. This says "Go on to slam unless you are ashamed of your previous bid.") However, suppose you hold:

♠ Q 8 5 4   ♡ A K 6   ◊ K Q 6   ♣ K Q 2

Now if partner jumps to 2 notrump over your 1 club opening, you cannot leap to slam. It is not the lack of controls (aces) that worries you, but the possible shortage of power (points). You have 19 points, and partner may have 13, for a total of only 32. Therefore, you bid *4 notrump*, which says "Go on to slam if you have the maximum for your previous bid, but not if you have the minimum." Note that this auction:

YOU	PARTNER
1 club	2 notrump
4 notrump	

is *not* Blackwood, but a quantitative slam try. A bid of 4 notrump is Blackwood if made right over a *suit* bid by partner; it is quantitative if made right over a *notrump* bid by partner.* This sort of quantitative slam try can be made in a major suit as well as in notrump, by jumping to five. However, an auction like this one:

YOU	PARTNER
1 heart	3 hearts
5 hearts	

is very rare, since in suit bidding you must worry about controls even when assured about power. Still, the auction above would be proper if you held:

♠ A 2   ♡ A 10 8 4 3   ◊ A 10 4   ♣ A 10 4

You have all the controls yourself, and wish to ask partner only about his point count. With 15 or 16 points he should bid

---

* There are, unfortunately, some exceptions to this rule. If either partner has opened with a two-bid in a suit, or made a jump shift, then any 4 notrump bid is Blackwood. Thus, either of these:

YOU	PARTNER		YOU	PARTNER
2 spades	3 diamonds		1 club	2 hearts
3 notrump	*4 notrump*		2 notrump	*4 notrump*

asks for aces, even though 4 notrump comes right over a notrump bid.

slam; with 13 or 14 points he should pass your jump to 5 hearts.

• ASKING FOR ACES

BLACKWOOD

In bidding suit slams, worries about controls are far more common than concern about power alone. When your *only* problem is whether the enemy have two aces, you may use Blackwood. Suppose the auction goes:

PARTNER	YOU
1 diamond	1 spade
4 spades	?

You hold:

♠ K Q 10 8 4   ♡ K Q J 10 2   ◇ 2   ♣ K 3

Surely there is as much power in the partnership hands as you could need: your hand is worth 19 points after revaluation, partner promises 20 points with his rebid. Whether you play in game, small slam, or grand slam is all a question of aces. So you bid 4 notrump. If partner responds 5 *hearts,* showing two aces, you sign off at 5 spades; if partner answers 5 *spades* (three aces), you bid slam; and if partner bids 5 *clubs* (four aces), you bid a grand slam (in notrump, preferably), since you can count 13 tricks.

Note that the response to show all the aces is 5 *clubs,* not 5 *notrump.* This is to enable the Blackwood bidder to ask for kings if partner has four aces. Of course, the 5 club answer could show *no* aces as well, but your own hand and the auction will always tell you which partner holds. On the example above, for instance, a 5 club reply must show four aces. If partner has opened and jumped to game with no aces (and only one king), he deserves to be in a grand slam missing four aces, and so do you for playing with him.

ROMAN BLACKWOOD

Actually, it is so easy to tell from the auction *approximately* how many aces partner holds that a group of Italian experts devised a modification of Blackwood which gives some information about *which* aces responder holds when he shows two. This is called **Roman Blackwood**, and starts out, as usual, with the bid of 4 notrump.

Roman Blackwood Responses

5 Clubs = No or *three* aces
5 Diamonds = One or *four* aces
5 Hearts = Two aces—but not those below
5 Spades = Two aces: spades-diamonds or hearts-clubs

Five *hearts* shows two aces which are both majors (spades-hearts) or both minors (diamonds-clubs) or both red (hearts-diamonds) or both black (spades-clubs). Five *spades* shows two aces *unlike* in both rank and color. Here is an example hand to show how this works:

OPENER	RESPONDER
♠ K Q J 10 6 2	♠ A 8 7 3
♡ A K	♡ Q 8 4
◇ K Q 6 4 3	◇ 7 2
♣ ——	♣ A Q 7 5
1 spade	3 spades
4 notrump	5 hearts
6 spades	pass

Opener learns that he is missing an important ace, and cannot make a grand slam. The 5 heart response shows two *like* aces: probably, from opener's point of view, spades and clubs (like in color), possibly diamonds and clubs (like in rank). Had responder held the spade and *diamond* aces, he would have responded 5 *spades*. Opener, looking at his own ace of hearts, would know exactly which unlike aces responder held, and would confidently bid 7 spades.

The example above illustrates the advantage of Roman Blackwood. The disadvantage is that it is rather complicated, and seldom is necessary. I would never use these responses with a strange or occasional partner. It *is* impressive to ask a new partner, "Do you like Roman Blackwood?" He has probably never heard of it, and will now realize that you are much the more sophisticated player. However, if he unexpectedly answers that he admires the Roman variation and wants to play it, you had better tell him that you prefer the old-fashioned kind.

GERBER

Another ace-showing convention is called **Gerber** after the great Texas player who developed it. Here, instead of 4 no-trump, the bid of 4 *clubs* asks for aces, and responses are by the usual steps:

Gerber Responses

4 Diamonds = No or four aces
4 Hearts = One ace
4 Spades = Two aces
4 Notrump = Three aces

Some players employ Gerber *instead* of Blackwood. However, it is chiefly popular as an adjunct to Blackwood, for use when partner's last bid was in notrump. Here, a bid of 4 notrump would be quantitative, a slam try in notrump, so the jump to *4 clubs* should be used to ask for aces. For example, suppose partner opens 1 notrump and your hand is:

♠ K Q 6   ♡ K Q 9 8 6 4 2   ◇ K 2   ♣ 5

All you care about is aces, but you cannot bid 4 notrump. Right over 1 notrump, this would ask partner to bid 6 no-trump with a maximum or to pass with a minimum. There-fore, you jump to 4 clubs, Gerber. If partner responds 4 spades (two aces), you sign off at 5 hearts; over a 4 notrump response (three aces), you bid 6 hearts; and a 4 diamond reply (four aces) allows you to bid a grand slam.

Other auctions in which a jump to 4 clubs would be Ger-ber are:

OPENER	RESPONDER
1 spade	2 notrump
4 clubs	

OPENER	RESPONDER
1 diamond	1 heart
2 notrump	4 clubs

Note that in each case a bid of 4 *notrump* would be a quantitative raise in notrump, inviting 6 notrump, not asking for aces. My recommendation is that you use 4 clubs as Gerber only in those auctions in which 4 notrump would *not* be Blackwood.

After asking for aces with a bid of 4 clubs, you may then ask for kings. It is simplest to do this with the bid of 5 clubs. Partner shows the number of kings he holds by the same responses, now, of course, at the five-level.

WHEN NOT TO ASK FOR ACES

All these conventional devices for asking about aces—Blackwood, Roman Blackwood, Gerber—are fine when you have no worries about *power,* and when your only concern about *controls* is the number of aces in partner's hand. However, do not overuse them. If you are not sure that your side has 33 points, you would be foolish to inquire about aces, since the answer will not resolve your problem. Even if you are confident that the necessary 33 points are held, you should not ask about aces if you have two losers in an unbid suit, for then you could not tell whether to bid slam missing one ace—the enemy might cash the first two tricks. For example, if you open 1 spade with either hand below and partner jumps to 3 spades:

(1) ♠ K Q 9 8 2   ♡ A 7 4   ◊ A 8 4   ♣ K 2
(2) ♠ K Q J 8 7 4   ♡ Q 3   ◊ A K Q 2   ♣ 4

you should *not* launch into Blackwood. Partner would answer 5 hearts (two aces) with either of these hands:

(a) ♠ A 10 6 5   ♡ K 8 2   ◊ J 5 3   ♣ A J 6
(b) ♠ A 10 6 5   ♡ J 8 2   ◊ 3   ♣ A Q J 6 5

How can you tell whether to bid slam?

Note that hand (a) will make slam opposite example (2) but not opposite example (1); hand (b) will make slam opposite example (1) but not opposite example (2). The point is that using Blackwood (or Roman Blackwood or Gerber) with either example (1) or (2) is futile, since you are concerned with more than the number of aces partner holds. With example (1), your main worry is whether partner has a *maximum* jump raise like (b) or a *minimum* like (a)—is there enough power? With example (2), your worry is about controls, but *specific* controls—has partner two aces *and* control in hearts?

If you use Blackwood or any other ace-showing gadget properly, you will never have a problem over partner's response. If your side has three aces, you will bid slam; if you are missing two aces you will not. It is as simple as that. However, nothing is more common in the average bridge game than for the Blackwood bidder to go into an agonized huddle after the response, wondering whether to bid slam missing one ace. Will there be enough tricks? Will the enemy cash the A K of some suit? It is now too late to find out, for the unfortunate, tortured player who is glaring fiercely at his cards, or imploringly up at the ceiling, has asked the wrong question. He wanted to learn how many *points*, or *which* controls, partner holds, and he has found out, instead, how many aces his side has. Almost always, he should have used the cue-bidding approach to slam instead of Blackwood.

• CUE BIDDING

A cue bid is one made without any intention of suggesting the bid suit as trump. The simplest example of a cue bid is the bid in an enemy suit:

PARTNER	OPPONENT	YOU
1 spade	2 hearts	*3 hearts*

Obviously, you do not want hearts to be trump; if you did, you would *double*, for if you can make 3 hearts you can set 2 hearts doubled 4 tricks. Your cue bid shows not *length* in hearts but *control* of hearts—you have the ace or, more likely, a void. Since you have made no effort to find a trump suit, your cue bid inferentially shows magnificent support for spades. Since you have not merely jumped in spades, forcing to game, your cue bid strongly suggests slam. For the auction above, you might hold:

♠ K Q 10 7 3   ♡ ——   ◇ A K 10 2   ♣ Q J 9 4

Observe that your cue bid will *keep you out* of slam if partner opened with:

♠ A J 8 6 2   ♡ A K 3   ◇ Q 4   ♣ 8 5 2

Partner knows that his heart honors are wasted, for your control must be a void; he will sign off by rebidding 3 spades, and will reject all slam tries. The whole auction might go:

PARTNER		YOU	
♠ A J 8 6 2		♠ K Q 10 7 3	
♡ A K 3		♡ ——	
◇ Q 4		◇ A K 10 2	
♣ 8 5 2		♣ Q J 9 4	

PARTNER	OPPONENT	YOU	OPPONENT
1 spade	2 hearts	3 hearts	pass
3 spades	pass	4 diamonds	pass
4 hearts	pass	4 spades	pass

Over partner's 3 spade rebid, you bid 4 diamonds. This is another cue bid showing control, not length, since the trump suit—spades—is firmly set. Partner cue-bids *his* heart control, more to warn you than to encourage you. And you sign off at game.

Note that had you used Blackwood instead of cue bidding, partner would have shown two aces, and you would have had to guess in the blind whether to bid five, six, or seven. Yet even 5 spades is in jeopardy.

Cue bidding for slam is frequently used when the opponents have never been in the auction. Most suit bids show *length,* not control, since the first order of business is to find a trump suit. However, after a trump suit is finally and certainly set, any *new* suit must be a cue bid. Thus in this sequence:

YOU	PARTNER
1 spade	3 spades
4 diamonds	

your 4 diamond bid is a cue bid. Spades must be a good trump suit (you have at least four and so has partner; your side has at least eight trumps). It is worse than futile to continue the search for trumps—you have found it. Lord knows, it is hard enough to find *one* trump suit, and there is no bonus for finding another. Therefore, if you hold this hand:

♠ Q J 10 8 4   ♡ 4 2   ◇ A K J 8 3   ♣ 2

and hear partner jump to 3 spades over your 1 spade opening, you bid *4 spades.* You know *where* to play—spades—and *how high* to play—game—so no purpose is served by "showing" your diamonds. You are showing them to the enemy—partner will be dummy. If you bid 4 diamonds here, you are *not* suggesting diamonds as trumps, you are cue-bidding, suggesting a slam. For this cue bid (1 spade—3 spades—4 diamonds) you might hold:

(a) ♠ A K 10 8 2   ♡ K Q 10 2   ◇ A 3   ♣ 5 3

This cue bid tells partner two things: you are interested in slam (or else you would have gone right to game); you have *control* of the suit you bid (the ace or a void). It also asks partner two things: Does he have maximum values for his previous bidding, in which case he also is interested in slam? Does he have a control to show you? Let us see how you would respond to partner's cue bid (he opens 1 spade, you answer 3 spades, partner cue-bids 4 diamonds) with these hands:

(1) ♠ Q J 8 3   ♡ A J 2   ◇ J 8 3   ♣ A 8 4
(2) ♠ Q J 8 3   ♡ A 2   ◇ K Q J 5 2   ♣ 8 4
(3) ♠ Q J 8 3   ♡ 8 4   ◇ K 8 7 2   ♣ A K J

(1) Bid *4 spades*. You have a minimum jump raise with flat distribution, and so are not interested in slam. Partner's cue bid does not oblige you to show a control in answer; if he were interested entirely in your aces, he would use Blackwood. You will show an ace only if you wish to encourage partner to bid slam.

(2) Bid *4 hearts*. You have maximum values with a strong playing hand, so cooperate in partner's effort to sound out a slam. Observe that you do so by cue-bidding a control, not by raising partner's diamond "suit." Spades, not diamonds, will be trump.

(3) Bid *5 clubs*. With close to a maximum jump raise, make the encouraging cue bid.

(a) ♠ A K 10 8 2   ♡ K Q 10 2   ◇ A 3   ♣ 5 3

YOU	PARTNER
1 spade	3 spades
4 diamonds	P
P	

Suppose you hold hand (a) and hear the preceding answers to your cue bid. What do you do? If partner bids 4 spades, you pass; there are either too few points or too few

aces for slam when partner is unwilling or unable to cue-bid
an ace. If partner bids 4 hearts, you sign off at 4 spades;
partner has the wrong ace, and you can bid no higher without
a control in the unbid club suit. If partner bids 5 clubs, you
jump to 6 spades; there are enough points, enough aces, and
first- or second-round controls in all suits.

It is possible to cue-bid second-round controls (kings,
singletons), but only after you or partner have already shown
first-round control of the same suit. Thus, responder on this
auction:

OPENER	RESPONDER
1 diamond	1 heart
3 hearts	3 spades
4 clubs	5 clubs

shows first-round control of spades, second-round control of
clubs (opener has the *first*-round control), and a strong interest in slam. He might hold:

♠ A 4 2   ♥ K Q 10 8 4   ♦ 6 2   ♣ K J 4

Here, responder cannot quite yet jump to slam, for he is worried about *diamond* control; no one has cue-bid this suit. If
opener holds:

♠ K Q 2   ♥ A 9 7 2   ♦ Q J 10 6 4   ♣ A

he will sign off by returning to the trump suit—5 hearts.
When *two* suits have been cue-bid, neither partner may bid
slam without at least the king, or a singleton, in the third
suit.

Here are some further examples of cue-bidding auctions:

OPENER	RESPONDER
♠ K 8 4	♠ A Q J 10 7 3
♥ A K Q 6 5	♥ 8 2
♦ 8	♦ 7 5
♣ J 8 4 3	♣ A K Q
1 heart	2 spades
3 spades	4 clubs
4 hearts	5 clubs
6 spades	pass

When opener raises responder's jump shift, the trump suit is
set, so 4 clubs is a cue bid. Opener has solid values for slam,

and encourages by showing his heart control. Responder repeats his club cue bid, this time showing the king, and pinpointing his worry about diamonds. Opener jumps to slam, for he has the needed second-round control of the missing suit.

OPENER	RESPONDER
♠ A K 9 8 4 3	♠ Q 10 6 2
♡ ——	♡ Q 2
◊ K Q 8 7 5	◊ A 6
♣ A 2	♣ K Q 10 7 4

1 spade	3 spades
4 clubs	4 diamonds
4 hearts	5 clubs
7 spades	pass

Responder's answering cue bids show the two key cards that opener needs—the diamond ace and the club king—so opener can count 13 tricks and bid the grand slam.

OPENER	RESPONDER
♠ Q 2	♠ J 8 6 5
♡ A K Q J	♡ 4
◊ A K J 10 8 7 4	◊ Q 9 5 3
♣ ——	♣ A K J 4

2 diamonds	3 diamonds
3 hearts	4 clubs
4 hearts	5 clubs
5 diamonds	pass

Here the partnership has enormous overlapping power, but avoids the losing slam, since neither partner can do more than encourage violently with repeated cue bids. Neither dares go to slam without a control in the unbid spade unit.

OPENER	RESPONDER
♠ A Q J 8 3	♠ K 10 4 2
♡ Q 3	♡ A 8 4 2
◊ A Q J 2	◊ 7 3
♣ A 3	♣ K Q 2

1 spade	3 spades
4 diamonds	4 spades
5 clubs	5 hearts
6 spades	pass

Responder does *not* cue-bid his ace in answer to 4 diamonds, since he does not wish to encourage opener to try for slam. However, when opener persists with a second cue bid, responder reassures him about the heart control, and opener's worries are over.

It is most important to realize when a new suit is a cue bid and when it is not. The crux of the matter is *whether the trump suit has been settled beyond all doubt*. Consider these auctions:

	OPENER	RESPONDER
(1)	1 spade	2 spades
	3 *hearts*	
(2)	1 diamond	3 diamonds
	3 *spades*	
(3)	1 heart	2 spades
	3 hearts	3 spades
	4 *clubs*	

None of these are cue bids, since the trump suit may be in doubt. In auction (1) opener might have a 4-card spade suit, and, fearing a 3-card raise, be trying for game in a new suit. In auction (2) opener may be trying for the easier game contract in spades or notrump even though a diamond fit has been found. In auction (3) no suit has been supported, and opener is continuing the search for the proper trump. In none of these auctions is there any implication that opener is interested in slam. These bids show *length*, not *control*, in the suit bid; they suggest *that* suit as *trump*. Cue bidding takes place only after the trump suit has been irrevocably settled.

One of the few occasions in which a cue bid can be made *before* a suit has been supported occurs when you have opened 1 notrump (or 2 notrump) and partner forces with three of a suit:

YOU	PARTNER
1 notrump	3 hearts
4 *clubs*	

YOU	PARTNER
2 notrump	3 spades
4 *diamonds*	

In each of these auctions, partner has asked you to choose between game in his suit or notrump. You have answered that you have good support for his suit, and have settled it as trump. In addition, you state that you have maximum values for your opening, with the ace of the suit you cue bid, and urge partner to try for slam if he has any interest in such a high contract. Thus:

OPENER	RESPONDER
♠ A Q 8 4	♠ K J 9 6 3
♡ K J 2	♡ A Q 3
◇ J 7 6 3	◇ 4
♣ A K	♣ Q 10 9 5

1 notrump	3 spades
4 clubs	4 hearts
5 hearts	6 spades

Opener shows, with his cue bid, a magnificent maximum containing spade support and the club ace. Responder, who would have passed a raise to game, is encouraged to cue-bid his ace in return, and jumps to slam on the third round since he holds the key singleton in the unbid suit. Note that opener dares not go beyond game before responder evinces slam interest; the 3 spade response could be made with a hand that will yield only a play for game, not slam. For example:

OPENER	RESPONDER
♠ A Q 8 4	♠ K J 9 6 3
♡ A K J	♡ 8 4
◇ K 2	◇ 6 5
♣ A K 7 2	♣ 10 8 5 3

2 notrump	3 spades
4 clubs	4 spades
pass	

Opener cannot become too enthusiastic despite his enormous power. After all, he showed most of his strength with his first bid. Therefore, he indicates his slam interest with a cue bid, and subsides when partner firmly declines the invitation by returning to the agreed-upon suit. After a rigidly limited *notrump* opening, it is always *responder* who must decide whether slam is in view.

• SLAMS BASED ON "FIT"

There is actually a third factor, in addition to power and controls, which affects slam bidding. This is how much of the power is wasted or duplicated—how well the partnership hands *fit*. Consider these two partnership hands:

	OPENER	RESPONDER
(1)	♠ A Q 10 9 7 4	♠ K J 8 6 2
	♡ ——	♡ A Q 10
	◇ K J	◇ A Q
	♣ A 10 9 8 2	♣ 7 5 3
	OPENER	RESPONDER
(2)	♠ A 10 7 6 5 2	♠ K 9 8 3
	♡ ——	♡ 8 6 4 2
	◇ A 7 3	◇ K 2
	♣ Q J 7 5	♣ K 8 4

In (1), the partnership has 39 points worth of power: opener has a 21-point hand, responder an 18-point hand, once the trump fit is found. A slam contract is sure to be bid, but is almost impossible to make. In contrast, in (2), the partnership has only 26 points after revaluation. It is not easy to bid even a game with these cards. Yet a slam will most probably be made.

The explanation lies in the manner in which the partnership hands fit together. The hands in (1) have enormous duplication of values: all those trump honors and length are not needed; the 6 points in hearts opposite opener's void are all waste; the partnership counts 12 points in diamonds but wins only 2 tricks since the honors fall on each other and the shortness is duplicated; responder is weak and long in opener's side club suit.

Hands (2) have no waste whatever: the spade honors are just sufficient to draw trumps; there is no useless heart honor opposite the void; responder's doubleton produces a trick; responder has an honor to solidify opener's side suit.

Of course, the examples above are extremes. The monstrous duplication of (1) and the magic fit of (2) are both very rare. Normally there is moderate waste in the partnership's power, and the figure of 33 points for slam allows for it. However, this means that a slam may be made easily with fewer than 33 points if there is very little waste, and it may require much more than 33 points if there is a great deal of waste. Therefore, bear in mind those features of the hands above which are favorable and unfavorable. These are danger signals, pointing to excess duplication:

Too Many Trumps: Suppose you hold A Q 10 9 6 of hearts and partner opens 2 hearts: your queen and your fifth trump are waste, since four to the ace would solidify partner's long suit.

Shortness Facing Shortness: Suppose partner bids three suits. You yourself have a singleton in the fourth suit: it is wasted, for partner is short there also.

Three Small Cards Facing Length: Suppose partner bids two suits. You have good support for one, but three little cards in the other: be wary of slam, for you have neither an honor to fill out partner's length nor the shortness to allow him to ruff.

Honors Facing Shortness: Suppose partner cue-bids a suit in which you hold A K: your 7 points are wasted, for he is void. Likewise, it is a sign of waste to be void in a suit which partner bids strongly or cue-bids.

In contrast, be most aggressive in your slam bidding when you have fitting honors to partner's second suit (a doubleton king is the ideal holding, for this might either solidify the suit or allow him to ruff it out). Most important, fall in love with hands that have voids or singletons in *enemy* suits (where partner is unlikely to hold honors), or with hands that have three or four little cards in a suit in which partner has a singleton or void.

So crucial is the distributional fit of partnership hands for slam bidding that you must sometimes go out of your way in the auction to indicate to partner where you are short. The general principle is that if you bid three suits, one with a jump, you have no more than a singleton in the fourth. Thus:

YOU	PARTNER
1 diamond	1 spade
3 hearts	3 notrump
4 spades	

You mark yourself with at most a singleton club on the auction above. What should partner do, on this auction, with these hands?

   (1) ♠ Q 10 7 6 2 ♡ K 7 4 ♢ 8 7 3 ♣ K Q
   (2) ♠ Q 10 7 6 2 ♡ K 7 ♢ K 3 ♣ J 7 5 3

He should *pass* with hand (1), but bid *4 notrump* with hand (2), intending to reach a small slam unless two aces are missing. Each example is worth 12 points once spades are supported, and this is in the slam range (your jump shift promises 20 points at least). The difference is that hand (1) should fit terribly with your distribution (partner's doubleton faces your singleton; he has wasted honors in clubs; he has the worst holding opposite your side diamond suit), while hand (2) should fit magnificently (partner has little waste in clubs; he has both a fitting honor and a doubleton opposite your side suit). For *your* auction, you might well have:

   ♠ A K J 5 ♡ A Q 3 ♢ A 10 9 5 4 ♣ 2

Notice how each of the preceding examples will play facing this hand.

Let us examine your bidding with these cards. You open 1 diamond and partner responds 1 spade. Now your hand is worth 21 points, justifying a leap to 4 spades. Instead, however, you force with a jump shift and next support spades—this is to mark your singleton (by bidding three suits including a jump) and so allow partner to determine how well the hands fit. It is clear, therefore, that if you bid:

YOU	PARTNER
1 diamond	1 spade
4 spades	

you have no singleton. Your hand might look like:

   ♠ A K J 7 ♡ K 2 ♢ A J 8 4 ♣ A 8 4

High cards anywhere in partner's hand will fit with yours. The only suit in which partner must pay special attention to his holding is diamonds, your side suit. Honors, or shortness, here will be particularly welcome.

• GRAND SLAMS

Nearly everything said so far about small slams applies to grand slams as well. Distributional fit is a key factor in deciding whether to go all the way. Cue bidding is the most likely route, since, particularly for *grand*-slam bidding, you want to locate specific controls in partner's hand. However, if your sole concern is the *number* of controls that partner holds, you can employ Blackwood (or some fancy variation if you prefer), bidding 4 notrump and then 5 notrump to check on kings.

ASKING FOR KINGS

It is important to remember that *only when you are interested in a grand slam* do you use the Blackwood 5 notrump. Partner's response must be at the six-level, so you are asking a question when the answer cannot interest you unless there may be enough power (37 points) and enough controls (all four aces) for seven. This has an interesting corollary: When you ask for kings with 5 notrump, you guarantee that your side has all the aces; therefore partner may bid a grand slam all by himself.

This is quite different from the situation when you bid 4 notrump to ask for aces. Here, you are the boss; *you* will decide whether or not to bid six. In contrast, when you ask for kings, partner is allowed to exercise his judgment. Consider this auction, for example:

OPENER	RESPONDER
♠ K 5 2	♠ A 8
♡ A K J 7 3	♡ Q 4
◇ 8 4	◇ A K Q J 10 7 2
♣ A Q 2	♣ 9 3
1 heart	3 diamonds
3 hearts	4 diamonds
4 notrump	5 hearts
5 notrump	7 *diamonds*

Responder decides, quite properly, that if opener is interested in a grand slam, then a grand slam can be made even if a king is missing. He has a solid 7-card suit, which opener cannot be sure of, and the undisclosed queen of opener's suit. Therefore, if seven cannot be made, opener has no business inviting it. Actually opener bid 5 notrump merely so that responder could bid seven; he himself could not count 13 tricks even if the response showed two kings. He relied on partner to bid the grand slam with a long, solid suit once reassured that there was no ace missing and that the opening bid was a strong one.

THE GRAND-SLAM FORCE

In order to ask for kings (and, as we have seen, to invite a grand slam) with 5 notrump, you must first ask for aces. Even if you hold all the aces yourself, you must not bid:

YOU	PARTNER
1 spade	3 spades
5 notrump	

It is necessary first to bid 4 notrump and then, when partner answers 5 clubs, to bid 5 notrump. The auction above is not Blackwood at all, but a rare device called the **grand-slam force**.

The grand-slam force asks partner exclusively about his holding in the trump suit. Your jump to 5 notrump after a suit has been established forces partner to bid *seven* if he has two of the three top honors in trumps, but to bid *six* if he lacks two top trump honors. Here is an example of this convention in operation:

OPENER	RESPONDER
♠ 5 3	♠ A K
♡ A K 7 3	♡ Q 10 8 6 5 2
◇ A 6	◇ K Q 10 7 3
♣ K J 9 7 3	♣ ———
1 club	1 heart
3 hearts	3 spades
4 diamonds	5 notrump
7 hearts	

When opener cue-bids his diamond ace, responder's problem is entirely concerned with the trump suit. (Opener could just as easily hold A K in clubs and K J in hearts.) The jump to

5 notrump forces opener to bid the grand slam, since he holds two of the three top honors in the agreed-upon suit.

Now you know all about the grand-slam force. However, be sure to remember that your partner may never have heard of it. This is a fine gadget to have in your bag of tricks, but use it only when playing with a regular partner with whom you have discussed it, or with a player you trust absolutely. (And just about the only time you should trust a strange partner absolutely is if you should happen to be playing with me.) It is far better to settle for a sure small slam than to risk baffling your partner with a weird and wonderful new bid.

THE ODDS

Actually, you must be willing to play most of your potential grand slams in six-contracts. This is because the basic odds of the scoring table do not favor grand slams. Suppose you know that you can make a vulnerable small slam in spades, and are wondering whether to bid seven. What can you gain—what can you lose? The gain, if you bid seven and make it, is exactly 750 points (the difference between the 1500 grand-slam and 750 small-slam bonus). The loss, if you go down, is 100 points to the enemy, plus the 750-point slam bonus, the 500-point rubber bonus, and the 180 points for trick score which you could have had—a total of 1530 points. Thus you risk a loss of over 1500 points to gain 750 points.

The odds are 2 to 1 against you. If you bid three grand slams and make two of them, you would have been slightly better off to settle for three small slams. You will lose heavily in the long run if you bid grand slams which require a finesse for a missing king. With nine trumps missing the queen, you should not want to risk a seven-bid. Even if all you need is a three-two division of five outstanding cards, you should not be too pleased with a grand-slam contract.

There is a simple rule for bidding seven: you must be able to count 13 tricks. When in doubt, don't.

PART 2 • COMPETITIVE BIDDING

(See Book One, Chapters 9 and 10)

Competitive bidding—auctions in which *both* sides are fighting to name the trump suit—separates the wolves from the sheep in bridge more than any other phase of the game. There is a lot more to bidding besides finding out what contract your side can fulfill. To be a wolf, you must also be concerned with what the enemy can make: by proper defensive bidding, you may confuse their auctions, and you may lose fewer points by going down in a contract of your own than by letting the opponents play a game or slam. And when the opponents contest the auction on hands that belong to you, you must not behave like a sheep to be fleeced. You must know when to double them, and when and how to bid on to your own contract.

For convenient reference, this Part is broken down into five main topics: special methods for entering the auction over enemy openings; sacrifice bidding; bidding when you or the opponents have a part score; reopening the auction when the enemy stop at a low contract ("balancing"); doubling for penalties.

CHAPTER 5

When the Opponents Open the Bidding

The basic weapons which you have for entering the auction over an enemy opening bid—the overcall, the takeout double, the notrump overcall, the cue bid, the preemptive double jump—have been described in Book One, Chapter 9. Here you will examine two new devices to add to your arsenal. Also, we will consider how to defend against 1 notrump openings and against preemptive openings, with some special weapons for these awkward auctions.

• THE UNUSUAL NOTRUMP OVERCALL

When you hold two long suits, you should almost always climb into the auction over an enemy opening. If partner fits one of your suits, you will be able to win a surprising number of tricks even if your side has fewer high cards than the enemy; and thousands of points may be at stake, for often both sides can make high contracts when the distribution is freakish. Therefore, your first duty with such a hand is to bid both your suits.

If you hold the major suits, this can usually be done economically:

OPPONENT	YOU	OPPONENT	PARTNER
1 diamond	1 spade	1 notrump	pass
2 clubs	2 hearts		

In the auction above, you are able to show both suits and stay at the two-level. Even if the opponents had bid more vigorously, you would probably have been able to suggest your second suit at the three-level. However, contrast this with your position when your two suits are minors:

OPPONENT	YOU	OPPONENT	PARTNER
1 spade	2 diamonds	2 notrump	pass
3 hearts	4 clubs		

Here, you are forced to the *four*-level even though the opponents have not jumped. And they are much more likely to bounce right into game when they have the major suits—you might well be faced with the choice of bidding at the five-level or suppressing one of your suits.

To take care of these difficult minor two-suiters, a special convention has been devised—the **unusual notrump overcall**. Under certain circumstances, a notrump overcall is "unusual" and acts as a takeout double for the minor suits. When? There is nothing unusual about this overcall:

OPPONENT	YOU	OPPONENT	PARTNER
1 heart	1 notrump		

This shows the normal 16 to 18 points with a stopper in hearts. But what about:

YOU	OPPONENT	PARTNER	OPPONENT
pass	pass	pass	1 heart
1 notrump			

You cannot hold 16 points, since you passed originally. Any notrump overcall by a passed hand is unusual. Likewise,

OPPONENT	PARTNER	OPPONENT	YOU
1 heart	pass	1 notrump	*2 notrump*

You cannot want to play notrump in this auction, for then you would double 1 notrump. Any notrump overcall right over an enemy notrump bid is unusual. Similarly:

OPPONENT	PARTNER	OPPONENT	YOU
1 heart	pass	3 hearts	*3 notrump*

You surely do not expect to play 3 notrump against an opening bid on your left and a jump response on your right. Any notrump overcall when the opponents have bid very strongly must be unusual. Finally:

OPPONENT	YOU	OPPONENT	PARTNER
1 spade	*2 notrump*		

This auction sounds as though you hold 22 points or more. However, you practically never will hold such strength against an enemy opening bid, and can double or cue-bid if you do. It is far more useful to treat the *jump* to 2 notrump over an opponent's major-suit opening as unusual.

We have seen the four situations in which a notrump overcall is unusual: (1) any notrump overcall by a passed hand; (2) any notrump overcall of a notrump bid; (3) any notrump overcall when the enemy have shown great strength; (4) the jump overcall of 2 notrump after a major-suit opening. What does such a bid promise?

REQUIREMENTS

Think of the unusual notrump as an *overcall in both minor suits at once*. To use it, you must hold at least 5-card length in each, just as you would have to have for an overcall in either suit. Usually, this bid is based on 11 cards in the minors; five clubs and five diamonds is the bare minimum distributional requirement.

How much high-card strength is required? This depends on two factors: your playing strength, and the extent of risk.

Playing strength means length and solidity of suits. Consider these examples:

(a) ♠ 2   ♡ ——   ◇ Q J 10 9 7 2   ♣ Q J 10 7 6 2
(b) ♠ 2   ♡ 2   ◇ K Q J 9 7   ♣ K 10 8 7 6 2
(c) ♠ 3 2   ♡ 2   ◇ A Q 10 9 2   ♣ K Q 9 8 2
(d) ♠ K Q   ♡ K   ◇ Q 8 7 6 2   ♣ J 9 7 6 2

Hands (a) and (b), with their freakish distribution, have considerably more playing strength (although fewer points) than (c) and (d). Hand (c) has considerably more offensive power than hand (d)—each has 11 high-card points, but hand (c) has its honors concentrated in the long suits where they will do most good.

Extent of risk means the level at which you must bid, and the vulnerability conditions. Obviously, it requires greater offensive strength to force partner to bid at the four-level than at the two-level; and you must be more cautious when vulnerable, both because the penalties are greater and because the opponents are more anxious to double you. The **rule of 500** is a good guide to the unusual notrump overcall. That is, assume that partner holds his usual:

♠ 7 6 5 4   ♡ 5 4 3   ◇ 5 4 3   ♣ 5 4 3

He must respond to your bid by choosing a minor suit. If he is doubled, will the set be greater than 500 points? The preceding examples (a) or (b) will probably win 8 tricks; you are safe at the four-level vulnerable or the five-level nonvulnerable. Example (c) will win only 6 or 7 tricks; it would be foolhardy to go to the four-level vulnerable (by an unusual 3 notrump overcall) and risky nonvulnerable. Example (d) will win no more than 5 tricks; the only unusual notrump overcall you might make with it would be 1 notrump (as a passed hand) nonvulnerable.

The normal range of strength goes from a near bust with two 6-card suits up to a minimum opening bid with two 5-carders. Your primary purpose is not so much to bid and make game as to interfere with the opponents and suggest a possible sacrifice should *they* reach game. However, you may take advantage of the unusual notrump overcall with a powerhouse like:

♠ A   ♡ 2   ◇ K Q J 9 3   ♣ A Q J 10 7 6

Bid 2 notrump over an enemy 1 heart opening. Remember, though, that partner does not expect such great strength. You must bid vigorously later to show him that you have a most unusual "unusual" notrump overcall.

RESPONDING TO THE UNUSUAL NOTRUMP

When partner uses the unusual notrump, you are forced to respond just as if he had cue-bid or made a takeout double. (Of course, you are allowed to pass if your right-hand opponent takes action.) What you must do is to choose between partner's two suits, to give a preference as if partner had bid both minors. That is, if you hold:

♠ J 64   ♡ K J 10 9 7   ◇ 8 4 3   ♣ K 2

when your left-hand opponent opens 1 notrump and partner overcalls 2 notrump, you respond *3 diamonds*. You are not bidding a suit of your own; partner has overcalled in clubs and diamonds simultaneously, and you are choosing one of *his* suits. Occasionally you may have to express a preference with a doubleton. Thus, you should be pleased with the hand above: it has reasonable support for one minor and a valuable honor in the other. If you have much more useful strength than in the example above, you should consider giving a *jump* preference. Suppose you hold:

♠ J 10 8 6 4   ♡ A 10 3   ◇ 2   ♣ K J 64

Your left-hand opponent opens 1 spade; partner overcalls 2 notrump; right-hand opponent passes. Respond *4 clubs*. To see why, pretend that the auction has gone:

OPPONENT	PARTNER	OPPONENT	YOU
1 spade	2 diamonds	pass	pass
2 hearts	3 clubs	pass	?

Would you not bid 4 clubs here, to try for game with your excellent support, your valuable singleton, your side ace? Partner's unusual notrump overcall is the equivalent of the auction above, and your action should be the same. Actually, the only question on either auction is whether to jump all the way to 5 clubs; if vulnerable, this would certainly be proper. If partner holds, as he well might,

♠ 2   ♡ J   ◇ A J 8 7 5 3   ♣ A 10 9 8 5

you have a chance to take *12* tricks. Yet he would have to pass if you responded only 3 clubs to his 2 notrump overcall. He must fear that you hold a poor supporting hand like:

♠ K J 8 6   ♡ K Q 10 7   ◇ 7 4   ♣ Q 6 4

Note that this example hand has 11 high-card points where the previous one had 9, but that it is worth much less. Honors in the major suits are usually wasted opposite an unusual notrump overcall unless they are aces. The only useful values in the hand above are the club queen, the club support, and the doubleton diamond. Remember, you could have a much poorer hand than this one and bid 3 clubs.

Therefore, when partner uses the unusual notrump most of the responsibility for getting to game or taking a sacrifice rests with *you*. He is not expected to bid again unless you jump; you know what he has, while he has no idea what you have. Consider this deal, which was bid at rubber bridge with North-South vulnerable:

NORTH
♠ A 8 6 2
♡ Q J 8 5
◇ K J 10 2
♣ 6

WEST
♠ Q 10 9 4
♡ K 9 6 4 2
◇ 9
♣ 9 4 3

EAST
♠ ——
♡ 7 3
◇ A J 7 6 4 3
♣ K Q 10 8 5

SOUTH
♠ K J 7 5 3
♡ A 10
◇ 8 5
♣ A J 7 2

SOUTH	WEST	NORTH	EAST
1 spade	pass	3 spades	3 notrump
pass	4 clubs	4 spades	5 clubs
double	pass	pass	pass

The result was a five-trick, 900-point set—and South could have been defeated in 4 spades. East, of course, was the culprit. He forgot that West's 4 club bid was forced and promised nothing. Any drastic action must be taken by the *partner* of the unusual notrump overcaller.

The example above illustrates one of the pitfalls of the device. It is tempting to "raise" partner when you hear him bid a suit in which you hold 5 cards, forgetting that you have already, in effect, bid the suit yourself.

Another danger is that of partnership misunderstanding between an unusual and a natural notrump overcall. You must be sure that you and partner have discussed the four positions in which a notrump overcall is unusual. Under no circumstances should you use this convention with a strange partner. It is far too disaster-prone when confusion sets in.

OVER AN ENEMY UNUSUAL NOTRUMP

Even if you do not care to adopt the unusual notrump yourself, you must be prepared to cope with its use by the opponents. Here are the three main principles to follow:

1. If you have good support for partner's suit, make your normal raise, or jump-raise (when you can do so at a reasonable level).

2. If you have a strong hand in high cards, double the notrump overcall.

3. Do not allow the overcall to stampede you into a high bid in a *new* suit; be cautious unless you are sure of a fit.

To illustrate, suppose the auction has gone:

PARTNER	OPPONENT	YOU	OPPONENT
1 heart	2 notrump	?	

What should be your action with these hands?

(a) ♠ A J 8 6 2   ♡ Q 10 4 3   ◇ 7 4   ♣ 8 5
(b) ♠ A K J 6 3   ♡ K Q 4 3   ◇ 7 4   ♣ 8 5
(c) ♠ A J 10 5   ♡ A 8 5   ◇ 10 5   ♣ K 10 7 5
(d) ♠ K J 8 6 4 2   ♡ 7 5   ◇ Q J 7   ♣ J 3

(a) Bid 3 hearts. Your single raise shows good support with about 8 to 11 points, when made at the three-level.

(b) Bid 4 hearts. This is the equivalent of a normal jump raise to 3 hearts over 1 heart.

(c) Double. Partner should treat this like the redouble over an enemy takeout double. He may double any takeout himself, or pass it around to see if you want to double.

(d) Pass. It is annoying to be unable to bid your long suit, but the level is too high. Remember, the spades and hearts are not góing to split in friendly fashion. (Remember this too whenever you get to be declarer after an opponent's unusual notrump overcall.)

• THE WEAK JUMP OVERCALL

The jump in a new suit over an opponent's opening, the jump overcall:

OPPONENT	YOU	OPPONENT	YOU
1 heart	2 spades	1 spade	3 diamonds

is generally used to show a strong hand with a magnificent suit. Only if you skip *two* levels is it preemptive. However, many players are now using the auctions above to show weak hands containing long suits. This is the useful gadget called the weak jump overcall.

If you and partner have agreed upon the weak jump overcall, you can bid some strong hand, such as:

♠ K Q J 10 8 6 4   ♡ 2   ◇ A Q 5   ♣ K 2

by doubling an enemy opening and jumping in spades at your *second* turn. Actually, the fact that the rare hands suitable for the *strong* jump overcall are so easily and satisfactorily handled with a takeout double is what led bridge theoreticians to look for another meaning to give this almost idle jump bid. The usefulness of the weak jump overcall can be seen by comparing these two examples:

(1) ♠ A Q 10 8 4   ♡ K 3   ◇ A 8 7 3   ♣ 7 4
(2) ♠ K Q 10 9 7 4   ♡ 5   ◇ J 10 7 3   ♣ 7 4

Your right-hand opponent opens the bidding 1 heart. Under the normal rules for defensive bidding, as described earlier in Book One, Chapter 9, you should overcall 1 spade with either hand. However, your *objective* in overcalling is quite different in each case. With hand (1), you have a fighting chance to make game if partner has a little strength, and you may certainly be able to outbid the opponents to make a part score. With hand (2), though, you will be unable to make more than the opponents unless partner is very strong. Your object in overcalling is more to interfere with the enemy, tell partner what to lead, and suggest a possible sacrifice in the likely event that the opponents reach game.

If you have agreed to play the weak jump overcall, you can distinguish between these two hands. With example (1), you still bid 1 spade; with example (2), you jump to 2 spades. The simple overcall now promises a 5-card suit in a hand of close to opening bid strength. It is your point count, not so much your suit, which induces you to enter the auction. The jump overcall promises a good-looking 6-card suit (or a magnificent 5-carder) with very little outside strength. It is your suit, not your points, which tempts you into the bidding.

SIMPLE OR JUMP OVERCALL?

The principal difference between a simple overcall and a weak jump overcall is in *defensive* strength. Look again at our two examples:

(1) ♠ A Q 10 8 4   ♡ K 3   ◇ A 8 7 3   ♣ 7 4
(2) ♠ K Q 10 9 7 4   ♡ 5   ◇ J 10 7 3   ♣ 7 4

Suppose that partner's hand, opposite one of these, is:

♠ J 5 3   ♡ 10 8 2   ◇ K 9 5   ♣ A 9 6 3

What can your side make? Holding either hand (1) or (2), you can take about 8 or 9 tricks at spades. What can the enemy make? If you hold hand (1), the opponents can make about 7 or 8 tricks at hearts; your side owns the contract. In contrast, if you hold hand (2), the opponents can surely make 4 hearts, probably 5 hearts, conceivably even a slam. Thus, partner's action with the hand above will depend on whether you have made a simple or a jump overcall. Should the enemy bid 4 hearts, he will sacrifice if you have jumped, for then he knows that you have very little defensive strength. However, he will feel confident of defeating them if you have merely overcalled; his ace and king added to your defensive strength make a sacrifice unnecessary.

You must decide whether to make a jump overcall or a simple overcall mainly on the basis of your defensive strength. This is best measured by the quick-trick table:

A K = 2	A = 1	K = ½
A Q = 1½	K Q = 1	

With a total of 2½ or more quick tricks, never make a jump overcall. With 1 quick trick or fewer, always prefer the jump. Tend to jump with 1½ quick tricks, and not with 2 quick tricks; here, though, you can be influenced by other factors. If your honors are clustered in your long suit, you have poorer defense and should feel like jumping; scattered honors should induce you not to. If partner is a passed hand, you may try for the preemptive value of the jump overcall with greater quick-trick strength; if he has not passed, a jump overcall with 2 quick tricks might cause your side to miss a good game contract.

No one is vulnerable; your right-hand opponent deals and opens 1 diamond. What is your action with these hands?

(a) ♠ K Q J 10 6 ♡ 8 4 ◇ 6 ♣ 10 9 8 7 3

(b) ♠ A J 5 ♡ Q 8 4 ◇ 3 ♣ A K Q J 7 3

(c) ♠ 8 4 ♡ K Q J 9 7 6 ◇ A 10 2 ♣ 7 5

(d) ♠ Q J 10 9 7 6 3 ♡ 2 ◇ 7 2 ♣ A 9 8

(e) ♠ K 6 ♡ A J 10 6 4 3 ◇ J 5 ♣ Q 10 2

(f) ♠ 8 5 ♡ A 4 ◇ J 8 6 ♣ Q 10 7 6 3 2

(a) *Jump to 2 spades.* With this weak defensive hand, you want to impede the opponents (the jump does an effective job of this) and to suggest a sacrifice. You may jump to the two-level in a 5-card suit when it is a very strong one.

(b) *Double.* With great high-card strength plus a powerful suit, a simple overcall is insufficient, while the jump overcall is unavailable since it now is preemptive. Actually, the double would be preferable even if the jump overcall showed strength, for if partner can *rebid* a major suit after you jump in clubs you will have found your best spot.

(c) Overcall *1 heart.* With 2 quick tricks, you are far from weak defensively, so prefer the simple overcall. However, if partner had passed originally (or if your ace were in hearts), you might well jump to 2 hearts even with this much defense.

(d) *Double-jump to 3 spades.* With a true preemptive hand, the kind you would have opened with a three-bid, use the normal *double* jump overcall even though the single jump is weak. Contrast this example with hand (a) to see the distinction.

(e) Overcall *1 heart.* This hand has only 1½ quick tricks, but the spread-out honor cards give it too much defense for a jump. Without the jack of diamonds and queen of clubs, 2 hearts would be proper.

(f) *Pass.* When you lack the defensive strength for a simple overcall, and your suit is too ragged for a jump overcall, you should remember that no one is forcing you to bid. (If I *had* to bid with hand (f), I would prefer 3 clubs to 2; it is more dangerous, but at least it could do some good.)

RESPONDING TO A JUMP OVERCALL

When your partner has made a weak jump overcall, you become the captain of the partnership, just as you do if he uses the unusual notrump. That is, you make almost all decisions: whether or not to compete further, whether or not to sacrifice, whether or not to double the opponents. Partner is never expected to bid again, and this is true even if you raise his suit:

OPPONENT	PARTNER	OPPONENT	YOU
1 diamond	2 spades	pass	3 *spades*

Your 3 spade bid above is not a try for game but a mild additional preemptive bid. You definitely do *not* want partner to bid 4 spades either as a sacrifice or in an attempt to make it. Quite likely, you are prepared to double the enemy if they reenter the auction at the four-level; you might hold:

♠ 7 3   ♡ K Q 10 6   ◇ A J 10 4   ♣ A 10 5

Note that this hand is not nearly strong enough to produce game opposite a jump overcall. Partner has a minimum *responding* hand (6 to 9 points, usually) in high cards, so you need a strong opening yourself to think of game. Of course, if you have a good support and a singleton on the side you may make game on fit instead of power. We will see later, in Chapter 6 on "Sacrifice Bidding," that you usually jump right to game or higher with such hands, regardless of point count. However, if it is your high cards which tempt you to bid, remember that partner has shown weakness, not strength, by his jump.

When your right-hand opponent bids a new suit over partner's jump, you should almost always pass. Partner has robbed the enemy of a great deal of bidding room and forced them to grope blindly for their best contract. If you take action, you dissipate this advantage considerably. Study this example deal:

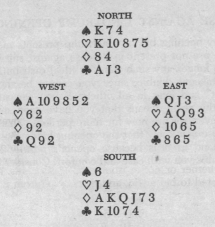

```
                        NORTH
                     ♠ K 7 4
                     ♡ K 10 8 7 5
                     ◇ 8 4
                     ♣ A J 3
        WEST                            EAST
     ♠ A 10 9 8 5 2                  ♠ Q J 3
     ♡ 6 2                           ♡ A Q 9 3
     ◇ 9 2                           ◇ 10 6 5
     ♣ Q 9 2                         ♣ 8 6 5
                        SOUTH
                     ♠ 6
                     ♡ J 4
                     ◇ A K Q J 7 3
                     ♣ K 10 7 4
```

With neither side vulnerable, the auction goes:

SOUTH	WEST	NORTH	EAST
1 diamond	2 spades	3 hearts	?

Would you feel like bidding 3 spades here with the East hand? You certainly should not. If you pass, South is forced to bid again; probably he will bid 4 diamonds. Now, North-South are in the rough—the only game they can make is 3 notrump, yet they will probably end up going down at 4 hearts or 5 diamonds.

In contrast, if you bid 3 spades with the East cards you take South off the spot. Now he can pass around to his partner. North will either double and collect 300 points or bid 3 notrump and make game. West's jump overcall makes it virtually impossible for the opponents to reach a good contract *unless East acts*. Notice, too, that only a *jump* overcall would give North-South a problem.

When partner uses the weak jump overcall, you have other actions available besides the preemptive raise or the jump to game. You can bid notrump (usually after partner jumps in a minor suit) or force by bidding a new suit. However, these bids are very rare, requiring great strength since partner is so weak. Ninety-nine times out of a hundred, your proper response will be a preemptive raise or a pass—and most often the latter.

• DEFENSE AGAINST 1 NOTRUMP OPENING BIDS

An enemy opening bid of 1 notrump presents many problems which are not present in defense against suit openings. There is no longer any such thing as ideal distributional pattern for a takeout double, since you cannot be short in the enemy "suit" and long in all others; if you can support all four suits, this really means that you have good support for none. And overcalls are now far more perilous. This is not so much because *you* know that the opening bidder has a strong defensive hand as it is because opener's *partner* knows it, and can double you with ease and comfort. Consider this deal:

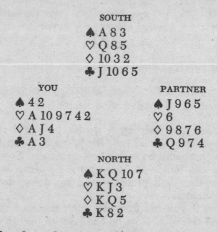

SOUTH
♠ A 8 3
♡ Q 8 5
◇ 10 3 2
♣ J 10 6 5

YOU
♠ 4 2
♡ A 10 9 7 4 2
◇ A J 4
♣ A 3

PARTNER
♠ J 9 6 5
♡ 6
◇ 9 8 7 6
♣ Q 9 7 4

NORTH
♠ K Q 10 7
♡ K J 3
◇ K Q 5
♣ K 8 2

With both sides vulnerable, South deals and opens 1 *spade*. You overcall 2 hearts, and, although you *could* be in trouble, nothing bad happens. North bids 2 spades, neither you nor partner ever bids again, and the opponents achieve a small profit if they stop at a part-score contract.

Now suppose South opens properly with 1 notrump. If you overcall 2 hearts, disaster strikes. North *doubles*, since he can count up that his side has many more points than yours, and nearly as many trumps. You take a 500-point penalty on a part-score hand. The danger of the overcall is that opener's partner knows his side's full strength; when you are in trouble, you get doubled. And when you get doubled, partner always puts down a worthless hand, for there are no cards left for him to hold. What is more, your overcall seldom shows

a profit even when partner holds a fair hand. Exchange
partner's hand with North's in the example, so that your side's
cards are:

YOU	PARTNER
♠ 4 2	♠ A 8 3
♡ A 10 9 7 4 2	♡ Q 8 5
◊ A J 4	◊ 10 3 2
♣ A 3	♣ J 10 6 5

Now you will make 2 hearts if you play carefully. But you
will not be doubled, since North has a terrible hand. And
had you passed instead of overcalling, the deal would have
been played at 1 notrump. You would have defeated this contract at least 2 tricks, for an easy 200 points.

THE OVERCALL

It *can* be right to overcall against a notrump opening, but
only if you have wild distribution—singletons or voids which
will kill the enemy high cards. I would bid 2 hearts over 1
notrump with:

♠ 7   ♡ Q J 10 9 8 5 4   ◊ 3   ♣ K 10 8 6

Here, if I am doubled there is a good chance that the enemy
have made a mistake. The test of an overcall is whether you
would *welcome* a penalty double on your left. With the hand
above, you would. With the earlier example:

♠ 4 2   ♡ A 10 9 7 4 2   ◊ A J 4   ♣ A 3

you turn pale when doubled, for you know that you are in
for a big set—all the enemy high cards will cash. Thus, you
should not overcall with this relatively even distribution—
just pass and hope that your heart lead will defeat the contract. Actually, it makes some sense to *double* 1 notrump.
This could be disastrous if partner has nothing, but it could
produce a big profit when partner has the balance of power.

THE DOUBLE

The double of a 1 notrump opening is for *penalties,* not
takeout. There are two types of hand which call for this
action:

(a) ♠ A Q 4   ♡ Q 10 9 6   ◊ K J 4   ♣ A J 2
(b) ♠ K Q J 9 7 5 2   ♡ A 10   ◊ A 8   ♣ J 2

Example (a) is a 1 notrump opening of your own—you have as much strength as the opener. Why do you expect to defeat him, to take more tricks than he does? Because your strength is *behind* his; your finesses will work while his will fail. To be sure, you will not set 1 notrump if the missing 6 points or so are all in dummy. However, if they are evenly split between opener's partner and yours, you should collect a reasonable penalty. And you may reap a rich harvest when your partner has most of the missing cards.

Example (b) is an even better penalty double, although it has fewer high cards. Here your principal advantage is that you are *on lead*. Almost surely, you will win 8 tricks with your own cards, and any useful honors in partner's hand will increase the profit. A solid or semisolid suit on lead, with a control or two on the side, is the best recipe for a juicy double of 1 notrump.

It is important to note that neither example is much of a double if the auction goes:

OPPONENT	PARTNER	OPPONENT	YOU
1 notrump	pass	pass	?

Hand (a) is now *in front* of the opener, and you will defeat him only if you are lucky enough to find partner with almost all the missing cards. You will do better to pass. Hand (b) is no longer on lead. It is too much to expect that partner will guess to start spades, and with any other lead the contract is likely to make. You should overcall 2 spades. A double in this position is always an out-and-out gamble, and should be made only on favorable vulnerability (they are, you are not). However, *right over* the opener, a double can pay rich dividends.

When you double, partner is expected to *pass* with any fair hand, and with any evenly distributed hand no matter how weak. That is, with either:

(c) ♠ 8 4 3   ♡ J 7 4   ◇ 9 7 6 2   ♣ 9 8 3
(d) ♠ 8   ♡ K 7 5 4 3   ◇ Q 9 2   ♣ Q 9 8 3

partner must leave in your double of 1 notrump. With hand (c) he should not really expect a profit. If you have doubled with great high-card strength, the contract will likely make— but if partner takes out, your side is in for a disastrous penalty anyway. And if you have a long suit to lead, you may surprise partner by defeating 1 notrump all by yourself.

With hand (d), partner should not be astounded if your side can make game. However, he passes anyway—and gleefully—for he is going to tear Declarer limb from limb, no matter which sort of double you have.

Partner *is* allowed to take out your double, but only with a very weak *unbalanced* hand like:

♠ —— ♡ 7 4 3 ♢ 1 0 9 7 6 5 2 ♣ 1 0 9 8 3

Here, he should bid 2 diamonds when you double 1 notrump. If you have doubled with a strong balanced hand, you were not going to defeat 1 notrump; yet 2 diamonds will probably make. In any event, it cannot be a disastrous contract.

THE LANDY CONVENTION

The double of 1 notrump is not for takeout, but nearly 100 per cent for business. Therefore, it is well to have a takeout bid available in addition. Not, of course, for hands which can support all four unbid suits—with these balanced hands, you double if strong enough or pass otherwise. You need a takeout bid when you want partner to choose a *major suit*. That is, if you hold, over an enemy 1 notrump opening:

♠ A Q 10 6 4 ♡ K J 10 3 ♢ K 10 4 ♣ 2

you cannot double. With fewer points than opener, and no very long suit to run, you have no reason to expect to defeat 1 notrump. Yet you would like to compete. It is even conceivable, although far from likely, that your side can make game. Certainly you could own the hand for a part score if you find partner with a fit and a few high cards. This is true because you hold the high-ranking major suits—the opponents will have a *minor*-suit fit, and have to go one level higher to outbid you. You can get into the auction with this sort of hand if you play the **Landy Convention.**

This is the artificial bid of 2 clubs over a 1 notrump opening to ask partner to take out into a major suit—like Stayman over the opponent's notrump opening instead of over your own. This conventional bid bears no relationship to your club holding. In fact, the fewer clubs you have, the better. What you do need is length in hearts and spades, the suits you are asking partner to choose between.

The basic requirement is at least 4 cards in each major suit. With two 4-card suits, you should have about 14 points to bid 2 clubs. However, this high-card minimum can be lowered drastically if you have greater major-suit length. As a rough guide, take 2 points off the 14-point requirement for each card over eight that you hold in hearts and spades combined. That is, these are all minimum 2 club bids over an opponent's 1 notrump opening:

♠ K Q 8 4   ♡ A J 6 3   ◇ A 8 4   ♣ 5 2
                                        14 points—8 cards

♠ K Q 8 4   ♡ A J 6 3 2   ◇ Q 8 4   ♣ 2
                                        12 points—9 cards

♠ K Q 8 4 2   ♡ A J 6 3 2   ◇ 8 4   ♣ 2
                                        10 points—10 cards

♠ K Q 8 4 3 2   ♡ Q J 6 3 2   ◇ 4   ♣ 2
                                        8 points—11 cards

♠ Q J 8 4 3 2   ♡ Q J 6 5 3 2   ◇ 4   ♣ ——
                                        6 points—12 cards

How do you respond when partner bids the Landy 2 clubs? You should treat this much as you do the unusual notrump overcall, here, of course, choosing a major suit instead of a minor. That is, if you hold:

♠ A 10 6   ♡ 8 7   ◇ J 7 5 3   ♣ Q 10 7 6

when the auction goes:

OPPONENT	PARTNER	OPPONENT	YOU
1 notrump	2 clubs	pass	?

bid *2 spades*. You are not allowed to pass, and you should not want to bid diamonds when you have reasonably good support for one of partner's suits. Notice that this hand belongs in 2 spades opposite all of the earlier examples of 2 club bids.

On rare occasions, you may make a *jump* response in a major suit, trying for game. This should not be predicated on point count, since opener has more than enough points to stop a game bid on power. It should be based on fit—length in one major suit and a high honor or a singleton in the other. Compare these two hands:

(1) ♠ A 10 9 6   ♡ K 7   ◇ 7 5   ♣ J 7 6 4 3
(2) ♠ A 10 9 6   ♡ 8 7 4   ◇ K 9 2   ♣ K Q 6

In response to a Landy 2 club takeout, example (1) is much more valuable than example (2), since it has four surely useful features: the spade ace, 4-card spade support, the heart king, the doubleton heart. In example (2), only the spade features are certain to produce tricks. Therefore, give a **jump preference** to 3 spades with example (1) only. To understand this, match up these hands with the previous examples of partner's 2 club bids.

It is possible to respond to Landy by bidding a minor suit, particularly diamonds (since the 2 diamond response is cheap). A typical hand would be:

♠ 8 4   ♡ 7 3   ◇ K Q 10 9 6   ♣ J 8 7 2

You certainly do not want to bid a 2-card major. If partner has a freak, he can bid spades or hearts himself. However, you should show 3-card support for one of partner's suits rather than bid a minor of your own. This is true even with:

♠ 8   ♡ 10 6 2   ◇ J 10 8 6 4 3   ♣ Q 9 2

Respond 2 *hearts*. You are probably in trouble, and if you bid 2 *diamonds* the enemy may smell blood and start doubling, where you might escape with an immediate heart bid. In addition, partner is likely to bid spades over diamonds— give him your preference at the two-level, not the *three*-level.

What would be your action when your right-hand opponent opens 1 notrump, neither side vulnerable, and you hold:

   (1) ♠ K 8 4 3   ♡ Q 7 6 2   ◇ Q J 8   ♣ K J
   (2) ♠ Q 7 4   ♡ K J 10 8 4 2   ◇ Q 6 2   ♣ A
   (3) ♠ A 10 4   ♡ 8 3   ◇ A K Q J 8 4   ♣ 6 2
   (4) ♠ Q 10 9 4 3   ♡ A Q 10 8 7 6   ◇ 5   ♣ 6
   (5) ♠ 5   ♡ 6   ◇ Q 10 9 4 3   ♣ A Q 10 8 7 6

(1) *Pass*. Twelve points is not enough for the 2 club takeout when you have flat distribution, particularly with such bare major suits.

(2) *Pass*. You stand to lose too much by overcalling, and have little to gain. If you want to gamble, then double.

(3) *Double*. You have 7 tricks all by yourself, and anything partner can contribute will increase the yield.

(4) Bid 2 *clubs*. It would not be wrong to overcall 2 *hearts*, but it is better to bid both suits at once. However, be

sure that partner knows that you are playing Landy. If you have never discussed the convention with him and he passes you in 2 clubs, do not send me the bill.

(5) Bid 2 *notrump*. You cannot overcall 2 clubs, for this shows major-suit length. A jump overcall to 3 clubs is possible, but the unusual notrump overcall is preferable (if partner will understand it) since it offers partner a choice of two suits.

• DEFENSE AGAINST PREEMPTIVE OPENING BIDS

Enemy openings of three or higher are designed to give you irritating problems. And they will. If there were any surefire method for handling preemptive openings, the opponents would stop opening them. The truth is that you will always be forced to guess more or less in the dark: if you enter the auction at such a high level with a fairly strong hand, you may find partner with worthless cards and suffer a huge penalty; yet if you pass, you may let the opponents steal a hand in which your side can make game. All I can do for you is to give you some principles to follow in your guesswork, so that you will be right most of the time.

Let us suppose that your right-hand opponent opens with a bid of 3 diamonds. Just as if the opening bid were 1 diamond, the two chief actions available are the double (for takeout) and the overcall. Of course, each is now made at a much higher level, and so requires greater strength. An overcall of, say, 3 hearts promises more than a good-looking suit; it is a serious attempt to reach game.

OVERCALLING THE PREEMPTIVE OPENING

Start out by assuming that partner holds a minimum (6 to 9 points) responding hand. This is the normal expectation if you are strong (that is, you have 16 high-card points; the three-bidder has about 8 points; if partner has half the remainder, he too has 8 points). When this strength in partner's hand, along with a doubleton in your suit, is enough to let you make 9 tricks, overcall at the three-level. Consider these hands:

(a) ♠ K 2   ♡ K Q J 8 5 2   ◇ 10 4   ♣ Q 8 7
(b) ♠ A 5   ♡ A Q 10 8 5 2   ◇ 10 4   ♣ K J 7
(c) ♠ A 5   ♡ A K Q 10 5 2   ◇ 10   ♣ K Q 7 4

What is your action over 3 diamonds? Pass with example (a), for your 13 points will not come close to producing 9 tricks if partner has the expected 6 to 9 points. You could overcall 1 heart, but not 3 hearts. But overcall 3 hearts with example (b). Your 16 points give you safety at the three-level if partner has his fair share of the missing honors. With example (c), jump to 4 hearts, since this is what you can make if partner has his 6 points or so.

Partner's action, in response to your overcall, is based on the same assumption. If he holds:

♠ Q976   ♡ 96   ◇ Q84   ♣ A632

and hears you bid 3 hearts (or 4 hearts) over a 3 diamond opening, he should pass. He should not feel that he owes you a bid because he has 8 points that you do not know about; he must realize that you *assumed* that he had this much strength. Of course, if his hand is worth 10 points or more, he will raise 3 hearts to game; and he may try for slam over 4 hearts with about 12 useful points. Note, however, that for these actions he needs substantially more points than you expect him to hold.

What happens when partner holds *fewer* points than you anticipate? Then you will go down. If you bid 4 hearts over 3 diamonds, get doubled, and lose 500 points when partner has:

♠ 864   ♡ 764   ◇ J853   ♣ 632

you can apologize to soothe partner's feelings. Actually, though, he owes *you* an apology for producing such a horrible dummy. You were merely unlucky on this occasion. After all, if the enemy did not achieve an occasional triumph, they would never preempt. And if you base your bidding on the fear that partner has nothing at all, you will be talked out of too many sound game contracts.

DOUBLING THE PREEMPTIVE OPENING

The takeout double starts with the identical assumption of minimum responding strength in partner's hand. It has the same 15-to-16-point minimum as does the overcall, so that you will have safety at the three-level opposite the expected 7 or 8 points. The difference between the double and the overcall is one of hand pattern—now you have no long suit

of your own; you want to play with partner's longest side
suit as trump.

Thus, if the opponent to your right opens 3 diamonds and
your hand is:

(d) ♠ K Q 8 4   ♡ Q J 7 3   ◇ 4 2   ♣ A J 6
(e) ♠ A Q 8 4   ♡ K J 10 3   ◇ 4 2   ♣ A J 6
(f) ♠ A Q 8 4   ♡ K Q 10 3   ◇ 2   ♣ A Q J 6

Pass with example (d); you could double *1* diamond, but
lack the strength to force partner to bid at the three-level.
Double with example (e), and pass partner's response; if he
has what he is entitled to, your side can make about 9 tricks.
With example (f), double and raise partner's response to
game; you will make it if partner has close to his normal
expectancy.

Partner responds to your double by bidding a suit at a
minimum level when he has only the point count you expect;
he jumps in a suit when he holds 10 points or more. In
choosing the suit for his response, he should give preference
to an unbid *major*, for, since he is guessing anyway, he might
as well guess the suit in which game is most easily made.
Thus, if you double 3 diamonds and partner holds:

(g) ♠ J 10 4 3   ♡ 6 4   ◇ Q 5   ♣ K 10 9 8 2
(h) ♠ J 10 4 3   ♡ A 4   ◇ Q 5   ♣ K 10 9 8 2

he should respond *3 spades* with hand (g), and *4 spades*
with hand (h). Does it make partner nervous to jump to
game in a 4-card suit, jack high, that you have never bid?
Well, it is reasonable for him to be worried, but he should
make his jump in a firm tone anyway—you must be prepared
with excellent support for any unbid majors, for these are the
suits that you are begging partner to bid. Nervous or not,
partner must decide with hand (h) that your side has enough
power for game, and that 4 spades is the most likely game
to make. Really, he has no problem. However, if you double
3 diamonds and he holds:

(i) ♠ J 10 4 3   ♡ A 8 6 4   ◇ Q 5 3   ♣ K 10

he has a nasty decision to make: in which major suit should
he bid game? His proper action is to let *you* choose; he should
bid 4 *diamonds*, a cue bid. You will now bid game (or try
for slam) in your better major suit. Thus:

YOU	PARTNER
♠ Q 9 8 2	♠ J 10 4 3
♡ K Q 5	♡ A 8 6 4
◇ 2	◇ Q 5 3
♣ A Q J 8 4	♣ K 10

OPPONENT	YOU	OPPONENT	PARTNER
3 diamonds	double	pass	4 diamonds
pass	4 spades	all pass	

Partner has another possible action in response to your double: he is allowed to *pass*. Of course, your double is for takeout, not for penalties; therefore, if partner passes *he* is making the penalty double. Virtually never would he do this if you make a takeout double of a *one*-bid. However, when you double *three*, you have considerable high-card strength. And the enemy are in a relatively high contract which your side needs only 5 tricks to defeat. So if you double 3 diamonds and partner holds:

♠ A 4   ♡ 8 6 4   ◇ Q J 9 4   ♣ 10 6 5 3

he should pass for penalties. He should never do this with a weak hand, because he is afraid to bid; he should be more afraid to pass and let the enemy make game in a doubled part score. In the example above, though, he feels confident of a juicy set. He can win 3 defensive tricks, and you should be able to win at least three yourself in order to have the strength for a takeout double. The essential features of his penalty pass are: (1) Two or three defensive tricks, including some length in trumps, so that the contract will certainly be defeated, and (2) no great length in an unbid major suit, so that your side is unlikely to score more points in its own contract.

DOUBLES AND OVERCALLS IN FOURTH SEAT

It is a great deal safer to enter the auction when a preemptive opening has been passed around to you in fourth seat:

OPPONENT	PARTNER	OPPONENT	YOU
3 diamonds	pass	pass	?

Now you know that opener's partner does not have a power-house. You can expect *your* partner to have a trifle more, perhaps 9 or 10 points. Thus, you can *reopen* the auction with a double or an overcall whenever you have 13 points or more and the correct pattern: a long, strong suit for an overcall; good support for unbid suits, particularly unbid majors, when you double. Let us look again at two earlier examples:

(a) ♠K 2 ♡K Q J 8 5 2 ◇10 4 ♣Q 8 7
(d) ♠K Q 8 4 ♡Q J 7 3 ◇4 2 ♣A J 6

With neither hand are you strong enough to act *directly over* a 3 diamond opening. However, in the *reopening* position it is proper to bid—3 hearts with (a), and "double" with (d). Partner is expected to give you leeway when you *reopen* with a double or an overcall. You have already assumed that he has 9 or 10 points; he should go to game only when he holds substantially more.

It is because fourth seat can reopen with somewhat weaker overcalls and take-out doubles that you can afford to pass moderately strong hands in the dangerous *direct* position. This is particularly important when you hold length and strength in the enemy suit:

♠A 7 3 ♡K 6 ◇A Q 10 9 ♣10 7 5 3

If your right-hand opponent opens 3 diamonds, you should *pass* with the hand above. You would dearly love to double for penalties, but if you say "I double for penalties" the opponents will call for the police; and if you merely say "Double," partner will take out into a major suit. Suppose that the full deal is:

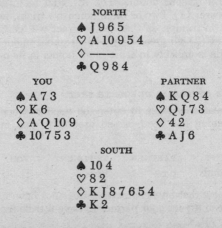

NORTH
♠J 9 6 5
♡A 10 9 5 4
◇——
♣Q 9 8 4

YOU
♠A 7 3
♡K 6
◇A Q 10 9
♣10 7 5 3

PARTNER
♠K Q 8 4
♡Q J 7 3
◇4 2
♣A J 6

SOUTH
♠10 4
♡8 2
◇K J 8 7 6 5 4
♣K 2

If you double, the auction will proceed:

SOUTH	YOU	NORTH	PARTNER
3 diamonds	double	pass	4 diamonds
pass	?		

Partner cue-bids, thinking vaguely of a possible slam contract in hearts or spades. And you start regretting your double, for now your side is headed for a substantial loss. However, had you *passed:*

SOUTH	YOU	NORTH	PARTNER
3 diamonds	pass	pass	double
pass	pass	pass	

Partner reopens with a takeout double, and you convert it into a penalty double by passing. When you are long in the enemy suit, partner will always take out a double, for he is short. But if you pass, partner is quite likely to reopen with a double—since he is short in the enemy suit, he has the right pattern for this action.

THE FISHBEIN CONVENTION

Most bridge players (correctly, in my opinion), use the double of an opening three-bid for takeout, giving partner the option of passing only when he has length in trumps. However, some experts prefer to treat the double as strictly for penalties. Then there is need for an artificial takeout bid. The most common of these devices is the Fishbein Convention—the use of the overcall in the *next higher suit* as a takeout double. Thus:

OPPONENT	YOU
3 clubs	3 *diamonds*

(or 3 *hearts* over 3 diamonds; 3 *spades* over 3 hearts; 4 *clubs* over 3 spades.)

All these overcalls are artificial (not promising great length in the suit bid) and forcing, if you have agreed to play Fishbein. Partner must take out with an unbid suit or "raise" your overcall. As usual, he gives preference to a major-suit takeout, and is careful to bid game when he has unexpected strength.

This convention is employed only in the direct position. A *reopening* double:

OPPONENT	PARTNER	OPPONENT	YOU
3 diamonds	pass	pass	*double*

is still for takeout. Therefore, a reopening overcall, even of 3 *hearts* in the auction above, is natural and nonforcing.

There are two popular variations of Fishbein. In one, the bid of 3 notrump is used for takeout—all suit overcalls are natural. In the other, the cheaper *minor* suit is used for takeout (3 *diamonds* over 3 clubs, 4 *clubs* over the other three-bids) and major-suit overcalls are natural. In each case, doubles are for penalties.

Obviously, it is most important to agree with partner which, if any, of these devices you are using. (In the absence of discussion, you should assume that all overcalls are natural, and that the double is for takeout.) If you wish to use an artificial takeout bid, I recommend the "cheaper minor"; major-suit and notrump overcalls are too valuable to give up. However, my advice is to use no conventional bids over enemy three-bids; and to use takeout (sometimes called "optional") doubles. True, it is delightful to be using one of these gadgets if your right-hand opponent opens 3 diamonds and you hold either of these hands:

(1) ♠ K Q 10 6   ♡ A J 10 4   ◇ ——   ♣ A Q 10 7 3
(2) ♠ K 6   ♡ A 7   ◇ K J 10 8 4   ♣ Q 7 5 3

You are in a position to make a decision for the partnership —using a takeout bid with example (1) and a penalty double with example (2). Most often, though, you will hold a hand like:

(3) ♠ K Q 10 6   ♡ A J 10 4   ◇ K 4   ♣ A 10 7

Now you have no idea whether to double for penalties or to use a takeout device. With the great majority of strong hands, you will want to solicit partner's opinion, and you can do this only if you play the "optional" takeout double. Partner will bid a major suit if he has one, but has the option of passing the double with length in trumps and poor offensive prospects.

OTHER ACTIONS OVER THREE-BIDS

We have seen that the takeout double of a three-bid strongly invites partner to respond in a major suit. Therefore, it is very dangerous to double when there is an unbid major for which you have little support. Suppose that your right-hand opponent opens 3 diamonds and you hold:

(a) ♠ K 4   ♡ A Q 10 8 6   ◊ A J 3   ♣ K 10 4
(b) ♠ K 4   ♡ K 10 4   ◊ A J 3   ♣ A Q 10 8 6

With neither hand is it comfortable to double, even though you have sufficient strength, since partner is likely to answer in spades—even to jump to 4 spades with a 4-card holding. You can overcall 3 hearts with example (a); the suit is a trifle short, but this action is reasonable. With example (b), you should overcall 3 *notrump*. Partner's expected 7 or 8 points, added to your 18, should give you a good play for this game contract. Actually, 3 notrump is very often the best spot to play a game when you have protection in the enemy suit. The opponent with the dangerous long suit is weak in high cards, and if you can hold off your stopper in his suit you will usually shut him out. In fact, it is probably correct to bid 3 notrump over 3 diamonds with both examples above.

Similarly, if your opponent opens 3 spades and you have:

♠ A Q 8 4   ♡ K 2   ◊ A Q J 2   ♣ K 7 3

the winning action is likely to be 3 notrump. A double is un-thinkable, for this is not for penalties—it begs partner to take out in hearts, the unbid major. If the opening were 3 *hearts*, the example above would be a fine double. You are well pre-pared for a spade response, and have no great desire to play in notrump with such tenuous protection in the enemy suit.

Obviously, the 3 notrump overcall is dangerous, for you can take a large penalty when partner does not have his share of the missing cards. Still, there is no safety in *any* action after an enemy preempt. You have to go with the odds, accepting an occasional disaster in order to achieve your best results in the long run.

The strongest action over an opponent's preemptive open-ing is the cue bid:

OPPONENT	YOU	OPPONENT	PARTNER
3 diamonds	*4 diamonds*		

This indicates that you would have opened with a two-bid had you had the chance. For this bid, you might hold:

♠ K Q J 8 7 4   ♡ A K Q 10 4   ◊ ——   ♣ A 6

Observe that it is wrong to bid 4 *spades* with this hand, and not only because spades might be the wrong suit. You are too *strong* merely to jump to game—remember, this says that you can make 10 tricks if partner has 6 or 7 points, not that you can make game opposite nothing. Thus you will miss a slam if partner has some strength, for he will pass.

In answer to your cue bid, partner will take out into an unbid suit when he is very weak. If he would have made a *positive* response to a two-bid, he jumps in his longest suit. Occasionally, he may even cue-bid himself:

OPPONENT	YOU	OPPONENT	PARTNER
3 diamonds	4 diamonds	pass	*5 diamonds*

This means that partner wants to go to slam, but has no idea *where;* you should bid your best suit in reply. There is a rare auction in which you repeat *your* cue bid:

OPPONENT	YOU	OPPONENT	PARTNER
3 diamonds	4 diamonds	pass	5 clubs
pass	*5 diamonds*		

This tells partner to take a choice between the two unbid suits. This might be your action with the spade-heart two-suiter in the earlier example. However, beware of multiple cue bids when playing with an inexperienced partner. He may suddenly decide that you want to play in diamonds—and it is most unpleasant to struggle in a 5 diamond contract with a void opposite two small trumps. It is less delicate but much safer to pick a suit yourself.

OVER OPENING FOUR- AND FIVE-BIDS

Obviously, it is even more difficult to handle enemy opening four-bids and five-bids than it is to cope with their three-bids. Most often, you will have to let yourself be shut out of the auction. Even when you have considerable high-card strength, you will probably have to settle for a small profit through doubling the opponents, for you have too little room to find a trump suit.

Of course, you can take a stab at a game contract if you have a powerful suit along with a good hand. For example, bid 4 spades over a 4 heart opening with:

♠ A Q J 9 6 4   ♡ 2   ◇ K J 8 3   ♣ A Q

You should bid 4 spades over 3 hearts, counting on partner for a few high cards, so you certainly will bid it over 4 hearts. Actually, you can bid a strong suit a little more freely over a game bid, since there is a chance that you are taking a good sacrifice. Thus, nonvulnerable against vulnerable opponents, bid 4 spades over 4 hearts with:

♠ K J 9 8 6 4 3   ♡ ——   ◇ K J 3   ♣ Q 5 4

The double of an opening four-bid or five-bid is still, in theory, for takeout. Therefore, you will double a 4 diamond opening with:

♠ A Q 6 4   ♡ K J 10 3   ◇ 2   ♣ A Q J 4

Observe that your side can probably make a major-suit game if partner has a smattering of high cards and some length in hearts or spades. However, because of the level at which you are doubling, you need great high-card strength (usually 16 points or more). For this reason, partner can safely pass for penalties even when very weak, counting on you for the tricks to defeat the contract. This will be his action unless he has a convenient major suit to bid, or unless he has freak distribution.

If you double 4 clubs or 4 diamonds, partner will take out only when holding a good-looking heart or spade suit; usually he will pass. If you double 4 *hearts,* partner is unlikely to take out unless he can happily bid 4 spades. And if you double 5 clubs or 5 diamonds, partner will leave the double in unless he has a wildly distributed hand. Thus, your double will turn out to be for penalties most of the time. However, you should not double merely because you are long in trumps —this is just the time that partner will have the pattern to take out. Your double should be based on high-card strength, so that you are safe whether partner bids or passes. For instance, if your right-hand opponent opens 5 clubs, and you hold:

(1) ♠ A K 6   ♡ A Q 10 7 4   ◇ K J 4   ♣ 7 2
(2) ♠ A 10 6 2   ♡ 7 3   ◇ Q 10 4   ♣ Q J 9 7

double with example (1), but not with example (2). You will almost certainly set 5 clubs with either hand, but it is too dangerous to double with the second. Partner is probably void in clubs and may become too excited to pass if he thinks that you have great strength. Take a sure profit and pass—you have not even given up the chance for a huge set, for *partner* may double if he has most of the missing honors.

One high preemptive opening bid is given different treatment—the opening bid of 4 spades. Here there is a ready-made takeout bid available. This is the overcall of 4 notrump, which uses up no bidding room. Therefore, if you bid 4 notrump, partner will respond at the five-level in his best suit. If you double 4 spades, this is strictly for penalties. Partner needs extremely freakish distribution to override your decision and take out into a suit.

This overcall of 4 notrump is used only over 4 *spades*. Over 4 hearts, it is the unusual notrump asking for a takeout in a minor suit.

CHAPTER 6

Sacrifice Bidding

There are many positions in bridge in which you should deliberately bid more than your side can make. You are willing to be doubled and set, since you will lose fewer points this way than by allowing the enemy to score game or slam.

Consider this deal:

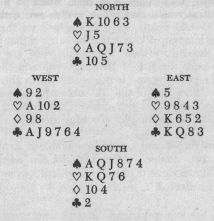

NORTH
♠ K 10 6 3
♡ J 5
◇ A Q J 7 3
♣ 10 5

WEST
♠ 9 2
♡ A 10 2
◇ 9 8
♣ A J 9 7 6 4

EAST
♠ 5
♡ 9 8 4 3
◇ K 6 5 2
♣ K Q 8 3

SOUTH
♠ A Q J 8 7 4
♡ K Q 7 6
◇ 10 4
♣ 2

North-South are vulnerable, East-West are not; what is par for each side? North-South can take 10 tricks at spades, so their best result is to bid and make 4 spades. East-West can take 9 tricks at clubs, so their best result would be to buy the contract for 3 clubs. However, this is surely impossible: South opens 1 spade, West overcalls 2 clubs, North jumps to 3 spades, forcing to game. East cannot buy the hand with even a 4 club bid, down only one for a good result, since opener will go on to 4 spades.

Now, though, East or West can **sacrifice** at 5 clubs. If this is doubled, it will be set two tricks for 300 points, not nearly as costly a score as allowing the vulnerable opponents to make game. And perhaps North-South will be pushed to 5 spades and go down. Thus, best bidding on both sides will produce 300 points for North-South. They will score more than twice this many points if allowed to play in 4 spades; East-West could lose much less (or even show a profit) if allowed to play 3 or 4 clubs, or if North-South go to 5 spades. All this is easy to see when looking at four hands, but each player's decision in reaching the par result may be difficult.

• WHETHER TO SACRIFICE

The decision to sacrifice is based on three factors: (1) the vulnerability conditions, (2) your offensive strength, (3) your defensive strength. Vulnerability is actually not so important as it might appear on the surface. When the opponents are vulnerable and you are not, a sacrifice against a game contract looks attractive: if they make, say, 4 hearts, they score 120 plus 700—820 points; even if you are set three tricks doubled, you lose only 500 points. The catch is that after you have given the enemy their 500 points, they are still vulnerable; the odds are 3 to 1 that they will win the rubber anyway. This *second* game is not really worth the full 820 points scored, since half of the 700 rubber bonus was earned previously by making the *first* game. Thus, a game bid and made is worth 350 points plus the trick score, or about 500 points in all.

This means that if you are not vulnerable it is preferable to go down two doubled rather than let the enemy make game, while down three doubled is neither a loss nor a gain. And this is unaffected, in rubber bridge, by the *opponents'* vulnerability.

When *you* are vulnerable and the opponents are not, down two doubled costs you 500 points, which is no bargain. With these vulnerability conditions, a sacrifice bid is rare. However, if *both sides* are vulnerable, the rubber game is worth about 650 points (500 bonus plus trick score) so a two-trick set is again preferable to an enemy game.

If you and partner have a trump fit, a combined count of 21–22 points should let you take 8 tricks, for a profitable sacrifice at the four-level; 23–24 points should produce 9 tricks and a good five-level sacrifice. Consider the East hand in our earlier example:

♠ 5 ♡ 9 8 4 3 ◇ K 6 5 2 ♣ K Q 8 3

When partner overcalls 2 clubs, this hand is worth 10 points. Partner's hand probably has a value of at least 13 or 14 points for play at clubs (10 or 11 for his overcall, plus an extra 2 or 3 points once a fit is found). The combined hands should count to somewhere between 23 and 26 points, for a one-trick or two-trick set at the five-level. Thus, a 5 club sacrifice should cost less than the value of an enemy game.

However, it will cost less only if the opponents can *make* their game contract. Therefore, you must assess your side's defensive, as well as offensive, strength. After all, when your hands are worth 9 tricks on offense, they may win 4 tricks on defense. You must consider the *nature* of your points. High-card points in side suits or in the enemy suit are usually just as good on defense as on offense. In contrast, high cards in your own long suit are probably worthless in defense. So are side long suits, and voids or singletons. Values like these suggest sacrifice bidding. Let us look again at the East-West hands of our first example:

WEST	EAST
♠ 9 2	♠ 5
♡ A 10 2	♡ 9 8 4 3
◇ 9 8	◇ K 6 5 2
♣ A J 9 7 6 4	♣ K Q 8 3

The West hand above should not consider a 5 club sacrifice even after East raises the suit. West has 13 points for offense —a reasonably strong count. However, 8 of these points—the two aces—are just as good on defense. If East has a smattering of high cards in the unbid suits, an enemy game will be defeated.

In contrast, East has the sort of points which suggest a sacrifice. His 5 points in clubs are wasted on defense; his singleton spade is hardly an asset if spades are trumps. Since 7 of his 10 points are useful only on offense, *East* should diagnose the 5 club sacrifice against the opposing 4 spade game. In fact, the auction should go:

SOUTH	WEST	NORTH	EAST
1 spade	2 clubs	3 spades	5 clubs

Notice East's jump to 5 clubs at his first turn to bid. Since he intends to sacrifice against a game contract, he does so *immediately*. This has the advantage of preventing any further enemy exchange of information, and may even stampede inexperienced opponents into going to five of their suit. It would be less effective, although not wrong, for East to pass over 3 spades and then to sacrifice when South bid 4 spades. However, it would be an error for East to bid 4 clubs over 3 spades. This action helps the opponents (South can now pass if he wants to), and misleads partner. It describes a hand like:

♠ J84   ♡ Q943   ◇ KQ   ♣ Q 10 6 3

With the hand above, East would *not* want to sacrifice against a 4 spade contract, since he has too much defensive strength. However, he should raise partner's overcall so that *West* can sacrifice if his strength is entirely offensive.

Suppose that the auction goes:

OPPONENT	PARTNER	OPPONENT	YOU
1 club	1 spade	2 hearts	?

What would be your action with these sample hands?

   (a) ♠ Q 10 8 6 3   ♡ 4   ◇ K J 8 7 4   ♣ 5 3
   (b) ♠ Q 10 6   ♡ 4 2   ◇ A Q J 2   ♣ 8 5 3 2
   (c) ♠ Q 10 6   ♡ Q J 10 7   ◇ K J 3   ♣ Q J 10

   (a) Jump to 4 spades. You intend to sacrifice against an enemy contract, so do it right away.
   (b) Bid 2 spades. This will enable partner to sacrifice if he has a long suit, good distribution, and little defensive strength.
   (c) Pass. You have no intention of sacrificing, and certainly should not encourage partner to sacrifice when your hand is so powerful defensively, and so weak offensively.

• WHEN YOUR SIDE OPENS WITH A THREE-BID

Sacrifice bidding is much less common when *your* side has made the opening bid. Unlike an overcall, which is limited in high cards but promises strong distribution, an opening bid usually contains considerable defensive strength. Thus, opener's partner can never be confident that the opponents can make game. It is up to the opening bidder himself to sacrifice if he has a strictly offensive hand.

Exactly the opposite is true, however, when the opening is preemptive. An auction like this one:

OPENER	OPPONENT	RESPONDER	OPPONENT
3 spades	4 hearts	pass	pass
4 spades			

is an abomination. Opener announced with his three-bid that he had the right sort of hand for a sacrifice—a long suit with little defense. For the rest of the auction, no matter how it develops, all action must be taken by *responder*. Opener, in effect, is barred from the bidding; he has no idea what partner's hand is, while responder knows exactly what opener has.

Of course, the corollary is that *you* must be very alert to diagnose a sacrifice when your *partner* opens with a three-bid. If the auction goes:

PARTNER	OPPONENT	YOU	OPPONENT
3 spades	double	pass	4 hearts
pass	pass	?	

and your hand is:

♠ J 6 3   ♡ 10 7 4   ◇ A Q J 7 4   ♣ 6 2

you should sacrifice at 4 spades. Your distribution is not particularly strong for offense, but partner's is, and there is no prospect of defeating the enemy game, for partner can take at most 1 defensive trick and you are most unlikely to win more than 2. In fact, you should have bid 4 spades *right over the double*. When you are going to sacrifice eventually, it is most effective to do so as soon as possible, cutting away the enemy bidding room. With the hand above, you should bid 4 spades at your first turn even if your opponent passes over partner's three-bid. This sort of **anticipatory sacrifice** can be a deadly weapon, for the opponents cannot be sure that you are sacrificing. If their strength is divided evenly, you may escape without a double, down two for a 100-point penalty when the enemy can make game.

This principle of taking your sacrifice as early as possible can result in a spectacular-sounding auction like this one:

PARTNER	OPPONENT	YOU	OPPONENT
3 hearts	3 spades	*5 hearts*	

For the bid above, you might hold:

♠ 3   ♡ Q 8 5   ◇ A K 10 8 4   ♣ 10 7 5 3

You can tell from your hand that the opponents are going to bid 4 spades and make it. Since you have no intention of letting them buy the contract so cheaply, you should sacrifice immediately. This will surely give your left-hand opponent a nasty problem. He is certain to hold a fairly strong hand with spade support for his partner, and he has to guess whether to show it at the five-level. If he does, you may well defeat 5 spades (and I have seen opponents crowded into *slam* contracts by bids like this), earning a plus score on a losing hand.

The theory of sacrificing after a three-bid—that the *partner* of the bidder must do all sacrificing, and that he should bid right away as high as he is willing to go—applies to nearly all other preemptive bids as well. That is, if your partner has made a weak jump overcall, or a double jump overcall, or an unusual notrump overcall, he is not expected to bid again; *you* must do the sacrificing. For example, suppose you hold:

♠ 83   ♡ 108643   ◇ K 2   ♣ Q 1095

The auction proceeds:

OPPONENT	YOU	OPPONENT	PARTNER
1 spade	pass	3 spades	3 notrump
double	?		

Partner has used the unusual notrump, presumably in order to suggest a minor-suit sacrifice. You should comply with the suggestion, for you have magnificent support for one minor and a useful honor in the other. Therefore, sacrifice *right away* by jumping to 5 clubs. Similarly, holding:

♠ A 1084   ♡ 42   ◇ K 10974   ♣ 75

Your left-hand opponent opens 1 club, partner jumps to 2 spades (weak), right-hand opponent bids 3 hearts. Jump to 4 spades, sacrificing immediately. A 3 spade bid is a waste of breath, and if you sacrifice at 4 spades later, the opponents will have exchanged more information and will know what to do. The "premature" sacrifice forces them to guess in the dark.

• SACRIFICING AGAINST A SLAM

The most profitable occasion for a sacrifice bid occurs when the opponents have bid a makeable slam. A nonvulnerable slam is worth approximately 1000 points; a vulnerable slam may be worth 1500 points. Thus, you no longer have to worry about going down only two tricks. It is a triumph to take a penalty of 700 points when the enemy were about to make a vulnerable slam. True, a succession of triumphs like this will send you to the poorhouse. Still, you have saved a huge number of points—and if you sacrifice against your opponents' slams and they let you play yours unmolested, you will be a big winner in the long run.

The crucial consideration is whether the opponents can actually make the slam that they have bid. If they can, it is almost impossible for your side to lose too much by sacrificing in a suit in which you have found a fit. Therefore, if the enemy auction takes a slammish turn (an opening two-bid facing a positive response; a jump-shift response to an opening one-bid, etc.) try to get into the auction, particularly if nonvulnerable, in order to investigate a sacrifice.

However, it is embarrassing to take a "phantom" sacrifice against a slam which was not going to make; what is worse, it is expensive. And if you sacrifice whenever the opponents bid slams, they may count on it and reach reckless contracts relying on you to sacrifice. Therefore, it is best to let the opponents play their six-bids, even though your side has found a fit, if you can win 1 trick on defense. If partner cannot win a defensive trick, it is up to *him* to sacrifice.

Let me illustrate many of the principles discussed so far in this section with a wild hand from actual play:

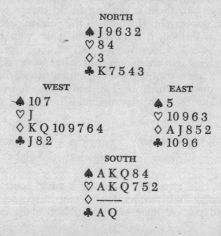

```
                    NORTH
                 ♠ J 9 6 3 2
                 ♡ 8 4
                 ◇ 3
                 ♣ K 7 5 4 3

    WEST                          EAST
 ♠ 10 7                        ♠ 5
 ♡ J                           ♡ 10 9 6 3
 ◇ K Q 10 9 7 6 4             ◇ A J 8 5 2
 ♣ J 8 2                       ♣ 10 9 6

                    SOUTH
                 ♠ A K Q 8 4
                 ♡ A K Q 7 5 2
                 ◇ ——
                 ♣ A Q
```

West was dealer, nonvulnerable against vulnerable opponents, and opened 3 diamonds. If East had passed, South would have cue-bid 4 diamonds. When North responded in spades, South would probably jump to 7; if he bid only six and East then sacrificed at 7 diamonds, South would likely have bid 7 now. Even if East had jumped to 5 diamonds at his first turn, it would have done him no good. South would have cue-bid 6 *diamonds,* and the same auction would have followed.

However, when I held the South hand, the auction went:

WEST	NORTH	EAST	ME
3 diamonds	pass	7 *diamonds*	?

East decided, correctly, that he could not defeat a slam, and so sacrificed immediately. There I was with one of the best hands I ever held, and the auction was up to the seven-level before it was my turn to bid. Probably I should have doubled and taken a profit, but I knew I was being robbed and I just could not stand it. So I bid 7 hearts—down one, when I could have scored some 2400 points in spades.

• WHEN THE OPPONENTS SACRIFICE

You may conclude, after the last example, that I am not the one to tell you how to handle enemy sacrifice bidding. Still, when the opponents bounce into a high contract before you have ever bid, there is nothing to do except to guess, and hope you guess right. However, if the auction proceeds in a more normal fashion, it is possible to make your decision on a logical basis.

The underlying assumption is that when your side wins the hand for a game contract and the opponents sacrifice, you will always double them or bid one more yourself—you will never allow them to play undoubled. That is, suppose that the auction goes:

YOU	OPPONENT	PARTNER	OPPONENT
1 spade	2 clubs	3 spades	5 clubs

Clearly, your side owns this hand for a game contract—you have an opening bid, partner has a jump response. Therefore, you and partner must either double 5 clubs or bid 5 spades. On the auction above, you have three choices: you can bid 5 spades, you can double 5 clubs, you can pass and leave the decision to partner. Let us examine all three actions.

If you bid 5 spades, you must have a strong *offensive* hand. Either you are sure that you can take 11 tricks because you have substantial extra values, or you have so little defense that you are worried that 5 clubs might actually be made. You might hold:

(1) ♠ A K J 9 7 4   ♡ K Q 10 7   ◇ 8 7   ♣ 2
(2) ♠ K Q J 8 6 5   ♡ 7 3   ◇ K J 10 8 4   ♣ ——

With example (1), you are confident of making 5 spades (even a slam is not impossible; you would cue-bid if you held a side ace), and so are unwilling to accept a small penalty in exchange for your game. With example (2), you are by no means sure of holding your losers to two, but you have such poor prospects for defense that the risk of going to five is less than that of allowing the enemy to buy the contract. Notice two features which these examples have in common: very powerful *offensive* distribution (a long, strong trump suit, uneven shape), extreme shortness (a singleton or void) in the enemy suit.

Contrast the preceding examples with the next two, with which you should *double* a sacrifice bid of 5 clubs on the same auction:

(3) ♠ A 10 7 6 4   ♡ A Q 5   ◇ J 8 4   ♣ Q 4
(4) ♠ K J 8 7 5   ♡ 4   ◇ A Q 10 6   ♣ K Q J

Here you can see the two reasons for an immediate double of an enemy sacrifice. Example (3) presents almost no prospect for making 11 tricks; you may not defeat 5 clubs by many tricks, but you must take what points you can. A five-level contract of your own cannot be contemplated when you have such flat distribution and such a minimum of high cards. Example (4) is no minimum—your side might easily make 5 spades. However, this hand is so strong defensively that you should do better with the double. Your club holding is crucial here—partner surely has only a singleton at most, so your K Q J are practically wasted for offense (the ace would be preferable); but you will win two trump tricks on defense. Partner should respect your penalty double and pass, unless he holds extremely freakish distribution with a void in the enemy suit.

• THE FORCING PASS

Often, you will hold a hand which fits into neither category. It is not so strong offensively or so weak defensively that you must bid on in your suit; nor is it so weak offensively or strong defensively that you must double. Here, you *pass*.

YOU	OPPONENT	PARTNER	OPPONENT
1 spade	2 clubs	3 spades	5 clubs
pass			

This is called the **forcing pass**. You and partner are committed to doubling 5 clubs or bidding 5 spades. If you choose to do neither, partner must do one or the other. Hence, your pass is forcing; partner is not allowed to pass also. The pass in this position is moderately strong action. It invites partner to bid at the five-level, so you must not have a flat-looking minimum. Two typical hands for the preceding auction would be:

(5) ♠ A Q 10 8 4   ♡ A J 7 3   ◊ K 3   ♣ 8 4
(6) ♠ A Q 10 5 3   ♡ 6   ◊ Q J 7 6   ♣ A 10 4

Note that these examples are strong enough, either in distribution or in high cards, to make an 11-trick contract reasonable. However, each one has substantial defensive prospects as well. If partner's jump raise was based largely on distributional values, which are useless on defense, he will go on to 5 spades. If he has high-card strength, he will double. Contrast these hands:

(a) ♠ K J 8 7 3   ♡ 8 4   ◊ A 10 9 8 3   ♣ 5
(b) ♠ K J 8 7   ♡ K 10 4   ◊ A 9 8 3   ♣ Q 5

With example (a), partner will bid 5 spades if you pass, for his values are distributional. With example (b), partner will double, for he has high cards which will be just as useful on defense as on offense.

The first example in this chapter presents a good illustration of this type of decision. The auction should probably go:

OPENER	RESPONDER
♠ A Q J 8 7 4	♠ K 10 6 3
♡ K Q 7 6	♡ J 5
◇ 10 4	◇ A Q J 7 3
♣ 2	♣ 10 5

OPENER	OPPONENT	RESPONDER	OPPONENT
1 spade	2 clubs	3 spades	5 clubs
pass	pass	*double*	

Observe opener's pass and responder's double. Opener has good offensive distribution, and so cannot even consider doubling himself. However, with a bare minimum in high cards and respectable defensive strength, he should not bid 5 spades (as he would if his heart king were the ace). Thus, he compromises with a forcing pass. Responder's decision is also close, but since he has a great deal of his count in high cards, and since he is not at all happy about contracting for 11 tricks, he doubles. If his queen of diamonds were the king, he might well bid 5 spades, for then he could confidently expect to make this contract once partner encouraged with a pass.

The forcing pass is, of course, used in the same fashion when the opponents sacrifice against a *slam* contract. That is, on this auction:

OPENER	OPPONENT	RESPONDER	OPPONENT
1 spade	3 clubs	3 hearts	5 clubs
6 hearts	pass	pass	7 clubs
pass			

opener is inviting responder to bid a grand slam if he has maximum values. In order to do this, opener *must* have first-round control—the ace or a void—in the enemy suit. On the auction above, opener is forced to double 7 clubs if he holds, say, a singleton small club. And even with the club ace he should double unless he himself holds a tiptop maximum for his earlier bidding. The higher the level at which the opponents sacrifice, the stronger must you be to use the forcing pass.

If *your* side has taken a sacrifice against an enemy game contract, there is no such thing as a forcing pass after the opponents bid on. Suppose you hold:

♠ A J 10 8 7 4   ♡ 2   ◇ Q J 9 7   ♣ Q 4

The auction goes:

OPPONENT	YOU	OPPONENT	PARTNER
1 club	1 spade	2 hearts	2 spades
4 hearts	4 spades	5 hearts	pass
pass	?		

You should *pass*. Partner's pass over 5 hearts is in no way forcing, since the hand clearly belongs to the enemy and your side is merely sacrificing. (Had your opponent passed over your 4 spade sacrifice, that *would* have been forcing on the opening bidder since *their* side owns the hand.) As a general policy, when your sacrifice has pushed the opponents to five of a major suit you should let them play there undisturbed. They get no extra bonus for making a five-bid, and they may well go down.

• FREAK HANDS

Finally, there is a rare, but extremely important, type of auction in which it is not clear which side owns the hand and which side is sacrificing. Both sides have a fit, and the distribution is freakish. The golden rule here is to bid one more yourself, to buy the contract rather than let the enemy play. For example suppose you hold:

♠ A Q 9 7 5 3   ♡ 8 4   ◇ K Q 10 5 3   ♣ ——

The auction goes, with both sides vulnerable:

YOU	OPPONENT	PARTNER	OPPONENT
1 spade	double	4 spades	5 hearts
5 spades	6 hearts	pass	pass
?			

Bid 6 spades. You can have no idea whether you can make the contract—probably you cannot; and there is no way to tell if the enemy can make 6 hearts—the chances are that they cannot. But if both slam contracts are down one, you have

lost only a few hundred points by bidding on, while it will
cost you somewhere from 1000 to 3000 points if you let
them play the hand when one or both contracts can be made.
So important is this kind of "insurance policy" that I would
probably bid 7 spades if the opponents went to 7 hearts.
The whole hand could be:

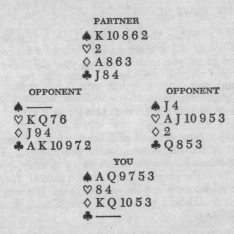

PARTNER
♠ K 10 8 6 2
♡ 2
◇ A 8 6 3
♣ J 8 4

OPPONENT
♠ ——
♡ K Q 7 6
◇ J 9 4
♣ A K 10 9 7 2

OPPONENT
♠ J 4
♡ A J 10 9 5 3
◇ 2
♣ Q 8 5 3

YOU
♠ A Q 9 7 5 3
♡ 8 4
◇ K Q 10 5 3
♣ ——

Here, you can make 7 spades against the likely club lead;
the opponents can make 7 hearts if you lead spades. I would
rather be in the position to make a grand slam if the opponent goes wrong than in that of trying to guess the right
lead in order to score 100 points, with more than 2000 points
to lose if I go wrong.

These wild, freak hands do not occur often, but there are
huge numbers of points at stake when they do. Winning
bridge players have a simple policy for these hands—get to
be declarer. Then your losses will be in pennies and your
profits in dollars.

CHAPTER 7

Part-Score Bidding

● ENEMY PART SCORES

When the opponents have a part score, particularly one of 40 or more so that two of a major suit will give them game, you must loosen up your defensive bidding. This is true of both doubles and overcalls. For instance, a hand like:

♠ 84   ♡ K Q 8 6 2   ♢ Q 10 8 3   ♣ K 4

is normally a poor overcall of 2 hearts after a 1 spade opening. That is, the risk outweighs the possible gain. However, if the opponents have a part score of 40 or more, you should overcall. Now the possible gain is much greater, for you may push the enemy to 3 spades and set them. Without the part score, this would be a paltry gain; now it saves game. Likewise, this hand:

♠ 10 8 4   ♡ K J 3   ♢ A Q 10 3   ♣ Q 9 2

is not a normal takeout double of a 1 spade opening. However, the chance of gain is so great when the opponents are on score that you should take this action. As a guide, reduce the point requirement for a double or an overcall by about a queen; reduce the suit requirement for a *two*-level overcall to that for a *one*-level overcall.

Partner must make some allowance for the fact that you have to enter the auction a little less cautiously. With a hand like:

♠ A 75   ♡ A 10 5 4   ♢ K 9 2   ♣ J 7 3

he would normally tend to commit your side to game if you either doubled a 1 spade opening, or overcalled 2 hearts. In a part-score situation, he should give you leeway—bidding 3 hearts on either auction. When you have a normal double or overcall, you should carry on to game, while you would pass if you have shaded your bid in order to compete. Actually, if you have a normal double or overcall you should try to bid twice even if partner does not act. For example, with:

♠ 3   ♡ K Q J 9 7 4   ◊ A 9 7 3   ♣ 10 5

if the auction goes:

OPPONENT	YOU	OPPONENT	PARTNER
1 spade	2 hearts	2 spades	pass
pass	?		

rebid 3 hearts when the opponents are on score. Partner may have been reluctant to compete for fear that your suit was ragged. Likewise, with:

♠ 3   ♡ A 10 9 3   ◊ K Q 10 4   ♣ K J 9 6

on this auction:

OPPONENT	YOU	OPPONENT	PARTNER
1 spade	double	2 spades	pass
pass	?		

double again. Partner was probably unwilling to respond at the three-level for fear that you had doubled merely because of the enemy partial.

Be sure, however, that you do *not* bid again at your next turn if your first action was predicated on the score. For example, suppose that you have doubled a 1 club opening (the enemy have a 40 partial) holding:

♠ A 10 8 4   ♡ Q 8 6 3   ◊ A J 5   ♣ J 2

The auction proceeds:

OPPONENT	YOU	OPPONENT	PARTNER
1 club	double	2 clubs	2 hearts
3 clubs	?		

It is tempting to bid 3 hearts. But you must *pass*. If you bid here, it means that you are trying for game with a sound double, not protecting against the enemy partial. Remember, partner knows as well as you that 3 clubs gives the opponents game. With any sort of reasonable hand, *he* will bid again. Generally speaking, the burden of protecting against the part score falls on the player whose pass will end the auction. If you act when partner would have another chance to bid anyway, you show extra values; but you promise nothing much extra if you act in the passout position. Thus, if the auction had gone:

OPPONENT	YOU	OPPONENT	PARTNER
1 club	double	2 clubs	2 hearts
pass	pass	3 clubs	pass
pass	?		

it would be proper for you to bid 3 hearts even after your subminimum double. Partner knows that you are not trying for game once you pass him in 2 hearts.

Another reason for indicating to partner (and he to you) whether you are bidding with sound values or merely competing, is that you both must know when to double the opponents. Quite often, an enemy part score helps *you* to collect a sizable penalty. Partly, this is because the opponents may be tempted to overbid when game is so easy to make. And partly it is true because it is now much less dangerous for you to double a part-score contract. Since you are no longer doubling them into game, it will not be very expensive even should they make their contract. However, a double *can* be disastrous if the opponents are able to redouble or make overtricks. And this can happen if you compete too vigorously in the **direct position**, as opposed to the **passout position**, leading partner to expect many more high cards than you actually hold. Get into the auction freely, but when you have entered light, pass at your next turn to warn partner against taking drastic action.

The same general principles apply when your side has opened the bidding and the opponents, who are on score, compete. Any action taken *when partner has another chance to bid* promises normal sound values. In contrast, bids made when a pass would end the auction show nothing extra, but are protection against the enemy partial. For instance:

YOU	OPPONENT	PARTNER	OPPONENT
1 spade	2 hearts	3 *clubs*	

Partner's 3 club bid shows a strong hand, a lively interest in game. Two hearts puts the opponents out, but partner need not bid for this reason—you are still at the table and will protect. The corollary is that in this sequence:

YOU	OPPONENT	PARTNER	OPPONENT
1 spade	2 hearts	pass	pass
2 *spades*			

you promise no extra strength or interest in game, for you are protecting in the passout position.

Are you interested in game on this auction?

YOU	OPPONENT	PARTNER	OPPONENT
1 heart	2 diamonds	2 hearts	3 diamonds
3 *hearts*			

You should be, yes. There is no need for you to bid, since partner has another chance. Therefore, partner should go on to game with a maximum raise. In contrast, if you pass over 3 diamonds and partner reopens by bidding 3 hearts, he is *not* looking for game—he is protecting, and may have a minimum.

Finally, a word of advice about opening the bidding when the opponents have a partial: except in fourth seat, *lighten your requirements slightly*, just as you do for doubles and overcalls. This is because you are going to enter the auction anyway, and an opening bid works out to be safer than an overcall. For example, holding:

♠ A K 8 5 3   ♡ 8 4   ◇ 6 2   ♣ K J 9 4

open 1 spade. If you pass, you will probably have to overcall 2 spades later, and you are in much greater jeopardy. Vulnerability does not affect this opening. Actually, I would prefer to be *nonvulnerable* if I passed this hand (of course, I would not), since a later *vulnerable* overcall would produce too heavy a strain on my heart.

● **YOUR OWN PART SCORE**

OPENING THE BIDDING

Strangely, you should *not* open light when your side has the part score. True, you can make game with a two-level contract if you have a 40 partial. However, unless you are playing against rabbits, you will never buy the contract that cheap. You have a far better chance to buy the hand at the two-level when you do *not* have a partial; when you have one, you will be pushed to three or four. What is more, a competitive auction is more likely to come to a violent climax —partner doubling the opponents, or they doubling you. So you open only with the normal strength; if anything, you should tend to pass any doubtful hand.

Whether you open, then, is not much affected by your own part score, but *what* you bid often is—particularly when you have a partial of 60 or more. There are two related reasons for the changes: (1) Any suit you bid is a serious, not a tentative, suggestion of a trump; this is just as true of minor suits as of majors, since it is now as easy to make game in clubs as it is in spades. (2) You no longer have to worry about your rebid, since you can pass a new suit response which fills the part score. Thus, if you hold:

♠ A K J 5   ♡ 8 7 4   ◇ 10 8 6   ♣ A Q 7

you should normally open 1 club, but with a 60 part score you should bid 1 spade instead. It is no longer *safe* to bid a 3-card club suit, for partner will not be so anxious to find another suit. It is no longer *necessary* to bid a short club, since you now have an entirely satisfactory rebid over a 2 diamond or a 2 heart response—you will pass. Similarly, holding:

♠ Q 8 4   ♡ K Q 10 3   ◇ A 3   ♣ K 8 5 3

open 1 *heart*, not 1 club, with a big part score. There is no need to prepare a rebid, for you will pass a 2 diamond response. The club suit is no longer biddable—to open in *any* 4-card suit, when you have a big partial, you require two of the four top honors (just as you do normally for the major suits). A side advantage of opening the last two examples in a major suit is that it makes it harder for the enemy to compete. Obviously, they can more readily enter the auction over 1 club than over 1 heart or 1 spade.

Still, you cannot open in a *weak* 4-card major simply because you are on score. Partner is even more likely to raise with 3-card support, so you must have two honors. What should you open, then, if you have a 60 partial and deal yourself a hand like this one?

♠ Q 8 4 3   ♡ K 4   ◇ A K J   ♣ J 10 7 5

No suit is long or srong enough to bid, so you open with 1 *notrump*. This does not promise 16 to 18 points now. It can be any strength—as little as 13, as much as 20—in a balanced hand. Remember, partner no longer needs to know your point count to determine whether to go to game; 1 notrump *is* game. He can pass with even distribution, or take out into any long suit, and you will be in a reasonable contract. Of course, if the opponents compete you will bid again when you hold a powerful hand, and pass if you have a minimum count. Actually, 1 notrump is a most convenient opening when you have a big partial; it makes the auction easy for your side while making it very hard for the enemy to compete.

RESPONDING

Responding to partner's opening bid is likewise affected when you have a partial. The main difference is that your response shows *where* you want to play without much regard for *how high*. You should not bid weak suits, but you can suggest a long strong suit regardless of point count. Consider your response with these two hands after partner opens 1 heart:

(a) ♠ Q 8 4   ♡ 7 2   ◇ K 8 7 4   ♣ A Q 4 3
(b) ♠ 8 4   ♡ 7 2   ◇ K 8 4   ♣ Q J 9 8 4 3

Normally, you would respond 2 clubs with (a), and 1 notrump with (b). That is, your first duty is to let partner know that you have a strong hand by going to the two-level with (a), or warn him of a minimum by staying at the one-level with (b). However, your bids are reversed when you have a 60 partial: you respond 1 notrump with (a) and 2 clubs with (b). It is not nearly so important to show your point count, since any contract is a game; and you must make an immediate suggestion of where to play, since any response may, and likely will, be passed. Note that your responses are very natural when you have a partial—you want to play 1 notrump with (a) and 2 clubs with (b), so that is what you bid.

Never bid a 4-card suit at the two-level, and be very cautious in bidding one even at the one-level. That is, if partner opens 1 club and you hold:

♠ J 8 4 3   ♡ 6 4 2   ◇ A J 3   ♣ K Q 5

do not bid 1 spade, as you normally would. Raise to 2 clubs. Observe that you can give a single raise with 11 points. Your responses no longer show your point count, they indicate a reasonable spot in which to play the hand.

SLAM BIDDING

Slam bidding is both helped and hindered by your own part score. The fact that the auction may end at any moment, the minute the contract is enough for game, can cost you a slam bonus. For this reason, the most slammish bids—opening two-bids and jump-shift responses—must still be *forcing*, even though they fill the part score. For example, if you hold:

     ♠ 7 4   ♡ J 6 3   ◊ 10 8 6 3   ♣ 9 7 5 2

and partner opens 2 spades when you are 40 on score, respond 2 notrump. After all, partner may have been dealt:

     ♠ A K J 6 5 2   ♡ A   ◊ A K Q J 2   ♣ 4

He can bid 6 diamonds at his next turn, and reach a good slam. Likewise, if you have opened 1 spade with:

     ♠ A Q 7 4 3   ♡ 4 2   ◊ K J 3   ♣ K 6 4

and partner jumps to 3 hearts, rebid 3 notrump even though 3 hearts is enough for game. Partner must be given some way to investigate slam without risking a pass.

Since two-bids and jump shifts are still forcing, they should not be shaded. If you are 40 on score, it is tempting to open 2 spades with:

     ♠ A K Q J 4 2   ♡ A 3   ◊ A 6 4   ♣ J 5

After all, you can make 2 spades all by yourself: what if partner passes one? However, you must open only *1* spade, for three reasons. First, the danger of getting to a poor slam is too great, for partner will expect greater strength. Second, partner will strain to make a response when you are on score; he will bid if he has any card which might take a trick, passing only with a complete bust. Third, if partner *does* pass 1 spade, you are better off than if you had opened 2, for then you would get to at least *3* spades and go down.

The same reasoning applies to the jump-shift response. It is wrong to bid 3 hearts over 1 spade with:

     (c) ♠ 7 4   ♡ A Q J 10 8 3   ◊ A J 5   ♣ 8 2

True, with a partial you would respond 2 hearts with much less high-card strength:

(d) ♠ 7 4   ♡ Q J 10 8 4 2   ◇ K 10 5   ♣ 8 2

However, bidding 2 hearts with a moderately strong hand does not give up on slam, even when you are on score. If partner has a strong opening bid with a fit for hearts, for example:

♠ A K 10 8 3   ♡ K 9 5   ◇ Q 3   ♣ A Q 6

he will bid 3 hearts over two. This is a mild slam try, for it is a bid over game. If you hold hand (c) above, you will then move toward slam, while if you have a doubtful response like (d), you will pass.

It is by giving you these easy, cheap slam tries—bidding more than you need for game—that a part-score actually helps slam bidding. With a 60 partial, these are slam tries:

OPENER	RESPONDER
1 notrump	2 *notrump*
1 diamond	1 spade
2 spades	3 *spades*

In each auction above, opener's strength is largely unknown. He has simply bid game in what looks to him like the best spot. Responder has an opening bid or better of his own, and makes a tentative try for slam. Opener will pass with a minimum hand, and the partnership is at a safe level; opener, with a strong hand, will bid on toward slam.

There are two auctions in which a bid over score is *not* a slam suggestion. These are responder's single or jump raises of opener's suit:

OPENER	RESPONDER
1 spade	2 spades
1 spade	3 spades

Even if your side has a 70 partial, both responses above show the normal value—6 points or more for the single raise, 13 points or more for the jump raise. Thus, if you hold:

♠ K 10 7 3   ♡ 8 4   ◇ K J 7 3   ♣ 8 5 2

raise 1 spade to 2 no matter what the score is. If you pass 1 spade, you will not buy the contract there. All you do is make it easy for the opponents to compete.

AGAINST COMPETITION

When you are on score, you must expect vigorous enemy competition. Do not let them steal from you. If your side owns the hand (that is, has substantially more than half the high cards) bid up as high as you are willing to go. Then if the opponents bid higher, double them. For example, suppose you hold:

♠ A 10 6 3   ♡ K J 9 4   ◇ J 10 3   ♣ 8 6

The auction goes:

PARTNER	OPPONENT	YOU	OPPONENT
1 spade	2 clubs	2 spades	3 clubs
pass	pass	3 spades	pass
pass	4 clubs	?	

Double. This is your side's hand, for you have 9 high-card points opposite partner's opening bid. Probably you cannot make 4 spades, since partner showed a minimum by passing over 3 clubs. Thus, although you allowed yourself to be pushed to the three-level, you should go no higher. Make the enemy pay for the privilege of robbing you—this is akin to the situation in which they have sacrificed against a game.

Once in a long while, the opponents will have freakish enough distribution to make their contract, but you must accept this gracefully. They are usually overbidding to protect against your partial, and they will not be so gay on the next hand if you sting them for 300 or 500 on this one.

CHAPTER 8

"Balancing" Bids

• WHEN AN ENEMY ONE-BID IS PASSED

There are two types of auctions in which you should be a little more free than usual to compete with the opponents, even when they do not have a partial. The most common of these occurs when an opening suit bid is passed by responder:

OPPONENT	PARTNER	OPPONENT	YOU
1 heart	pass	pass	?

Here the odds are very great that your side can make more than the enemy. And this is true even when your own hand is fairly weak. Suppose, on the auction above, you hold:

♠ Q 10 7 4 3   ♡ 2   ♢ A 8 7 3   ♣ 10 6 4

You should reopen the auction by overcalling 1 spade, counting on partner to hold considerable strength. Why must partner be strong? Because there are 40 high-card points in the deck, and they must be somewhere. Assume that opener has an above-average count of 15; responder, who passed, has perhaps 3 or 4; you have 6 high-card points. This means that partner probably has close to 15 points—almost surely as much as 13, perhaps 16 or 17. Why, then, did he pass over 1 heart? Because he had length in hearts and no good suit of his own. The whole deal might be:

NORTH
♠ 9 8 2
♡ 10 8
♢ J 10 6 5 2
♣ Q J 7

PARTNER   YOU
♠ K J 6   ♠ Q 10 7 4 3
♡ Q 7 6 5 3   ♡ 2
♢ K Q   ♢ A 8 7 3
♣ K 8 5   ♣ 10 6 4

SOUTH (DEALER)
♠ A 5
♡ A K J 9 6
♢ 5 4
♣ A 7 3 2

Note that partner must pass over 1 heart, both because he fears a diamond response if he doubles and because he hopes for a substantial penalty if the opponents get too high. He is **trap-passing**. Despite your weakness, your side can make 3 spades, while the opponents will make 1 heart if you let them play. You must reopen with a **balancing** overcall, deducing that partner has the balance of the missing strength. (Here, opener has an unusually powerful hand, responder has close to a maximum pass; still, see what is left for partner.)

Since you will balance with an overcall with the slightest excuse, you must reopen with a takeout double whenever you have close to the strength for an opening bid. Twelve points, or even a good-looking 11 points, is enough. You must have a heavy preference for balancing with a double:

OPPONENT	PARTNER	OPPONENT	YOU
1 heart	pass	pass	*double*

when you have the required count. First, you want to let partner know that you have some strength of your own; you are not merely **protecting** in case he is trap-passing. Second, if partner *is* trapping, you put him in the position to pass your double for penalties. Some of the fattest penalties in bridge come when one partner trap-passes over an opening bid and the other can muster up a balancing double. After all, opener can often win only 3 or 4 tricks, and when his partner has nothing he is in serious trouble.

AFTER PARTNER REOPENS

When your partner reopens the auction, you must realize that his doubles and overcalls may be very light. If he overcalls, you must be particularly careful. Consider the hand which trap-passed in our earlier example:

♠ K J 6   ♡ Q 7 6 5 3   ◇ K Q   ♣ K 8 5

When partner reopens with 1 spade, you can do no more with this hand than raise to 2 spades (in fact, it would not be inconceivable to *pass*). After all, partner has already played you to have considerable strength, even though you have never bid. And if he had enough power for game, he would almost surely have balanced with a double, not an overcall.

When partner reopens with a double, do not leap into game with 11 or 12 points, for he may have no more than you. Tend to make a minimum response, to see if partner will bid again. When he *has* a normal double, instead of merely a balancing double, he will rebid. Then you can look for game. Suppose the auction goes:

OPPONENT	YOU	OPPONENT	PARTNER
1 diamond	pass	pass	double
pass	?		

What is your response with these hands?

(1) ♠ K J 8 6   ♡ 7 4   ◇ Q 8 3   ♣ K J 10 3
(2) ♠ A 3   ♡ K 4   ◇ K J 9 6 5   ♣ Q 10 5 3
(3) ♠ Q 3   ♡ K 8 6   ◇ K J 6 3   ♣ A J 10 5

With example (1), bid only 1 spade. Had partner doubled *directly over* the opening, you should jump to 2 spades, but you must give him leeway when he balances. If your side has a game, partner will bid again.

With example (2), pass for penalties. Partner's high cards added to your great defensive strength should yield a big set.

With example (3), jump to 3 notrump. You do not have enough sure trump tricks to pass, but your side must have a good play for game.

RARE REOPENING BIDS

There are other balancing actions besides the double and the overcall. The strongest is the cue bid:

OPPONENT	PARTNER	OPPONENT	YOU
1 heart	pass	pass	*2 hearts*

This is still forcing to game, but you may have to relax the high-card requirements slightly in the reopening position. For example, with:

♠ K Q 10 9 7 5 4   ♡ ——   ◇ A Q 10 7 6   ♣ 3

you should bid 2 hearts on the auction above. An overcall is, of course, impossible. A double is poor, for there is a much greater chance that partner will pass for penalties when you *reopen* with a double; and you have no wish to defend with this freak. A jump overcall to 2 spades does not do this hand justice. Whether you play your jump overcalls to be strong or preemptive normally, in the balancing position they should look like:

♠ K Q J 8 7 4   ♡ 2   ◇ A J 5 3   ♣ 7 4

This is a reopening jump to 2 spades when a one-bid is passed around to you. You should have the minimum count for a balancing *double*, but a long, strong suit and offensive distribution.

The *reopening* overcall of 1 notrump:

OPPONENT	PARTNER	OPPONENT	YOU
1 spade	pass	pass	1 notrump

no longer promises 16 to 18 points. It should be a hand with some strength in the enemy suit and 9 or 10 to 13 points in high cards. For example, balance with 1 notrump on the auction above if you hold:

♠ A Q 5   ♡ J 6   ◇ K J 7 4   ♣ 10 8 7 2

Why not double? Because you are not anxious to hear a response in hearts, the unbid major suit, and because the 1 notrump overcall describes your hand in one bid.

When you do hold the 16-to-18-point hand in the reopening position, double first and then bid notrump at your next turn. This may get you up to 2 notrump, and seems like an overbid. However, partner almost surely has a little something, and the fact that all the enemy cards are massed in opener's hand is very favorable for your side.

Finally, there are a few rare hands with which you should not reopen at all, but pass and allow the opponents to play their contract of one. Roughly, these fall into two groups. The first type is so weak that you would have passed a one-bid yourself, or a bare 6 or 7 points with no long suit. That is, holding:

♠ J 8 5 3   ♡ Q 6 4   ◇ K 7 3   ♣ 10 5 4

or less, do not balance over any opening bid. If partner is trapping, and he probably is, you will set the opponents for a small plus score. You really did not expect a profit when you saw your cards, so you should settle for a small one.

In addition, you should pass instead of balancing with almost any hand that contains 4 or 5 cards in the enemy suit. On the auction:

OPPONENT	PARTNER	OPPONENT	YOU
1 heart	pass	pass	?

pass both of these hands:

♠ 6 3   ♡ Q 10 9 6   ◇ A K 3 2   ♣ Q 10 4
♠ A J 8   ♡ K Q 10 7 4   ◇ K 8 6   ♣ J 3

There is no chance that partner has passed with a good hand, since he is not long in hearts when you are. Therefore, let the opponents struggle with their misfit. When long in the enemy suit, reopen only with 15–16 points or more, a hand that has real prospects of game in notrump.

• OTHER BALANCING AUCTIONS

There are other occasions in which the enemy auction tells you that partner has a good hand, even though he has never bid. Such auctions have two aspects in common:

1. The opponents have passed out at the two-level
2. The opponents have found a suit fit

The simplest example goes:

OPPONENT	YOU	OPPONENT	PARTNER
1 heart	pass	2 hearts	pass
pass	?		

In this position, you should reopen the auction rather more
often than not. The opponents are most unlikely to hold a
preponderance of the high cards (if opener had more than 11
to 13 or 14 high-card points, he would have had enough to
try for game; if responder had more than 6 to 8 high-card
points, his total count would have been too great for a single
raise). They have somewhere between 17 and 20 of the 40
high-card points in the deck. Let us assume that they have
20. This means that if you hold:

♠ Q 9 8 4 3   ♡ 6 2   ◇ K J 4   ♣ Q 5 3

you can bid 2 spades, counting on partner to have 12 points
in high cards, since you have only 8. The whole deal could
be:

NORTH
♠ J 7
♡ K 9 7 3
◇ 7 5 3
♣ K 10 8 4

YOU	PARTNER
♠ Q 9 8 4 3	♠ A 10 5
♡ 6 2	♡ J 5
◇ K J 4	◇ Q 8 6 2
♣ Q 5 3	♣ A J 7 6

SOUTH (DEALER)
♠ K 6 2
♡ A Q 10 8 4
◇ A 10 9
♣ 9 2

Take careful note that it is not just luck to find partner with
with all those cards. Try to give his club ace to one of the
opponents: if South had it, he would surely bid over 2 hearts;
if North held it he would be much too strong for a single
raise. It is hard to give even the diamond queen to either
opponent. On this deal, North-South can make 2 hearts, and

you can make 2 spades. So, although neither you nor partner were strong enough for a bid on the first round, together you have enough to compete effectively.

Of course, in the example above you have a convenient 5-card spade suit to bid. What, though, if you held your partner's cards:

♠ A 10 5   ♡ J 5   ◇ Q 8 6 2   ♣ A J 7 6

and he yours. The auction would still go:

OPPONENT	YOU	OPPONENT	PARTNER
1 heart	pass	2 hearts	pass
pass	?		

The opponents could still make 2 hearts, and you 2 spades. Here, you should *double*. This is a balancing double, for takeout. (You will never want to double the opponents for penalties at the two-level, after an opening bid and a raise.) Since the enemy have found a fit, your side is overwhelmingly likely to have a fit also. Partner will bid his suit in response to your double, and your fit will be found. There is no particular difference in strength between the balancing overcall and the balancing double. Typically, one member of the partnership will have the high cards, the other will hold the suit. (If one had both, he would bid on the *first* round.) If you hold the suit, you bid it; with the high cards, you double.

It is most important to understand the objective of these balancing bids. You are *not* trying to get to game, or even to outbid the opponents. Your object is to push them to the three-level where you have a fighting chance to defeat them. This means that if the auction goes:

OPPONENT	PARTNER	OPPONENT	YOU
1 spade	pass	2 spades	pass
pass	3 diamonds	3 spades	?

your only choice is whether to say "Pass" or "No bid." You may not double, or bid 3 notrump, or bid 4 or 5 diamonds. Partner has accomplished what he set out to do—to push the enemy one higher. Whatever strength you have, partner has already bid for you. If you act here, you are punishing partner for competing, and even if your bid gets a good result, you will make partner afraid to balance with you again.

WHETHER TO BALANCE

In deciding whether to balance, the sound of the opponents' auction is more important than the look of your hand. You must learn to distinguish between these two auctions:

	OPPONENT	PARTNER	OPPONENT	YOU
(1)	1 club	pass	1 heart	pass
	2 hearts	pass	pass	?
(2)	1 heart	pass	2 clubs	pass
	2 hearts	pass	pass	?

In auction (1), the opponents have stopped short after finding a fit. Probably, your side has a fit too, and about half the cards. So balance with either of these hands:

♠ A 10 6 3   ♡ 7 5 4   ◇ K 8 4   ♣ K J 5
♠ K 3   ♡ 8 2   ◇ Q J 9 7 5 3   ♣ Q 6 2

doubling with the first hand, overcalling with the second.

In contrast, do not dream of balancing with either hand on auction (2). The opponents have *not* found a fit, so you may have none either. They probably have stopped short because they had a misfit, not because they lacked high cards, so there is no reason to expect strength in partner's hand.

The crux, then, is whether the opponents have found a fit. If they have, be very alert to balance. You should pass only when you have no long suit, and are reluctant to double because you have less than 9 or 10 points. Here, it is usually right to sell out, hoping that the opponents have made a mistake.

The only auction on which you should consider reopening when the opponents have *not* found a fit is one like:

OPPONENT	YOU	OPPONENT	PARTNER
1 spade	pass	1 notrump	pass
pass	?		

Here you can count on partner to have some high cards, since both opponents have advertised minimum holdings. However, there is no presumption that your side has a fit. Therefore, you balance only when you have a long suit in a hand that did not have enough strength for an immediate overcall. You might bid 2 diamonds now with this earlier example:

♠ K 3   ♡ 8 2   ◇ Q J 9 7 5 3   ♣ Q 6 2

However, on this type of auction you will balance only with an overcall. If you reopen here with a *double*, it is for *penalties*. You are not balancing at all. You passed at your first turn with a strong hand and length in the enemy suit, and now you are springing your trap. This is true of any reopening double when the opponents have not found a suit fit.

Once in a long while, you will reopen the auction after the opponents have passed out in a low contract; then they will bounce into game. If they make their contract, you will look foolish, so avoid partner's accusing eye. However, do not let a rare disaster of this sort (which is really your opponents' fault, not yours) stop you from balancing. You will be a big winner over the years if you do not let the enemy buy their part-score contracts at the one- or two-level. Get in there and fight.

CHAPTER 9

Penalty Doubles

There are really three distinct types of penalty doubles. These are **offensive doubles** (your side owns the hand and the opponents are competing; you expect to earn more points doubling than by bidding on), **defensive doubles** (the opponents own the hand, but you think they have gone too high, and so double), and **lead-directing doubles** (the opponents own the hand, and you expect to beat them only if partner leads a specific suit). These three sorts of doubles have almost nothing in common, so I will treat them separately.

• OFFENSIVE DOUBLES

We have already seen one of the common positions for an offensive double—when the opponents have sacrificed against your game contract. The other position occurs when your side opens the bidding and the opponents enter the auction. Right there, with their first bid, the opponents are in their greatest danger of a crushing penalty. The biggest sets of all come from doubling overcalls; knowing when to double is essential to winning bridge.

WHEN TO DOUBLE OVERCALLS

There are three ingredients which go to make up a successful double of an enemy overcall. They are listed below in the order of their importance:

1. **Shortness in partner's suit**
2. **Strength in high cards**
3. **Length in the enemy suit**

(Note that your trump holding is the least important factor of all.)

Shortness in partner's suit is crucial because it suggests that the hand is a misfit. If you have no fit, neither do the opponents. In addition, you will earn a bigger score by doubling than by bidding on yourself, since in a misfit hand neither side will win as many tricks as its high-card points indicate. Holding:

♠ 5   ♡ A Q J 4   ◇ K 10 7 4   ♣ Q 8 7 5

you should double an overcall of 2 diamonds if partner opens 1 spade, but *not if he opens 1 heart*. Opposite a 1 heart opening bid, your hand should produce at least game. Thus, even a 500-point set will not be a net gain. And you are unlikely to collect this much, for the opponents probably have a fit when you have one. In contrast, your hand may well have no game opposite a 1 *spade* opening, so a 300-point set will show a profit. And you should not be surprised to collect 700 points, for the hand may be a complete misfit all around the table. As a rough guide, *never* double an overcall with 4 or more cards in partner's suit, *seldom* double with 3 cards, *be willing* to double with 2-card length, *be eager* to double with a singleton or void in partner's suit.

Overall high-card strength is the second factor to consider. The penalty double of an overcall promises a strong responding hand of 10 points or more, so that your side has a clear majority of the high cards. This requirement is important because partner or either opponent may take out into another suit. Thus, a hand like:

♠ 3   ♡ 6 5   ◇ K J 9 8 5 4   ♣ 10 6 4 2

is a horrible double of an enemy 2 diamond overcall. Obviously you can defeat 2 diamonds, but nine times out of ten someone will run out. Now the most likely result is that *your* side will suffer a heavy loss. If the opponents take out in hearts, partner will double or bid on, expecting some useful cards in your hand. The opponents will either make a doubled contract or collect a big penalty. If partner takes out himself, the disaster will be just as great. In contrast, a hand like:

♠ 3   ♡ A 10 5   ◇ K J 9 4   ♣ Q 10 6 4 2

is a fine double of 2 diamonds (when partner opens 1 spade). You can hurt the opponents if the double stays in, and you have a useful hand if someone runs out.

Length in the enemy suit should not be the *reason* for your double. However, it is your protection against Declarer winning too many trump tricks. You cannot afford to double an overcall with only two trumps. Three-card length is not really satisfactory, but occasionally serves. Ideally, you will hold four trumps. Of course, you can double an overcall with 5-card length in the enemy suit; here, though, you should start to worry about having *too many* trumps. A double with *six* trumps will almost never be left in by everyone around the table. Suppose partner opens 1 spade, and right-hand opponent overcalls 2 diamonds. You hold:

♠ 2   ♡ K 3   ◇ A Q 9 8 6 4   ♣ J 6 5 2

It is very tempting to roar "DOUBLE," but this is unlikely to yield a big profit, for you have too many diamonds. Partner probably has a hand like:

♠ A Q 7 5 4   ♡ A 10 8 4   ◇ ——   ♣ K 9 7 3

He will take out your double to 2 hearts; now your side has to struggle to earn even a small plus score. However, if you pass 2 diamonds, partner will reopen with a takeout double. You lick your chops and convert it into a penalty double by passing again. It is winning policy not to double an overcall when your hand is suitable for play only in this one contract.

Partner opens the bidding 1 spade, and your opponent overcalls 2 diamonds. With which of these examples should you double?

(1) ♠ K 8 4   ♡ A Q 7 2   ◇ A 8 6 3   ♣ 8 2
(2) ♠ 8 4   ♡ A Q 7 2   ◇ Q J 8 6   ♣ Q 8 2
(3) ♠ 3   ♡ 8 4   ◇ Q 10 9 7 4   ♣ K 10 9 5 3
(4) ♠ 3   ♡ K 8 4 2   ◇ Q 9 7   ♣ A Q 9 5 3

Do not double with example (1). You will surely defeat 2 diamonds, but you will not set it enough to make up for the game you can make. The tipoff is your support for partner's spade suit, and your diamond holding (your ace will be just as useful on offense as on defense).

Double with example (2). Here, you do not have spade support, and your diamond honors are *intermediates,* much better for defense than offense.

Pass with example (3). You would dearly love to defend against 2 diamonds doubled, but your best chance to bring this about is to pass. You are not nearly strong enough to double.

Double with example (4). Your diamond holding is 1 card shorter than you would like, but this is the least important ingredient of a double. All the other features are ideal: you have a singleton spade and considerable high-card strength. In addition, you are doubling two of a *minor*, which will not give the opponents game if they should happen to make the contract. This is not a prime consideration, since the odds are 20 to 1 that 2 diamonds will go down if partner stands for your double.

TAKING OUT PARTNER'S DOUBLE

When should partner take out your double, and when leave it in? He should decide almost entirely on the basis of his length in the enemy suit. After all, if the opponents play 2 diamonds doubled, *your side* is really playing with diamonds as trumps, since you must win 7 tricks to show a decent profit. He should expect you to have four trumps, and if he is void or has a singleton he should look for a different trump suit. Your double is a suggestion, not a command. However, with two or three trumps, he should be happy to accept your suggestion and play for penalties.

Let me put it this way: Opener should always take out a double if void in trumps, always leave it in with three trumps. He should usually take a double out with a singleton trump; usually leave it in with a doubleton. The factors which affect his decision with a singleton or doubleton are the offensive strength of his distribution (long suits) and the defensive strength of his high cards. Suppose you open 1 spade, your left-hand opponent overcalls 2 clubs, and partner doubles. You hold:

(a) ♠ J 9 6 5 3   ♡ A K Q 9 4   ◇ A   ♣ 7 2
(b) ♠ A K 7 6 3   ♡ A Q 5   ◇ K 7 4 2   ♣ J

Example (a) is the rare sort of hand with which you take out, even with a doubleton. The possession of a *side* 5-card suit (for which partner likely has a fit) should always tempt you to take out. Another indication is that your honors are not in spades, where partner is short, but in hearts where they may not cash on defense. In contrast, example (b) is the exceptional hand with which you leave in the double although holding a singleton trump. You have strong spades opposite partner's shortness, and your side honors are first- and second-round winners which are good for defense. Even your jack of clubs may be useful. And your side 4-card suit is a minor, so that game will be hard to make even if partner has a fit.

When you decide to take out partner's double, try to bid a new suit. Remember, he is very likely to have a singleton in your first suit. Thus, if you open 1 spade with:

♠ K Q 7 5 4 2 ♡ K J 10 3 ◇ 2 ♣ K 5

when partner doubles an enemy 2-diamond overcall, take out to 2 *hearts*, not 2 spades. (It should not occur to you to leave the double in.)

• DEFENSIVE DOUBLES

It is much more difficult to determine whether to double the opponents when *they* have a majority of the high cards, and own the hand. Actually, it is seldom that you can collect a really big set from a defensive double. The opponents are much more likely to go down 1100 in 2 diamonds (after an overcall) than in 6 diamonds, for by the time they reach a high contract they know a great deal about their combined strength. Of course, they may have overbid—and you may set them one or two tricks. But you will not often do better than this. Thus, a defensive double aims at a profit of about 200–300 points (the difference between two down doubled and undoubled).

THE ODDS

Since this is all you have to gain, it is mathematically disadvantageous to double part-score contracts. Suppose you hold:

♠ A Q 10 8 ♡ A 2 ◇ J 3 ♣ K 7 6 5 4

The auction goes:

OPPONENT	YOU	OPPONENT	PARTNER
1 spade	pass	2 diamonds	pass
2 spades	pass	3 spades	pass
pass	?		

Probably you will defeat this contract, but you should not double it. The odds are too heavily against you. The double will cost you about 500 points if the contract makes (for the opponents score a game as well as extra trick score and the bonus of 50). It gains 50 points for a one-trick set or 200 points for a two-trick set. So if you double five times and the opponents make their contract once, you break about even. Therefore, do not double part scores defensively (that is, when the opponents own the hand); be free to double part scores *offensively*, when your side has many more high cards than they have.

Much the same applies to doubling slam contracts. Here again, there is too much to lose compared to the small gain. Suppose your opponents get to 6 spades, and you are sitting behind Declarer with:

♠ A Q 9   ♡ 10 8 6 4 2   ♢ J 5 3   ♣ 8 7

If you double, and Declarer has the spade king, as you expect, you gain 50 points. But if the king turns up in dummy along with the jack or ten, you lose at least 230 points. I say "at least" because dummy may redouble, and now your double costs 590 points. Worse still, your double tells Declarer where the trumps are. So the enemy may make a redoubled slam when they might go down without the double. Then the double costs over 1600 points—the 50 points or even 200 points you might gain are not nearly enough to pay for this risk.

The fact is that you should double only *game* contracts. Here the odds are about even. There is still the risk of telling Declarer where the cards are, but if you double intelligently you will show a big profit in the long run.

WHEN TO DOUBLE GAME

Two equally important factors determine whether or not you should double the opponents in game:

1. **The nature of their bidding**
2. **How the missing cards in their key suits are divided between you and partner**

Notice that your point count is immaterial. This is of great importance in deciding to double an enemy overcall *offensively*, but hardly enters into your calculations in deciding whether to double an enemy game defensively.

The first consideration is whether the opponents have stretched to reach game after both opener and responder limited their hands, or whether they have bounced into game on an auction in which either opponent may have extra values. Contrast these two sequences:

	OPENER	RESPONDER
(1)	1 spade	2 diamonds
	3 spades	4 spades
(2)	1 spade	2 spades
	3 spades	4 spades

You have to be a madman to double on auction (1), for opener has 17 points *or more,* responder has 10 points *or more;* the enemy total count is at least 27 and could be as high as 32 or 33. They will probably redouble if you double, and make their contract even against unlucky breaks.

However, it is very tempting to double auction (2). Opener is limited, since he could not jump to game when raised; responder is limited, since he did not bid a new suit. The total enemy count is probably somewhere between 25 and 27 points. Neither opponent can have the *extra* values for a redouble, and unlucky breaks will surely defeat the game.

Let us look at another pair of auctions:

	OPENER	RESPONDER
(3)	1 diamond	1 heart
	2 hearts	3 hearts
	4 hearts	
(4)	1 diamond	1 heart
	3 hearts	4 hearts

On auction (3), the opponents have stretched to reach game after limiting their hands. They cannot stand bad breaks, so double if they are going to get them. But do not double auction (4), almost regardless of your hand. Opener is somewhat limited, but responder may have almost enough for slam. Then a double will be disastrous.

Of course, you must not double the opponents whenever they creep into game. They will go down only if the missing cards are divided unluckily for them. If they are, you should know it, and double. Suppose the auction goes:

OPPONENT	PARTNER	OPPONENT	YOU
1 heart	pass	1 spade	pass
1 notrump	pass	2 hearts	pass
3 hearts	pass	4 hearts	?

Should you double with either of these hands?

(a) ♠ 8 4 2   ♡ A K 5   ◇ K 7 4   ♣ Q 9 6 2
(b) ♠ K J 10 8 5   ♡ ——   ◇ Q J 10 6   ♣ Q 7 5 4

You certainly should double with example (b). Both opponents have limited strength, so they need favorable breaks to make their contract. You can see that spades split badly, and that any finesse they need here will fail; and they are getting the worst trump split possible. I would expect at least a two-trick set on this auction.

However, you should definitely *not* double with example (a). The fact that you have a lot of high cards is not a bad break for the opponents—they knew that they did not hold these cards, and finding them all massed in one hand is rather favorable for them. What *can* hurt them is bad splits in their suits, and losing finesses. But their trumps divide evenly; so do spades, and any finesse they need here will succeed, since you have no honor behind the spade bidder. Holding hand (a), I would bet 2 to 1 that the opponents will make their game.

Let us look at another limited auction:

OPPONENT	YOU	OPPONENT	PARTNER
1 spade	pass	1 notrump	pass
2 hearts	pass	3 spades	pass
4 spades	?		

Should you double with either of these hands?

(c) ♠ J 10 9 6 3   ♡ 8 4   ◇ A 8 6   ♣ 5 4 2
(d) ♠ 8 4 3   ♡ A 8 4   ◇ A 8 6   ♣ A 5 4 2

Yes. Double with example (c), but not with (d). The opponents are getting *good* breaks if you hold hand (d) since you will never get partner in to lead toward your aces. You would have a better chance to defeat the contract if you had less. In contrast, the enemy have run into bad luck on hand (c). They hoped to lose no spade tricks; instead, they may lose two. Notice the difference between your *unexpected* trump tricks in example (c) and your aces in example (d) which the opponents know they are going to lose.

The same principle holds true for doubling 3 notrump contracts. On the auction:

OPPONENT	PARTNER	OPPONENT	YOU
1 spade	pass	2 clubs	pass
2 spades	pass	2 notrump	pass
3 notrump	pass	pass	?

double if you hold:

(e) ♠ 2   ♡ K 7 4   ◇ J 10 9 7 5   ♣ K J 9 4

But do not dream of doubling if you hold:

(f) ♠ K 7 4   ♡ A Q 2   ◇ A J 6 2   ♣ 8 5 3

With example (f), I would expect the opponents to make overtricks despite my strength. All their suits split, all their finesses work, and I will never get my partner on lead to play to my tenaces in the red suits. Example (e) is much weaker (which is good for our side, since our strength is evenly divided), but almost assures a set. Their suits split badly, and all their finesses figure to fail.

In short, double defensively only when the opponents creep into game and are getting evil splits in their long suits. Do not double part scores or slams; do not double games bid with jumps; do not double because you have a beautiful collection of high cards—you would be better off with less.

• LEAD-DIRECTING DOUBLES

Occasionally, the penalty double is used more or less artificially to tell partner which suit to lead. Of course, you must hope to defeat the enemy contract with this lead, but your primary purpose is not to increase the *size* of the set, but to make a set possible.

DOUBLING 3 NOTRUMP

The first such situation occurs if you double 3 notrump when neither you nor partner have been in the auction. Here:

OPPONENT	PARTNER	OPPONENT	YOU
1 spade	pass	2 clubs	pass
2 notrump	pass	3 notrump	*double*

your double calls for the lead of *dummy's first bid suit*—clubs. To double on the auction above, you might hold:

♠ A 5 2   ♡ 3   ◇ 8 7 6 3   ♣ K Q J 9 4

You have a good chance to defeat 3 notrump if partner leads clubs. This is by no means certain, but what is sure is that you will *not* set the contract with partner's normal lead. You double not to earn an extra 50 points, but to have some prospect of a set.

If your side *has* been in the auction, the double of 3 notrump changes in meaning. When partner has bid a suit, your double demands that he lead it. Likewise, if you have bid a suit, your double forces partner to open it. Would he not do so anyway? Not necessarily; the auction may have gone:

OPPONENT	YOU	OPPONENT	PARTNER
1 heart	2 diamonds	double	pass
3 clubs	pass	3 notrump	pass
pass	?		

If your hand is:

♠ 3   ♡ A 7 3   ◇ A Q J 10 9   ♣ 10 7 5 2

you had better double and command a diamond lead. Otherwise, partner—who has heard Declarer double you in diamonds—may decide on a surprise attack in spades. The woods are full of partners who trust Declarer instead of you, so take no chances.

DOUBLING A SLAM

The double of a slam contract is used similarly to demand a specific opening lead. (I said earlier that the odds are wrong for slam doubles, but this is when you are trying to gain 50 points or so; if you defeat a slam *because you have doubled it*, the double gains over 1000 points.) Here, the double calls for:

1. The first side suit bid by dummy or, if none has been bid—
2. The most unusual lead

Let us see an example:

OPPONENT	YOU	OPPONENT	PARTNER
1 diamond	1 heart	2 spades	pass
4 notrump	pass	5 hearts	pass
6 spades	*double*		

Your double demands that partner lead *diamonds*. Your hand might be:

♠ 7 5 3   ♡ A J 10 8 7 5   ◇ ——   ♣ Q J 10 3

With a diamond opening, you can ruff and hope to defeat the slam with your ace. If you do *not* double, partner will surely lead hearts, the suit you bid. Thus, if you double a slam after overcalling, when dummy has bid no side suit:

OPPONENT	PARTNER	OPPONENT	YOU
1 diamond	pass	3 diamonds	4 hearts
5 diamonds	pass	6 diamonds	*double*

you *forbid* partner to lead your suit, hearts. He must guess whether you want spades or clubs. If *his* hand is:

♠ J 9 8 6 5 4 2   ♡ Q 2   ◇ 8 4   ♣ 9 5

he should open a spade, expecting you to be void. Your hand, for the auction above, might be:

♠ ——   ♡ K J 10 9 7 6 5 3   ◇ A 6   ♣ Q 7 6

Your double is far from a sure thing, since partner might not be able to read the spade lead. But if you do *not* double, partner will lead hearts. The greatly increased chance to defeat the slam is certainly worth the price if they make the contract.

And, after all, if you set every contract you double it is certain that you are not doubling nearly enough.

PART 3 • THE PLAY OF THE CARDS

CHAPTER 10

Play and Defense at Notrump

Inexperienced bridge players are likely to have an irrational dread of notrump. As declarers in suit contracts, they have a warm, secure feeling produced by their beautiful trumps; in notrump, they feel naked, exposed to awful, nameless perils.

In fact, it really is harder to win tricks at notrump than in a suit. A resourceful declarer can usually produce an extra trick or two from the same number of points when he has a good trump suit—he has, as we will see later, many more strings to his bow. However, for just this reason it is actually much easier to plan your play (or defense) in notrump. The techniques are simple, the choices few and clear cut.

Nine-tenths of all hands played in notrump resolve into a race between Declarer and defense to force out enemy high cards and take tricks with lower honors or small cards in long suits. Who will establish a long suit first?—that is the crux of most notrump hands. Declarer's chief advantage in the race is that he has more high cards with which to stop the opponents from winning tricks quickly. The defense, however, has a head start—they have the opening lead and can get to work on their suit first. Let me illustrate this with an example deal:

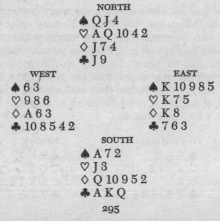

```
                    NORTH
                  ♠ Q J 4
                  ♡ A Q 10 4 2
                  ◇ J 7 4
                  ♣ J 9
     WEST                         EAST
   ♠ 6 3                        ♠ K 10 9 8 5
   ♡ 9 8 6                      ♡ K 7 5
   ◇ A 6 3                      ◇ K 8
   ♣ 10 8 5 4 2                 ♣ 7 6 3
                    SOUTH
                  ♠ A 7 2
                  ♡ J 3
                  ◇ Q 10 9 5 2
                  ♣ A K Q
```

South is declarer at 3 notrump, after East overcalls in spades. West opens the spade 6, racing to set up partner's long suit. Dummy plays the jack; East covers with the king; South wins the ace. Next, South works on his own long suit, leading the diamond 2. West plays low, dummy the jack, East winning the king. East returns the 10 of spades, forcing out dummy's jack and establishing his suit. Dummy leads a diamond, forcing out West's ace and establishing South's diamonds. Since West has no more spades, he leads the heart 9, hoping to give partner the lead. But Declarer wins dummy's ace, and cashes his high clubs and diamonds to make the contract.

Now, the play and defense described were both full of mistakes. I will refer back to this hand in later sections (so often, in fact, that you will probably be sick of it) to illustrate the proper techniques. What I want you to see now is the bare outline of the race. The defense pounds away at one of its long suits; Declarer plugs away at one of his. The defenders are able to set up their spades because they have the opening lead, and have two winners in Declarer's suit; Declarer has time to establish his diamonds because he has two winners in spades. Eventually, Declarer wins the race even though the enemy suit is established first; his opponents do not have enough side high cards for entries, and he takes his diamond tricks before they cash their spades. The vital factors are *stoppers* (winners in the enemy suit) and *entries*.

• PLANNING THE PLAY

When you are declarer in a notrump contract, you must plan your campaign the instant dummy goes down. Ask yourself two questions: (1) How many winners can I cash right away, and which long cards or intermediate honors can be established to bring the total to the required number? (2) Have I enough stoppers in the enemy suit to allow me to carry out my plan before they cash enough tricks to defeat me, and, if not, what can I do about it? Suppose that you are declarer with these hands:

YOUR HAND	DUMMY
♠ A Q 3	♠ 8 4
♡ A J 4 2	♡ Q 5
◊ 7	◊ A K J 8 5 3
♣ A 10 8 6 4	♣ 7 3 2

Your contract is 1 notrump (you have, say, a 60 partial). The opening lead is the spade 5. Dummy plays low, the 10 is played, you win the queen. You should think, "I have two spade tricks, one heart, two top diamonds, one club—six in all right now; I need one more. Extra tricks may be available in diamonds or clubs with a little luck, but there is a sure trick in hearts if I lead to dummy's queen. I have a second stopper in spades, so the opponents cannot take any tricks when they win the heart king."

Now, suppose your contract is 2 notrump. You need two extra winners, so a heart play will leave you a trick short—you must try clubs or diamonds. A successful finesse in diamonds will give you your contract, but this is only a 50 per cent chance. By giving up two club tricks, you will set up your two long clubs if that suit splits three-two; here the odds are 2 to 1 in your favor. Thus, it seems better to attack clubs. However, you must ask yourself whether you can afford to give up the lead twice. You have only one spade stopper left, so the enemy will cash their spades. How many? The opening lead was the spade 5, so the leader has at most a 5-card suit (he has led his fourth highest; with a 6-card suit he would have 2 cards left in his hand lower than the one he led, but only one such card—the 2—is missing). Therefore, you can afford to give up two clubs—the opponents can take only three spade tricks and two club tricks, and will not set you.

Finally, suppose that you are playing a contract of 3 notrump. You need 3 extra tricks. You might get them by giving up two clubs and then trying for your ninth trick in hearts or diamonds; but in the meanwhile the enemy will have won 5 tricks and beaten you. Therefore, you must go all out to establish the diamond suit, where you might win your needed tricks without surrendering the lead too often. It is not a good chance, but it is your only one.

Notice the steps in your process of reasoning. How many winners have I off the top? Where can I develop the balance that I need? How many tricks can the opponents take when I surrender the lead? To answer the last question, you may have to guess the length of the enemy suit. To do this, you look for the spot-cards *under the one led.* If there are none missing (the lead was the 2, or the 3 is led and the 2 is in your hand or dummy), then the leader should have a 4-card suit. Each missing spot warns of the possibility of a longer enemy suit. The auction may also help you in determining opposing suit length, for the odds are that an overcall would be made with a 6-card or longer suit.

Let us return to our first example hand. Here, Declarer is in 3 notrump with these cards:

DECLARER	DUMMY
♠ A 7 2	♠ Q J 4
♡ J 3	♡ A Q 10 4 2
◇ Q 10 9 5 2	◇ J 7 4
♣ A K Q	♣ J 9

The opening lead is the spade 6, in response to a spade overcall by the opponent sitting over dummy. Dummy's jack is covered by the king, and won by Declarer's ace. If you were declarer, would you start to work on your diamond suit or on dummy's heart suit, and why?

You have six top winners, and must establish three more. By forcing out the ace and king of diamonds, you have a 99 per cent chance of producing 3 extra tricks. However, you have only one spade stopper left, and your opponent, to overcall, surely has a 5-card suit at least. Therefore, this line of attack risks the loss of 5 tricks—two diamonds, three spades—before you can cash your 9. By going after hearts instead, you have slightly less chance of establishing 3 more tricks (it is more likely that the hearts split five-one than that the diamonds split five-zero). Here, though, you will have to surrender the lead only once; there is no risk at all that the enemy will win the race. Therefore, it is clearly best to attack hearts, not diamonds.

• PLANNING THE DEFENSE

The defense does not have the opportunity to plan its campaign so carefully, for neither player sees his partner's hand. However, each defender knows the objective—to establish a long suit before Declarer does.

For this reason, your opening lead against a notrump contract will usually be in your longest suit. If this suit is headed by a sequence of three honors, or by two touching honors with a third card just barely out of sequence (K Q 10, Q J 9), you lead the highest of your touching honors. If it is not headed by a sequence, you lead your fourth-highest card. Suppose the opponents bid 1 notrump—3 notrump, and you are on lead with:

 (1) ♠ K J 9 5 3 ♡ J 10 9 ◇ A 8 2 ♣ 6 3
 (2) ♠ J 10 8 5 3 ♡ J 10 9 ◇ A K 2 ♣ 6 3

You should lead spades, your long suit, with either hand. From hand (1), you lead the 5—you have no sequence, so you open your fourth highest. From hand (2), you lead the jack —your suit is headed by a "broken" 3-card sequence.

Of course, you do not always lead your longest suit. If the opponents have bid it, you should generally try to guess what partner's long suit is and lead that. For example, if the enemy auction goes 1 spade—2 diamonds—2 notrump—3 notrump, and you must lead with either hand above, do *not* lead spades. Try the jack of hearts. In trying to guess partner's suit, an unbid major is often a good gamble. The opponents might leave a long minor suit unbid, but they are likely to bid any major-suit length that they have. And if *they* are not long, partner is.

Likewise, when partner has bid a suit, you should have a strong tendency to lead his suit, not your own. This is not mandatory when partner has made an *opening bid*, since he promises a strong *hand*, not a strong *suit*. Then you are allowed to lead your long suit instead, but remember that you must lead *away* from your honors, while you can lead *up to* partner's. However, if partner has *overcalled*, he promises a long, strong suit and it is positively felonious to lead anything else. The only excuse is to be void of partner's suit, and even then you must be prepared to apologize. In our first example hand, the opening leader held:

♠ 6 3   ♡ 9 6 2   ◇ A 6 3   ♣ 10 8 5 4 2

He led the spade 6, not the club 4, because his partner had overcalled in spades. Often, half the purpose of an overcall is to tell partner what to lead. It is infuriating if he then opens some scraggly suit of his own, explaining sagely that the opponents had bid notrump over your suit. He is supposed to trust you, not the enemy.

Once the opening lead is made, the defense should have a heavy prejudice in favor of continuing to play the same suit each time it gains the lead. Defenders who try to establish *two* suits usually end up losing the race, and setting up neither. In contrast, defenders who plug away at one suit have a good chance of cashing long cards. I would estimate that in two-thirds of all notrump game contracts, the defense can establish a long suit, aided by its headstart of the opening lead.

The reason that far fewer than two-thirds of all notrump contracts are beaten is that the defender who holds the

established long cards often has trouble gaining the lead to
cash them. The problem is *entries*. There is a little more to
planning the defense than merely leading a long suit repeatedly until it is established. The key principle here is: when
working to set up *your* long suit, try to save your high-card
winners for entries after your little cards are high; when
working on *partner's* suit, try to use *your* entries early to
return his suit, saving *his* honors as entries. Our first hand
provides a good example of this:

DUMMY
♠ Q J 4
♡ A Q 10 4 2
◇ J 7 4
♣ J 9

YOU
♠ 6 3
♡ 9 6 3
◇ A 6 3
♣ 10 8 5 4 2

You lead the spade 6, to dummy's jack, partner's king,
Declarer's ace. Declarer leads the diamond 2. You must *hop
up with your ace* and return the spade 3. "Second hand low"
is not one of the Ten Commandments. The objective of your
defense is to set up partner's suit, so you must seize *your*
winners early and save partner's as entries. In this example,
your play will defeat the contract, since when partner wins
his diamond king *later*, his spades will be good.

This defense is really simple if you understand what your
objectives are. Do not consider yourself a demon defender
until you have made a play like the one following:

DUMMY
♠ A 5
♡ 8 6 2
◇ Q J 8 5 3
♣ A 10 6

YOU
♠ 7 6 4
♡ K 10 7 5
◇ K 6 4
♣ 5 4 2

Declarer opens 1 notrump; dummy raises to 3. Partner leads the spade queen, won in dummy. The diamond 3 is led. You must play your *king*. If Declarer holds the ace (or, worse still, if partner has the singleton ace), an embarrassing number of tricks will be made. However, you are trying to defeat the contract, and this cannot be done unless partner holds the guarded ace of diamonds. Even so, it cannot be done unless you save partner's ace to be the entry to his established spades. Therefore, climb up with your king, and apologize if it goes wrong. (Your play is correct even when it loses, but it is a waste of time to try to convince partner of this.)

On defense, it is not *always* right to continue playing the suit led originally. Sometimes, the opening lead is a false step, and the mistake may be corrected in time. Here is an instance of such a hand:

DUMMY

♠ 10 8 4
♡ J 5 3
◊ K J 9 6
♣ K 10 2

YOU

♠ A 3
♡ A 8 7 6 2
◊ Q 10 5
♣ 8 4 3

Declarer opens 1 notrump; dummy raises to 2 notrump; and Declarer bids 3. Partner opens the spade 2, and you win your ace. Shift to the 6 of hearts! Why? Because partner has only a 4-card suit. He leads his fourth-highest card; if he has a 5-card suit, he must hold a card lower than the one he led—but he led the 2. (The same would be true had he opened the 5 if Declarer played the 2 under your ace; with the 4, 3, and 2 in sight, partner must have only a 4-card suit.) Therefore, Declarer also has four spades, and this is the wrong suit to attack. Perhaps it is not too late to establish *your* length in hearts.

You must get in the habit of looking for the spots *under* the one partner leads. This will tell you whether it is certain, likely, or impossible that partner has a long suit. If it appears that partner's length is 5 cards or more, you should almost always continue his suit. But if partner led a 4-card suit, you should consider shifting, particularly when you know that the enemy has 4-card length also.

Another position in which you switch suits occurs when partner signals you to do so. Consider this hand, for example:

DUMMY
♠ J 2
♡ 7 6 5
♢ K J 6 2
♣ K 8 7 3

YOU
♠ 10 9 4
♡ K Q 10 4 3
♢ 8 7 4
♣ J 5

Against 3 notrump, you lead the heart king. Dummy plays the 5, partner the 2, Declarer the 9. *Switch to the spade 10.* Why? Because, beyond all doubt, Declarer has the A J of hearts, and another heart lead will go right into the gaping jaws of his tenace. These are partner's possible holdings in hearts:

(a) J 8 2   (c) J 2   (e) 8 2
(b) A 8 2   (d) A 2   (f) 2

With (a) or (b), partner must signal with the 8, to say "Come ahead." With (c), partner must drop the jack under your king, both to unblock the suit and let you know that he holds this card. And with (d) partner must *overtake* your king with his ace for the same two reasons. (Partner must *never* leave himself with a singleton honor in your long suit.) Therefore, partner must hold (e) or (f), and a continuation will be fatal.

It is easy to read partner's 2 as a discouraging signal, but what about a 4 or a 6—what is the dividing line between a high signal ("Come ahead") and a low signal ("Switch")? *There is none.* Partner should encourage with the highest spot he can afford, or discourage with the lowest spot he holds. Thus, if you lead the king and he holds Q 4 3 2, he plays the 4; if he holds 9 8 7, he plays the 7. How do you tell that a 4 is encouraging or a 7 discouraging? You look for the spot-cards *under his signal.* If partner plays the 4, and the 3 and 2 are missing, you continue the suit; but if partner plays the 7 and you see the 6 5 4 3 2, you switch. Suppose the heart suit in our last example is divided like this:

♡ 7 6 5

♡ K Q 10 4 3 ♡ 9 8

♡ A J 2

You lead the king; dummy plays the 5, partner the 8, Declarer the 2. Note that you can read partner's 8 as *discouraging*, since all the lower spots are in sight. You know that partner has signaled with his lowest card; therefore you must switch. The successful bridge player is that rare bird—the eagle-eyed spot watcher. What he looks for constantly are the missing small cards, cards *lower* than partner's or opponent's lead, cards *lower* than partner's or opponent's signal.

• HOLDING OFF STOPPERS (DECLARER)

We have seen that one of the key factors in the race between Declarer and defense is *entries*—communication between the defenders' hands or between Declarer and dummy. It does no good to establish long cards if you cannot gain the lead to cash them. The surest entry to established long cards is the highest card of the same suit. Suppose you lead the king of your long suit:

DUMMY

8 3

YOU   PARTNER

K Q J 10 7   6 5 2

DECLARER

A 9 4

If Declarer wins the ace, you have no difficulty about entries. Should you gain the lead, you cash all your winners; and if *partner* gains the lead, he returns your suit—there is no communication problem so long as partner has cards in your suit and you hold the highest card remaining in it. However, if Declarer plays properly he will deny you this communication by holding off—allowing you to win the first and second tricks, and taking his ace on the *third* round. Now partner has no cards of your suit to return if he gets the lead. To cash your established long winners, you will need an entry in a side suit.

This is the basic **holdoff play**. Declarer wins his stopper in the enemy suit at the last possible moment, hoping to exhaust one opponent of cards there, and thus to break communication. This is almost always Declarer's best policy and should be employed even with *two* stoppers. Consider our first example hand:

NORTH

♠ Q J 4
♡ A Q 10 4 2
◇ J 7 4
♣ J 9

WEST	EAST
♠ 6 3	♠ K 10 9 8 5
♡ 9 8 6	♡ K 7 5
◇ A 6 3	◇ K 8
♣ 10 8 5 4 2	♣ 7 6 3

SOUTH

♠ A 7 2
♡ J 3
◇ Q 10 9 5 2
♣ A K Q

West leads the spade 6; dummy plays the jack, East the king. South should *hold off* his ace and allow the king to win. We have seen that the contract will be defeated if South wins the ace and attacks diamonds. (West should rise with the ace to lead his second spade, and when East gets in with the diamond king, the defense can cash 5 tricks.) However, notice the effect of the holdoff play. South wins the *second* spade and leads diamonds. Now it does West no good to take his ace early, for he has no spade to return. Thus, when East wins his diamond king, the spades will not yet be established. Declarer has broken the defense's communication and won the race.

Although it is usually proper to hold off your stopper in the enemy suit, there are three types of hands—two rare and one common—in which it is wrong. One instance is when you suspect that the opponents' suit is blocked. For example:

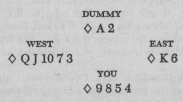

DUMMY
◇ A 2

WEST	EAST
◇ Q J 10 7 3	◇ K 6

YOU
◇ 9 8 5 4

The diamond queen is led by West. If you hold off dummy's ace, a second lead clears the suit, and West can cash his tricks whenever he gains the lead. This is not true if you take the ace immediately. If East plays the 6, his king blocks the run of the suit; and if East, properly, throws his king under the ace (refusing to leave himself with a singleton honor in partner's suit), your 9 provides a second stopper. The same is true in this similar combination:

DUMMY
◊ 9 5 4 3

WEST   EAST
◊ Q J 7 6 2   ◊ K 10

YOU
◊ A 9

West leads the 6, East plays the king, and you should win the first trick to block the suit. How do you know you should do this? In the first example, you knew East held the king because West lead the queen; in the second, you know East holds two honors because West did not lead the top of a sequence. If East has a doubleton, the enemy suit is blocked in each case *if you do not hold off.* And if East were to hold 3 cards in partner's suit, the holdoff is futile; for then you *cannot* break their communications. The tipoff is a doubleton ace opposite four—here it is often right to win your ace at once.

A second rare instance in which a holdoff is futile occurs when you know that one opponent holds all the missing high cards. For example, suppose East opens the bidding with 1 heart, and you become declarer at 3 notrump with:

DUMMY
♡ 6 5 4

WEST   EAST
♡ 9 2   ♡ Q J 10 8 3

YOU
♡ A K 7

West leads the 9, and East overtakes with the 10. The chances are that you should win the first trick. If your side has 26 points and East has an opening bid, West has no high cards at all. Therefore, it is a waste of time to hold off. The purpose of this play is to exhaust West of hearts so that he cannot play the suit when he gains the lead—but he will never be on lead again. As we will see later, you are likely to have other uses for your low heart on this type of hand.

By far the most common reason for refusing to hold off a stopper is that you are afraid of a switch to some other suit, and not afraid of the one led. For instance, suppose that you are declarer at 3 notrump with these cards:

DUMMY

♠ K 8 4
♡ 7 5 3
♢ A J 9 7 3
♣ J 8

YOU

♠ A 7 3
♡ A 2
♢ Q 10 8
♣ A K 7 5 2

The spade queen is led. Win your ace right away. The opponents have made a mistake by failing to establish their hearts —do not give them a second chance by leaving them on lead. You must make this hand if you attack diamonds at once, for even if the finesse fails you have all suits stopped and 9 tricks to cash. However, if you hold off in spades you may be defeated by a switch to hearts. Here is a somewhat more subtle example of the same general type:

DUMMY

♠ 8 6 5
♡ 7 4 2
♢ Q 8
♣ K Q J 4 3

WEST		EAST
♠ Q J 2		♠ K 10 9 3
♡ Q J 6 3		♡ K 9 8
♢ 9 5 3		♢ A 6 2
♣ 10 6 2		♣ 9 8 5

YOU

♠ A 7 4
♡ A 10 5
♢ K J 10 7 4
♣ A 7

West leads the heart 3 against your 3 notrump contract, and East plays his king. Normal play seems to be to hold off your heart ace twice and win the third heart. Then when you force out the ace of diamonds, the opponents cannot win any more tricks—you will make an overtrick since West has no entry to his fourth heart.

The trouble is that you will go down if the enemy is inspired to switch to spades at any point. Why should they? Well, West may decide that his heart suit is dead for lack of entries when you hold off twice; he should bury the hearts decently, and lead the spade queen in the hope of setting up tricks for partner. And East may decide at trick two that there is no future in hearts. He knows that partner has only four (the 3 was led, and the 2 is in dummy), and he, not partner, has the side entry, so he might well switch to his own suit.

To avoid this, you should win the first trick even though you have no further stopper. You, too, know that the lead was from a 4-card suit, so you are not afraid of hearts. On winning the diamond ace, the opponents can cash only 3 more tricks; your contract is safe. Had there been a missing spotcard under the one led, however, you would be forced to hold off and risk the switch to spades. Even here, though, you should hold off only once. Your reasoning should be that if East holds *two* hearts he is already exhausted in the danger suit, and if East holds *three* hearts then the suit is not dangerous after all.

• DEFENSIVE HOLDOFF

The holdoff play is available to the defenders as well as to Declarer. It is particularly useful when dummy has a long suit with few outside entries.

DUMMY

♠ Q 5 2
♡ 8 4
◇ K Q J 9 3
♣ 7 6 3

YOU

♠ K 8 4 3
♡ Q 10 3 2
◇ A 7 5
♣ 9 2

Against 3 notrump, partner leads the club king. You play the 2, and Declarer holds off. Partner continues with the queen, which also wins. Declarer takes the ace of clubs on the third round. Notice that this holdoff play has been successful, since you have both high-card entries and no more clubs to lead to partner. (Actually, Declarer could have won the second club, but was not sure whether you had two or three little cards in partner's suit.)

There is nothing you can do to stop Declarer from killing partner's clubs, but now you can get revenge by killing dummy's diamonds the same way. Declarer leads the 10 of diamonds, and you hold off your ace. A second diamond is played to dummy's jack; you let it hold. You win the third diamond with your ace, and Declarer has no entry to dummy to cash the two long cards. Incidentally, you have the same problem that Declarer had in clubs—has Declarer two little diamonds or three? Shall you win the *second* diamond or hold off to the third round? This is most important on defense for if you hold off *needlessly* on the second diamond (that is, if Declarer has only a doubleton, so that you can afford to win the second round), you may present Declarer with his ninth trick. Fortunately, you have a friend at the table; partner should tell you how many diamonds Declarer has.

He does this by signaling to tell you how many little diamonds *he* holds. With two, he plays high, then low; with three, he plays low, then high. If the diamonds are divided:

$$\diamond \text{ K Q J 9 3}$$
$$\diamond \text{ 8 2} \qquad\qquad \diamond \text{ A 7 5}$$
$$\diamond \text{ 10 6 4}$$

Declarer leads the 10, partner plays the *eight*, and you hold off. Declarer continues the suit, partner follows with the 2, and you hold off again. Partner signaled high-low showing two, so Declarer has three; you must not win your ace until the third round. But:

$$\diamond \text{ K Q J 9 3}$$
$$\diamond \text{ 8 6 2} \qquad\qquad \diamond \text{ A 7 5}$$
$$\diamond \text{ 10 4}$$

Declarer leads the 10 and partner plays the 2. Partner has signaled low-high showing three, so Declarer has the doubleton. You can win the second diamond.

Do not confuse this high-low or low-high signal with the more common one which means "Come ahead" or "Switch." Note that when, in the last example hand, partner led the king of clubs, you played the 2 from 9 2. A high spot means "Play this suit" and a low spot means "Consider switching suits" whenever this meaning is conceivable. However, when dummy has a long, strong suit, the defenders do not need signals to tell each other whether or not to attack it—Declarer, of course, is attacking it himself. Here the signals show your count, telling partner how many cards Declarer has in dummy's suit. Technically, high-low means that you have an *even* number of cards—2 or 4—while low-high means an *odd* number—3 or 5. However, the signal to show 4 or 5 is so rare that you need not worry about it. The thing to remember is to signal whether you have 2 or 3.

Defenders, like Declarer, should often hold off a *double* stopper in a long enemy suit. You can see clearly the mechanics and purpose of holdoff plays in this hand:

DUMMY
♠ A 6
♡ 10 7 4
◊ K J 10 7 5
♣ 6 4 2

PARTNER
♠ 8 3
♡ K 8 6
◊ 6 4 2
♣ Q J 10 8 3

YOU
♠ Q J 9 4
♡ 9 5 3 2
◊ A Q 8
♣ 7 3

DECLARER
♠ K 10 7 5 2
♡ A Q J
◊ 9 3
♣ A K 9

Against 3 notrump, partner leads the club queen. Dummy plays the 2, you the 3, Declarer the 9. Declarer wins the second club lead, and plays the diamond 9; partner follows with the 2; dummy plays the 5.

Notice what Declarer has done to you by holding off the first club trick. Had he won it, you could take your diamond queen and return partner's suit. Even if Declarer held off now, partner would win and continue clubs, establishing his

suit. Before Declarer could cash 9 tricks, partner would gain
the lead with his heart entry, and defeat the contract. Now,
though, you have no club to return. Partner's one side entry
is insufficient, since his long clubs will not be set up when he
wins his heart king. Declarer has broken your communications and shut out partner's suit by holding off.

You can still defeat the contract by doing the same to
dummy's diamonds. Hold off, letting Declarer's 9 win. Another diamond will be led to dummy's 10; now win your
queen. Declarer does not have another diamond to lead, in
order to force out your ace (you know this, for partner
played low-high). Thus, dummy's one side entry is insufficient, since dummy's long diamonds will not be established
when the spade ace is won.

You see here a common defensive technique. When Declarer takes a finesse *which he can repeat* (that is, he finesses
against the diamond queen by passing the 9; he can finesse
again by leading to the 10), you often let him "win" his first
finesse, and surprise him when his confident second finesse
loses. Unless you are very anxious to gain the lead early to
return partner's suit, you should make this play. However,
the finesse you let Declarer win must be one he can repeat.
For example:

DUMMY

A Q 8 4 2

PARTNER   YOU

J 9 3   K 10 4

DECLARER

7 5

If Declarer plays low to dummy's queen and you hold off,
you have thrown away a trick. This was your only chance to
capture an honor with your king. But:

DUMMY

A Q J 4 2

PARTNER   YOU

9 8 3   K 10 4

DECLARER

7 5

Now when Declarer plays low to dummy's queen, you should almost surely hold off. You will get a chance to capture dummy's jack later. In the meantime, you have deprived Declarer of an entry to dummy, and he may embarrass himself coming back to his hand to repeat his "successful" finesse. Incidentally, you must learn to make this play with a smooth wrist action; half the effect is lost if your hesitation betrays the location of the missing king. Your nerve and reflexes are likely to be tested in a deal like this one:

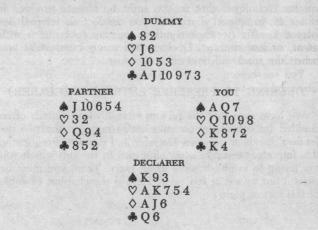

DUMMY
♠ 8 2
♡ J 6
♢ 10 5 3
♣ A J 10 9 7 3

PARTNER
♠ J 10 6 5 4
♡ 3 2
♢ Q 9 4
♣ 8 5 2

YOU
♠ A Q 7
♡ Q 10 9 8
♢ K 8 7 2
♣ K 4

DECLARER
♠ K 9 3
♡ A K 7 5 4
♢ A J 6
♣ Q 6

Partner leads the spade 5 against 3 notrump. You win the ace and return the queen, Declarer holding off. Declarer takes his king on the third round, and leads the queen of clubs. You must let it hold! True, Declarer could play dummy's ace next and drop your king, but this will not happen unless you are holding your cards sloppily, or have hesitated before holding off. Normally, Declarer will finesse again, and you will have shut out dummy's long suit. In any event, if you win your king on the first round, Declarer will make his contract; the overtrick he can score by guessing that your king is now unguarded is inconsequential.

This deal illustrates also another useful defensive play, a device to prevent Declarer from holding off. At trick one, instead of winning your spade ace you should play the *queen*. If partner holds the king, this will cost you nothing; when Declarer has the king, he is under great pressure to win it immediately. After all, from his point of view your partner is likely to have the missing ace; if he holds off his king, he may never win it. And if Declarer takes his king early, you can afford to win the first club trick, play your ace of spades and then your low one, allowing partner to run his long suit.

The key features which identify this defensive maneuver are the holding of A Q or, rarely, A J in partner's suit, coupled with the fact that *you* have the fast entry in the most dangerous enemy suit. This play must be part of your routine technique; that is, you must be able to produce it smoothly, in natural rhythm. If you conduct an internal debate and, after twenty seconds or so, play your queen with an air of low cunning, Declarer will surely guess what you have done, and will hold off his stopper.

• DUCKING TO PRESERVE ENTRIES (DECLARER)

We have seen that the race to establish long suits is often decided by *entries*—by communication between the two defenders' hands or between Declarer and dummy. Frequently, it is important to make a winning card in the suit which you are trying to establish serve as an entry. Then, you must be careful not to win it too early. Here is the simplest example of this sort of play:

YOU	DUMMY
♠ A K 5	♠ 8 6 3
♡ A J 10	♡ 5 4
◇ 7 4	◇ A K 8 6 3 2
♣ Q J 8 4 2	♣ 7 5

A low heart is led against your 3 notrump contract, and the king is played on your right. You have 5 top tricks, with a sixth available in hearts so long as you win the king with your ace (you do not hold off, for this would cost you a trick). The extra three tricks must come from dummy's long diamonds. The odds are better than 2 to 1 that the missing five diamonds are divided three and two; thus, after the suit has been played three times all of dummy's little diamonds will be high. However, if you play a diamond to dummy's king, cash the ace, and lead a third round, it will do you no good to have established the suit—you have no entry, and will be unable to cash the little cards.

The solution, of course, is to lead a small diamond and play low from dummy, **ducking** the first trick. On regaining the lead, you will lead to dummy's king and cash the ace. Notice that you have now won the *third* round of the suit in dummy. If the suit has split in a civilized fashion, you can cash three long diamonds, for the lead is in dummy when the suit becomes established. You have made use of your entry when you needed it.

Here is a similar example:

YOU	DUMMY
◇ 8 4 2	◇ A 10 7 5 3

Now you must duck *twice*. Lead a low diamond, and play low from dummy. On regaining the lead, give the opponents their second diamond trick. Finally, lead to dummy's ace at the *third* round, and the ace will serve as the entry to the established long cards.

This ducking play can be crucial even when dummy has a side entry. Suppose you reach an overly ambitious 3 no-trump contract with these cards:

YOU	DUMMY
♠ A 8 6 2	♠ 9 3
♡ A K 4	♡ 7 6 5
◇ 6 4	◇ A 9 7 5 2
♣ A Q 4 2	♣ K 8 3

The heart 2 is led, and you win the queen with your ace. (You do not hold off, since you are not afraid of the 4-card heart suit, and would not welcome a switch to spades.) To win 9 tricks, you must establish dummy's diamonds, hoping that the six missing ones are split three and three—the odds are nearly 2 to 1 against you, but this is your only chance. To cash in on your luck, if the diamonds do split evenly, you must husband your entries to dummy.

You must duck the first diamond. Next, lead to dummy's ace, and play a third round—holding your breath. With luck, the last two diamonds will be high, and you *still have an entry to them*—the king of clubs. Notice that you would have been one entry short had you won dummy's ace prematurely on the first round of the suit.

The same sort of play should be made if dummy has the king instead of the ace:

YOU	DUMMY
◇ 6 4	◇ K 9 7 5 3

Suppose that the ace is in front of the king, and that the suit splits evenly. If you lead to dummy's king, which holds, and then concede a trick, you will require two more entries: one to get there and concede another diamond, the other to get back to cash the long cards. However, if you concede the *first* diamond and next lead to dummy's king, you need only one side entry in order to run the suit.

• DUCKING ON DEFENSE

Of course, it is legal for these ducking plays to be made by the defenders, as well as by Declarer. Actually, your opening lead against notrump is frequently an example of this. If you hold:

    ♠ 8 6 3   ♡ 5 4   ◇ A K 8 6 3   ♣ 7 5

and are on lead against 3 notrump (the enemy bid 1 notrump—3 notrump), you open the diamond 6. This is a ducking play. You hope that partner will gain the lead early and return your suit; then when you cash your king and ace, your little cards will be high. Had you led out your king and ace, as you would against a suit contract, you would have no entry to your long winners.

Now suppose that *partner* is on lead after you have overcalled. He dutifully opens the diamond 7-spot, and you see:

DUMMY
♠ Q 10 2
♡ K J 5
◇ J 4
♣ Q J 10 9 3

YOU
♠ 8 6 3
♡ 6 4
◇ A K 8 6 3 2
♣ 7 5

Dummy plays the jack. You must make a ducking play, just as you would have on opening lead. Signal with your 8 to tell partner to come again. You hope that he will gain the lead in a side suit, and that he has the missing 5 of diamonds to lead to you. If you were to win your king or ace prematurely, partner would have no diamond left to lead, and your long suit could be dead for lack of an entry.

Here is another typical variation of this same play:

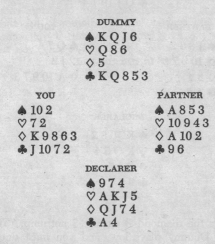

DUMMY
♠ K Q J 6
♡ Q 8 6
♢ 5
♣ K Q 8 5 3

YOU
♠ 10 2
♡ 7 2
♢ K 9 8 6 3
♣ J 10 7 2

PARTNER
♠ A 8 5 3
♡ 10 9 4 3
♢ A 10 2
♣ 9 6

DECLARER
♠ 9 7 4
♡ A K J 5
♢ Q J 7 4
♣ A 4

You lead the diamond 6 against 3 notrump. Partner wins the ace and returns the 10; Declarer covers with the queen. You must *duck*, and save your diamond king as the entry to your long cards. If you win the king here and return the 9, you set up your suit but then never regain the lead to cash your tricks; however, if you duck and leave partner with his 2 of diamonds, he will return it on winning his spade ace—now *all* your diamonds are good.

You may notice that Declarer made an error. He should have held off his diamond stopper, playing the 7 on partner's return of the 10. This would break your communications. However, Declarer's mistake will cost him nothing if you fail to duck and preserve your entry.

If, in the example above, *you*, instead of partner, had held the spade ace, you would have won Declarer's queen with your king and have returned the diamond 9 to establish your suit. However, it can be right to duck even when you hold a side entry:

DUMMY

♠ A 5
♡ A 8 3
◇ K 6 2
♣ Q J 10 7 4

PARTNER   YOU

♠ J 8 3 2   ♠ Q 7 4
♡ 10 9 7 6   ♡ J 2
◇ 8 4   ◇ A 10 9 7 3
♣ A 6 5   ♣ K 8 3

DECLARER

♠ K 10 9 2
♡ K Q 5 4
◇ Q J 5
♣ 9 2

Partner leads the diamond 8 against 3 notrump. (You have overcalled.) Dummy plays low, and you must duck. Now when Declarer leads clubs, partner will rise with his ace, using *his* entry early since he is working on *your* suit, and return the diamond 4. You can establish your diamonds while retaining the club king as an entry to them. Observe that Declarer would have won the race had you taken your ace immediately and returned your suit. Partner would not have a diamond left to play on winning his club ace; thus, you would be short one entry to cash your long cards.

It is harder to see and harder to do, but the position is identical if you hold the diamond king and dummy the ace—you must duck the first trick. Again, you must leave partner with a small diamond to return when he gains the lead; otherwise, you will not set up your suit in time. There is a ducking play similar to this one available in the first example hand of this chapter, the one I promised to bore you with:

DUMMY

♠ Q J 4
♡ A Q 10 4 2
◊ J 7 4
♣ J 9

PARTNER   YOU

♠ 6 3   ♠ K 10 9 8 5
♡ 9 8 6   ♡ K 7 5
◊ A 6 3   ◊ K 8
♣ 10 8 5 4 2   ♣ 7 6 3

DECLARER

♠ A 7 2
♡ J 3
◊ Q 10 9 5 2
♣ A K Q

We have seen that when partner leads the spade 6, dummy plays the jack, and you cover with the king, Declarer should hold off. This is so that when you return the suit and Declarer wins the *second* round, partner has no spades to play on winning his diamond ace. But you should have *ducked dummy's jack*, forcing Declarer to win the first spade trick. Now partner has a spade left, so that if Declarer attacks diamonds partner can defeat the contract by rising with his ace and establishing your suit.

. Another advantage to ducking the spade jack is that this play denies Declarer a later entry to dummy. Suppose that you allow dummy to win the first trick, and Declarer attacks the proper suit—hearts. He enters his own hand with the club ace and leads the heart jack. You *hold off* your king. Thus, Declarer has no entry to dummy's hearts, and you can set him if he tries to establish his own diamonds.

To finish with this deal once and for all, 3 notrump *can* be made by best play even against best defense. Declarer should not play dummy's jack to the first trick, but win the ace in his hand instead. Now he finesses in hearts. You hold off, but he finesses again, and the Q J of spades are still in dummy, providing a sure entry to the established hearts. This way, Declarer must make four heart tricks, three club tricks, and two spade tricks, or nine in all.

• OTHER ENTRY PLAYS (DECLARER)

As we have just seen, Declarer has methods other than ducking plays to produce extra entries to dummy. (I refer to entries to *dummy* because it is usually the strong hand which becomes declarer. If you should become declarer when dummy holds most of your side's strength, your problem will be entries to your own hand. Obviously, all the same techniques can be employed.) In the preceding example, Declarer intended to establish dummy's length; therefore, he saved a side entry for later use. This play is seen in its simplest form here:

YOU	DUMMY
♠ A J 8 3	♠ 9 5
♡ A K 5	♡ 8 6 3
◇ 10 7 2	◇ K Q J 6 4
♣ A 7 3	♣ K 6 2

In 3 notrump with a club lead, you win the ace in your hand to preserve dummy's entry in case the enemy hold off the diamond ace. Now change dummy's king of clubs to the Q J:

♣ A 7 3	♣ Q J 2

You must still win your ace, for the identical reason. It is merely a little harder to see. Similarly, playing 3 notrump with:

YOU	DUMMY
♠ A Q 3	♠ K J 4
♡ A J 9 6 3	♡ 7 5
◇ A J 10 2	◇ 6 3
♣ 9	♣ Q J 10 8 6 3

If a spade is led, you must win the *ace* in your hand to save two entries to dummy. Then overtake your club 9 with dummy's 10 to force out one club honor; lead your spade 3 to dummy's jack and force out the other; then the spade king is the entry to enable you to cash the long clubs. If the spades were:

♠ A Q 4   ♠ K 10 3

you should still win with the ace. Now, after forcing out a club honor, you might lead the 4 and finesse dummy's 10 in an attempt to develop the needed extra entry. Your left-hand opponent could spike your guns by playing his jack on your 4, but, in practice, he seldom does.

Notice that you must *overtake* your club 9. If you did not, the enemy could hold off, leaving the lead in your hand. Now you would need *three* entries to dummy, and you have not got them. This type of play must often be made:

YOU	DUMMY
♠ A J	♠ Q 10 9 6 4
♥ A 7 3	♥ K 8
♦ A 10 7 6 4	♦ 5 3 2
♣ J 8 4	♣ Q 9 2

Your contract is 1 notrump, and the heart queen is led. Your best chance is to work on dummy's spades (by the time your diamonds are established the enemy will probably have 7 tricks; in any case, you would still need a second trick in spades to take 7 yourself). Win the heart ace in your hand, saving dummy's king. Lead your ace and then jack of spades, *overtaking* with dummy's queen. Why? Because the opponents will hold off in spades—if you win your jack, you would need *two* side entries to establish the spades. However, if they hold off after you overtake, you are in dummy and can force out the king without using your entry. Here is a spectacular example of the same play:

YOU	DUMMY
♠ A K 7 3	♠ 8 6 2
♥ A K 6 4 2	♥ 5 3
♦ K	♦ A J 10 9 7
♣ K 10 4	♣ Q J 5

The correct play for 3 notrump against a low club lead is to win the club *king* in your hand (guaranteeing a later entry to dummy) and then overtake the diamond king with dummy's ace. Now you can lead the diamond jack to force out the enemy queen—9 tricks are certain, and 10 probable.

Another variation on the same theme:

YOU	DUMMY
♠ Q 8 4	♠ A 3
♡ J 10	♡ K Q 9 8 2
◇ A Q J 8 2	◇ 7 5
♣ A K 3	♣ 9 8 6 4

Playing 3 notrump, you receive a low spade lead. Hopefully, you duck in dummy—if you can save the ace as an entry to the hearts, your contract is sure. However, the king wins to your right and a spade is returned, knocking out dummy's side entry prematurely. How do you proceed?

It is futile to attack hearts now, for the enemy will kill that suit by holding off one round. Instead, play a diamond from dummy and finesse your queen. It holds, so you must return to dummy to repeat the finesse. Lead your heart jack and *overtake it* with the queen. If the opponents hold off the ace, you are in dummy to lead diamonds; if, instead, they win the ace, you can next overtake your 10 with dummy's king to run the heart suit.

How would you play a 3 notrump contract with these cards?

YOU	DUMMY
♠ A K 3	♠ 7 6 5
♡ K 5 2	♡ 6 4 3
◇ A Q J	◇ 8 3 2
♣ K Q J 7	♣ A 8 4 3

The spade jack is led, and you hold off (if the queen had been played to your right, you would win the first trick for fear of a heart switch, but you are willing to leave your *left*-hand opponent on lead). You win the spade continuation. What now?

You have 7 top tricks, and can win two more in diamonds if the king is to your right, by finessing twice. However, this requires two entries to dummy. The chances are that you can get to lead twice from dummy if you play correctly. Cash the king and queen of clubs. When both opponent's follow suit, overtake your jack with dummy's ace and take your first finesse in diamonds. Now you can lead your club 7 to dummy's 8 and finesse diamonds again.

Note the management of the club suit. When you have a four-four fit with dummy, you can almost always produce a "hidden" extra entry by proper handling of the honors and spot-cards. After all, on the *fourth* round that the suit is played, the opponents probably have no more; here, even a 3 in dummy may become an entry if you have the 2 in your own hand. A suit like this one:

YOU: K J 9 2   DUMMY: A Q 10 3

may yield *four* entries. You can overtake the king with the ace, the jack with the queen, the 9 with the 10, and the 2 with the 3. Indeed, it would be a pity if you were dealt such a suit and did not need all those entries—such a flamboyant line of play is hard to resist.

• ENTRY PLAYS ON DEFENSE

Spectacular entry-producing plays like the last example can seldom be made on defense, for it is not possible to know your partner's exact spots. However, you may occasionally go through similar contortions in order to avoid blocking the run of partner's suit. The simplest case is:

DUMMY
♡ 8 5 3

PARTNER   YOU
♡ Q J 10 7 2   ♡ K 9

DECLARER
♡ A 6 2

Partner leads the heart queen; dummy plays low. You must jettison your king right now. Why? Because Declarer will hold off his ace; if you win the second heart, you will be unable to continue the suit and drive out the enemy stopper. If you and partner both play properly—you overtaking the queen with your king, he overtaking the 9 with his 10— you will be able to establish the long suit without blocking it. We have seen this general principle earlier: never retain a singleton honor in partner's suit. This is easy enough to understand when the honor is the ace or king, but it is just as true of, say, a jack:

DUMMY

♡ Q 3

PARTNER   YOU

♡ A 10 7 6 4 2   ♡ J 9

DECLARER

♡ K 8 5

Partner leads the heart 6, and dummy plays the queen. You must unblock by throwing the jack. Notice that if you gain the lead subsequently and play the 9, partner can overtake with his 10 and run the entire suit even if Declarer holds up his king. However, had you retained your jack, partner could not overtake without setting up a second trick for Declarer.

An obvious extension of this principle is that when you have three cards in partner's suit, two of which are honors, you must play an honor to the first trick (otherwise you would be left with a singleton honor on the third round).

DUMMY

♡ K 3

PARTNER   YOU

♡ A 9 7 6 2   ♡ J 10 4

DECLARER

♡ Q 8 5

When partner leads the 6 and dummy plays the king, you drop your jack. If you gain the lead, you return the 10, and partner can run his suit without danger of blocking. A *triple* unblocking play like the following one should be quite routine for an experienced defender:

DUMMY

♡ 10 2

PARTNER   YOU

♡ K Q J 6 4   ♡ 9 8 7 5

DECLARER

♡ A 3

Partner leads the heart king, you drop your 9, and Declarer holds off. Partner continues with the queen, you play the 8, and Declarer wins his ace. Partner obtains the lead subsequently and plays the heart jack—you unblock the 7. Now partner's 6 drops your 5 and the run of the hearts is uninterrupted. Observe that this management of spot-cards is necessary—it is dangerous to retain even 8's and 7's in partner's long suit.

As a defender, you may be called upon to make a play we saw, earlier, made by Declarer—overtaking partner's honor so that your opponent cannot profit by holding up his stopper. An obvious example:

DUMMY

♠ A 6
♡ 7 4 3
◇ Q J 10 9 7 4
♣ A Q

YOU

♠ J 2
♡ Q 10 9 6 5 2
◇ A K 3
♣ 10 4

Partner leads the heart jack against 3 notrump, after you overcall. If you play the 6, Declarer may hold off with A K 8; now partner cannot continue, and Declarer will have time to knock out your diamond stoppers before your hearts are established. You must, of course, overtake partner's jack. Now Declarer cannot hurt you by holding off—you are on lead, and can continue your long suit.

It is easy to overtake a jack when you hold Q 10 9. But would you overtake if partner led the *queen* and you held:

♡ K 10 9 6 5 2

You still should, and for the same reason: Declarer might hold off with A J 8, and win the race. If you overtake, there is no danger, for *you* can continue the suit and set the contract.

Safeguarding your own communications by these overtaking or unblocking plays is not your only entry problem on defense. You must also concern yourself with disrupting the enemy communications—usually, attacking the side entries in dummy. Occasionally this must take precedence even over pounding away at your side's long suit:

DUMMY

♠ A
♡ 8 6 3
◇ K J 9 7 5 2
♣ 7 5 4

YOU

♠ K 10 9 2
♡ 7 5
◇ A Q 4
♣ J 8 6 3

Against 3 notrump (Declarer opens 1 notrump, dummy raises to 3), partner leads the heart jack, won by Declarer's queen. Declarer leads the diamond 10 and lets it ride. You hold off, hoping that Declarer has only a doubleton. However, a second diamond is played and partner shows out— you now win your queen. Here you must lead a spade, knocking out dummy's side entry prematurely before the diamond suit is established. Note that you had to delay the establishment of partner's hearts; the first order of business is to choke off dummy's menacing suit.

The defense above is obvious and simple. However, change the dummy slightly and it becomes more difficult:

DUMMY

♠ A 4
♡ 8 6 3
◇ K J 9 7 5 2
♣ 7 5

YOU

♠ K 10 9 2
♡ 7 5
◇ A Q 4
♣ J 8 6 3

You still hold off the first diamond and win the second. You still attack dummy's side spade entry. But now you must lead your spade *king*. A low spade lead might be won by Declarer; only the king is certain to knock out dummy's ace. Of course, this gambit of sacrificing your king may present Declarer with an extra spade trick; however, it will surely cost him 3 tricks in diamonds, so you are guaranteed a profit.

A common variation of this defensive maneuver occurs in dummy's long suit itself. Second hand sacrifices an honor to force out dummy's ace, preventing Declarer from making a ducking play:

DUMMY

A J 10 7 4

YOU

K 3

PARTNER

Q 9 2

DECLARER

8 6 5

Declarer leads the 5. If you play small, dummy will finesse the 10, and the suit is established. (Even if partner holds off his queen, Declarer can duck the second round, saving dummy's ace for the vital entry.) You should put up your king. Now if Declarer holds off the ace, your side will win 2 tricks. And if Declarer wins the ace prematurely, partner can hold off his queen and shut out the whole suit. Of course, this type of defensive play is futile when dummy has a sure side entry. It becomes proper only when Declarer must employ a ducking play, trying to use the ace of dummy's long suit as the vital entry to established low cards.

Many of these defensive techniques can be seen in the following example deal:

DUMMY

♠ 7 4 2
♡ 6 4 3
♢ A J 10 9 8
♣ A 2

PARTNER

♠ 8 3
♡ Q J 10 8 5
♢ Q 4 2
♣ 10 8 6

YOU

♠ 10 9 6 5
♡ K 7
♢ K 7 3
♣ K J 5 4

DECLARER

♠ A K Q J
♡ A 9 2
♢ 6 5
♣ Q 9 7 3

Partner leads the queen of hearts against 3 notrump. You unblock your king, and Declarer holds off. Now you switch to the king of clubs, forcing out dummy's ace. Declarer returns to his hand with a high spade to lead the 5 of diamonds. Partner dashes up with his queen—and the contract is set. Declarer can take only four spades, two clubs, one heart, and one diamond; he is a trick short.

Study the three key defensive plays. *First*, you unblocked your heart king on the opening lead. If you had not, Declarer could—and should—win the trick and start diamonds immediately. This way he would make an overtrick. Second, you sacrificed your club king to knock out dummy's side entry. Had you continued hearts, Declarer would win and establish diamonds while the entry remained. And had you led a *low* club, Declarer would win his own queen, saving dummy's vital entry. *Third*, partner rose with his diamond queen to force dummy's ace. Had he played low, dummy would finesse. Now if you were to take your king, Declarer would win 11 tricks. Of course, you should hold off, but this presents Declarer with a second diamond trick, for 9 in all.

The fact is that 3 notrump can be made, even against this virtuoso display of defensive technique. It might amuse you to try to work it out as a double-dummy problem. Here is a clue: the solution will be found in the last section on notrump play, the one devoted to endplays.

• AVOIDANCE PLAYS (DECLARER)

As declarer in a notrump contract, you will frequently meet situations in which one of your opponents is dangerous and the other is safe. That is, only one of your opponents can hurt you—by cashing long cards, by leading through an honor in your hand or dummy. The other opponent, if he gets the lead, can do nothing which will set your contract. Here is a deal which illustrates two such positions:

YOU	DUMMY
♠ Q 8 4	♠ K 5
♡ A K 2	♡ Q 7 5
◇ A 5 4	◇ K 8 6 2
♣ K J 10 3	♣ A 9 6 4

Your left-hand opponent leads the spade 3 against your 3 notrump contract. If you play low from dummy and win the queen in your hand, both opponents are equally dangerous. That is, either opponent can, on gaining the lead, cash the spade ace—or lead to partner's ace—dropping dummy's king. Now the whole spade suit can be run against you.

However, if you play dummy's king to the first trick, as you should, one opponent becomes safe and the other dangerous. When the opening lead was away from the ace, dummy's king holds the trick, and you have the Q 8 left in your hand. Here, it is safe to let your *left*-hand opponent regain the lead. If he cashes his ace, you will play your 8; if he underleads again, you will win with your queen. Your *right*-hand opponent, though, is dangerous. He can lead *through* your queen to partner's ace; if he gains the lead, the spade suit can run against you.

These roles are reversed if dummy's king loses to the ace on your right. Suppose the spade jack is returned; you hold off, and left-hand opponent follows with the missing 2. You win the third round of spades with your queen. Now *left*-hand opponent can bite you; he has two long spades to cash when he gains the lead. *Right*-hand opponent is toothless, since he has no more spades to return to partner.

All this is important as well as interesting because your plan to take 9 tricks must involve a finesse against the queen of clubs. You have two ways to take this finesse (cash your king and then pass the jack; or cash dummy's ace and lead low toward your 10) and no idea where the queen is. What you *do* know is which opponent will win the queen if either type of finesse loses. Thus, you can arrange your finesse so that, if it loses, the *safe* opponent will be on lead. That is, if dummy's spade king holds, cash the ace of clubs and lead your 10. But if the spade king loses and you hold off to the third round, cash your club king and lead your jack. In either case, 9 tricks are virtually assured even if you lose to the club queen. You will lose to the safe opponent.

Of course, you will not always have a convenient two-way finesse to take when you are trying to keep the dangerous opponent off lead. However, there are several other devices available to Declarer in these avoidance positions. A common one is a type of ducking play:

YOU	DUMMY
♠ Q J 8 2	♠ A 10 9
♡ A Q 2	♡ K J 4
◇ K 9 3	◇ A 10 7 6 2
♣ K J 6	♣ 8 4

The club 5 is opened on your left, and you win the 10 with your jack. Clearly, the A Q of clubs are behind your king, so your *right*-hand opponent, who can lead through your king, is dangerous. Therefore, you must *not* try for your extra tricks in spades—the finesse here loses to the dangerous opponent. Instead, you will give up a trick in diamonds to establish dummy's long cards. You must be careful, though, to lose this trick to your *left*-hand opponent, who is safe.

Thus, go to dummy with the heart jack and lead the diamond 2. Your right-hand opponent cannot afford to play an honor (unless, unluckily for you, he has both the queen and the jack), so he will play low. You play your 9, ducking the trick to your safe left-hand opponent. The general principle is to put the opponent to whom you wish to concede a trick in *fourth* seat, while keeping the dangerous hand in *second* seat on the crucial trick.

In the example above, we saw a second type of avoidance play—avoiding, if possible, a finesse which would lose to the dangerous opponent. This consideration may induce you *not* to finesse even when you must attack a suit in which you normally would. For instance:

YOU	DUMMY
♠ A Q 7	♠ K 9 4
♡ A 10 5	♡ 8 4
◇ 8 4 2	◇ A K J 7 3
♣ Q J 10 3	♣ A 8 4

You are declarer in 3 notrump after your right-hand opponent overcalled in hearts. The heart 9 is opened on your left, and you hold off your ace, winning the third round. Now you must dig two extra tricks out of clubs or diamonds. Unfortunately, both finesses go into the danger hand. The club finesse looks particularly uninviting, since your right-hand opponent probably has the club king for his overcall; therefore, you will attack diamonds.

With eight cards missing the queen, your best chance to avoid a diamond loser is to finesse. But here you are willing to lose a diamond (all you need to make your contract is *four* diamond winners) so long as you lose it to your safe *left*-hand opponent. Therefore, you do not finesse. You cash the ace and king. If the queen drops, fine. If it does not, you hold your breath and give up the third round, hoping that it loses to the safe hand. You are perfectly willing to lose a trick unnecessarily to the tripleton queen on your left; you must guard against a doubleton queen on your right.

The same reasoning which, above, leads you to avoid a

normal finesse may, on a different deal, lead you to take a
finesse when you ordinarily would not:

YOU	DUMMY
♠ A 8 3	♠ K 7 5
♡ K 2	♡ 7 4
◇ A J 8 6 2	◇ K 10 7 3
♣ K 8 4	♣ A Q 9 2

Left-hand opponent leads the spade 2 against 3 notrump.
You play low from dummy; the queen comes up on your
right, and you take your ace. Why not hold off? Because you
are afraid of a shift to hearts if it comes *through* your king.
This fear of a heart play from your right-hand opponent conditions your play in diamonds. You lead low to dummy's
king, and return the 3—you will finesse the jack unless the
queen appears. Again, this is not the most likely method for
winning five diamond tricks; with 9 cards, you usually play
to drop a missing queen. However, you are willing to lose a
trick in diamonds. Your play is designed to deny your dangerous right-hand opponent any chance to lead hearts through
your king.

Similarly, you might well finesse against a missing jack
with a combination like:

YOU	DUMMY
◇ 8 4	◇ A K Q 10 2

if your left-hand opponent is dangerous. In contrast, you
might refuse to finesse against a missing king with:

YOU	DUMMY
◇ Q J 10 6 3	◇ A 8 4 2

if you were willing to lose a trick to your left-hand opponent
but not to your right-hand opponent.

Here is an example hand which presents a wide choice of
finesses. The basis on which you decide which to take is:
which can you *lose* without surely losing your contract as
well?

YOU	DUMMY
♠ K 10	♠ A Q 9 3
♡ K Q 5	♡ 7 6
◇ 10 8 7 3 2	◇ A K J
♣ A 9 6	♣ K J 5 3

The heart 4 is opened against 3 notrump, the 10 is played to your right, and you win the king. Clearly, the heart ace is behind your queen; you may go down at once if your right-hand opponent wins a trick. Therefore, you dare not finesse to dummy's jack of diamonds or jack of clubs. Instead, go to dummy with a high diamond, and lead a spade, finessing your 10.

Notice that if *this* finesse loses, you are still alive and kicking, for your *left*-hand opponent cannot hurt you. If he leads another heart, you are home free with your ninth trick. Probably, he will get off lead with a diamond. Go up with dummy's remaining high honor. If the queen falls you have 11 tricks; if it does not, you can attack clubs. Lead low from dummy and finesse your club 9. When this drives out the queen, you have 9 tricks; if it loses to the 10 (in the safe hand) you still have the chance of dropping the club queen. Even if this fails also, you can hope that the diamond queen is to your left. And if nothing at all works, give up bridge for a week or two—you are on an unlucky streak.

The consideration of whether a key finesse will lose to the safe or to the dangerous opponent will occasionally determine whether or not you make a holdup play in the enemy suit. For example:

YOU	DUMMY
♠ A 7 2	♠ K Q 3
♡ K Q 5	♡ 9 6 2
◇ A K 5	◇ 10 8 4
♣ Q 10 9 2	♣ A J 8 3

The heart 4 is opened, and right-hand opponent follows suit with the 10. How should you play to make 3 notrump? If you win this trick, you will have a guarded honor remaining, which will protect you if your left-hand opponent regains the lead. But this is no protection at all, actually, since your only play in this straightforward hand is to tackle clubs—and the club finesse goes into the *dangerous* hand. Of course, the finesse may succeed; then any old play will land 10 tricks. However, you can virtually ensure your contract even if the finesse loses by holding off in hearts, letting the enemy 10 win the first trick. This will disrupt communications if your right-hand opponent has a doubleton; he will have no hearts to lead when he wins his club king. And if he has *three* hearts, then left-hand opponent started with only 4 cards, not enough to defeat you even if he runs his suit.

Exchange your club queen with dummy's ace:

YOU	DUMMY
♣ A 10 9 2	♣ Q J 8 3

Now you should win the first heart trick. The finesse, if it loses, loses to your *left*-hand opponent. Your guarded heart honor gives you complete protection.

The whole point is that although you cannot know *whether* a finesse will lose, you can tell *whom* it will lose to. This can affect your line of play even when you have a sure stopper left in the dangerous enemy suit. In the following hand, it helps you to solve the most common problem of all declarers —which suit to attack first.

DUMMY
♠ A 8 4
♡ A 8 7
◇ Q J 2
♣ A 10 7 2

LEFT-HAND OPPONENT	RIGHT-HAND OPPONENT
♠ Q 10 7 6 5	♠ J 9 3
♡ 9 5 2	♡ Q J 10 4
◇ A 3	◇ 10 9 7 5
♣ 9 5 4	♣ K 3

YOU
♠ K 2
♡ K 6 3
◇ K 8 6 4
♣ Q J 8 6

The spade 6 is opened against your 3 notrump contract, and you win the jack with the king. A count of winners reveals that you must attack both minor suits in order to establish 9 tricks; should you start with clubs or with diamonds?

This is a critical decision, for you are in danger of losing the race; you have one stopper remaining, but two enemy cards to force out. You are willing to give your dangerous left-hand opponent the lead *early*, while you still have protection in spades; however, if he gains the lead *late*, after your last stopper is gone, you will be set. Suppose you take the club finesse at trick two: the king wins to your right; you hold off dummy's ace on the spade return, winning the third round; sooner or later you must play diamonds, and since left-hand opponent has this entry, you are defeated by the long spades.

Of course, it is unlucky to find both missing cards placed badly. (With the club king on your left, the finesse would succeed; with the diamond ace on your right, the spade suit would be dead for lack of an entry.) However, if you play this hand correctly, there is no need to be lucky. Start with the *diamonds*, forcing out the enemy ace. Hold off in spades, winning dummy's stopper on the third round. Now come back to your hand and take the club finesse. It loses to your safe right-hand opponent, who has no spades to return. You have won the race and made your contract even though the key cards were badly placed.

What if these cards were reversed: the diamond ace on your right, the club king on your left? You will still make your contract by playing diamonds first, for *left*-hand opponent cannot gain the lead with his club king—the finesse will work. Remember that although you cannot know where the missing ace and king are, you do know who will win the trick if the finesse fails. Since the finesse will lose to the safe opponent, take it *late* when you have no stopper left in the danger suit. You cannot tell who will win the missing ace, so force it out *early* while you have a stopper remaining.

Here is the identical principle in reverse:

DUMMY

♠ J 8 3
♡ A 4
◇ J 6 4
♣ K J 10 8 3

LEFT-HAND OPPONENT

♠ K 10 2
♡ Q J 10 7 2
◇ Q 8 2
♣ 7 5

RIGHT-HAND OPPONENT

♠ 9 6 5 4
♡ 9 6 5
◇ K 9 5 3
♣ A 2

YOU

♠ A Q 7
♡ K 8 3
◇ A 10 7
♣ Q 9 6 4

The heart queen is the opening lead against your 3 notrump contract. You have four top winners, with four more available in clubs after the enemy ace of clubs is forced out. The ninth trick can surely be produced in spades, even should the finesse lose. However, here again you may have to surrender the lead twice when you have only one remaining stopper in the enemy suit. Therefore, the *order* in which you force out the opponents' entries is crucial.

It seems natural to attack the long club suit first, but this is wrong, and will fail. Right-hand opponent wins the ace, and returns hearts, establishing his partner's suit. Eventually, you must take the spade finesse; it loses to the dangerous left-hand opponent, and you are down. Instead, you should finesse in spades *first*. The king wins on your left, and hearts are continued—you hold off your king to the third round of the suit. Now you play clubs. The ace wins to your *right*, so your contract is safe.

Note that here, too, you would make 3 notrump if the key cards were reversed. Then the spade finesse would succeed, and you could switch briskly to clubs establishing your 9 tricks. What if *both* entries were to your left in the dangerous hand? Then you would go down no matter which suit you attacked first. You are entitled to complain about your bad luck, but only if you made the proper plays and gave yourself every chance to be fortunate.

Obviously, there is no rule to tell you whether to knock out an enemy ace before you take a finesse. It can be correct to do either first. The determining factor is: Which opponent will the finesse lose to? If it will lose to the *safe* hand, take it last; if it will lose to the *dangerous* hand, the one with length in the danger suit, take it first. And when you have a choice of several finesses to take, you decide on the same basis: a finesse which loses to the dangerous hand must be taken early while you have a stopper left; a finesse which loses to the safe hand is best taken late, when that opponent is exhausted in the danger suit.

• DEFENSE AGAINST AVOIDANCE PLAYS

These avoidance plays are of little use to you as a defender. We have already seen the only methods by which a defender can keep a dangerous dummy off lead—holding off with stoppers, and forcing out a dangerous side entry early.

You seldom have the luxury of deciding which suit to attack first, and you can see by looking at dummy whether, or which way, to finesse.

What the defense *can* occasionally do, though, is to prevent Declarer from making an avoidance play. There are two techniques for this which complement each other: (1) If Declarer is trying to keep *you* off lead and to lose a trick to partner, you may stop him by putting up an honor, playing second hand *high*. (2) If Declarer is trying to keep *partner* off lead and lose a trick to you, you may stop him by unblocking or discarding an honor which would otherwise win an unwanted trick. For example, consider this combination of cards:

DUMMY

A 8 5 3 2

(1)   YOU   PARTNER

J 7   Q 10 6

DECLARER

K 9 4

Suppose that Declarer must establish this suit without allowing partner to gain the lead. If he plays in straightforward fashion—king, ace, and then small—he will be defeated. So he attempts an avoidance play, leading the 2 from dummy; if partner plays the 6, Declarer will follow with the 9, ducking the trick to you. Partner can scotch this by putting up either honor. Now Declarer cannot pass the trick to you.

Next let us make a slight change:

DUMMY

A 8 5 3 2

(2)   YOU   PARTNER

Q 7   J 10 6

DECLARER

K 9 4

Again, dummy leads the 2; partner rises with an honor to prevent Declarer from passing the lead to you; Declarer wins his king. Right here, you must throw your queen under the king! If you hold onto it, following with the 7, Declarer next leads his 4; when your queen appears, he lets you win it.

Partner cannot overtake, and the key trick is lost to *you* instead of to partner.

Here is a full deal which illustrates all these techniques:

DUMMY
♠ A K 7 5 3
♡ 7
◇ K 4
♣ A 10 7 6 2

YOU
♠ Q 8 4
♡ A Q 6 4 2
◇ J 10 5
♣ Q 5

PARTNER
♠ J 10 6
♡ 10 9 5 3
◇ Q 9 3
♣ J 9 4

DECLARER
♠ 9 2
♡ K J 8
◇ A 8 7 6 2
♣ K 8 3

You open the heart 4 against 3 notrump; partner's 9 loses to Declarer's jack. With seven top winners, Declarer can make his contract by conceding a trick in any one of his three long suits. However, he will be defeated unless he can contrive to lose this trick to *you*, not to partner. Suppose he attacks the clubs:

♣ A 10 7 6 2

♣ Q 5   ♣ J 9 4

♣ K 8 3

If he leads the king, you must unblock your queen at once. (This cannot cost, since if partner does not have the jack, your queen will be lost anyway.) If, instead, Declarer goes to dummy and leads the 2, partner must be careful to play his 9. Now when Declarer wins the king, you must again throw away your queen.

Suppose Declarer attacks diamonds, not clubs:

◇ K 4

◇ J 10 5   ◇ Q 9 3

◇ A 8 7 6 2

Here, the proper defense is more complex. Declarer leads the 2—if you follow with the 5, you are lost. When partner plays the 9 to the next trick, Declarer ducks and you must take your 10 or jack. Even if partner properly puts up his queen on the second round, Declarer can win and concede the third trick to you. However, if you play your 10 to the first trick you are safe. Dummy wins the king and returns the 4; Declarer cannot duck partner's 9, since you can play your 5 under it. Actually, partner should put up his queen at the second round (in case you have J 10 alone). Now when Declarer takes the ace, you unblock the 10; partner's 9 wins the third trick.

Finally, consider the spade suit:

$$♠ A K 7 5 3$$

$$♠ Q 8 4 \qquad\qquad ♠ J 10 6$$

$$♠ 9 2$$

If Declarer leads the king and cashes the ace, you must be careful to throw away your queen, allowing partner to win the third round.

Can Declarer make his contract against best defense? Yes. He can concede a trick to *you* in the spade suit above by leading twice *toward* dummy's honors. Then if you play your queen to the first or second round, he can let you win it. And if you save the queen, you will win the third round.

Declarer can succeed in the club suit with a similar play:

$$♣ A 10 7 6 2$$

$$♣ Q 5 \qquad\qquad ♣ J 9 4$$

$$♣ K 8 3$$

He starts the suit by leading his 3 toward dummy's ace, so that if you unblock the queen he can allow it to hold. When you play the 5, he takes dummy's ace and returns the two. Partner must play his 9 and Declarer can safely duck, forcing you to win the queen.

If Declarer does find a winning approach, your only defense is not to play against him too often. However, most declarers will give you an opportunity to defeat a contract like this one. Then you and partner must both be alert to your respective roles—he to put up his high cards in second seat, you to throw away your blocking honors.

• ENDPLAYS (DECLARER)

The **endplay** is an advanced technique with which Declarer can occasionally produce one extra trick. This is done, usually toward the end of the hand's play, by forcing the defenders to lead a key suit, presenting declarer with a trick which he could not make on his own.

When the honors in a suit are divided between the two opposing sides, neither partnership holding a sequence of three honors, then the side which *starts* the play of this suit is likely to lose a trick. For example:

NORTH

♡ J 7 3

WEST   EAST

♡ A 10 6 4   ♡ K 9 5

SOUTH

♡ Q 8 2

There is no way for North-South to win a trick in this suit by attacking it themselves. (If South leads the 2, North's jack loses to the king, and the A 10 are still behind the queen. If South leads the queen, West takes his ace; the K 9 are still behind the jack.) However, if either West or East starts hearts, North-South are assured of a trick. (If West leads the 4, North plays low and East must put up his king to stop the queen from winning; now the queen forces out the ace, and the jack is high.)

Look at the last combination of cards from the standpoint of the East-West partnership. There is no means by which they can play this suit themselves without losing a trick. But they can take all the tricks if they can induce either North or South to lead the suit first.

Similarly, when your partnership holds in a suit either:

DUMMY   DUMMY

Q 5   J 2

or

DECLARER   DECLARER

A 4   A K 5

you have almost no chance to produce an extra trick by attacking the combination yourself. Your plan must be to force the opponent who holds the missing honor to lead the suit for you.

Let us change these combinations slightly:

DUMMY		DUMMY
5 4		5 2
DECLARER	or	DECLARER
A Q		A K J

Now you have a tenace, and so there is a 50 per cent chance for an extra trick by means of a finesse. Even here, though, it can be to your advantage to force the enemy to start the suit. If your left-hand opponent leads into your tenace, you have your extra trick 100 per cent of the time, regardless of the location of the missing honor. Thus, whenever you need 1 more trick to fulfill your contract, and you must try to take it with an honor that is not quite high, you should start thinking of how to persuade the enemy to lead the key suit to you—of how to work an endplay. Here is a simple example.

DUMMY
♠ 7 5
♡ K 7 6
♢ A K Q 2
♣ Q 8 4 2

WEST
♠ K 10 9 6 2
♡ 5 4
♢ J 10 7 6
♣ 6 3

EAST
♠ J 8 4
♡ J 10 9 3 2
♢ 9 5
♣ 10 9 5

SOUTH
♠ A Q 3
♡ A Q 8
♢ 8 4 3
♣ A K J 7

Your contract is 6 notrump (6 *clubs* would be easier—a suit slam generally is). West opens the heart 5, properly refusing to lead away from an honor against a notrump *slam*—he does not have to establish a long suit to defeat you, for he needs only 2 tricks.

Your first step is to count your top winners: four clubs, three diamonds, three hearts, one spade—11 in all. Where is your twelfth trick? If the missing diamonds divide three-three (or if the opponent with four diamonds unwisely discards one), dummy's 2 will be high. Failing this, you can try to win your spade queen.

You should start out by cashing your four club tricks, giving the enemy an opportunity to err in discarding. However, West correctly throws away two small spades, East his fifth heart. Next, you cash your two remaining heart honors—West discards another spade. Now you attack diamonds, taking dummy's ace, king, and queen. When East shows out on the third round, you realize that your queen of spades is the last hope for the fulfilling trick. Should you finesse?

No! There is no need to gamble when you have a sure play available. Lead dummy's last diamond, discarding your small spade. West wins, and is *endplayed.* You know that he has no more diamonds, hearts, or clubs; therefore he must lead spades into your tenace. Wherever the spade king is, you make your queen and your contract.

Before you finesse in at attempt to produce the trick that makes the contract, think, "Is there any way in which I can force the proper opponent to lead this suit to me?" The "proper" opponent is the one who must lead *into* your tenace, not through it; in the example above, if East proved to have the fourth diamond you would not put him on lead with it, since a spade lead *through* your A Q cannot help you. Even if you can give the lead to the correct opponent, you must first take away his safe exit cards. That is, it would be futile to give West the lead in diamonds before cashing your clubs and hearts, for then he would lead one of those suits instead of spades. The two elements of a successful endplay are (1) first eliminating the suits that the enemy can play safely, and (2) then giving the lead to the proper opponent.

Of course, if you have one of those combinations which will yield an extra trick if *either* opponent starts the suit, you need not worry about giving the lead to a specific hand. For instance:

DUMMY
♠ J 8 3
♡ A 9 4
◇ K Q 9 5
♣ 8 6 3

WEST   EAST
♠ A 10 2   ♠ K 9 6
♡ J 8 3   ♡ Q 7 5 2
◇ 7 6 4   ◇ 10 8 2
♣ Q 9 5 4   ♣ J 10 7

YOU
♠ Q 7 5 4
♡ K 10 6
◇ A J 3
♣ A K 2

West opens the 4 of clubs against your 3 notrump contract.
You count 8 fast tricks, but have no obvious chance for a
ninth. An attack on spades will fail since you must give up
3 tricks before establishing one; the enemy will then have
two club tricks in addition, or five in all. And there is no real
possibility of digging the extra trick out of hearts no matter
how you play this suit.

Is this a hopeless contract then? Not at all—you will make
it if you play correctly. Your strategy must be to force either
opponent to start the heart or spade suit for you. Win the
opening lead; cash three rounds of diamonds, so that the
enemy cannot play this suit; now, take your remaining club
honor, and give up the lead with your low club. The opponents can win their two club tricks (no more, since you know
that West has no spot-card lower than the one he led, and
thus started with a 4-card suit). Then they are endplayed—
with no more clubs or diamonds to lead, they must present
you with your ninth trick by attacking hearts or spades.

You see in this example a very common endplay technique
—giving the lead to the opponents *in their own suit*, after
taking away their safe exit cards. When you have this play in
mind, you will not hold off your stoppers in their suits to

the last moment; you must save a *low* card in the enemy suit with which to give up the lead. This can be seen in the previous hand—had you held off in clubs, you would have been forced to start either hearts or spades yourself. The same principle holds true here:

DUMMY

♠ K J 2
♡ 8 5 3
◇ A 8 2
♣ K Q 7 2

WEST

♠ 10 8 7 6
♡ 9
◇ 7 5 4 3
♣ J 10 9 6

EAST

♠ A 5 3
♡ K J 10 7 6 4
◇ K 9
♣ 8 4

YOU

♠ Q 9 4
♡ A Q 2
◇ Q J 10 6
♣ A 5 3

After East opens the bidding with 1 heart, you become declarer at 3 notrump; West leads the heart 9. If East signals with the 7, you can make the contract by holding off; West is forced to switch, and you then have time to force out both the spade ace and diamond king before the hearts are established. However, East should overtake the 9 with his 10. Now the normal holdoff and avoidance techniques are useless. East will continue hearts, and it does you no good to take the finesse into the danger hand first; you know, from the opening bid, that the missing ace is there too. How can you win 9 tricks without allowing East to gain the lead twice and run his hearts?

Your tricks must be two in spades after forcing out the ace, two in hearts, three in clubs, one top diamond plus a second diamond made by an endplay. Since you need your low heart in order to put East on lead late in the play, you win the first trick. A spade to dummy's king knocks out the ace, and you take the heart continuation, again refusing to hold off. Next you cash two high spades and the three top clubs. East must come down to five cards: the K 9 of diamonds and three established hearts. Now you play your carefully preserved low heart. East wins his three heart tricks, but is then forced to lead away from the king of diamonds, presenting you with your ninth trick.

Notice that East can be endplayed even though he originally has enough established tricks to defeat your contract. He cannot hold all his winners; in order to keep his guarded king, he must discard good cards. This will be true no matter how many winners he has so long as these two conditions obtain: you are within 1 trick of your contract; your opponent has a king or queen which he must guard. Under these circumstances, you can almost always endplay your opponent with one of his winners, forcing him to lead away from his guarded honor to give you your extra trick.

Our final example of an endplay is a deal we presented earlier as a problem:

DUMMY
♠ 7 4 2
♡ 6 4 3
♢ A J 10 9 8
♣ A 2

WEST
♠ 8 3
♡ Q J 10 8 5
♢ Q 4 2
♣ 9 7 6

EAST
♠ 10 9 6 5
♡ K 7
♢ K 7 3
♣ K J 10 4

YOU
♠ A K Q J
♡ A 9 2
♢ 6 5
♣ Q 8 5 3

An inspired defense gives you rough going in your 3 notrump contract. West leads the heart queen, East unblocks the king and you hold off. East shifts to the club king, knocking out dummy's entry. You return to your hand with a spade in order to start diamonds, and West alertly puts up his diamond queen, forcing you to win dummy's ace prematurely. The position now is:

```
                        DUMMY
                        ♠ 7 4
                        ♡ 6 4
                        ◇ J 10 9 8
                        ♣ 2

        WEST                            EAST
        ♠ 8                             ♠ 10 9 6
        ♡ J 10 8 5                      ♡ 7
        ◇ 4 2                           ◇ K 7
        ♣ 9 7                           ♣ J 10 4

                        YOU
                        ♠ K Q J
                        ♡ A 9
                        ◇ 6
                        ♣ Q 8 5
```

Your best chance for a ninth trick is to force East to give dummy a diamond trick. To do this, you must take away all his safe exit cards and then give him the lead. Play the low club from dummy and *duck*. East wins, and (best) takes his diamond king, then exits with a spade. Now you cash your three spades, your heart ace, your club queen. Finally, you lead your low club—East wins, and has nothing to play except a diamond to dummy's high jack.

Note that you must take your high spades and heart before leading the last club. Otherwise, East could safely exit in one of these suits. Note, too, the key maneuver of ducking the second round of clubs early in the play. This was to make sure that you endplayed the correct opponent. Had you, instead, cashed your high heart and spades and then played queen and a low club, you could be defeated. East should drop a club *honor* under your queen and allow West to win the third round with his 9. Now, West would cash two high hearts and set you. (He, of course, discarded his little diamond on your high spades.)

• DEFENDING AGAINST ENDPLAYS

In the preceding example we see one of the two chief methods of defending yourself against a declarer who is trying to endplay you: throwing away the high card with which Declarer can force you on lead, hoping that partner can win the trick instead. Suppose that you are defending against a contract of 1 notrump:

DUMMY
♠ A Q
♡ 8 4 3
♢ J 7 5 4
♣ 10 5 4 2

YOU
♠ K 10 5
♡ K Q J 7 2
♢ A 8
♣ Q 9 3

You opened the bidding 1 heart, Declarer overcalled 1 notrump, and everyone passed. Partner leads the heart 9; your jack loses to Declarer's ace. Declarer leads the king of diamonds. You win your ace, and cash four heart tricks. You exit with the diamond 8; Declarer wins the queen and leads to dummy's jack. You discard a low spade and the position is now:

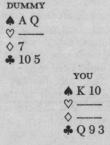

DUMMY
♠ A Q
♡ ——
♢ 7
♣ 10 5

YOU
♠ K 10
♡ ——
♢ ——
♣ Q 9 3

Dummy leads the 5 of clubs to Declarer's king, and Declarer cashes the club ace. He is about to endplay you, giving you the lead with your high club to force you to play into dummy's spade tenace. Therefore, you must throw your club queen under Declarer's ace! You hope that partner holds the missing jack (he probably does, since Declarer did not finesse). And if Declarer has the club jack after all, you have lost nothing. The contract would surely have been made if you had retained your queen. At least, Declarer will not have the satisfaction of endplaying you.

A second defensive technique is to *unguard* an honor when you are in danger of being forced to lead away from it in an endplay. Consider this example:

DUMMY
♠ A K J 4
♡ 8 3
♢ Q 7 4 2
♣ A Q 9

YOU
♠ 8 7 6
♡ K Q J 9 6 2
♢ K 3
♣ 5 3

PARTNER
♠ 10 5 3
♡ 10 7 4
♢ J 10 8 6
♣ 8 7 4

DECLARER
♠ Q 9 2
♡ A 5
♢ A 9 5
♣ K J 10 6 2

The contract is 6 notrump. Six *clubs* would be better, for Declarer could win your heart lead, draw trumps, discard his heart on dummy's fourth spade, and lead up to dummy's diamond queen for his twelfth trick. However, Declarer cannot make a straightforward play in *notrump* after you lead the heart king. His best chance is for an endplay—forcing you on lead with your heart winner at the eleventh trick, and hoping that you must play away from the diamond king.

Thus, Declarer wins the first trick, then cashes five clubs and four spades. You must discard down to 3 cards. If they are:

♡ K   ♢ K 3

Declarer throws you in with the heart, and you must give him his contract by leading diamonds for him. What could you do to prevent this? You could have held *two* hearts and the blank king of diamonds. Of course, Declarer could now lay down his ace of diamonds and drop your king, but there is no way for him to know what you have done. That is, there is no way unless you help him by going into an anguished trance before unguarding your king. If you discard your diamond 3 early and without pain, Declarer will almost certainly go wrong by trying to endplay you when you hold the setting tricks.

Have you noticed that there is another way to set this contract? You and partner could discard on the clubs and spades to come down to this end position:

DUMMY

♡ 8

◇ Q 7

YOU   PARTNER

♡ 9   ♡ 10

◇ K 3   ◇ J 10

DECLARER

♡ 5

◇ A 9

Now *partner* wins the heart trick, and leads toward your diamond king. This is a good theoretical illustration of the first method for combating endplays—discarding honors. You have to throw away both your jack and queen of hearts, saving a low one. This defense will surely defeat the slam, but in real life it is usually impossible to discard in such an ideal fashion. Even if you guess that partner holds the heart 10 and are expert enough to unblock both your heart honors (as no doubt you are), your partner will cross you up anyway by discarding his "worthless" hearts. If he is anything like *my* partners, he is not thinking about anything at all—he is full of self-pity because of his horrible hand, and is simply waiting for the contract to be made so that he can begin his lamentations. Little does he suspect that *his* discards may be the crux of the defense. Thus, you are usually on your own, and must decide whether or not to unguard your diamond king.

I say "whether or not" because it is not always right to make the expert play. If Declarer has never in his life tried for an endplay and really is unwilling to believe that such a thing exists, it is a terrible error to blank your king no matter with what superb insouciant air. Declarer will cash his ace, and look at you in gratified astonishment when your king drops. Never waste a million-dollar defense on a five-and-ten-cent declarer.

CHAPTER 11

Play and Defense at Suit Contracts

• PLANNING AS DECLARER

It is more difficult to plan your play in suit contracts than it is at notrump. The reason is that there are usually more ways to win tricks. In notrump, you can win only high cards or long cards, so contracts are hard to fulfill but easy to plan. In suits, you can win extra tricks by trumping, so contracts are easier to make; but there are more decisions to be made before you come up with the correct line of attack.

Roughly, there are four methods of playing suit contracts. Each one has its own problems and techniques, and we will examine them individually.

1. **Ruff losers with dummy's trumps**
2. **Establish a long side suit in your own hand or dummy**
3. **Win honors which are nearly high**
4. **Win the small trumps in your own hand by ruffing**

The single most important quality of a good declarer is that he knows which of these four campaigns he is embarked on. If he keeps his eye on the method he has selected for producing extra winners, he is likely to make his contract, even if he makes a technical error or two. But if he adopts a common fifth approach, much favored by my partners—

5. **Try a little of each, and hope for the best**

he will probably go down. Suppose that you are declarer in 4 spades with these cards:

DECLARER	DUMMY
♠ A K 8 7 6	♠ 9 5 3
♡ 2	♡ A 8 5 3
◇ A Q	◇ J 10 7 5 3
♣ A Q 8 5 2	♣ 6

The opening lead is the spade queen. What is your plan? It is not simple to answer this question, because all four lines of play are available.

Trumping in dummy. Win the spade king. Cash the club ace and ruff a club. Come back to your hand by ruffing a heart, and ruff another club. Now, if all goes well, you can come to your hand again with a high diamond, and lay down the ace of spades. If the club king has not dropped, you can concede a trick to it, and lose one trump, one club, and one diamond.

Setting up a long suit. Above, you combined trumping in dummy with establishing your long clubs. Instead, you could work on dummy's diamonds. Win the spade king and cash the ace. Play ace and queen of diamonds, conceding the king. Now you can go to dummy's heart ace and run the diamond suit, discarding your low clubs. This way, you lose one spade and one diamond.

Finessing. Win the spade king, and lead to dummy's heart ace. Play a club and finesse your queen. If it holds, ruff a low club in dummy and lead a diamond toward your queen. If lucky, you may lose only one trump trick, and make 12 tricks.

Trumping in your hand. Win the spade king, lead to dummy's ace of hearts, and ruff a heart. Cash ace of clubs, and ruff in dummy. Ruff another heart. Ruff another club. Ruff the last heart. If no one overruffs at any stage, you have won 8 tricks, and can cash the aces of diamonds and spades for 10.

Now, I do not propose to analyze here which of these four lines of attack is the best. What I want you to realize is that you must adopt one of them, and *you must know which it is.* Let me show you the complete deal:

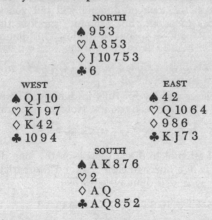

```
                    NORTH
                  ♠ 9 5 3
                  ♡ A 8 5 3
                  ◇ J 10 7 5 3
                  ♣ 6
     WEST                           EAST
  ♠ Q J 10                       ♠ 4 2
  ♡ K J 9 7                      ♡ Q 10 6 4
  ◇ K 4 2                        ◇ 9 8 6
  ♣ 10 9 4                       ♣ K J 7 3
                    SOUTH
                  ♠ A K 8 7 6
                  ♡ 2
                  ◇ A Q
                  ♣ A Q 8 5 2
```

Note that all four plans will work. However, the actual South tried the fifth approach. He won the spade opening lead, led to the heart ace, and ruffed a heart. He cashed the club ace and ruffed a club. Now he finessed the queen of diamonds. West won, and led a second trump. Declarer had to lose a spade and two more clubs, for down one. On a hand in which all four reasonable plans succeed, he went down because he tried no one of them, but, instead, a little of each.

This is the sort of disaster which is easily avoidable. All you have to do is decide—even before you play a card from dummy—which of the four basic plans you will adopt. In later sections, I will try to show you the proper techniques and precautions to adopt for each plan. But this will all be wasted if you do not make up your mind, consciously, which it is that you are trying to do.

• PLANNING ON DEFENSE

Planning your defense against a suit contract is not usually so difficult a job as planning the play. Sometimes you go after ruffing tricks of your own, by leading a short suit. But most often, you adapt your defense to counter Declarer's line of play. If he is trying for ruffing tricks, you play trumps whenever it is your turn. If he is trying to set up a long suit in dummy for discards, you usually attempt to cash out your winners in a desperate hurry before Declarer throws away his losers. If he must try to win tricks with nearly-high honors, you defend quietly, sitting back and waiting for your winners. Almost always, the look of dummy will tell you which of these defenses to adopt. For example, suppose the enemy auction goes 1 spade—2 spades—4 spades. This dummy comes down:

♠ J 8 4 3   ♡ 2   ◇ A 7 5 2   ♣ 10 5 3 2

Clearly, Declarer will try for ruffs in dummy. Therefore, the defense is in a hurry to lead trumps. Now, suppose dummy is:

♠ Q 7 5   ♡ 5 3   ◇ K Q J 10 7   ♣ 8 3 2

Declarer will attempt to discard losers on the long diamonds. The defense is in a hurry to cash club and heart tricks before they disappear. And if dummy looks like:

♠ A Q 5 2   ♡ 10 3 2   ◇ J 5 2   ♣ Q 8 3

Declarer can neither ruff nor discard losers. The defense is not in a hurry to do anything; it should be passive. Thus, the distributional pattern of the dummy usually tells the defense what to do. And any doubts are dispelled by Declarer's first lead. For example, if dummy is:

♠ K85   ♡ 42   ◇ A J 7 6 2   ♣ 8 3 2

Declarer may plan to use either the heart shortness or the diamond length. If he leads hearts, the defense should play trumps; if he leads diamonds, the defense should try to cash outside winners. We will examine defensive techniques in some detail later. However, three-quarters of your job is simply to realize what Declarer is up to—and thus to know what the objective of the defense must be.

THE OPENING LEAD

Actually, the hardest play to make on defense is the opening lead. Since you do not see the dummy first, you cannot be sure what your objective is—to stop ruffs, to cash out quickly, or to stay quiet and wait for your tricks. A trump lead, for instance, is the best way to stop ruffs or stay quiet, but it forfeits virtually any chance for a successful defense if it turns out to be a deal (probably the most common type) in which you must take your own winners quickly. However, if you lead a side suit in which you have an honor, trying to cash in a hurry, you may lose the setting trick when all you had to do was sit and wait. What you must do in selecting a blind opening lead (that is, a lead when partner has not bid) is to compromise between two qualities—attack and safety. "Attack" means "How likely is it that this lead will produce fast tricks?" "Safety" means "How likely is it that this lead will cost a trick which would otherwise be won?"

Unfortunately, attack and safety are often in conflict. Suppose that the enemy auction has gone:

DECLARER	DUMMY
1 spade	2 diamonds
3 spades	4 spades

You are on lead with this hand:

♠ Q 8 4   ♡ K J 4   ◇ Q 5 3   ♣ 7 6 3 2

Clearly, you must open hearts or clubs. The 4 of hearts lead is excellent for attack, since it will produce 2 or 3 tricks immediately if partner has the ace, or set up two possible winners if partner has the queen; but it is terribly dangerous, for if partner has neither honor you allow Declarer to win the first round with the queen—and now you may never make your king. In contrast, the 2 of clubs lead is completely safe, for you cannot lose a trick when you lead from nothing; but it is not at all attacking, since even if you find partner with an honor you may not produce a winner. Thus, you cannot have both attack and safety—which do you choose?

On the auction above, I would go for the attacking heart lead. Against *game* contracts (and even more urgently, against small slams) I tend to make aggressive leads, (1) because the opponents are likely to have the fulfilling tricks if I do not take mine first, and (2) because we do not figure to have the lead often—the opening lead may represent half of our opportunity to set up or cash winners. In contrast, I weigh safety much more heavily in defense against *part-score* contracts. The opponents do *not* have an abundance of points, and there is less need to gamble with the opening, for we rate to be on lead often again. Thus, against 2 spades, I would lead clubs.

Another factor which induces me to attack is my holding in dummy's suit—diamonds. It looks as though the diamonds will provide discards, since the finesse (if there is one) works, and the suit splits evenly. If I held *four* diamonds to the Q J, I would try the safe club lead instead, since there would appear to be less chance that our winners will vanish if they are not cashed early. Thus, you can see in this example the two main considerations in choosing between attack and safety: How high is the enemy contract? How well does dummy's side suit split?

Of course, it is ideal if you can attack with safety. This is possible when you have a sequence of 3 cards headed by an honor (K Q J, Q J 10, J 10 9). Leading the top of a sequence is completely safe as well as highly attacking, which is why these openings are so highly recommended. When the third card is just out of sequence (K Q 10, Q J 9, etc.), the lead is just as attacking and nearly as safe. So it is still an excellent one.

The best opening lead of all is the king from an A K combination. This is highly attacking, obviously, and safe as well. The greatest advantage of this opening, though, is that it holds the lead; you get to see the dummy, and can then make an intelligent decision instead of guessing. Therefore, if you have an A K, be thankful and lead the king. When you choose a different opening, it is brilliant when it works, but it is plain foolishness when, as is usual, it does not.

Another lead which is attacking while safe is a small singleton. The safety is qualified, though, if the opponents have bid the suit, since you are likely to spare Declarer a guess when partner has some intermediate honor holding. And for the attack to be successful you need useless trumps to ruff with. (It is pointless to open a singleton when holding queen-jack-small in trumps, for instance.) In addition, partner must be able to gain the lead to give you a ruff, so the *weaker* your hand the more promising is a short suit opening. Notwithstanding these limitations, though, the lead of a singleton is usually your best bet. This is particularly true when the enemy have bid strongly and confidently, so that high cards alone will not defeat them.

Similarly, a low *doubleton* is safe and mildly attacking. It is not nearly so likely to produce a ruff as is a singleton—therefore, it is not a very attractive lead in a suit the opponents have bid. However, a doubleton in a unbid suit is an excellent opening, particularly if you have a weakish hand with worthless trumps.

A 2-card sequence (K Q, Q J, J 10, etc.) is practically as useful for attack as is a 3-card sequence. It is not so safe, but it *is* a lot safer than leading from a single honor. (Some days, it will seem that whenever you lead the queen from queen-jack-small, the A 10 are in dummy, and Declarer has the king. Still, this will not happen very often, and you cannot be concerned solely with safety.) Against a suit contract, lead the top honor of a 2-card sequence (against no-trump, you would lead fourth best).

This concludes the list of good leads—those which are both safe and attacking. All other openings are either dangerous or unproductive, so you must decide on the basis we have discussed whether to be aggressive or passive. In general, suits in which you have great length are safer and less attacking. If you lose an honor by leading from it, you probably would not have won it anyway; but if you set up a winner, it may not cash. Shorter suits are more dangerous and attacking. Thus, if you must lead one of these suits:

♡ Q 10 5   ◇ Q 10 8 6 4

the heart 5 is the more attacking, the diamond 6 the safer, opening. When you decide to lead away from an honor, for example against 4 spades with:

♠ J 8 6 2   ♡ Q 7 4   ◇ J 6 4   ♣ K 5 3

the lead from the queen is safest (since if partner has no honor, you were probably not going to win a trick anyway), while the lead from the king is most attacking. The lead away from the jack is poorest, since it is neither safe nor attacking. Usually, the lead from the queen should be preferred, since it is mildly aggressive while relatively safe.

The same is true of leading doubleton *honors*. King from king-small is a desperate attacking lead, reserved for almost hopeless positions. Jack from jack-small is poor, for it often costs a trick and seldom gains one. Queen from queen-small is reasonable, if no better lead is available.

Ace from ace-small looks safer than it actually is. True, you will not lose your ace, but an ace should do more than win a trick—it should capture an enemy honor. In addition, it is valuable as a *control*—the enemy cannot win a trick in this suit without giving you the lead. Thus, the lead of an ace almost always costs you a trick indirectly, by losing its side advantages. If you obtain a ruff, you often are merely recovering the trick you gave up.

For the reasons above, avoid, whenever possible, leading any suit in which you hold the ace. Naturally, this does not apply when you have the king as well, or when partner has bid the suit strongly enough to suggest that *he* holds the king.

When partner *has* bid a suit, you should, of course, tend to open it. If you have an *excellent* lead of your own—an A K, a 3-card sequence, a singleton—you might well ignore partner's bid. Otherwise, keep him happy by leading his suit. Occasionally, you may make an exception when your holding includes partner's ace. Then, try to open some other suit, unless partner has promised great strength in his own. That is, if partner has made an opening bid, he does not necessarily have the king of his suit; but if partner has *overcalled*, he promises a strong suit and you should lead it.

Finally, let us specify which *card* to lead in the suit you select. From A K, the *king*. From any two- or three-card sequence, the *top*. From any doubleton, the *top*. From any 4-card or longer suit not headed by a sequence, the *fourth best*. (However, if headed by the ace, lead the *ace* when you must open the suit.) From the king or queen, or jack or ten and two small, the *lowest card* (the *ace* from ace and two small). From three small cards, lead the *top*. (A controversy has been raging for years in the bridge world whether to lead the top or the bottom card of three little ones. Most players lead high, so I recommend this here. In any event, this is a mighty poor opening lead, so you should not have the problem often.)

Note that the fact that partner has bid a suit has no bearing on which *card* you lead, although it may well affect which *suit* you open. Someone, somewhere, invented a slogan, "Lead the top of partner's suit." If there is any justice, he will spend eternity leading the queen from queen and two small, and finding:

NORTH
84

WEST   EAST
Q52   A 10 9 7 6

SOUTH
K J 3

• PLAN ONE—USING DUMMY'S SHORTNESS

One of the most attractive plans of attack as declarer is to utilize a short suit in dummy and ruff losers. Usually, the greater trump length will be in your own hand. Thus, every ruff in dummy represents an extra winner, for your own length is maintained. Whenever there is a side suit in which your own hand is longer than dummy, you should consider this plan. This is obvious when you hold a real two-suiter:

YOUR HAND   DUMMY
♠ A K Q 9 6   ♠ J 10 5
♡ A K 7 4 2   ♡ 8 5
◊ 5   ◊ A 6 4 2
♣ 8 3   ♣ J 9 5 4

In 4 spades, against a diamond lead, you clearly should make use of the fact that your hearts are longer than dummy's. Not only can you win tricks with two of dummy's trumps (in addition to your five), but in the process you

will establish your fifth heart. Thus, you win the lead, cash
the ace and king of hearts, and ruff a low heart with dummy's spade 10. If the hearts have not split evenly, return to
your hand with a high trump, and ruff the fourth round of
hearts with the jack. Almost surely, you will make an overtrick. Two precautions were necessary—first you did not draw
trumps immediately, since you need trump length in dummy
for this plan; second, you trumped the third round of hearts
with an *honor* in dummy to protect against an overruff. Actually, a very careful declarer would take a third precaution in
case the enemy hearts split five-one; he would cash only *one*
heart honor and then lead a low heart, conceding a trick.
Now he is sure to be able to ruff his remaining low hearts in
dummy. So in this simple hand, we see three of the techniques associated with the plan of ruffing in dummy: (1)
taking care to leave enough trumps in dummy; (2) protecting, if possible, against overruffs; (3) protecting, if possible,
against having *your* honors ruffed. Now let us look at a less
obvious hand of the same type:

YOUR HAND	DUMMY
♠ K Q J 9 6	♠ 10 7 5
♡ A 8 6 2	♡ K 7 3
◇ 5 4	◇ A 2
♣ A K	♣ 8 7 5 4 2

How do you play 4 spades against a diamond lead? The
average declarer draws trumps, and complains about his bad
luck when hearts split four-two and he goes down. A slightly
more sophisticated declarer might give himself the extra
chance of setting up dummy's club suit. But you, I trust,
realize that the contract can be made easily by ruffing a heart
in dummy. Win the lead, cash the ace and king of hearts,
and give up a heart trick. Now if the hearts have not split,
you can ruff the fourth heart with dummy's spade 10. Observe that it is not necessary to have a very short side suit in
dummy, or a very long one in your hand, in order to adopt
this plan. All you need is *greater* length in your own hand
than in dummy. Once you look for this, the correct approach
becomes obvious. All you need to do is to play hearts till you
can ruff, and be sure to leave a trump in dummy to ruff with.

Actually, you can rarely afford to draw all the enemy
trumps immediately when you plan to ruff in dummy. You

must realize how many times you intend to ruff, and keep the necessary number of trumps in dummy. In the previous example, it is dangerous to lead even one round of trumps before clearing hearts. The opponents might win the ace and play a second round of trumps; when they win their heart trick, they might be nasty enough to play a third round—and there goes your ruff. Suppose you are declarer in 6 diamonds with these cards:

YOUR HAND	DUMMY
♠ A K J 7 4	♠ 2
♡ 8 3	♡ A K J 5
◇ K Q J 7 2	◇ 10 9 6 5
♣ A	♣ K 10 5 4

a club is led, and you win your ace. What is your plan, and can you play trumps immediately? You intend to ruff spades in dummy. You need trump only twice, for one spade can be discarded on dummy's club king. Therefore, you can play trumps—so long as you leave two in dummy. Lead your diamond king, but stop playing trumps if the opponents hold off the ace (they might win a second trump lead and play a third round). Cash the ace of spades and ruff a spade with the 9 of diamonds. Ruff a low club back to your hand, and play a second spade, ruffing with dummy's 10. Now, you can switch back to trump leads, for you have done all the necessary ruffing in dummy.

Note that the enemy ace of trumps, in the preceding example, made it difficult for you to draw exactly as many rounds of trumps as you could afford. When *you* have the ace to control your trump suit, you can time the play more comfortably. Consider this example:

YOUR HAND	DUMMY
♠ A 8 7 3	♠ K 6 4 2
♡ A 8 5 3	♡ 6 2
◇ K 3	◇ A 8 4
♣ K J 5	♣ A 8 6 3

The queen of hearts is led against 4 spades. Your plan is to ruff hearts twice in dummy, so you must leave two trumps there. If you draw *no* trumps, the third or fourth round of hearts may be overruffed; if you draw *all* the trumps, there will be only one trump left in dummy; clearly you want to draw exactly two rounds. But if you cash the ace and king of spades and then concede a heart, the opponents will play a third trump. Therefore, you give up a heart first, ducking the opening lead. Win the *second* heart, now cash two high trumps, and go about your business of ruffing in dummy. You are no longer concerned about an overruff, since the only missing trump is high anyway.

Next, let me change the dummy hand slightly:

YOUR HAND	DUMMY
♠ A 8 7 3	♠ 9 6 4 2
♡ A 8 5 3	♡ K 6
◇ K 3	◇ A 8 4
♣ K J 5	♣ A 8 6 3

Your problem in 4 spades is still how to draw exactly two rounds of trumps. If you win the heart lead and play ace of spades followed by a low spade, the opponents may win and play a third round of trumps; yet if you do not lead any spades, the opponents may overruff. The solution is to win the heart lead and give up a trump trick immediately, playing low from both hands and retaining the ace. You will win whatever they return and *now* cash your ace of trumps. You have drawn the two rounds of trumps; and can start your ruffing, ignoring the missing high trump.

We have seen that you must worry constantly about over-ruffs, particularly when trumping the third or fourth round of a suit. The obvious countermeasures, ruffing with honors or drawing the enemy trumps, are not always available. For example, suppose you are declarer in 6 hearts with:

YOUR HAND	DUMMY
♠ A	♠ 10 8 7 6 5 3
♡ A K Q 10 9	♡ J 7 5
◇ A 6	◇ 8 4
♣ A K 7 6 2	♣ 5 3

The spade king is led and your ace wins. You plan to establish your side club suit by ruffing in dummy. Since you may have to ruff twice, you cannot draw trumps. Take your ace and king of clubs and lead a third round. When left-hand opponent follows, trump with dummy's jack. If right-hand opponent follows suit, clubs have split and you can now draw trumps. But what if he shows out?

You may still make your slam if you play carefully. Come back to your hand with a high diamond, and lead the fourth round of clubs. Instead of trumping it in the dummy, and risking an overruff, discard a low diamond. Then you will be able to trump a *diamond* in dummy without such grave danger of an overruff. This technique of transferring a ruff into a different suit by discarding a loser must be in your bag of tricks. Notice, though, that you would not have the opportunity to use this device if you had not taken earlier precautions: ruffing the third round of clubs high, postponing trump plays until you had taken your ruffs.

There is one last worry which goes along with the plan of ruffing losers in dummy. This is making sure that you have sufficient entries to your own hand. If you intend to ruff twice in dummy, you must get to your hand *three* times—twice to lead the suit and once more to draw the enemy trumps. In the following example, you are declarer in 4 hearts:

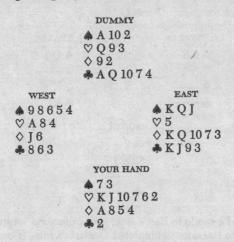

```
                    DUMMY
                 ♠ A 10 2
                 ♡ Q 9 3
                 ◇ 9 2
                 ♣ A Q 10 7 4

    WEST                          EAST
 ♠ 9 8 6 5 4                   ♠ K Q J
 ♡ A 8 4                       ♡ 5
 ◇ J 6                         ◇ K Q 10 7 3
 ♣ 8 6 3                       ♣ K J 9 3

                  YOUR HAND
                 ♠ 7 3
                 ♡ K J 10 7 6 2
                 ◇ A 8 5 4
                 ♣ 2
```

West leads the diamond jack (East opened the bidding 1 diamond). Your best plan is to ruff twice in dummy—how do you go about it? Not by drawing trumps, surely; you must clear the diamonds and do your ruffing first. However, there are hidden dangers lurking in this line of attack. When this deal was actually played, Declarer went down by losing a trick to

West's trump 8, even though he held an apparent abundance
of trump honors.

He won the lead with his ace, and played a second diamond. East won, and shifted to the spade king, taken by
dummy's ace. Now Declarer had to get to his hand to ruff a
diamond, so he cashed the club ace and trumped a club. He
ruffed a diamond—West discarded his last club—and dummy
was on lead again. Declarer returned to his hand by trumping
another club with the heart *10* (for fear of an overruff), and
West discarded. Now the last diamond was ruffed in dummy,
and Declarer still had the problem of entry to his own hand,
this time to draw the trumps. He played the heart queen,
won by West's ace, and the position was:

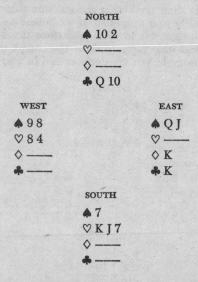

```
                    NORTH
                    ♠ 10 2
                    ♡ ——
                    ♢ ——
                    ♣ Q 10

        WEST                    EAST
        ♠ 9 8                   ♠ Q J
        ♡ 8 4                   ♡ ——
        ♢ ——                    ♢ K
        ♣ ——                    ♣ K

                    SOUTH
                    ♠ 7
                    ♡ K J 7
                    ♢ ——
                    ♣ ——
```

West led a spade to East's jack, and a diamond return (a club
would do the same) completed Declarer's ruin. If he trumped
low, the heart 8 would make immediately; if he trumped
high, it would win a trick later. By using ruffs as entries to his
hand, Declarer weakened his trump holding fatally.

The winning play is to *duck* the opening diamond lead.
Then the diamond ace can be used as the vital extra entry,
to ruff the third round of diamonds. Now Declarer can trump

a club low for the second entry, to ruff the last diamond. And after forcing out the trump ace with dummy's queen, Declarer can afford to ruff with an honor to gain the lead a third time and draw trumps.

You can see how important it is to have side entries to your hand when you plan to do a lot of ruffing in dummy. Often, you must be careful to win the opening lead in dummy, in order to have a high card in your own hand for use as an entry. And the device used in the example above— letting the enemy win the first round of a suit in which dummy has a doubleton and you the ace—is the most common method for producing an extra entry.

Actually, ducking the opening lead has the additional advantage of concealing your plan from the opponents. When Declarer, in the previous example, won the diamond ace and returned a diamond, he made it obvious that he was attempting to ruff in dummy. The defense did not have to sit still and wait for this to happen.

• DEFENSE AGAINST PLAN ONE

Let us move you into the East seat on the last deal. You see:

DUMMY

♠ A 10 2
♡ Q 9 3
◊ 9 2
♣ A Q 10 7 4

YOUR HAND

♠ K Q J
♡ 5
◊ K Q 10 7 3
♣ K J 9 3

Partner opens the jack of your diamond suit against 4 hearts. If Declarer takes his ace and plays a diamond right back, you should not dream of shifting to the spade king. After all, what is the hurry to cash spade tricks—where can Declarer discard his spade losers? You have the club suit so well stopped that Declarer must fail if he tries to use dummy's *length.* In any event, he has not led to dummy's long club suit; he has cleared dummy's *short* suit. Since Declarer is trying for ruffs, you switch to trumps. Partner takes his ace of trumps and returns a trump. Now dummy has only one trump left with which to ruff two losing diamonds.

This line of defense should be obvious to you because Declarer played diamonds, and particularly because you are not afraid of dummy's *length;* if Declarer can get rid of losers, it must be by using dummy's shortness. This is not at all so clear from partner's point of view. He sees:

DUMMY

♠ A 10 2
♡ Q 9 3
◇ 9 2
♣ A Q 10 7 4

PARTNER

♠ 9 8 6 5 4
♡ A 8 4
◇ J 6
♣ 8 6 3

Suppose he leads the diamond jack and it holds the trick (you have played the 7). For all *he* knows, Declarer can use that menacing club suit to discard his losers. Therefore, partner should shift to spades, trying to cash side winners before they disappear.

Since you can tell the instant dummy goes down what Declarer's plan must be, you should overtake partner's diamond jack with your queen. If Declarer ducks now, *you* are on lead, and know to shift to trumps. Partner will then follow your defense, winning his ace and continuing with a second trump lead.

This defense—shifting to trumps—is your only effective counter to Declarer's plan of ruffing in dummy. The problem is one of diagnosis. Both you and partner must think in terms of what Declarer's plan will be; once you decide that he will try to use dummy's shortness, it is easy enough to find the trump switch. Occasionally, though, it may be important to have the trump lead come from the correct hand. For example:

```
                    DUMMY
                    ♠ J 2
                    ♡ 10
                    ◇ A J 8 7 5 3
                    ♣ J 5 4 3
      YOU                            PARTNER
      ♠ Q 9 4                        ♠ 8 5
      ♡ K Q J 6 3                    ♡ A 9 7 5
      ◇ 10 2                         ◇ K Q 9 4
      ♣ Q 9 8                        ♣ 10 7 6
                    DECLARER
                    ♠ A K 10 7 6 3
                    ♡ 8 4 2
                    ◇ 5
                    ♣ A K 2
```

You lead the king of hearts against 4 spades. When dummy
appears, you should feel like switching to trumps, since dummy's singleton is menacing, while dummy's long suit is
ragged, and has no side entry. However, if *you* lead trumps,
you stop a heart ruff at the cost of a trump trick, so you gain
nothing. Partner should overtake your heart king with his ace
to lead trumps himself. He knows as well as you that dummy's singleton is dangerous, and he knows better than you
that dummy's length is harmless. Thus, he too is aware that a
trump switch is mandatory; since it is clearly better to lead
through Declarer's strength, he must seize the first trick. Incidentally, he should play the spade 5, not the 8. When
switching to trumps, do not lead the top of two small spots.
In this hand it is immaterial, but occasionally the difference
between saving an 8 and a 5 may be crucial toward the end
of the play.

Since it is so often proper to *switch* to trumps in defense,
why is not a trump *opening lead* more highly recommended?
The reason is that Declarer does not always want to ruff in
dummy. If his plan is to use dummy's *length* for discards,
instead of shortness for ruffs, then *he* wants to draw trumps
and the defense is in a hurry to play side suits. That is, if you
lead a trump against a 4 spade contract and this dummy
comes down:

♠ A 8 4   ♡ 6 2   ◇ A Q J 10 6   ♣ 8 5 3

you have probably lost all chance to win your heart and club honors before Declarer discards his losers. There is usually time to *switch* to trumps after dummy's appearance makes it seem desirable, while there is seldom time to cash winners in a hurry if you have led trumps originally and given Declarer the ball.

Still, there are rare occasions when the enemy auction makes it glaringly obvious that Declarer will try for ruffs in dummy. Then you may start the proper defense with a trump opening lead. The most common instance is when you have great high-card strength in a side suit that Declarer has bid. Suppose that the opponents' auction goes:

DECLARER	DUMMY
1 spade	1 notrump
2 hearts	3 hearts
4 hearts	

You are on lead with:

     ♠ A Q J 9   ♡ 8 4   ◇ J 10 9 3   ♣ Q 5 4

Sitting behind Declarer with four spade tricks, you feel sure that he cannot make his contract without ruffing in dummy. So lead the 4 of hearts. This could be wrong, for conceivably dummy might have a long club suit; then a diamond lead would be the winning defense. However, the odds are great that Declarer will want to use dummy's marked shortness in spades. The whole hand may be:

DUMMY
     ♠ 4
     ♡ Q 10 7 3
     ◇ K 7 6 4
     ♣ K 10 3 2

YOU	PARTNER
♠ A Q J 9	♠ 7 5 3
♡ 8 4	♡ A 6 5
◇ J 10 9 3	◇ Q 8 2
♣ Q 5 4	♣ J 9 7 6

DECLARER
     ♠ K 10 8 6 2
     ♡ K J 9 2
     ◇ A 5
     ♣ A 8

If the defense falls fast asleep, Declarer will win 11 tricks. Suppose you lead the jack of diamonds. Declarer takes dummy's king (saving the entry to his hand) and leads a spade. You win and, mistakenly, play a second diamond. Now Declarer can ruff all four spades in dummy and lose only to the ace of hearts at the end. Had you shifted to trumps when you won your spade trick, you could have taken two trumps out of dummy. Declarer would still make 10 tricks, though, by ruffing two spades and conceding one more, setting up his fifth spade.

You will defeat the game with an original trump lead, but only if partner cooperates. The defense must lead *three* rounds of trumps. If partner wins your opening with his ace and returns trumps, he will never regain the lead to play the third round. Thus, he must hold off, ducking the first trick. When you win your spade, you lead trumps again; partner takes his ace, and is on lead to play the third round.

Actually, this play of ducking the first round of trumps when you hold the ace and two small is the correct defense in many other situations. Obviously, it is wrong when you urgently need to play two rounds of trumps; but it is often necessary when, as is usual, the defense wants to play *three* rounds. Thus, if you decide to make a trump opening lead with this holding, you almost always lead low. Likewise, when Declarer leads trumps, it is seldom right to win your ace right away if you have two low ones with it. Consider this deal:

DUMMY
♠ 7 6 5 4
♡ 5 3
♢ A 8 5
♣ Q 7 6 2

YOU
♠ A 8 2
♡ Q J 10 7
♢ J 7 3
♣ A 10 4

PARTNER
♠ 9 3
♡ 8 4 2
♢ Q 10 6 4
♣ J 9 8 3

DECLARER
♠ K Q J 10
♡ A K 9 6
♢ K 9 2
♣ K 5

You lead the heart queen against the 4 spade contract; Declarer wins his ace, and leads the spade king. He plans to ruff two hearts in dummy, but is worried about an overruff of the fourth round; thus, he wants to draw two rounds of trumps first. If you win your spade ace immediately, Declarer's plan will succeed. Partner's spade 9 will fall on the second trump trick, and Declarer can now ruff out his hearts safely. However, if you *duck* the first trump lead, you will set the contract. When Declarer plays the second trump, you win your ace and lead a third round; and if no second trump is led, partner can overruff dummy on the fourth heart lead.

Can Declarer make this contract? Yes, but not after leading trumps. He should take both heart honors at once, and ruff a low heart. Then he cashes the ace and king of diamonds, and leads the fourth heart. When you play the jack, he discards dummy's losing diamond—transferring the dangerous heart ruff into a safer diamond ruff.

Even this line of play can be defeated if your opening lead is a low trump, as it should be if the auction went:

DECLARER	DUMMY
1 spade	2 spades
3 hearts	3 spades
4 spades	

Note that you will not set the contract by leading ace and then a low trump—Declarer will be able to ruff both losing hearts. And notice, too, that when you lead a low trump, partner must play his 3, not his 9. Here is one of the deals in which it is crucial for him to retain his high spot-card in trumps.

The real lesson, though, is the importance of the ace of trumps. The player who holds it controls the suit, and can determine when and how often trumps are drawn. So do not be in a hurry to win the trump ace early, as a defender. This is one ace that you cannot possibly lose. Therefore, take it at *your* convenience, not at Declarer's.

• PLAN TWO—USING DUMMY'S LENGTH

In the most common lines of play, Declarer takes advantage of the distribution of dummy. We have seen him making use of a side suit in which dummy has fewer cards than he has. Just as easily, he may use a suit in which dummy has more cards than has his own hand—here, to discard losers instead of to ruff them. Of course, such a suit must have either extra honors which will be high when Declarer has no cards remaining, or great length (usually 5 cards or more) so that the little cards can be established. For example, suppose that you are Declarer in this ambitious 4 spade contract:

YOUR HAND	DUMMY
♠ 10 8 6 4 3	♠ A K Q
♡ 8 4	♡ Q J 7 3
◇ A K 6 5	◇ 3
♣ A 2	♣ 10 9 8 6 4

The heart 2 is led, and dummy's jack loses to the ace on your right; a spade is returned. Here, dummy's shortness is of no use since you cannot afford to ruff with dummy's honors. Dummy's length, though, may produce the extra winners you need. You might obtain a discard by leading toward the queen of hearts. However, this is not a good line of attack, since, with 8 tricks, you need two more and this aims at only one. Two extra tricks might be available in *clubs*. Lead to your club ace and concede the second club. If the opponents lead another trump, win in dummy and lead the third round of clubs, trumping in your hand. If the enemy clubs split three-three, dummy's remaining two clubs are good; you lead to the last high trump and cash them. What if clubs do not split? Then you go down, but at least you tried.

In this example, you see both sorts of length in dummy which can be productive: a 5-card or longer holding in which the small cards can be established as in the club suit, or intermediate honors, as in the heart suit, which may provide discards. When such length is available, using it will most often be your best plan. You should think about these hands much as you do about a notrump contract. How many winners have I? Will this suit provide the extra tricks that I need? Then go about establishing the winners, drawing trumps, and cashing the tricks—usually in that order.

Just as in notrump contracts, you may have to worry about cashing your tricks before the opponents get theirs—it may be a race. And many of the methods which help you win the race at notrump are important in *suit* contracts played according to this plan. For example, suppose you are declarer at 4 hearts:

YOUR HAND	DUMMY
♠ 2	♠ K Q J 10
♡ A K J 7 5	♡ 10 8 3
◇ A 6 5	◇ J 10 4 2
♣ A 8 6 2	♣ K 9

The opening lead is the diamond 9; how do you plan the play? You have 7 sure tricks, and there is no need even to consider using dummy's shortness in clubs, since dummy's length in spades will provide the 3 tricks you need. The danger is that the enemy will win two diamonds and one spade before you can take your discards; then a losing heart finesse will set you. Obviously, the K Q of diamonds are behind dummy; if you play the 10 and win the queen with your ace, you are likely to go down if your left-hand opponent has the spade ace. Then he will lead through dummy's diamond jack before you can take your discards.

The solution is to hold off your diamond ace. Cover the lead with dummy's 10, and let the queen hold to your right. This does not gain a trick directly, for your right-hand opponent will not lead away from his diamond king. But it gains *time;* now you can knock out the spade ace while retaining control of the dangerous suit. You will win your ten tricks before the opponents take their four.

You have a similar problem as declarer at 4 spades here:

YOUR HAND	DUMMY
♠ A 10 9 8 6	♠ K J 2
♡ A J 5	♡ 8 3
◇ A 5 2	◇ K Q J 10 6
♣ 10 5	♣ K 6 2

The heart 2 is opened, and the king is played to your right. What is your plan? You have five diamond tricks, four spade tricks (even if you lose to the queen), and one heart, for 10. But you must draw trumps before running the diamonds, and if you lose to the spade queen, the enemy may cash 4 tricks—one spade, one heart, two clubs—before you take your discards. Here, this danger is present only if your left-hand opponent regains the lead to play *through* dummy's club king. So you must use avoidance technique, keeping the dangerous opponent off lead, as you often do at notrump. When you play trumps, you will lead your 10 and pass it, so that the finesse, if it loses, will lose to the safe hand. This is not enough, though, since the dangerous left-hand opponent might then gain the lead with a high heart. You take care of this possibility by holding off on the opening lead, losing the heart trick also to the safe right-hand opponent. Win the *second* heart with the ace, and lead your spade 10, letting it ride if it is not covered. This way, you are virtually certain to win your tricks before the enemy can take theirs. Note, incidentally, that you do not ruff a heart in dummy; this would jeopardize your chances. Your plan is to use dummy's length, not its shortness.

In using long honors in the dummy, you can occasionally show a profit from conceding an unnecessary trick to the opponents if, in the process, you get 2 tricks back. For example, suppose that you are declarer at 6 hearts against the diamond queen lead:

YOUR HAND	DUMMY
♠ A	♠ Q J 7
♡ A Q J 7 6 2	♡ K 8 4
◇ A 7 4	◇ K 6 5 3
♣ A K J	♣ 6 5 3

When this hand was actually played, Declarer won his diamond ace, drew trumps, led a second diamond and ducked, conceding the trick. The defense continued diamonds, won by dummy's king. Had the suit split three-three, Declarer could have discarded his club jack. It did not, so he was forced to finesse in clubs; this failed also—down one. Now, of course, Declarer first complained bitterly of his bad luck, and next bawled his partner out for putting him in slam. However, he should really have used the third conversational gambit of unsuccessful declarers, "Sorry, partner, I pulled a wrong card," for his contract was ice cold.

You see, I am sure, that all you have to do to win 12 tricks is to take two high clubs, two diamonds, six hearts, and *two* spades. Win the diamond in your hand, cash your ace and queen of hearts and your ace of spades. Lead to dummy's heart king. Play the spade queen and discard your losing diamond (unless the king covers). Now the spade jack is high in dummy, and you can discard your losing club as well. Thus, by conceding an unnecessary spade trick, you get rid of two losers for the price of one. And if the spade king is to your right, you can ruff it out, setting up a discard at no cost whatever. To make this contract, you need only realize that you can use dummy's spade length (the spades there are not very long, but they are longer than *yours*, which is what counts), and take mild precautions to save entries to the dummy.

In the next example, the principle of play is the same, but it is a little harder to see. Here, you are declarer in a less spectacular contract—2 diamonds:

YOUR HAND	DUMMY
♠ A	♠ J 10 9 2
♡ 8 7 6 4	♡ A 10 2
◇ A K 10 7 5	◇ Q J 4
♣ 10 6 3	♣ J 8 5

The opening lead is the king of clubs, followed by the ace and a low club won by the queen to your right. Now, a trump is led. How do you play?

Were it not for the trump switch, you could use dummy's shortness in hearts. You could take the heart ace and concede two heart tricks; if the suit did not split evenly, you could ruff the fourth round in dummy. However, this will no longer work, since the enemy will have led three rounds of trumps by the time you have given up two heart tricks. The solution is to use dummy's length instead.

Win the trump lead carefully in your own hand, saving dummy's honors as entries. Cash the spade ace, and lead to the jack of diamonds. Play the spade jack from dummy, and discard a losing heart (unless it is covered—then ruff). Go back to dummy with the queen of trumps and lead the spade 10, throwing another heart. This way, you will promote your eighth trick in dummy's long spade suit. Notice, though, that you must be sure to save three entries to dummy—two to lead spades, one to get back to cash the trick you worked so hard to establish.

Just as entries to your *own hand* are your worry when you plan to use dummy's shortness, entries to *dummy* are your constant preoccupation when you plan to use dummy's length. (This is the main reason that these two lines of attack

are, as we will see later, mutually exclusive—you can sometimes do either, but you can almost never do both at once.)
With enough entries to dummy, you can occasionally set up
the most anemic 5-card suit:

YOUR HAND	DUMMY
♠ 3	♠ 8 7 6 4 2
♡ A K Q J 7 4 2	♡ 10 9 8
◊ K J 2	◊ A 8 4
♣ A K	♣ 10 5

In 6 hearts against the queen of clubs lead, your plan should
be to establish dummy's fifth spade for your twelfth trick.
Win the ace, and lead your low spade. A club is returned,
won in your hand. Lead the 2 of hearts to dummy's 8, and
ruff a spade with the trump *ace*. Play the 4 of hearts to
dummy's 9, ruff another spade *high*. Overtake the trump 7
with the 10 and ruff the fourth round of spades. Now dummy's last spade is probably good (for the seven enemy spades
are most likely to divide four-three), and you have the diamond ace as the entry to it. Notice the care that you had to
take to keep four entries to dummy, ruffing with honors to
save your more valuable little spots. This is a common entry-
saving method. Another device for producing an extra entry
to dummy we have already seen in notrump play:

YOUR HAND	DUMMY
♠ A K J 10 9 2	♠ Q 3
♡ K 6 5	♡ A 9 2
◊ 8 4	◊ A 9 6 5 3
♣ 8 6	♣ 10 9 2

Against your 4 spade contract, the defense cashes two clubs
and leads a third round which you trump. Clearly, you must
try to establish a long diamond in dummy so that you can
discard a heart. How do you go about it? Not, I hope, by
leading to the diamond ace and conceding a second diamond.
Now you can get back to dummy with the spade queen to
ruff out the third round; if the suit splits three-three you are
home. However, the normal four-two division defeats you.
You can reach dummy with the heart ace to ruff the fourth
round, but you are an entry short, since you cannot go to

dummy again to cash the fifth card. To ruff twice and still get back, you need *three* entries.

You have them if you use the ace of diamonds properly. Concede the *first* diamond. Then the ace of diamonds is the entry for the first ruff; the spade queen is the entry for the second ruff. After drawing trumps, you can go to the ace of hearts to cash the fifth diamond.

Actually, there is another technique concealed in the proper play of the last two examples, which is frequently necessary when using dummy's length. You must delay drawing trumps so that you can use winning trumps in dummy as *entries.* Of course, you must draw the enemy trumps before you cash long cards, but setting up dummy's length is the first order of business. *After* establishing the winners in dummy, you can often accomplish the next two items on the agenda (pull the trumps; go to dummy and take your discards) at the same time, by drawing trumps *ending up in dummy.*

In the following example, your contract is 6 clubs, and the king of hearts is led:

YOUR HAND	DUMMY
♠ A Q 7 4 3	♠ 2
♡ A 2	♡ 8 5 3
◇ 2	◇ A Q J 10 4 3
♣ A K 10 7 6	♣ Q 9 5

The proper plan to bring home this ambitious slam is, of course, to use dummy's long suit. Win the opening, play to the ace of diamonds, and lead the diamond queen—letting it ride for a finesse if it is not covered. (If you finesse on the *first* round, you are down immediately should the king win, for a heart will be cashed. This way, you throw your heart loser on the diamond queen and may make the contract even though the finesse loses.) Suppose that the diamond king wins to your left; you trump the heart return. Now you must draw trumps and get to dummy to run the diamonds. Cash your ace of clubs, your king of clubs, and lead to dummy's queen. If the trumps split reasonably, you are home free. You have five trump tricks, five diamond tricks, and two side aces.

Observe that you do not need a ruff in dummy to take 12 tricks. In fact, it would be fatal to ruff, for the minute you shorten dummy's trump holding, the diamond suit is dead for lack of an entry. You could no longer draw trumps *ending up in dummy*. This deal is a good example of the importance of knowing what your plan is. The better line of play is to use dummy's *length*, going right after diamonds; however, it might work to use dummy's *shortness*, ruffing spades immediately in the hope that the king falls. What has to be wrong is to do a little of each. The trump length in dummy is precious when you are trying to use dummy's length; if this is your plan, the last thing you should want to do, ordinarily, is to trump in dummy. In fact, these plans are so much opposed to each other that—as we will see—the *defense* should occasionally force you to ruff in dummy when you are planning to set up a long suit there.

Thus, you have to decide, often before playing to the first trick, which plan you will adopt. Although you cannot use *both* the length and shortness of dummy, occasionally you will be able to use *either*. Then, your choice is made according to the location of entries—with many entries to dummy and few to your own hand, you plan to set up the length for discards; with many entries to your hand and few to dummy, you plan to use the shortness by ruffing. Which would be your plan in 4 spades, against a diamond lead, with these cards?

YOUR HAND	DUMMY
♠ K Q J 8 4	♠ A 7 5
♡ 6 4	♡ Q 9 8 7 5 3
◇ K 7 4	◇ A 8 2
♣ 8 5 2	♣ A

If you plan to ruff clubs in dummy, you need three entries to your hand. Therefore, rise with the diamond ace and cash the ace of clubs. Come back to your diamond king and ruff a club. Return to your hand with a trump, and ruff the second club (perforce with dummy's ace of trumps). Here your trouble starts, for you have no good way to come to your hand a third time in order to draw trumps. You cannot afford to ruff with an honor, and will have to be very lucky to avoid going down.

The better plan is to set up dummy's hearts—for you have more entries in *dummy*. Now, you must win the diamond opening in your hand to save dummy's honor. Concede a heart. If the opponents continue diamonds, win in dummy and concede another heart. They will cash a diamond, and shift to clubs, knocking out dummy's side entry. Ruff the third round of hearts (with an honor if necessary). Then draw trumps ending up in dummy, cashing your king and queen, finally leading to the ace. This approach requires only normal splits in the two long suits.

Let us exchange dummy's ace and your 8 of clubs:

YOUR HAND	DUMMY
♠ K Q J 8 4	♠ A 7 5
♡ 6 4	♡ Q 9 8 7 5 3
◇ K 7 4	◇ A 8 2
♣ A 5 2	♣ 8

To make 4 spades against a diamond lead now, your better plan is to use dummy's *shortness*, since you have an extra entry to your hand. You are most unlikely to be able to use dummy's *length*, for you are short an entry there.

Notice that you have to choose your plan before playing even one card. If you intend to *trump* losers, you must win the opening in dummy, saving your own entry for later, and lead clubs. If you intend to *discard* losers, you must win the opening in your hand, saving dummy's entry, and lead hearts. Should you play to the first few tricks without a clear idea of what you plan to do, you will almost certainly go down.

• DEFENSE AGAINST PLAN TWO

When dummy has the sort of length which can provide discards, the defenders must be just as alert to spot it as is Declarer. In fact, they are in *better* position than Declarer, since they can tell whether dummy's long suit splits evenly and whether finesses win or lose. For example, suppose that you are sitting behind dummy with:

DUMMY
♠ A Q 10 9
♡ 10 5 3
◇ 7
♣ 8 7 6 5 3

YOU
♠ 7 4 3 2
♡ K 6 4
◇ A 5
♣ J 10 9 4

Partner leads the diamond 6 and you win the ace. If *spades* are trumps, you are not worried about dummy's length, for the side club suit will not split evenly and any finesse there loses. Thus, you should shift to trumps; dummy's shortness is the only danger.

In contrast, if *clubs* are trumps, you should be terrified of dummy's length. Now the side suit is spades, and here the division of your side's honors and length must be perfect for Declarer. If he has any three spades, he will get one discard; if he has any doubleton spade, he can get two discards. Therefore, you must desperately cash your winners before they disappear—shift to hearts.

Taking your tricks in a hurry before Declarer can discard his losers is the prime method of defense when dummy has dangerous length. Suppose you are defending against a 4 heart contract:

DUMMY

♠ Q 10
♡ A 8 4
♢ K J 10 9 3
♣ 7 5 4

YOU

♠ K 8 3
♡ 7 5 2
♢ Q 4
♣ A K J 8 2

You lead the king of clubs; partner plays the 6, Declarer the 3. You continue with the ace, partner drops the 9, Declarer the queen. What now? Right here, the difference between the average defender and a thoughtful one shows up. The wooden defender continues with the jack of clubs ("It can't do any harm," he thinks) or shifts to trumps ("When in doubt, lead trumps," he learned at his mother's knee) or even commits the foolishness of leading diamonds ("Through strength," he mutters). You, I trust, will not think of slogans but of what Declarer's plan will be; and you will conclude that he will try to use dummy's length. What is more, your own holding tells you that he will succeed unless you cash your side winners first. So you shift to the 3 of spades. If Declarer's hand is:

(a) ♠ J 7 4 ♡ K Q J 6 3 ♢ A 8 2 ♣ Q 3

you can defeat the contract with two spade tricks, but only if
you take them right away. When Declarer's hand, instead,
is one of these:

(b) ♠ A 7 4   ♡ Q J 10 6 3   ◇ A 8 2   ♣ Q 3
(c) ♠ A 7 4   ♡ K Q J 10 6 3   ◇ 8 2   ♣ Q 3

you will defeat 4 hearts with a spade switch if Declarer misguesses and plays the 10 from dummy, allowing partner's
jack to force his ace. Declarer must lose to the heart king in
(b), or the diamond ace in (c), and now your side has a
spade trick to cash also. What if Declarer plays dummy's
queen when you lead spades, or holds the A J himself? You
have lost nothing, for Declarer would have been able to discard his losing spades anyway; you could not defeat the contract.

Occasionally, this defense—cashing out in a hurry—requires
desperate measures. Consider this example. The auction goes:

DECLARER	PARTNER	DUMMY	YOU
3 hearts	3 spades	4 hearts	pass
pass	pass		

Partner leads the king of spades, and you see:

DUMMY
♠ A 8 6
♡ A Q 5
◇ 7 6 4
♣ A Q J 9

YOU
♠ J 9 4
♡ 9 3
◇ J 8 5 2
♣ K 8 4 3

Dummy's ace wins the first trick. Declarer draws trumps,
playing the ace, and then low to his 10—partner shows out,
discarding a small spade. Now Declarer leads the club 10
and finesses; you win your king. What do you lead?

Clearly, you must cash three more tricks right here, for dummy's clubs will provide discards. Since partner almost surely has a 6-card spade suit (to overcall at the three-level) a spade return is useless; you must take three *diamond* tricks immediately if you are to defeat the contract. Therefore, shift to diamonds, and lead the *jack*. When you urgently need 3 tricks in one suit, your best bet is to lead an honor, so that you can repeat a finesse. The whole deal may be:

DUMMY

♠ A 8 6
♡ A Q 5
♢ 7 6 4
♣ A Q J 9

PARTNER

♠ K Q 10 7 5 3
♡ 6
♢ A Q 10
♣ 7 5 2

YOU

♠ J 9 4
♡ 9 3
♢ J 8 5 2
♣ K 8 4 3

DECLARER

♠ 2
♡ K J 10 8 7 4 2
♢ K 9 3
♣ 10 6

Notice that a low diamond return will not succeed. Declarer will duck, allowing partner to win the 10, and the defense can take only two diamonds before Declarer gets his discards. However, it does Declarer no good to duck the *jack*, for then you are on lead to continue the suit.

Do you see how Declarer can make his contract? He is in no jeopardy unless *you* gain the lead to play through his diamond king; if he plays cleverly, he can keep you off lead. He should duck the king of spades lead, even though he holds a singleton! Now he can discard a low club on the spade ace, and take a backward finesse in clubs—cashing dummy's ace and leading the queen. If *this* finesse loses, the safe opponent is on lead: the contract is secure.

We have seen, in the deal above and in earlier examples, how Declarer should use avoidance techniques to keep a dangerous opponent off lead. Just as in notrump, the defense must try to counter his plan. For instance:

DUMMY
♠ 9 8 6
♡ 10 2
♢ A 10 7 5 3
♣ A K J

PARTNER
♠ A J 10
♡ A K 8 7 6
♢ Q 9
♣ 7 5 2

YOU
♠ Q 7 5 2
♡ Q J 5 2
♢ J 8 2
♣ 9 4

DECLARER
♠ K 4 3
♡ 9 4
♢ K 6 4
♣ Q 10 8 6 3

You and partner have allowed the enemy to steal the contract for 2 clubs (you can make 3 hearts). However, it will not be a total loss if your side manages to win all its potential tricks —two hearts, one diamond, three spades—before Declarer gets discards on dummy's diamonds. To do this, *you* must contrive to gain the lead, and then you must play your queen of spades.

When this deal was actually played, partner's hand cashed the king-ace of hearts and shifted to trumps. Dummy won and led the diamond 3; your hand played the 2, and Declarer put in his 6, ducking the trick to the safe opponent. Now, of course, the defense was helpless to stop Declarer from making 9 tricks.

On the diamond lead, your hand should play the 8, to make it hard as possible for Declarer to pass the lead to partner. If Declarer takes the king, partner must be alert to throw away his queen, so that Declarer cannot duck the *second* round to him. To be sure, Declarer would succeed, as the cards lie, by playing low on your 8, but he cannot be sure of this.

Actually, the defense can always take its winners first if partner lets *you* win the second heart trick. On his opening lead of the heart king, you must signal with the *queen*. This promises the jack (since otherwise you cannot afford to throw the queen), so partner underleads his ace to give you an entry. Now, the queen of spades lead ensures the set. Note the feverish activity of the proper defense against menacing length in dummy. If you sit back and wait for your tricks, a clever declarer will almost always make his contract; you have to fight for your entries and your winners. Here is another example of active defense:

DUMMY

♠ Q 8 3
♡ J 5
◊ K Q J 9 7 4
♣ A 4

YOU

♠ 9 5
♡ A 9 6 3
◊ A 5 3
♣ K 10 7 6

Partner leads the 2 of clubs against the 4 spade contract. Declarer wins dummy's ace, plays a spade to the 10 in his hand, and leads a low diamond. When you win your ace, what should you do?

The way to cash out your winners in a hurry is to take your club king, and then *underlead* your ace of hearts. If partner has the heart king, it makes no difference whether you lead the ace or underlead it. However, if partner holds the *queen*, the underlead is your only chance—you must hope that Declarer misguesses, playing low in the expectation that *you* have the queen and partner the ace. You almost never underlead an ace on the *opening lead*, but must be prepared to do so later in the play when you need 2 tricks in a hurry. The whole deal may be:

DUMMY
♠ Q 8 3
♡ J 5
♢ K Q J 9 7 4
♣ A 4

PARTNER
♠ 7 6 2
♡ Q 8 7 4
♢ 10 2
♣ Q 9 5 2

YOU
♠ 9 5
♡ A 9 6 3
♢ A 5 3
♣ K 10 7 6

DECLARER
♠ A K J 10 4
♡ K 10 2
♢ 8 5
♣ J 8 3

Actually, trying to cash tricks in a hurry is only one of *two* good lines of defense against dummy's length. The other method is to attack the entries in dummy so that Declarer cannot use the length after he sets it up. This defense could (and really should) be used in the preceding example deal.

Partner leads the 2 of clubs and let us suppose that Declarer ducks, letting you win your king. Return a club, knocking out the ace in dummy before it can be used as an entry. Declarer plays a trump to his hand and leads diamonds. Partner should follow with his *10*, starting a high-low signal to show a doubleton (actually, any *even number* of cards) in dummy's long suit—this is just as important in suit play as in notrump. Thus, you know enough to duck the first round of diamonds and win the second round, so that Declarer does not have a *diamond* entry to dummy. Finally, you attack the *trump* entry. This cannot be done by leading trumps, for Declarer will win in his hand, then clear trumps *ending up* in dummy. You do it by *making dummy ruff*. Cash the club king and lead a third round (Declarer must have a third club, for partner led the 2, showing a 4-card suit). Now dummy's long suit is useless, for Declarer has no side entry to it, and cannot end up in dummy after drawing partner's three trumps.

You see in this example the three methods of attacking dummy's entries: forcing out the side entries early, holding off in dummy's long suit, making dummy ruff. The third device goes against normal instincts—you hate to play a suit in which dummy is void. Remember, though, that as *declarer* you never want to ruff in dummy if your plan is to use the length there; thus, on *defense* it must occasionally be a good idea to force Declarer to do what he does not want to do himself.

Let me repeat an example deal I used earlier to demonstrate proper play as declarer, this time to see the best defense:

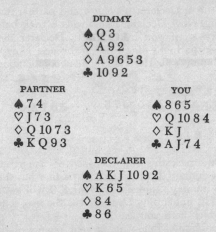

DUMMY
♠ Q 3
♡ A 9 2
◇ A 9 6 5 3
♣ 10 9 2

PARTNER
♠ 7 4
♡ J 7 3
◇ Q 10 7 3
♣ K Q 9 3

YOU
♠ 8 6 5
♡ Q 10 8 4
◇ K J
♣ A J 7 4

DECLARER
♠ A K J 10 9 2
♡ K 6 5
◇ 8 4
♣ 8 6

The contract is 4 spades. Describing the play earlier, I had the defense lead three rounds of clubs. Declarer ruffs, and can now set up dummy's fifth diamond for a discard if he takes care to duck the first round of diamonds, using the ace as an entry. Actually, proper defense will always defeat the contract.

Partner leads the club king, which holds (you signal encouragement with your 7). He continues with the club 3, his original fourth best; and you win the ace. Here, it is *safe* to continue a third club, but this is a waste of time since you know that Declarer will ruff (if partner held only three clubs originally, he would have continued with the queen). When dummy has a long suit, you cannot afford to play safe—you must either try to cash winners or to attack dummy's entries. Shift to hearts, doing both at once. Declarer takes his king, and concedes a diamond trick. Now lead a second heart, knocking out dummy's ace prematurely. Even if your side's diamonds split three-three, Declarer could not use dummy's length, for the vital side entry is gone.

Incidentally, in shifting to hearts above, you should lead your *10*. This is in case the hearts are:

$$♡ A 9 2$$

$$♡ K 7 6 \qquad ♡ Q 10 8 4$$

$$♡ J 5 3$$

If you lead the 4, Declarer plays low and partner must go up with the king. Now Declarer's jack wins a trick behind your queen. However, if you lead the *10*, Declarer must cover with the jack; partner's king loses to the ace. Now your Q 8 surrounds dummy's 9. Here is a similar combination:

DUMMY

$$◇ Q 7 5$$

YOU

$$◇ K J 9$$

If you must attack this suit, because of dangerous length elsewhere in dummy, lead the *jack*. If partner has the ace, he will capture dummy's queen, and your K 9 will swallow Declarer's 10. (If, unhappily, *Declarer* has the ace, it makes no difference which card you lead.)

The final example, following, is your review of the objectives and techniques both of Declarer and defense when dummy has useful-looking length:

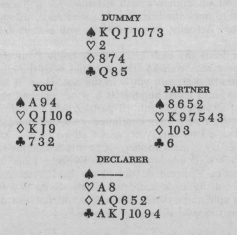

DUMMY

♠ K Q J 10 7 3
♡ 2
◇ 8 7 4
♣ Q 8 5

YOU

♠ A 9 4
♡ Q J 10 6
◇ K J 9
♣ 7 3 2

PARTNER

♠ 8 6 5 2
♡ K 9 7 5 4 3
◇ 10 3
♣ 6

DECLARER

♠ ——
♡ A 8
◇ A Q 6 5 2
♣ A K J 10 9 4

You open the queen of hearts against the 6 club contract, and Declarer wins his ace. (Note that you do not open the ace of spades; it is *Declarer's* job, not yours, to establish dummy's suit.) How should Declarer proceed?

He should plan, of course, to use dummy's length. Therefore, he must not ruff a heart in dummy. He leads the 4 of trumps, winning carefully with dummy's 8, preserving a later entry to the queen. Now, he plays the spade king, throwing a loser from his hand. He intends to win whatever is returned, cash his ace of trumps, and lead to dummy's queen—drawing trumps ending up in dummy. Then he can cash the long spades and discard the rest of his losers.

Suppose Declarer does lead to the club 8, and then throws a diamond on dummy's spade king. You win your ace; what do you lead now? You must not return a trump or a spade, waiting hopefully for a diamond trick—Declarer will be able to discard all of his diamonds. You must either try to cash out at once (leading a diamond in the hope that partner has the ace—not a good bet when Declarer has bid strongly) or attack dummy's trump entry by forcing a ruff. Clearly, the latter is more likely to succeed, so you lead a second heart. Declarer must ruff, and goes down when the clubs split three-one so that he cannot end up in dummy after drawing trumps.

However, Declarer could always make his contract. On dummy's lead of the king of spades, he must discard his *heart*. Now, when you lead a second round of hearts, he ruffs *in his hand,* saving dummy's precious trump length.

Properly played and defended, this deal is a contest over the entries to dummy. Declarer must safeguard them by careful management of spot-cards and by refusing to shorten dummy's trumps by ruffing. The defense attacks them by trying to force a ruff. Note how different all this is from the proper play and defense when Declarer's plan is to use dummy's shortness instead of its length.

• PLAN THREE—WINNING TRICKS WITH LOSERS

The first two plans for playing suit contracts are the best ones, but dummy does not always have the length to let you discard, or the shortness to let you ruff enough losers to make your contract. Then you must fall back on the expedient of trying to win your losers, to take tricks with honors that are nearly high. This can be done by taking successful finesses, but do not imagine that this section will deal with how to finesse. Instead, it will be devoted to how to avoid finesses, but win losers anyway.

Expert bridge players consider it an indignity to take a finesse, to pray, hopefully, for a favorable lie of cards. Of course, even experts must finesse—in establishing dummy's long suit, or in working on dummy's shortness, they may be compelled to start a suit in which there are honors which are not quite high. But, in general, they find it more aesthetic, and vastly more profitable, to induce the opponents to lead such suits to them. Consider this example, where you are declarer in a contract of 2 spades against the heart king opening:

YOUR HAND	DUMMY
♠ A J 9 4	♠ K 10 6 3
♡ A 9 6	♡ 7 5 2
♢ A J 4	♢ K 10 5
♣ J 7 2	♣ Q 8 4

You have 6 sure tricks, with possibilities in three suits. The average declarer tackles one suit after another and hopes for the best. He wins the opening lead with the ace, cashes the ace of spades, and leads the jack of spades for a finesse (a gypsy told him, long ago, that the queen lies over the jack). Unfortunately, this loses to the queen; the opponents cash two heart tricks and put Declarer back on lead with the third trump. Now, our declarer turns to the diamond suit, leading low from his hand, trancing, then putting in dummy's 10. The queen wins, and a diamond is returned. So, finally, Declarer must attack clubs; but he finds the honors divided and loses three club tricks, in addition to one diamond, one spade, and two hearts—down two. Of course, Declarer was unlucky, misguessing both two-way finesses; still, everyone has unlucky days. On your birthday, you are entitled to guess everything right, but for the rest of the year you had better play the hand more shrewdly. Let us see how an expert handles the same cards:

YOUR HAND	DUMMY
♠ A J 9 4	♠ K 10 6 3
♡ A 9 6	♡ 7 5 2
♢ A J 4	♢ K 10 5
♣ J 7 2	♣ Q 8 4

The first thing he does is to duck the king of hearts lead. It has been his experience that half the time he leaves an opponent on lead, his opponent obliges by making a mistake. This time, though, a heart is continued, and Declarer wins. He plays the third heart, putting the enemy on lead again. Here, they *must* give Declarer a trick by starting a new suit, for to play the thirteenth heart would present him with a ruff and discard. Suppose the opponents take their ace and king of clubs, then play a third club. Declarer wins, and cashes his two top spades. When the queen does not fall, he leads a third spade—and the enemy are on lead once more. They cannot play hearts or clubs without allowing him to throw a loser and ruff; they have no more trumps to play; so they must lead diamonds. This automatically "guesses" the diamond queen for Declarer, and he loses only two hearts, one spade, and two clubs. He has made his contract without ever taking a finesse!

If you are trying to develop extra tricks in a long suit, or in dummy's short suit, you must attack it yourself. But if you simply are trying to win an honor, your best bet is to force the enemy to play the suit to you. This is done in two steps: first, take away their safe plays; second, give them the lead. In the preceding example, there was not much trouble doing either, but you may often have more work to do. For instance:

YOUR HAND	DUMMY
♠ A 8 4 3 2	♠ J 9 7 6 5
♡ Q 5 2	♡ J 8 3
◇ A 8 3	◇ K 6
♣ K 2	♣ A 7 4

Your contract is 4 spades, and the diamond queen is opened. If the missing trumps split normally, two-one, you have 9 tricks—four spades, two clubs, two diamonds, and a diamond ruff in dummy. The tenth trick must be made with a heart honor so, of course, you plan to force the enemy to lead that suit. How? By making it unsafe for them to play anything else and then giving them the lead. Giving them the lead is no problem here, for you can concede a trump trick. However, if you play ace of spades and a low spade right away, there is no reason for the enemy to play hearts for you—they will continue diamonds, or shift to clubs.

Cash your trump ace, but do not concede the trump trick yet. First, take your club king, lead to dummy's ace, and ruff the third club. Then cash your diamond ace and ruff your last diamond in dummy. Now concede the trump loser. The remaining cards are:

YOUR HAND	DUMMY
♠ 8 4	♠ J 9
♡ Q 5 2	♡ J 8 3
◇ ——	◇ ——
♣ ——	♣ ——

The opponents are on lead, and cannot lead clubs or diamonds without presenting you with a ruff and discard; they have no more trumps; so they are forced to lead hearts. And you must make your game. The process of ruffing out a suit so that the enemy cannot play it is called **stripping**. It is common to most deals in which you cannot use length or shortness in dummy, but must try to win honors. This whole technique, inducing the enemy to play a specific suit for the good reason that anything else they lead will give you a ruff and discard, is called a **strip and endplay**.

Usually, the difficulty comes not with the strip but with the endplay—that is, in giving the lead to the opponents. The simplest methods, if they are available, are to endplay the enemy with a trump winner, or by playing a side suit in which both your hand and dummy will be void when the opponents win their trick. Each type can be seen in this example:

YOUR HAND	DUMMY
♠ Q J 9 5 4 2	♠ A 10 8 7
♡ 5	♡ A 6 4
◇ A J 3	◇ K 7 4
♣ K 9 7	♣ Q 10 2

Your contract is 4 spades, and the heart queen is led. Win the ace, and ruff a heart in your hand. Lead the spade queen to coax your left-hand opponent to cover; if he does not, rise with dummy's ace—a small trump is played to your right. Ruff dummy's last heart. Now the hearts are stripped; the enemy cannot play them safely. So concede the trump trick. If your left-hand opponent wins the king, he is endplayed; either a diamond or a club lead gives you the contract.

Suppose, though, that your right-hand opponent wins and leads a diamond through your A J. You play the jack hope-

fully, but the queen covers. Take dummy's king, cash your
ace, and give up the third diamond. Neither your hand nor
dummy has any diamonds (or hearts) remaining, so the opponents must play clubs for you or give you a ruff and discard. Either way, you lose only one club trick, and make your
contract safely.

It is not always so easy to give up the lead at the right
moment, particularly since you may also have to worry about
giving the lead to a specific opponent. How would you plan
the next example, in which you aré declarer at 6 spades
against the lead of the heart king?

YOUR HAND	DUMMY
♠ K Q J 8 7 6 3	♠ A 10 9
♡ 3	♡ A 7 6 5
◇ A 8 6	◇ K J 3
♣ 7 5	♣ A Q 9

Win dummy's ace, and ruff a heart in your hand (high, to
take care of a freak accident). Lead a spade to dummy's 9
and ruff another heart; lead to dummy's trump ace to ruff the
last heart. The position is now:

YOUR HAND	DUMMY
♠ K Q	♠ 10
♡ ——	♡ ——
◇ A 8 6	◇ K J 3
♣ 7 5	♣ A Q 9

You have stripped successfully; how do you endplay? To
lead ace, king, and a third diamond is wrong here, for you
are concerned with more than giving the lead to the enemy—
you must put your *right-hand* opponent on lead. If, instead,
your left-hand opponent is in, he can play *through* dummy's
clubs. Therefore, you lead a low club and play dummy's 9,
passing the lead to the correct opponent. He is helpless, for a
heart return lets you ruff in dummy and discard, a club return gives you a discard for your diamond loser, a diamond
return gives you a free finesse.

This device of ducking to put the proper opponent on lead
at the proper time (that is, after you have completed the
stripping process) is a common and useful one. However, it
requires, for guaranteed success, a high spot-card under the
honor—like the club 9 in the preceding example—so that you

can cover your opponent's card without wasting the honor. That is, with this combination:

YOUR HAND	DUMMY
6 5 3	A Q 7

you can duck successfully only if your left-hand opponent plays the 2 or 4 when you lead the 3. When a higher spot is played, it is pointless to duck, since the wrong opponent will be on lead. You may have to search for a different method of endplaying the proper opponent. Consider this deal:

DUMMY
♠ 5 4 3
♡ A 10 6
◇ K J 8
♣ 9 6 5 4

WEST
♠ K 10 7
♡ K Q J 5 3 2
◇ 6 4 3 2
♣ ——

EAST
♠ J 9 8 2
♡ 9 7 4
◇ 10 9 5
♣ Q J 10

YOUR HAND
♠ A Q 6
♡ 8
◇ A Q 7
♣ A K 8 7 3 2

Your contract is 5 clubs; the king of hearts is led. How should you play? Win the ace in dummy, and ruff a heart, starting to strip. Cash the ace and king of trumps. If *West* had the trump trick, you could play to the jack of diamonds, ruff out the last heart, cash your diamonds, and finally endplay him with the high trump. But East has the trump, and you cannot endplay *him*—he leads through your spades, not up to them. The ducking technique would be to play to the diamond jack, ruff the last heart, cash two diamonds ending up in dummy, and lead the spade 3. If East plays the 2, you can cover with your 6 to endplay West; but your spot is so low that East can set you by playing even his 8 on dummy's lead.

The best plan is to cash three diamonds, ending up in dummy, and lead the 10 of hearts. Do not ruff it, but throw away your 6 of spades. West is hooked—you have neither hearts nor diamonds in either hand, so a red-suit lead allows you to ruff in dummy and discard (you do not mind if East overruffs; this is his natural trump trick anyway). Therefore, West must lead into your A Q of spades. You have stripped the hand and endplayed him, passing the lead to the proper opponent by throwing a loser on a loser.

There are, then, four distinct methods for endplaying an opponent: with a high trump, with a loser in a suit in which your hand and dummy have the same number of cards, by ducking, by throwing a loser on a loser. In the following example, you can see all four techniques:

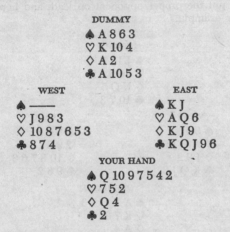

DUMMY
♠ A 8 6 3
♡ K 10 4
◇ A 2
♣ A 10 5 3

WEST
♠ ——
♡ J 9 8 3
◇ 10 8 7 6 5 3
♣ 8 7 4

EAST
♠ K J
♡ A Q 6
◇ K J 9
♣ K Q J 9 6

YOUR HAND
♠ Q 10 9 7 5 4 2
♡ 7 5 2
◇ Q 4
♣ 2

You are declarer in a contract of 3 spades, which East has incautiously doubled (he would have a better chance to defeat you if he had *fewer* high cards). The club 8 is led; you win the ace and ruff a club. Play to dummy's trump ace, and ruff another club. Now put East on lead with his trump king. He plays the king of clubs.

At this stage, you can make your contract in three different fashions. You can throw a heart loser, letting East hold the lead, and forcing a return in a red suit. Or you can ruff, and then play ace of diamonds followed by a low diamond—East is endplayed, forced to lead hearts. Or ruff and lead a heart, putting in dummy's 10 to duck the trick to East; he must then give you your ninth trick by playing hearts or diamonds.

The example above is an easy hand to make. You must take the precaution of ruffing out clubs, the only suit which

East can play safely. Then, you have four ways to pass the lead to him—with his high trump, by playing ace and then a low diamond, by ducking in hearts, by throwing a loser on a loser in clubs. Of course, you seldom have *all* these devices available, but one is enough—if it gives the lead to the right opponent at the right time.

The process of stripping to prepare for the endplay is usually simple—thinking of it is the hard part. However, there are occasional hands in which you are unwilling or unable to strip a hand completely. Then you must strip it as much as possible, put the proper opponent on lead, and hope for the best. For example:

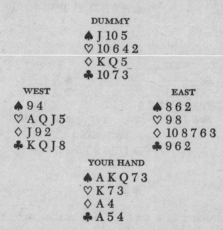

DUMMY
♠ J 10 5
♡ 10 6 4 2
◇ K Q 5
♣ 10 7 3

WEST
♠ 9 4
♡ A Q J 5
◇ J 9 2
♣ K Q J 8

EAST
♠ 8 6 2
♡ 9 8
◇ 10 8 7 6 3
♣ 9 6 2

YOUR HAND
♠ A K Q 7 3
♡ K 7 3
◇ A 4
♣ A 5 4

You become declarer at 4 spades after West has made a take-out double. The king of clubs is led; what is your plan? Leading up to the heart king is hopeless, as well as inelegant. You must contrive to force West to lead hearts to you—you must strip away the suits he can safely lead, and then endplay him. Throwing him on lead is not a problem if he has all the club honors, as is likely; you can duck the first club, win the second, and eventually endplay West with the third club. The difficulty is stripping the side suits. You can cash three rounds of diamonds all right, but you cannot cash three rounds of trumps. If you do, there are no more trumps in dummy, so when West is on lead with the club, he is not forced to play hearts—he can safely lead the thirteenth club. There must be trumps left in *both* your hands; then an off-suit lead will give you a ruff and discard.

Therefore, win the second club, and cash *two* high spades—your ace and dummy's 10. Play the three top diamonds, stripping this suit. Now lead the third club and pray. As you hoped, West has no spade to lead; a club lets you ruff in dummy and throw a heart loser from your hand, while a heart lead lets you make your king.

Thus, it is necessary to leave a trump in dummy when trying for a strip and endplay. If this means that you have to leave an enemy trump outstanding also, you must do so—perhaps the opponent that you endplay will not hold it. You may have to try for the same sort of partial strip in a side suit:

DUMMY

♠ A K 5
♡ A 8 7 2
♢ A K Q
♣ 8 5 2

WEST

♠ J 8
♡ K J
♢ J 10 6
♣ A Q J 10 9 2

EAST

♠ Q 10 9 6 3
♡ 10 3
♢ 9 7 4 3
♣ 6 4

YOUR HAND

♠ 7 4 2
♡ Q 9 6 5 4
♢ 8 5 2
♣ K 3

West, who has opened and rebid in clubs, leads the diamond jack against your ambitious 4 heart contract. Your only hope is to force West to lead clubs to you. Endplaying him will be easy, since he is almost certain to hold the trump king, but stripping is difficult, for how can you prevent him from leading spades?

Win the diamond, cash the ace of hearts, the ace and king of spades, and the two remaining diamond honors. Now give West his trump trick and cross your fingers. If he started with a doubleton spade, or if his remaining spade is the queen, he must now lead clubs to you. Of course, if he started with three small spades you will go down, but you have done your best.

The strip and endplay is the advanced play which comes up most frequently. And it is not difficult either to execute or to diagnose. Look back over all the examples in this section and see what they have in common: a dummy which will provide neither enough ruffs nor enough discards, whose long suit is generally trumps. Here you must plan to win tricks with your losers. Try it the expert way, making the enemy do your work for you.

• DEFENSE AGAINST PLAN THREE

When dummy has this friendly, toothless appearance—no menacing length, no dangerous shortness—your defense should take on a different tempo. In the last section on defense, when dummy had length which would provide discards, you were frantically busy: underleading aces, leading honors, shifting suits. Now, though, you must defend quietly; your main objective is to make safe plays, to avoid giving Declarer a trick. A "friendly" dummy is not necessarily weak in high cards, but it has no useful distribution. For example:

DUMMY
♠ A K Q 10 6
♡ K 6 5
♦ K Q
♣ A 9 5

YOU
♠ J 5
♡ J 4
♦ A 10 6 4 3
♣ Q 8 6 2

Dummy has opened 2 notrump; Declarer bid 3 spades; dummy raised to 4 spades. Partner leads the 2 of diamonds. Win the ace and *return a diamond*. Do not dream of switching suits; the diamond return is unproductive, but you are looking for safety. If you attack in hearts or clubs, it may well cost a trick. And there is no hurry, for where is Declarer going to discard losers? You can afford to sit back and wait for your tricks.

Contrast this with your position if Declarer had bid 3 *hearts* over 2 notrump and was raised to 4 hearts. Now you must certainly shift to clubs, for if spades is a *side* suit, dummy has teeth. Here, the shift to clubs is both safe and necessary; it is not that partner is any more likely to hold club honors, but that any club tricks that your side has must be set up at once, and that any club trick you lose by starting the suit would not have been won anyway.

The central idea is this: the side that first leads a suit will lose a trick by it about half the time. This will usually happen when neither side has a sequence of three honors in the suit led. Have you noticed how often your opening lead costs a trick? This is because you are starting a new suit without a sequence of honors.

Therefore, try never to break a fresh suit unless you have to; that is, unless you can see that Declarer's losers there can be discarded. When dummy has no menacing length, sit back, relax, and defend quietly. Here are three guides to quiet defense:

(1) Return the suit you or partner started. Even if opening that suit cost a trick, stick with it; do not cast about for another suit in which to lose another trick.

(2) If you cannot play the same suit, lead trumps. This is the suit in which the enemy figures to be most solid.

(3) If Declarer has started a suit, play it back to him. He has taken the curse off by leading it first.

Let us see a typical quiet defense:

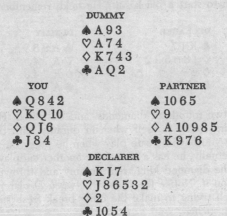

```
                    DUMMY
                   ♠ A 9 3
                   ♡ A 7 4
                   ◇ K 7 4 3
                   ♣ A Q 2

    YOU                              PARTNER
   ♠ Q 8 4 2                        ♠ 10 6 5
   ♡ K Q 10                         ♡ 9
   ◇ Q J 6                          ◇ A 10 9 8 5
   ♣ J 8 4                          ♣ K 9 7 6

                   DECLARER
                   ♠ K J 7
                   ♡ J 8 6 5 3 2
                   ◇ 2
                   ♣ 10 5 4
```

The contract is 2 hearts, and you lead the diamond queen (this is safer than a spade, since your side is more likely to have a sequence). Dummy plays low, partner signals with the 10. Continue with the jack of diamonds; dummy ducks again, Declarer ruffs. Now Declarer plays a trump to the ace and returns a trump—you are in again. First, cash your remaining high trump (so that you will not be put on lead with it) and exit with a third round of diamonds. Declarer ruffs, leads to the ace of spades, and returns a spade, finessing his jack. Win your queen and play a spade right back. Declarer must finally attack clubs, finessing dummy's queen; partner wins and can safely return either a club or a diamond. The contract is down one, because *Declarer* started both spades and clubs; your side played neither suit until Declarer broke it for you.

When this deal was actually played, your hand (West) attacked clubs, leading through dummy's A Q when in with the trump winner. Declarer ducked, and partner's king had to go up. Now partner's hand, not to be outdone, attacked spades. Declarer played low, West had to play the queen and it lost to the ace. Declarer made 9 tricks instead of 7, because the *defense* started both black suits. This defense was far too busy; it should have been obvious that Declarer had no discards, so that there was no need for attack. A dummy with even distribution should be a signal to both sides to try to force the other to start new suits.

Incidentally, do you see what Declarer could do to try to force you to start a black suit? He held, remember:

DECLARER	DUMMY
♠ K J 7	♠ A 9 3
♡ J 8 6 5 3 2	♡ A 7 4
♢ 2	♢ K 7 4 3
♣ 10 5 4	♣ A Q 2

You led two rounds of diamonds, and he ruffed. He should ruff a third round himself when in dummy with the trump ace. Now you have no safe play when he puts you in with a trump. Actually, he has a chance for another endplay later by playing the diamond king from dummy and throwing a losing club on it. Notice the contest between Declarer and defense, each trying to make the other break fresh suits. Here is another such:

```
            DUMMY
         ♠ A Q 7 3
         ♡ A 8 4
         ◇ J 8 3
         ♣ 10 5 4
  YOU
♠ 9 5
♡ K Q 10 6
◇ A 10 7 2
♣ Q 9 2
```

You open the heart king against the contract of 3 spades. Dummy wins, partner signaling with the 2. Now the diamond 3 is led to Declarer's king, and you take your ace. What now? Lead trumps, the safest play you have. Declarer draws two rounds of trumps, then leads toward the diamond jack; partner takes the queen. Bless him, he returns a heart; Declarer's jack loses to your queen. You cash the heart 10, then exit with the 10 of diamonds—ruffed by Declarer. Dummy is entered with a trump, and a low club is led to Declarer's jack. Win your queen and return *clubs*. This has been a perfect quiet defense: you have been in no hurry to dig out your tricks, but have waited for them, leading trumps or the suits Declarer has broken when no other safe play was available. You will set 3 spades two tricks.

Of course, Declarer did not play the hand very well. The full deal is:

```
              DUMMY
           ♠ A Q 7 3
           ♡ A 8 4
           ◇ J 8 3
           ♣ 10 5 4
  YOU                    PARTNER
♠ 9 5                  ♠ 6 2
♡ K Q 10 6            ♡ 9 5 2
◇ A 10 7 2           ◇ Q 9 5 4
♣ Q 9 2               ♣ K 8 7 6
              DECLARER
           ♠ K J 10 8 4
           ♡ J 7 4
           ◇ K 6
           ♣ A J 3
```

Let us see good play against good defense. First, Declarer lets you hold the heart king; if you continue hearts, he is home. However, you respect partner's 2, and shift—to trumps. Declarer draws two rounds of trumps, so that you cannot again have this safe play. Now he cashes the heart ace and puts you back on lead with a heart. You are forced to break a new suit; suppose you lead the 2 of clubs. Dummy plays low, partner the king, Declarer the ace. Declarer leads the 3 of clubs. You must be careful to hop up with your queen so that you have a safe exit card—the 9 of clubs. Declarer has forced you to start clubs, but now you force *him* to start diamonds. And the contract is down one.

Quiet defense, then, is the art of doing nothing. It is only when dummy has dangerous length that you must be spectacular. When dummy is flat, your only opportunities for brilliance come in defending against endplays. Here there are three techniques which may be useful. If you have a weak hand, so that partner is in danger of being endplayed, you must try to gain the lead at least once in order to play toward his strength. And if Declarer has stripped already and is preparing to endplay partner, you must put up as high a card as you can afford in order to make it difficult to pass the lead to partner's hand. When you have a strong hand and are about to be endplayed yourself, you have occasionally a desperation device available—throwing away the honor that Declarer plans to put you on lead with, hoping that partner can win the trick instead. Two of these techniques can be seen in this example:

DUMMY
♠ K Q 6 4
♡ 10 6 2
♢ 8 6 4
♣ K Q 6

PARTNER
♠ 8
♡ A Q J 7
♢ Q J 9 7
♣ J 9 5 2

YOU
♠ 7 5 2
♡ 9 5 3
♢ K 10 5 3
♣ 7 4 3

DECLARER
♠ A J 10 9 3
♡ K 8 4
♢ A 2
♣ A 10 8

On defense against 4 spades, partner opens the queen of diamonds. You must overtake with your king, to prevent Declarer from letting partner win. *You* must win a diamond trick to lead a heart to partner. If you do not overtake, Declarer ducks, wins the second diamond, and draws three rounds of trumps. Now he strips, ruffing the last diamond, and cashing the high clubs ending up in dummy. Here, the position is:

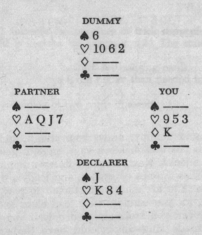

If declarer leads the 2 of hearts from dummy, you can recover by playing your 9, doing your best to prevent Declarer from cheaply passing the lead to partner. Note that if you follow lazily with the 3, Declarer puts in his 8 and partner is endplayed. Of course, Declarer can make his contract in the position above by leading dummy's *10*, and ducking. Then you would regret your failure to seize an entry in diamonds. Observe, too, how much work the *weak* hand may have to protect the strong hand against an endplay.

In the next example, you lead the king of clubs against an ambitious 6 heart contract:

```
                        DUMMY
                        ♠ A Q 4
                        ♡ Q 10 9 7 4
                        ◇ 7 4 3
                        ♣ A 10
        YOU                             PARTNER
        ♠ K 7 5                         ♠ J 9 6 2
        ♡ 6                             ♡ ———
        ◇ K J 10 5                      ◇ 9 8 6 2
        ♣ K Q 9 8 6                     ♣ J 7 5 4 3
                        DECLARER
                        ♠ 10 8 3
                        ♡ A K J 8 5 3 2
                        ◇ A Q
                        ♣ 2
```

Declarer wins in dummy, draws your trump, and ruffs out dummy's club (partner makes a vain effort to gain the lead by playing his jack). Next, Declarer finesses dummy's queen of spades, cashes the ace of spades, and leads a third spade to put you in. You are endplayed, forced to play diamonds into the A Q, for you cannot safely lead clubs and have no trumps. However, you are endplayed only if you have held on to your spade king—you should have thrown it away under dummy's ace! Partner could help you by signaling with his 9 when dummy's spade queen wins, but you should get rid of your king in any case. You should realize that the contract *must* make if you keep your king; your only chance is to throw it away.

Incidentally, Declarer can make it harder for you to make the correct play. If he cashes the queen and ace of spades *before* stripping the clubs, it is not so obvious that you must jettison your spade king to avoid the endplay.

All these techniques can be seen in our final illustration:

DUMMY
♠ Q J 9 2
♡ 7 6 5
◇ 7 4 3
♣ A Q 6

PARTNER
♠ 8 3
♡ A K Q 10 4
◇ K 10 9
♣ K 4 2

YOU
♠ 10 5
♡ 9 2
◇ J 6 5 2
♣ J 10 9 8 2

DECLARER
♠ A K 7 6 4
♡ J 8 3
◇ A Q 8
♣ 7 5

On lead against a 3 spade contract, partner cashes king, then queen, then ace of hearts (you signal high-low, then discard the 2 of diamonds to warn against a diamond switch). Partner leads a quiet trump, won in dummy; Declarer draws your remaining trumps with his ace. Now he finesses dummy's queen of clubs, cashes the ace, and leads the low club. If partner has retained his king, Declarer can throw his losing diamond and make his contract. However, you should have signaled with your club jack on dummy's queen—promising, like all signals with *honors*, a sequence headed by that card; then partner can safely throw his club king under dummy's ace. Suppose you both play properly—Declarer must ruff the third club, for he cannot let *you* gain the lead.

Next, he goes to dummy with a trump and leads the 3 of diamonds. If you follow low, he ducks with his 8, endplaying partner. However, if you are alert enough to put up your *jack*, his plan is foiled. He has to finesse his queen, and partner can safely exit with the diamond 10 after winning his king.

Actually, the best defense makes it unnecessary for you and partner to use such razzle-dazzle—signaling with jacks, throwing away kings, putting up honors in second seat. All you have to do is ruff partner's ace of hearts, seizing the lead at trick three to play a diamond through Declarer. This breaks up all endplays. And partner should not have led the ace of hearts, trusting you to ruff it; he should, instead, have led a *low* heart to the third trick, *forcing* you to make the right play.

• PLAN FOUR—WINNING EXTRA TRUMP TRICKS

The first three plans for playing suit contracts are by far the most common; one of them should be employed in close to 90 per cent of all deals. However, there is a rare fourth approach—producing extra trump tricks by ruffing repeatedly in your own hand. The usual occasion for this is when you have a long trump suit, but dummy is so short that you are unable to draw the enemy trumps. For example:

DUMMY
♠ A 7 3 2
♡ ——
♢ A K 8 2
♣ A 10 7 6 5

WEST
♠ K 9
♡ A J 9 3
♢ J 9 4
♣ K Q 9 3

EAST
♠ Q J 10 5
♡ 7 4
♢ Q 10 7 5
♣ J 8 4

YOUR HAND
♠ 8 6 4
♡ K Q 10 8 6 5 2   .
♢ 5 3
♣ 2

You opened 3 hearts, and partner showed his faith in you by raising to 4; West, who has less confidence in your ability, doubled and led the club king. You have five losers—three hearts, two spades—and no length or shortness in dummy to help you, no lower honors which might win through a finesse or endplay. Here, you must use the fourth plan.

Take dummy's ace, and ruff a club. Go to the diamond king, ruff a club. Play to the diamond ace, and ruff a diamond. Lead to the spade ace, and ruff the fourth round of clubs. Now you are down to the K Q 10 of hearts. Exit with a spade, and wait for two more trump tricks. You win six trumps in your hand, and four high cards in dummy, for 10 tricks in all. Your five losers—East's spades and West's trumps —all fall on the last few tricks.

Two other occasions for this plan are (1) a bad trump split, so that you cannot draw the enemy trumps, or (2) a concentration of trump honors in dummy which makes you unwilling to ruff there, and induces you to use your *own* shortness instead. Both can be seen in this example:

DUMMY

♠ A K 6
♡ 7 4
♢ K Q 7 3
♣ A Q 7 3

WEST

♠ Q J 9 8
♡ Q 10 3
♢ J 5
♣ J 10 9 5

EAST

♠ 5
♡ J 9 8 2
♢ A 10 9 4
♣ K 8 6 4

YOUR HAND

♠ 10 7 4 3 2
♡ A K 6 5
♢ 8 6 2
♣ 2

Your contract is 4 spades. West (who, impressed by your play on the last hand, does not double this time) leads the jack of clubs. Again, you have a lot of losers—two diamonds, two hearts, at least one spade. Here you can ruff one heart in dummy, but cannot ruff a second without losing an extra trump trick. However, if you think in terms of *winners,* your prospects improve: dummy has two high spades, one high club, one high diamond, and you have two high hearts; you can ruff once in dummy, and three times in your hand; and this adds to 10.

Suppose you win the club ace and ruff a club. Go to the spade ace; ruff a club. Lead to the spade king; ruff the last club. Cash ace and king of hearts and ruff a heart in dummy. Well played? No, not at all; you are going down, for the remaining cards are:

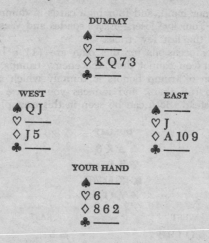

DUMMY
♠ ——
♡ ——
♢ K Q 7 3
♣ ——

WEST   EAST
♠ Q J   ♠ ——
♡ ——   ♡ J
♢ J 5   ♢ A 10 9
♣ ——   ♣ ——

YOUR HAND
♠ ——
♡ 6
♢ 8 6 2
♣ ——

You have won the first 9 tricks, but you will never get your
tenth trick with dummy's high diamond. When East wins his
ace, he plays the jack of hearts; West discards his diamond,
and has two high trumps left. In a normally played deal, Declarer has the long trumps at the close of play, and so is in
no hurry to cash his winners early. In contrast, when you are
using your trumps to ruff with, the *enemy* winds up with the
long trumps; therefore, you must be urgent about cashing
your side winners before the opponents discard their losers
—just as you are, more commonly, as a defender.

Thus, in the example above you should lead a diamond
after ruffing the second round of clubs. Cash dummy's diamond king as soon as you regain the lead, and then play as
described. Now you will win 10 tricks. On tricks twelve and
thirteen, West has two high trumps remaining, while East
has a high heart and a high diamond; four losers fall on 2
tricks.

The same technique of cashing side winners early must be
used in the second variation of this plan—the **crossruff**. Now,
you intend to ruff back and forth between dummy and your
own hand. Remember that the enemy will be discarding
while you ruff merrily with high trumps, so any side winners
you have saved will disappear on their long trumps. In the
deal below, you are in 4 spades, doubled by East with a roar
like a hungry lion's; West opens the diamond king.

```
                    DUMMY
                 ♠ J 5 4 3
                 ♡ ——
                 ◇ A 10 9 7 3
                 ♣ A 9 5 2

   WEST                        EAST
♠ ——                       ♠ A 10 8 7 2
♡ J 8 5 2                   ♡ K Q 10 7
◇ K Q J 5 4                 ◇ 8 6
♣ J 10 7 6                  ♣ Q 3

                 YOUR HAND
                 ♠ K Q 9 6
                 ♡ A 9 6 4 3
                 ◇ 2
                 ♣ K 8 5
```

Think about your winners: you have four in high cards, and
so need six in trump. Take the diamond ace, cash the ace
and king of clubs and the ace of hearts before the mice get
at them. Now ruff a heart in dummy, a diamond in your
hand, another heart in dummy, another diamond in your
hand. (On this third round of diamonds, East does not follow; if you had not cashed your high cards, he could discard
a club, but now he is helpless; his best play is to throw away
his last heart so that he can overruff dummy.) You lead a
heart and ruff with dummy's *jack*. If East overruffs with the
ace, you win all four trumps in your hand and two in dummy;
if he does not, you win three trumps in each hand. Either
way, you make your six trump tricks and your contract.

A third variation of ruffing in your own hand is called
dummy reversal. Here, you treat your hand as if it were the
dummy, using your own shortness to take ruffs; you treat
the dummy as if it were Declarer's hand, drawing the enemy
trumps with high honors there. Here is a simple illustration:

```
YOUR HAND              DUMMY
♠ A Q 8 6              ♠ K J 10 4
♡ 10                   ♡ A 7 3
◇ K Q 7 5             ◇ A 6 4
♣ 9 7 5 3            ♣ J 8 2
```

The king of hearts is opened against your 4 spade contract. Dummy has no helpful length, and its shortness is very hard to use. However, *your* shortness is readily available. Win the heart ace, ruff a heart. Cash the trump ace and lead to dummy's 10; ruff a second heart. Go to the diamond ace and draw trumps with dummy's honors. You make four trumps in dummy, two ruffs in your hand, and four side winners for 10 (11, if the diamonds break three-three). Notice that here there is no hurry about winning side tricks, because dummy, not the enemy, winds up with the long trumps. It is only when you are not going to draw the enemy trumps at all that you must cash out early.

In the example above, dummy's hand might easily have become declarer at spades, and then the proper play—ruffing in *your* hand—would be obvious and normal. Somehow it is harder to see when it is Declarer's hand that must ruff. Yet, when your trump suit is four-four, it is frequently correct to reverse the dummy. There are two signposts: (1) enough honors in dummy to draw the enemy trumps, and (2) flat distribution in dummy, and uneven distribution in your own hand. Actually, a dummy reversal may be indicated even when you have five trumps in your hand and three in dummy:

YOUR HAND	DUMMY
♠ A K J 8 2	♠ Q 10 5
♡ 10	♡ A 7 3 2
◇ K 7 5 3	◇ A Q 4
♣ 9 7 3	♣ J 8 2

Again, the king of hearts is led against 4 spades. Both indications of the dummy reversal are present: dummy is flat while *you* have the shortness; dummy's trumps are strong enough to draw the enemy's (if, as is normal, the enemy trumps split three-two). Thus, win the ace and ruff a heart. Cash ace of spades and lead to dummy's 10—making sure that the opponents' trumps split evenly. Ruff another heart. Go to dummy's diamond queen and ruff the fourth heart. Finally, lead to the ace of diamonds and draw the last trump with dummy's queen. You have 10 top winners, if you think to count them: three trumps in dummy, three ruffs in your hand, and four high side cards—five if the diamonds split. Still, this sort of hand must contain an optical illusion, for most declarers never see this line of play.

Another occasion for ruffing in your own hand is in the attempt to "finesse" against an enemy trump honor when there are no trumps left in dummy to lead. This is the rare, but spectacular, play known as the **trump coup.**

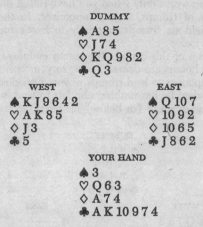

```
                      DUMMY
                    ♠ A 8 5
                    ♡ J 7 4
                    ◇ K Q 9 8 2
                    ♣ Q 3

   WEST                            EAST
♠ K J 9 6 4 2                   ♠ Q 10 7
♡ A K 8 5                       ♡ 10 9 2
◇ J 3                           ◇ 10 6 5
♣ 5                             ♣ J 8 6 2

                   YOUR HAND
                    ♠ 3
                    ♡ Q 6 3
                    ◇ A 7 4
                    ♣ A K 10 9 7 4
```

Your contract is 5 clubs (3 notrump or 5 diamonds would be easier) and the defense cashes king-ace of hearts and leads a third round, which you win. You play to the club queen, and back to your king—and West shows out. East's club jack is onside, but how can you finesse against it without a trump in dummy to lead through?

You can do it with a little luck, by getting down to East's length in trump. Go to the ace of spades and ruff a spade; play to the queen of diamonds and ruff another spade. Now cash ace of diamonds and lead to dummy's king. When East follows, you are home free, for the last two cards are:

```
                    ◇ 9 8

                                ♣ J 8

                    ♣ A 10
```

You lead the diamond from dummy; East must trump and you overtrump. Notice that if you had the third trump left in your hand:

```
                    ♠ 8
                    ◇ 9 8

                                ♠ Q
                                ♣ J 8

                    ♣ A 10 9
```

when you led the diamond from dummy, East would discard a
spade. You must ruff, and lead away from your ace to East's
jack. This coup works only when you have ruffed down to the
same number of trumps as your opponent. In the example
above, you held six trumps originally to East's four—so you
had to ruff twice.

A first cousin of this coup is the **trump endplay.** Here, the
enemy trump honors are *behind* yours, so your only hope is to
force your opponent to lead trumps to you. Obviously, he will
do this only when he has nothing else left to lead, so here too
you must come down to (or below) his length in trumps.

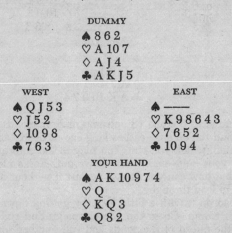

DUMMY
♠ 8 6 2
♡ A 10 7
◊ A J 4
♣ A K J 5

WEST
♠ Q J 5 3
♡ J 5 2
◊ 10 9 8
♣ 7 6 3

EAST
♠ ———
♡ K 9 8 6 4 3
◊ 7 6 5 2
♣ 10 9 4

YOUR HAND
♠ A K 10 9 7 4
♡ Q
◊ K Q 3
♣ Q 8 2

West leads the 10 of diamonds against your 6 spade contract.
You win in your hand, and cash the ace of spades, getting the
bad news. Lead to the heart ace; ruff a heart. Go to the ace
of clubs; ruff another heart. Next, cash two more clubs and
two more diamonds. The end position is:

WEST
♠ Q J 5

YOUR HAND
♠ K 10 9

Now you duck a trump trick to West, who must lead from
his Q 5 into your K 10. Again, this could not work if you have
four trumps at the end to West's three—then he would have a

side card to exit with. However, if you come down to his
level in trumps (and if his distribution is such that he cannot
ruff in early) you can recover from the bad break. It is always
profitable to make a slam, but to make one with two trump
winners behind you is triumph indeed.

• DEFENSE AGAINST PLAN FOUR

When Declarer is using his own trumps by ruffing, there is
not very much that the defense can do about it. Try not to
help him by leading suits which he can ruff; lead trumps
yourself if possible, just as if he were trying to ruff in dummy;
and try to withhold entries to dummy.

If Declarer is *cross-ruffing*, lead trumps whenever it is your
turn. When he has forgotten to cash his winners first, discard
your losers; when he has cashed his side high cards, discard
the suit that the hand to your right is ruffing, so that you will
be in a position to overruff. It is almost never profitable to
ruff ahead of Declarer or dummy (as opposed to *over*ruffing)
with a natural trump trick; it is usually better to discard. For
example:

DUMMY

♠ 10 7 5 3
♡ A J 8 7 6
♢ ——
♣ J 9 7 3

YOU

♠ A J 4
♡ 4 3
♢ K 7 2
♣ A 10 8 6 4

Against 4 spades, partner opens the king of hearts. Dummy
wins and leads a low heart, which Declarer ruffs. Next, Declarer cashes ace of diamonds and ruffs a diamond. A third
heart is lead from dummy. Do *not* ruff up with your ace of
spades to return a trump. Instead, discard your king of diamonds. Should Declarer try to ruff another diamond in
dummy, you can overruff and then play ace of spades followed by a low spade. The whole crossruff will collapse.

What you *can* often do on defense against any sort of hand
is to ignore Declarer's plan, disdaining to or despairing of

trying to counter it, and go after extra trump tricks of your
own. There are two different methods of establishing extra
trump tricks on defense; leading a suit in which you are
short, hoping for ruffs; leading a suit in which you are long
hoping to make *Declarer* ruff and thus promote your long
trumps.

Making Declarer ruff is usually the best chance to defeat
the contract when you hold four trumps. Consider this example:

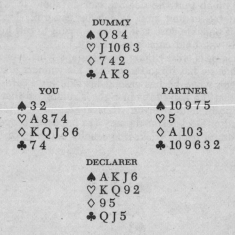

DUMMY
♠ Q 8 4
♡ J 10 6 3
◇ 7 4 2
♣ A K 8

YOU
♠ 3 2
♡ A 8 7 4
◇ K Q J 8 6
♣ 7 4

PARTNER
♠ 10 9 7 5
♡ 5
◇ A 10 3
♣ 10 9 6 3 2

DECLARER
♠ A K J 6
♡ K Q 9 2
◇ 9 5
♣ Q J 5

The contract is 4 hearts. Declarer has 10 tricks after drawing
trumps—three hearts, four spades, three clubs—but if you
defend cleverly, you can prevent him from drawing your
trumps. You lead the king of diamonds, followed by the queen
(partner signals 10-3), and continue a third diamond to
make Declarer ruff. Now Declarer is shorter in trumps than
you are; however, dummy still has enough trumps to draw
yours, so you have not yet accomplished your objective.
Declarer leads the heart king; you must hold off your ace;
Declarer leads the queen; you duck again. If a third round
of trumps is played, you can win, for Declarer has no more.
Now you play a fourth round of diamonds, forcing *dummy* to
ruff; your little trump becomes high, and you make your fifth
diamond to boot. Note that you had to hold off your ace until
the third round of trumps. Had you won it earlier and continued diamonds, *Declarer* would ruff; dummy would still
have enough length to draw your trumps.

This device of forcing Declarer to ruff, **pumping** the Declarer, as it is called, can be overdone. Remember, he wins a trick every time you pump him. If you hold four or five trumps with strong intermediates, for example: ♠ Q J 9 5 4 or ♠ K Q J 9, the odds are that you are helping Declarer by making him ruff. When he has this many *natural* trump losers, his best line of play is likely to be ruffing in his own hand anyway. The time you want to pump Declarer is when you have a large number of little trumps which are not busy guarding your honors—for example: ♠ 9 7 6 5 4 or ♠ A K 3 2. Then you can produce trump tricks which do not otherwise belong to you. When you do have the proper holding, though, start right out with the pumping defense with your opening, leading your longest suit regardless of your holding in it. For instance, on lead against 4 spades with:

♠ 10 7 5 3   ♡ 2   ◇ A Q 10 7 6 3   ♣ 10 2

open your ace of diamonds and continue with a diamond. Do not make the error of leading a short suit. When you hold four trumps, your prime chance for an extra trick is to pump Declarer. The whole hand might be:

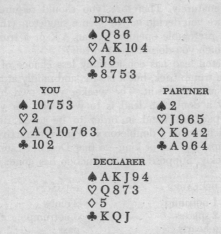

                DUMMY
              ♠ Q 8 6
              ♡ A K 10 4
              ◇ J 8
              ♣ 8 7 5 3

  YOU   PARTNER
♠ 10 7 5 3   ♠ 2
♡ 2   ♡ J 9 6 5
◇ A Q 10 7 6 3   ◇ K 9 4 2
♣ 10 2   ♣ A 9 6 4

              DECLARER
              ♠ A K J 9 4
              ♡ Q 8 7 3
              ◇ 5
              ♣ K Q J

Observe that a singleton (or doubleton) lead will do no good; Declarer can draw trumps, and concede the ace of clubs to take 10 tricks. However, diamond leads will be most effective. Declarer ruffs the second diamond, and is down to your size in trumps. If he draws your trumps, he is down two, for when partner gets in with the club ace, all your diamonds are high. Declarer's best bet is to stop playing trumps after drawing two rounds and discovering the bad split. He leads the king of clubs: you signal with the *10*, and partner must hold off his ace. Now Declarer must go down, for if he draws trumps he has too few tricks and if he plays another club partner will give you a ruff. Note your distributional signal —high-low in the suit Declarer plays—to show a doubleton.

Incidentally, do you see how Declarer could make this hand? He should discard a heart instead of ruffing the second diamond, thus preserving his trump length. A third round of diamonds does no good, for it can be ruffed in dummy. This is Declarer's principal counter against the pumping defense— throwing a possible loser instead of ruffing.

TRYING FOR RUFFS

When you are not long in trumps, you may want to lead a short suit and try for a ruff. A singleton lead has an excellent prospect—even if partner cannot win and give you a ruff at once, Declarer may have to ruin his line of attack by drawing trumps prematurely. Therefore, you should require a good reason before you decide *not* to open a singleton (this reason could be a preferable opening like an A K or a trump holding with which you do not want to ruff).

A doubleton lead has considerably less chance of producing an extra trump trick, but it is safe, and mildly attacking as well, if in an unbid suit. The weaker your own hand, the more likely a doubleton lead is to work out, for you need entries in partner's hand in order to be given ruffs. One feature which makes a doubleton lead more attractive is control in trumps—the ace or king—so that Declarer cannot draw trumps quickly. Suppose that the auction has gone:

DECLARER	DUMMY
1 notrump	2 clubs
2 spades	3 notrump
4 hearts	pass

You are on lead with:

♠ J 10 2   ♡ A 6 2   ◇ 9 3   ♣ A 10 7 4 3

Your choice is between the spade sequence and the double-ton diamond. (There is no reason to lead trumps, and in clubs you want the lead to come toward your ace.) Your hand is a little strong for a doubleton lead, since partner will be short of entries, but spades have been bid; the trump ace should persuade you to try the diamond opening. The whole deal is:

DUMMY

♠ Q 6 5
♡ Q J 7 3
◇ K Q 10 2
♣ 8 5

YOU	PARTNER
♠ J 10 2	♠ 9 8 4
♡ A 6 2	♡ 8 4
◇ 9 3	◇ A 7 6 5
♣ A 10 7 4 3	♣ J 9 6 2

DECLARER

♠ A K 7 3
♡ K 10 9 5
◇ J 8 4
♣ K Q

On the 9 of diamonds lead, dummy plays the queen—and partner must make the crucial decision. If he wins his ace and returns a diamond, you will not obtain a ruff; as you feared, partner is short of entries; and you cannot get him on lead again. However, if he ducks the first trick, signaling encouragement with his 7, you can play your second diamond when on lead with the trump ace; now he wins his ace and gives you the ruff.

How does partner decide that your lead is a *doubleton,* so that he must duck, not a singleton? He asks himself how many diamonds Declarer would hold if you have only one—here, the answer is four. On the auction, Declarer cannot hold four diamonds; therefore, your lead cannot be a singleton. This technique of holding off an ace opposite a doubleton lead is an important one, for the situation is fairly common.

One drawback of a doubleton lead is that Declarer (or dummy) may be short as well. However, this may put you in the desirable position of being able to overruff. For example, suppose on this auction:

DECLARER	DUMMY
1 heart	3 notrump
4 hearts	pass

you open a doubleton queen of spades from a very weak hand:

DUMMY
♠ K 7 6
♡ Q 8 6
◇ A Q
♣ K Q 9 5 2

YOU	PARTNER
♠ Q 3	♠ A J 10 8 5 4
♡ J 9 5	♡ 2
◇ 10 7 4 2	◇ 9 8 3
♣ J 8 6 3	♣ A 10 4

DECLARER
♠ 9 2
♡ A K 10 7 4 3
◇ K J 6 5
♣ 7

Your desperate lead may defeat the contract even though Declarer has a doubleton also. When Declarer lets you hold the trick, you continue with a second spade, partner wins his 10 and lays down the ace. If Declarer trumps with an honor, your jack of hearts will make a trick later; if he trumps with the 10, it wins a trick right away. Actually, though, Declarer should do neither; he must, instead, discard his losing club. This is always Declarer's best counter when he fears an over-ruff—throwing a loser instead of ruffing. However, partner can surely defeat the contract if he cashes his club ace before playing the third spade. Since Declarer will throw a loser instead of ruffing, the defense must cash all its winners before trying for an overruff.

In the following example, the defense must use both of the techniques already described, along with a new one. You start out by leading the top of your heart doubleton against a 3 spade contract:

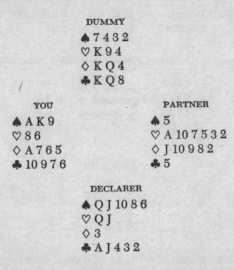

DUMMY
♠ 7 4 3 2
♡ K 9 4
◊ K Q 4
♣ K Q 8

YOU
♠ A K 9
♡ 8 6
◊ A 7 6 5
♣ 10 9 7 6

PARTNER
♠ 5
♡ A 10 7 5 3 2
◊ J 10 9 8 2
♣ 5

DECLARER
♠ Q J 10 8 6
♡ Q J
◊ 3
♣ A J 4 3 2

Dummy plays low, and partner ducks to preserve his entry. Declarer wins, and leads a sly 10 of spades; you take your king. Now be careful to cash your diamond ace, for you are going to try for an overruff, and so must take your side winners first. Next, lead your second heart to partner's ace; he returns a third heart. Here Declarer cannot discard a loser, since you have cashed out—he ruffs with the spade queen. Do *not* overruff. Simply discard, and wait for two tricks with your A 9 of trumps behind Declarer's jack. It is almost never proper to overruff with a natural trump winner. If you do here, you allow Declarer to force out your spade ace with his queen, which is what he intends to do with his queen anyway. In contrast, if you discard you have made Declarer waste his trump honor; and this produces an extra trick for your side.

There is another defensive method, similar to the overruff position, which can develop an extra trump trick out of thin air. This is to play a suit in which partner will ruff *ahead* of

Declarer (or dummy) and force the enemy to waste an honor. This is called the **uppercut**.

DUMMY
♠ 10 5 3
♡ A Q 7 4
♢ A K J 10 5
♣ 2

YOU
♠ K Q J 8 4
♡ J 10 8
♢ Q 3
♣ A 10 8

PARTNER
♠ A 7
♡ 9 2
♢ 9 8 4 2
♣ Q 7 5 4 3

DECLARER
♠ 9 6 2
♡ K 6 5 3
♢ 7 6
♣ K J 9 6

Against a contract of 3 hearts, you open your king of spades. Partner overtakes with his ace (this is almost always the correct action holding a doubleton ace) and returns his spade; you cash the jack and queen. You have 4 tricks on top, but no real hope for a fifth unless you can promote a trump winner. Therefore, cash your club ace and then lead a fourth round of spades. Partner ruffs up with his 9 of hearts, forcing out Declarer's king, and suddenly you have a sure trump trick.

Notice two features of this play. First, you must cash side winners before attempting it, for otherwise Declarer can discard a loser from either dummy or his own hand. Second, this device is a wild stab, made in an otherwise hopeless position. Never attempt it if there is some straightforward chance to defeat the contract with high cards; however, if you *must* produce a trump winner for the setting trick, this technique provides an extra opportunity.

The fact is that the whole line of defense which we have been examining—trying to make extra trump tricks—has an air of desperation about it. It has been consistently successful in our examples, but in real life it will not work so well. Partner will not always have the convenient entries to give you ruffs; Declarer will often be able to draw trumps, or will have solid enough trumps to prevent overruffs. Thus, doubleton leads are best when the enemy auction is so strong as to suggest that the defense cannot set the contract with high cards (like the auction in an earlier example which went: 1 heart—3 notrump—4 hearts). Normally, a suit in which you have some honors to set up is a preferable opening lead.

Of course, this does not apply to singleton leads. Here, the odds favor obtaining a ruff; and you may get two or three ruffs if you are both lucky and skillful. The skill comes in finding entries to partner's hand, and there is a special set of defensive signals for these situations.

When partner gives you a ruff, you frequently have a problem of which suit to lead next. You almost never want to play trumps, so you have two side suits to choose between (the *third* suit is the one you are trumping). The success of the defense usually hangs on this choice. Consider the following example, in which you open your singleton heart against the contract of 2 spades.

DUMMY

♠ Q 9 3
♡ K J 10 5
◇ J 9 4
♣ K Q 5

YOU

♠ K 7 2
♡ 2
◇ 10 8 6 3
♣ 10 9 8 6 2

PARTNER

♠ 6 5
♡ A 9 8 6 3
◇ A K 7
♣ J 4 3

DECLARER

♠ A J 10 8 4
♡ Q 7 4
◇ Q 5 2
♣ A 7

Partner wins the heart ace and gives you a ruff. Looking at all four hands, you can see the proper defense very plainly. You lead a diamond to partner's king; he returns a heart for you to ruff. You play to his diamond ace; he returns the fourth heart, and you must score your spade king on an over-ruff. However, it is not so simple at the table. Why should you guess to shift to diamonds—away from your ten, with the J 9 in dummy, into Declarer's possible strength—rather than to clubs, through dummy's strength? You should not have to guess, for partner can signal to tell you to shift to diamonds.

He does this with the heart he returns at trick two. You will ruff any spot-card that he plays, the 9, 8, 6, or 3, so the one he picks to lead is a signal. A *high* spot suggests that you shift to the *higher*-ranking of the two side suits; a *low* spot suggests a shift to the *lower*-ranking suit. Since partner wants a diamond switch, he returns the 9 of hearts, for diamonds is the higher ranking of the two remaining suits; if he held poor diamonds and the ace of clubs, he would have returned the 3 of hearts, asking for a switch to the lower-ranking suit. This is called the **suit-preference signal.**

Actually, a second type of signal is necessary for best defense in the example above. After partner has given you two heart ruffs, you put him on lead a third time with his diamond ace. Now *he* must guess: shall he play the fourth heart in the hope that you have a third trump and that it is high enough to overruff Declarer; or shall he, instead, play a diamond, hoping that you hold the queen? You can tell him to give you another ruff by using a signal known as the **trump echo.**

Ruff the first time with the trump 7; ruff the second time with the trump 2. This high-low signal in *trumps* means that you have a third trump and that you want to ruff with it. Suppose that you lead a singleton diamond against a heart contract and see:

DUMMY

♠ J 8 3
♡ 10 8 7 4
◇ A K 7 5
♣ K 2

YOU

♠ K 9 4
♡ 9 5 2
◇ 3
♣ Q 10 8 7 4 3

Dummy wins, and leads the heart 4—partner plays the queen, Declarer takes his ace. Now Declarer plays a low trump to dummy's 10 and partner wins the king. You should have followed with the heart 5 and then the 2, signaling high-low so that partner knows you want to, and can, ruff a diamond return. If, instead, you follow low-high—2, then 5—partner should *not* play a second diamond; you do *not* have a third trump to ruff with (or do not want to ruff).

Let us see another instance of the suit-preference signal:

DUMMY
♠ 2
♡ 7 5
♢ A K Q 8 7 4
♣ Q 10 6 2

PARTNER
♠ K J 8 6
♡ Q 10 9 6 4
♢ 2
♣ A 8 5

YOU
♠ A 10 7 4 3
♡ 8 3 2
♢ J 10 6 5
♣ 3

DECLARER
♠ Q 9 5
♡ A K J
♢ 9 3
♣ K J 9 7 4

Against a 5 club contract, partner (who has overcalled in hearts) leads his singleton diamond. Dummy wins, and leads a trump—partner is in with his ace, and must guess how to give you the lead. You must tell him by signaling with your jack or 10 of diamonds on the opening lead, asking for a shift to the *higher*-ranking spade suit. It is obvious that you cannot be telling partner to play another *diamond*, for he has no more and everyone knows it. In ruffing positions, your high signal (or *low* signal) is suit preference. Incidentally, partner could make sure by ducking the first trump trick. When he wins the second trump lead, you can signal with the spade 10, confirming that you want spades next.

Did you notice that Declarer can make his contract by breaking your communications before drawing trumps? He can cash A K of hearts and lead his jack; partner covers, and Declarer throws away dummy's singleton spade. Thus, Declarer loses the trick to the safe opponent; you can never gain the lead to give partner his ruff.

We have seen many different varieties of defensive signals in the course of this book. Be careful not to confuse one with another. The basic signal in bridge is the high spot-card to mean "Play *this* suit to me" and the low card to mean the opposite. A high spot-card can also mean "I have an even number of cards in this suit," but only when dummy's holding (or the bidding) makes it glaringly obvious that this is the long enemy side suit and you cannot want partner to attack it. A low spot-card can also mean "Shift to the lower-ranking suit," but only when partner has *no more cards* in the suit in which you are signaling, so that you cannot be telling him whether or not to continue playing it. If it is possible for a high signal to mean "Come ahead in *this suit*," then that is what it means. For example:

DUMMY

♠ 2
♡ Q 8 5
◇ J 7 4 3
♣ A Q 10 6 4

YOU

♠ A K 10 6 4
♡ 2
◇ Q 9 8 5
♣ 7 5 3

You open the spade king against 4 hearts, and partner signals with the 9. He is telling you to *continue spades*. (He may have four hearts to the king and want to make dummy ruff; or he may have clubs so securely stopped that he does not want any desperate switch to diamonds.) To have you switch to diamonds, all he had to do is signal with a *low* spade ("Do *not* continue this suit, partner"). You could figure out for yourself which suit to shift to.

Unless your opening lead is an obvious singleton, partner's signal says whether or not to continue playing the same suit—not which new suit to attack next. There is nothing in all of bridge quite so infuriating as to give partner a high card to tell him to continue, and then to see the wise look in his eye and the knowing smile on his lips as he shifts to a high-ranking suit. It has happened to me, and it will happen to you; but do not let it happen to your partner.

APPENDIX

Rules, Penalties and Proprieties

Contract bridge is a game with a strict set of rules. There is a National Laws Commission which publishes an official book of laws, covering proper procedure (and infractions) in the deal, auction and play. This is a fine book to own—a revised edition was issued in 1963. However, it is not really necessary as long as you are familiar with the rules and penalties governing the most common situations.

SOME IMPORTANT RULES

1. A redeal

There should be a new deal by the same dealer if it is discovered *before the deal is complete* that a card is exposed, or that the wrong deck was used, or that the proper procedure of shuffling, cutting or dealing has not been followed. There should be a redeal if it is discovered *before the play is complete* that one player picked up too many cards, another too few, or that the deck was imperfect. However, if one player discovers during play that he has only 12 cards and the missing card is found (for example, on the floor, or in the other deck) the deal stands, and the player is assumed to have held the card (that is, a revoke may be called if he has failed to follow suit when he could have done so with the missing card).

2. Changing a bid

A player may change a bid if he does so *without pausing*. (For example, your tongue slips and you say "1 heart I mean 1 spade." Your bid is 1 spade, and there is no penalty.)

3. Played cards

A defender's card is considered played if held so that *partner* could see its face. Declarer's card is considered played if he holds it face up touching (or near) the table. Dummy's card is considered played if touched by declarer, except to arrange the cards or to reach a nearby card. In addition, any card named by a player is considered played (but he may change an inadvertent designation if he does so without pausing). No played card can be changed, except to correct an illegal play (to correct a revoke, for example). However, if your *opponent* corrects such an error, you may change any card played subsequently to this trick.

4. Looking at tricks

After a trick has been gathered up and faced down, a player may inspect the cards—but not after either *he or his partner* has played to the next trick. Of course, when play is over, the tricks may be inspected to verify a claim of honors or of a revoke.

5. Dummy's rights

Dummy may call attention to leads out of turn or to revokes and may try to prevent them (tell partner where the lead is, or ask him if he has any cards in a suit when he fails to follow). However, he loses these rights and must be silent if he looks at his partner's cards or deliberately looks at either defender's hand.

6. Correcting the score

Any score may be corrected by mutual consent up until the time that the final net score of the rubber is agreed to. After this, the score stands as agreed.

COMMON INFRACTIONS IN BIDDING

1. A pass out of turn

If you pass when it was some other player's turn to bid, your pass is canceled, and the auction reverts to the proper player. The penalty depends on *whose* turn it was. If it was your right-hand opponent's turn, he makes any bid he chooses, and you *must* pass now. There is no further penalty. However, if it was your *partner's* turn when you passed, the penalty is greater. Partner may bid or pass as he chooses (but may not double or redouble), and you must pass for the rest of the auction. If partner then *passes* and you are the opening leader, declarer may call for or prohibit the lead* of any specific suit. (Exception: If you pass before any player has made an *opening bid*, the only penalty is that you must pass at your first turn.)

2. A bid out of turn

If you *bid* (as opposed to *pass*) out of turn, your bid is canceled, the auction reverts to the proper player, and there is a penalty. If no one else has either passed or bid (you mistakenly thought you were dealer and opened the bidding), then partner must pass for the whole auction, and you may do whatever you please at your proper turn. If someone else *has* bid or passed and you bid at your *right hand opponent's* turn, then (1) if he passes, you must repeat your bid and there is no penalty, or (2) if he takes any other action, you may do whatever you please and partner must pass at his *next turn*. Finally, if someone else has bid or passed and you bid when it is *your partner's* turn, then partner

---

* Whenever, in these rules, you are prohibited from leading a certain suit, you may not lead this suit for as long as you retain the lead. (You may not cash an ace, and *then* lead the prohibited suit.)

must pass for the whole auction and you may do what you choose; if partner is the opening leader, then declarer may call for or prohibit the lead of any specific suit. If you *double* or *redouble* at partner's turn, the rule is the same except that you may *not* double or redouble at your proper turn.

3. An insufficient bid

If you make a bid which is not higher than the previous bid (for example, bid 1 heart after your right-hand opponent opens 1 spade), your bid is canceled and you may do one of three things. (1) You may make the lowest sufficient bid in the same denomination (bid 2 hearts in the example above), in which case there is no penalty. (2) You may make any other sufficient bid—but you may not double or redouble—in which case partner must pass for the rest of the auction. (3) You may pass, in which case partner must pass for the rest of the auction; further, if partner becomes the opening leader, declarer may call for or prohibit the lead of any specific suit. These penalties sound fierce, but most often you will merely make your bid sufficient in the same suit and suffer no penalty at all.

In all three bidding infractions covered above, the non-offending side has the option of *condoning* the offense. For example, if you bid 1 club out of turn, or after a higher bid has been made, your *left-hand* opponent may, if he chooses, bid 1 diamond, simply accepting the irregular 1-club bid as normal. If he does take any action before attention is called to your offense, he waives all penalties and the auction now proceeds in normal order—your partner bids next. (Suppose you pick up your cards and say "pass," thinking that you dealt; but you did not. If your left-hand opponent passes after you do, no penalty may be called; the auction proceeds as if you *had* dealt.) However, if either opponent calls attention to your infraction, this demands that it be corrected; your left-hand opponent may no longer condone the offense.

COMMON INFRACTIONS IN PLAY

1. Exposed cards and penalty cards

Declarer may expose cards without penalty. If he drops a card accidentally, he need not play it. However, a *defender* is penalized for exposing a card in such a way that his partner could see it (or for naming a card in his hand) when it is not a legal play. Any such cards become "penalty cards."

A penalty card is left face up on the table, and must be played at the defender's first legal opportunity. If a defender has two or more penalty cards which can legally be played, *declarer* chooses the one to be played. And declarer has an option when the *partner* of a defender with a penalty card has the lead: declarer may, if he wishes, require or forbid the lead of the penalty card's suit. If declarer exercises this option, all cards of the suit he prohibits (or requires) led cease to be penalty cards and may be picked up.

2. Defender's lead out of turn

If a defender leads to a trick when it is not his turn to do so, declarer has two choices. (1) He can *accept* the lead, playing from his own hand or dummy, whichever follows after the offender. (If declarer does follow to the trick before attention is drawn to the irregular lead, then he *has* accepted the lead.) (2) Or, declarer can treat the card led out of turn as a penalty card. In this case, of course, declarer can exercise his option to require or forbid the offender's partner to lead the same suit; then the offender picks up his card and can play whatever he chooses in turn.

If the *opening* lead is made by the wrong defender, and declarer elects to accept it, dummy goes down before declarer plays. And if declarer spreads his cards, this accepts the lead and *he* becomes dummy. (He should not do this deliberately.)

3. Declarer's lead out of turn

If declarer leads to a trick improperly, either from his own hand or from dummy, the next opponent to play may accept the lead (and so does if he follows to the trick). However, if either defender calls attention to the improper lead, this demands that it be retracted—it can no longer be accepted. Now, if declarer has led from the wrong hand, he must, if possible, lead a card *of the same suit* from the proper hand. This is the only penalty; he need not play the card he led incorrectly. (If declarer leads at a defender's turn, and this lead is not accepted, there is no penalty.)

4. A revoke

If you fail to follow suit when you could have, you have revoked. Until *your side* plays to the next trick, you may (you *must*, if you become aware that you have revoked) correct your error. Of course, the opponents can then change any play they made after yours, and, if you are a defender, the card you played by mistake becomes a penalty card. Once your side plays to the next trick, your revoke is *established* and may not be corrected. Two tricks are transferred from your side to the opponents' and count as if won in play. However, you lose only those tricks won *after* the revoke (counting the trick of the revoke). That is, if your side won only one trick subsequently, you lose only one; if you won none, there is no penalty. And there is no penalty for a second revoke in the same suit by the same player.

There is no penalty for an established revoke by *dummy*—all players are responsible for seeing that dummy follows suit. (The same is true of a defender's *penalty card.*) No revoke on the *twelfth* trick is ever established—it is corrected if discovered. Then, the *partner* of the offender may be required by an opponent to play either of his two cards to the twelfth trick (if both could legally be played, and if he plays to this trick *after* the offender).

A revoke may be called until all players have abandoned their hands and the cards have been mixed together.

5. Disputed claims

Often, declarer will try to save time by claiming some number of the remaining tricks (if declarer shows his cards, this is considered to be a claim). The proper procedure is for play to halt temporarily. Declarer should leave his hand exposed and make a statement as to how he plans to play. The defenders may ask questions, and even show each other their cards; either one may require declarer to continue play.

Now, declarer must leave his hand exposed and play on. He must not vary from his stated line of play. And any doubtful decision (whether to finesse, whether to draw a missing trump, etc.) not covered by his original statement must be resolved in favor of the defending side.

When a *defender* makes a claim, he should show his cards to declarer only. However, if he exposes cards to partner in claiming, these do not become penalty cards; instead, declarer may treat all cards in the *other* defender's hand as penalty cards.

MORE ABOUT PENALTIES

1. Remarks and gestures

Obviously, it is illegal to give partner unauthorized information by remarks or gestures (for example, to say to partner, "lead trumps"; or to point to the score, reminding partner that your side has a partial). If the offense occurs during the *auction*, either opponent may require *both* partners of the guilty side to pass for the balance of the auction; and then if the offender later becomes a defender, declarer may call for or prohibit the lead of a specific suit whenever the offender's *partner* first is on lead. If the offense occurs during the *play*, offender's partner may be prevented from making a lead or play illegally suggested.

2. Assessing penalties

Any player (except dummy, if he has forfeited his rights) may call attention to an infraction of the rules. No bid or play should then be made until the players determine the facts and agree on the penalty (if they later discover that the penalty assessed was improper, it nonetheless stands). Either member of the innocent side may elect to waive the penalty; the two partners may *not* consult about the imposition of a penalty—if they do, they waive all penalties.

Should you waive penalties? Usually no, even among friends. Penalties are designed not as punishments, but to redress damage which your opponent may inadvertently have done. Of course, if it is glaringly obvious that you have not been damaged in any way, it is reasonable to waive a penalty. And it is courteous to waive a penalty if your side helped to induce the offense (for example, if by extraneous conversation during the auction you caused an enemy to bid out of turn or make an insufficient bid).

However, the safest policy is to exact almost all penalties. If penalties are frequently waived in your game, then awkward situations and arguments are bound to result when it is not clear whether, or how much, damage has been done to the innocent side. If you always go by the rules, there can never be hard feelings.

THE PROPRIETIES

The laws of contract bridge contain a section devoted to the proprieties of the game. Since bridge is played by human beings, not machines, situations arise which involve "ethics" rather than rules.

Ideally, all bids and plays should be made in the same manner and at the same tempo. All players should strive toward this, but, of course, it is impossible to realize completely. Long huddles, loud doubles, slow passes—these will give you information at the table that has nothing to do with the actual game. If this unauthorized information comes from *your partner,* you must bend over backward not to take advantage of it. However, if it comes from *an opponent,* you are entitled to use it at your own risk. And it is improper to attempt to deceive an opponent with mannerisms (for instance, by hesitating when you hold a singleton in the suit led).

In bridge, there is a great deal of partnership communication— in bidding, defensive signals, etc. It is highly improper to have special understandings with your partner of which the opponents are unaware. They are entitled to know just as much about the meaning of your bids and plays as your partner knows. If you are using some unusual convention in bidding or play, you must announce it to the opponents beforehand.

It is considered improper deliberately to violate a rule of the game. This means that you must not revoke consciously a second time in order to conceal a prior revoke; and it is unethical to bid out of turn or make an insufficient bid deliberately in order to bar your partner from the auction when you are afraid of his next action.

There is no penalty prescribed in the laws for violating any of the proprieties above. However, players who take flagrant advantage of their partner's mannerisms, or who have private understandings, or who intentionally violate the laws, get evil reputations. And soon enough they can find no one willing to play with them. You should be willing to give any opponent one bite, but against *constantly* unethical players your only defense is to refuse to cut into the same game again.

Chicago Bridge

Chicago is a form of bridge in which you play four deals instead of a rubber. It is designed for five- or six-handed games, so that no player who is out will ever have to wait for an hour or so until a lengthy rubber drags to a conclusion. In Chicago, the score is totaled after four deals; players who are out come in, and a new round is started.

In a five-handed game of Chicago (and in rubber bridge also), it is customary for each player to draw a card at the start. The one with the lowest card is out, the next-lowest is next to go out, etc.; thus, the rotation is established. After four deals, the player who was out replaces the one next in rotation. Usually, the two players to the right of the new dealer shift to produce new partnerships. Or, the four players may cut to establish partnerships on each round. In a *six*-handed game, the cut for rotation is the same but the two lowest players are out first, and will replace the next two lowest for the following round. Here it is usual to cut for partners on each round.

Each game is scored separately. A nonvulnerable game earns a bonus of 300 points (for example, if you bid four spades and make it, you score 420 points); a vulnerable game earns a 500-point bonus (for example, if you bid 3 notrump and make 5, you score 660 points). Vulnerability is determined by the number of the deal. For the first deal, neither side is vulnerable. On the second and third deals, the *dealer*'s side only is vulnerable. And for the fourth and final deal, both sides are vulnerable.

There is no bonus for a part score made on one of the first three deals—it carries over until wiped out by a game or until the four deals are over. If you complete a part score to make game, your game bonus is determined according to your vulnerability when you made the *last* score. A part score made on the *fourth* deal carries a bonus of 100 points.

If a hand is passed out, the deal does *not* shift; the same player deals again with the same conditions of vulnerability. This causes a change in strategy from rubber bridge. On the second or third deal, a player in the fourth seat after three passes will almost always open the bidding. The opponents are vulnerable and he is not; he opens to "kill" their vulnerability advantage. (In New York's Cavendish Club, perhaps the leading bridge club in the country, the rules are different: for the second and third deals, the dealer's side is *not* vulnerable and the opponents are. Thus the player in fourth position is vulnerable, and will not open light. The Cavendish rules seem to me to be superior, but they have not found general acceptance.)

Chicago scoring changes the odds on bidding game in certain

positions. When you are nonvulnerable and will become vulnerable on the next deal, it does not pay to bid a touch-and-go game; after all, a part score may be converted into a *vulnerable* game. Thus you will never stretch. In contrast, on the *fourth* deal the rewards for making game, compared to those for a part score, are greater than normal. So you tend to bid any game you can even sniff faintly.

Another change in the odds is for sacrifice bidding when nonvulnerable against vulnerable. In rubber bridge, you should hate to suffer a 500-point penalty to stop game—the vulnerability is the same for the next deal and you will probably lose the rubber anyway. But in Chicago, where the vulnerability changes with each deal, a nonvulnerable sacrifice of 500 points is a clear profit when the opponents are vulnerable.

If you play for stakes, you might note that Chicago scoring is somewhat inflated. That is, you are really playing for about 30% more than the same stake per point would be at rubber bridge.

Party Bridge

Party Bridge or **Progressive Bridge** is a popular form of competition in social (as opposed to tournament) bridge circles. How would you run such a game in your home?

Suppose there are 16 players—8 men and 8 women. Give each player an individual score or tally card. Have tables numbered from 1 to 4. Let the players choose their starting positions (or assign them), but each partnership should consist of a man and a woman.

First round: At each table, two mixed pairs play against each other. They cut, and high card deals first. Four hands are played and scored as in Chicago (see page 426). After the four deals, each player enters on his tally his total score and his opponents' total. (For example: WE, 820—THEY, 450). When all tables are finished, call the first change.

Changing: The winners at Table 1 stay there; the losers at Table 1 move to Table 4 (the highest number). At each other table, the *losers* stay put, while the winners move to the next lower numbered table (4 to 3, 3 to 2, 2 to 1). At every table, the partnerships shift—the woman who arrives at the table becoming the partner of the man who has remained there. And another round starts. Usually at least six rounds are played—each should take from 20 to 30 minutes.

Final Scoring: When the last round is over, each player totals all his scores and all his opponents' scores—the difference, plus or minus, is his score for the game. The highest plus is the winner, and you might have a consolation prize for the greatest minus too.

GLOSSARY

Above the line: Scoring of points other than those for fulfilling a contract (i.e., overtricks, penalties, bonuses).

Auction: (1) All the bids and passes made by the players; or the period during which they are made. (2) The game which preceded contract bridge, in which declarer's side received full credit for all tricks made, even overtricks.

Avoidance: Keeping a dangerous opponent from gaining the lead. (see p. 326)

Balance: Reopen the bidding when the opponents stop short, counting on partner for the missing strength. (see Chapter 8, Book II)

Balanced hand: A hand containing no very long or very short suit.

Below the line: Scoring of points won by fulfilling a contract.

Bid: (1) An agreement to win a specified number of tricks in a specified suit or notrump. (2) The statement of that agreement.

Blackwood Convention: The understanding whereby the bid of four notrump asks partner to show the number of aces he holds. (see p. 207)

Block: Interfere with the run of a long suit by causing a trick to be won in the wrong hand.

Book: Declarer's first six tricks, or, for the defenders, one trick fewer than enough to defeat the contract.

Broken sequence: Three cards of which the two highest-ranking are in sequence and the third is one card out of sequence (K-Q-10).

Business double: Penalty double.

Cash: Lead out winning cards.

Chicago: Four-deal bridge, as opposed to rubber bridge. (see appendix)

Come-on: A high card used as a signal to tell partner to play or keep playing that suit.

Contract: (1) The final bid of the auction. (2) The game which superseded auction bridge.

Convention: An agreement to give an unnatural or unusual meaning to a certain bid or play.

Coup: An unusual or spectacular (successful) play.

Cover: Play a higher card than the one played to a trick by right hand opponent.

Cross-ruff: To ruff back and forth between the partnership hands.

Cue bid: A suit bid which does not suggest that suit as trump, usually because that suit was first bid by an opponent, but occasionally because a different trump suit has already been agreed upon. In the second instance, a cue bid indicates an ace or void (rarely, a king or singleton) in the suit bid. (see p. 211)

Deal: (1) Distribute the 52 cards 13 to each player. (2) The cards so distributed.

Declarer: The player who plays both his own and dummy's cards.

Defender: An opponent of declarer.

Defensive bidding: Bidding by the side which did not make the opening bid.

Discard: To play (or the play of) a card in a suit which is neither the suit led nor trump.

Distribution: The way in which the 13 cards in a hand are divided among the four suits, or the way in which the 13 cards of a suit are divided among the four players.

Double: (1) Increase the penalties or trick score of the previous bid, should it become the contract. (2) The statement which does so.

Double finesse: Finesse against *two* missing cards.

Double jump: A bid two levels higher than needed to overcall the preceding bid.

Doubleton: A holding of two cards in a suit.

Down: Failing (by some number of tricks) to make a contract.

Draw trumps: Lead trumps until the opponents have no more.

Drop: Lead a high card, to which another hand must follow suit by playing a certain missing card.

Duck: Play a low card in preference to a very high one in following suit. (see p. 312)

Dummy: (1) Declarer's partner. (2) This player's hand, face up on the table.

Dummy reversal: The unusual line of play in which declarer ruffs with his own trumps and then draws trumps with dummy's. (see p. 403)

Duplicate bridge: A competition in which different players hold the same cards and have their scores compared.

Duplication: Overlapping (and thus wasted) values in the same suit, held by two partners.

Echo: The play of a high card followed by a low card used as a signal.

End play: Force an opponent to lose a trick by giving him the lead when he has no safe play. (see p. 337)

Entry: A card which will win a trick, thereby giving a certain hand the privilege of leading.

Equals: Two cards of the same suit which are adjacent in rank, or else now equivalent in value because all intermediate cards have been played previously.

False card: An abnormal play, made with intention to deceive.

Finesse: Attempt to win a trick (or establish a later winner) with a card which is not high, thanks to favorable location of a missing higher card.

Fishbein Convention: The understanding whereby the double of an opponent's 3-bid is for penalties and the overcall in the next higher suit is for takeout. (see p. 247)

Fit: (1) A suit in which two partners have together enough cards for a good trump suit. (2) The way in which the distribution or high cards of one partner's hand meshes with the other's hand.

Forcing bid: A bid which partner must not allow to become the contract.

Forcing pass: A pass made directly over an opposing sacrifice bid, which compels partner to bid on or to double—partner may not pass. (see p. 260)

Fourth hand: (1) In bidding, the player to dealer's right. (2) In play, the last player to follow to a trick.

Freak: A hand or deal with wildly unbalanced distribution.

Free bid: A bid made when partner would surely have an opportunity to bid again if one were to pass.

Game: (1) A unit of a rubber won by the first partnership to score 100 points below the line. (2) A contract which, if fulfilled, will bring a partnership to 100 points or more below the line.

Gerber Convention: The understanding whereby the bid of four clubs asks partner to show the number of aces he holds. (see p. 209)

Grand slam: A contract to take all 13 tricks.

Grand-slam force: The bid of 5 notrump used to ask partner to bid seven in an agreed-upon suit with sufficient trump honors. (see p. 222)

Guarded honor: An honor card with enough low cards in the same suit so that it cannot be dropped.

Hand: (1) The cards dealt to one player, or those he has remaining. (2) Any one specific deal of the 52 cards.

High card: (1) An honor. (2) A card which cannot be beaten by any card of the same suit now held by the opponents.

High-low: See Echo.

Hold off: Allow the opponents to win a trick when one could win it instead.

Honor: Any ace, king, queen, jack or ten.

Honors: Four of the trump honors in one hand (100 honors); all five trump honors or all four aces at notrump in one hand (150 honors).

Informatory double: See takeout double.

Jump bid: A bid at least one level higher than is necessary.

Jump shift: A single jump bid in a new suit made by a player who has previously bid a different suit or whose partner has done so.

Landy Convention: The understanding whereby the overcall of two clubs after an opponent opens with one notrump is for takeout. (see p. 239)

Lead: Play the first card to a trick; such a card.

Leave in: Pass, rather than *take out*, partner's double.

Level: The number of tricks bid.

Long cards: Low cards which become high because the opponents have no cards remaining in the same suit.

Loser: A card which may be captured by a higher card of the same suit held by an opponent.

Major suit: Spades or hearts.

Make: Win in play the number of tricks bid (or specified).

Match-point: (1) Unit of scoring in duplicate bridge, won by surpassing the score of another pair holding the same cards. (2) Duplicate Bridge.

Maximum: Having the greatest possible values for the bid made.

Minimum: Having the least possible values for the bid made.

Minor suit: Clubs or diamonds.

Negative response: A bid which denies strength, made in answer to a forcing bid from partner.

New suit: A suit which has not previously been bid.

Nonvulnerable: Not having scored a game.

Off side: (A card which is) in unfavorable position for a winning finesse.

On side: (A card which is) in favorable position for a winning finesse.

On score: Having a part score towards game.

Opening bid: The first bid of the auction.

Opening lead: The lead to the first trick.

Optional double: A takeout double which partner may well leave in, usually because it is made over a high bid.

Overcall: (1) Bid a suit after an opponent's opening bid, before partner enters the auction. (2) Such a bid.

Overruff: Ruff a trick with a higher trump after another player has ruffed also.

Overtrick: A trick made in excess of the contract.

Overtrump: See Overruff.

Partial: Part score.

Part score: (1) A score below the line of fewer than 100 points. (2) A contract which will earn such a score if fulfilled.

Pass: Make no bid, double or redouble.

Passed hand: A player who has passed when he could have opened the bidding instead.

Passed out: (A deal) thrown in because all four players in succession passed.

Penalty: (1) Score earned by defenders who set declarer. (2) After an infraction of the rules, the handicap placed by law on the offending side.

Penalty card: A card illegally exposed by a defender, left face up in front of him.

Penalty double: A double which is made in the expectation that the opponents will go down (as opposed to a takeout double).

Points: (1) Units of scoring. (2) Units of hand valuation, based on honor cards, distribution or both.

Preemptive bid: A high bid made not to show strength but to make it difficult for the opponents to compete.

Preference: A bid which chooses between two trump suits suggested by partner, not necessarily showing support.

Psychic bid: A bluff bid based on nonexistent values.

Pump: Shorten an opponent's trump holding by forcing him to ruff. (see p. 409)

Quantitative try: A bid which asks partner to go on (usually to slam) if he holds maximum values, no matter where.

Quick tricks: High cards or combinations which will probably win tricks the first or second time a suit is played.

Raise: (1) A bid in the same suit (or notrump) as partner's last bid. (2) To make such a bid.

Rebid: (1) A player's action at his second turn to bid. (2) Bid one suit twice.

Redouble: Multiply by two the value of the trick score or of the penalty score after an opponent has doubled.

Respond: Make a bid not independently, but in answer to some action by partner.

Responder: The partner of the opening bidder.

Reverse: Rebid in a new suit higher in rank than one's first suit, and at a higher level. (see p. 182)

Revoke: Fail to follow suit when holding a card of the suit led.

Roman Blackwood: A variation of the Blackwood Convention. (see p. 208)

Rubber: (1) A series of deals which ends when one side wins two games, after which the score is totaled. (2) The final game of this series, for winning which a bonus is scored.

Ruff: Play a trump when another suit is led.

Rule of 11: A principle which obtains when the lead was the fourth-highest card of a long suit: subtract the spot led from 11; the remainder is the number of cards of the same suit not in the leader's hand which are higher than the one he led.

Rule of 500: A principle of preemptive bidding: to lose no more than 500 points (two tricks doubled vulnerable, or three tricks doubled nonvulnerable) even if partner contributes no additional winners.

Run a suit: Keep on playing winning cards of one suit.

Sacrifice: Overbid deliberately, expecting to go down, but to lose less in penalties than the value of an opposing contract. (see Chapter 6, Book II)

Second hand: (1) In bidding, the player to dealer's left. (2) In play, the player who is second to follow to a trick.

Separate suits: Two suits which do not adjoin in rank, so that both suits could be bid at the same level if partner responds in a suit which ranks in between.

Sequence: Two, or more commonly *three*, cards consecutive in rank.

Set: (1) Defeat a contract. (2) The score for defeating a contract.

Set up: Establish (a long suit, or honors) as winners, by forcing out superior enemy cards.

Shift: Play a different suit from the one started by the partnership.

Short club: The opening bid in a three-card club suit. (see p. 178)

Shut-out bid: A preemptive bid.

Side suit: (1) A suit other than the trump. (2) A four-card or longer suit held along with a longer one bid first.

Signal: A play, or sequence of plays, which is given a specific conventional meaning by a partnership.

Sign-off: A bid which is intended to discourage partner from bidding on.

Singleton: A holding of only one card in a suit.

Slam: A contract to take 12 or 13 tricks.

Small slam: A contract to win 12 tricks.

Solid suit: A suit which can be run without loss.

Split honors: Play one of several honors in sequence when following to a trick as second hand.

Spot card: A card other than an honor.

Squeeze: Force an opponent to discard a vital card thereby causing him to lose a trick.

Stayman Convention: The understanding whereby the bid of two clubs over partner's one notrump opening asks him to bid a major suit. (see p. 199)

Stopper: A card in the opponents' suit which will win a trick.

Strip: Play as Declarer so that neither dummy nor declarer's hand has any card remaining in a certain suit or suits.

Strong hand: A hand which has more values than those needed for the bid made.

Suit-preference signal: A signal which tells partner not whether or not to continue the suit of the card played, but which suit to switch to. (see p. 416)

Support: (1) Enough cards in partner's suit to warrant a raise. (2) A bid which shows such values.

System: A complex of partnership understandings which define the meaning given to many different bidding sequences.

Takeout: (1) A bid in a different denomination from that bid by partner. (2) A bid which forces partner to bid a new suit.

Takeout double: A double made in the expectation that partner will respond by bidding a suit or notrump, as opposed to a penalty double.

Temporizing bid: A bid made in an unplayable suit, in order to show strength or mark time before suggesting where to play the contract.

Tenace: Two honors not in sequence.

Third hand: (1) In bidding, dealer's partner. (2) In play, leader's partner.

Top of nothing: (The lead of) the highest of worthless cards.

Touching suits: Suits adjacent in rank (♠ ♡, ♡ ◇, ◇ ♣).

Trap pass: A pass made with a strong hand in the expectation of later making a penalty double.

Trick: Four cards played in succession, one from each hand.

Trump: (1) The suit named in the contract. (2) Any card of that suit (which ranks higher than any card of another suit). (3) Ruff.

Trump coup: The unusual play in which declarer forces a defender to ruff and be overruffed, thereby capturing a trump honor. (see p. 405)

Trump echo: The high-low signal used in the trump suit to indicate possession of another trump. (see p. 416)

Unbalanced hand: A hand containing a very long or a very short suit.

Undertrick: A trick bid, but not taken in play.

Unguard: Discard a small card so that an honor is no longer guarded.

Unusual notrump overcall: An overcall in notrump used as a take-out bid, usually asking partner to bid a minor suit. (see p. 224)

Uppercut: As a defender, ruff ahead of declarer or dummy, forcing that hand to overruff with a high trump, and thus producing a trump winner for partner. (see p. 414)

Void: The holding of no cards in a suit.

Vulnerable: Having scored one game.

Weak jump overcall: A jump overcall used, by partnership agreement, as a preemptive bid. (see p. 231)

Winner: A card which cannot be captured by a higher card of the same suit held by an opponent.

Work count: The 4-3-2-1 valuation of honor cards.

Yarborough: A hand which contains no honor card.

CONTRACT BRIDGE SCORING

A. TRICK POINTS FOR MAKING A CONTRACT

(below the line)	First odd trick	Each subsequent trick
Notrump	40	30
Spades or hearts.......	30	30
Clubs or diamonds.....	20	20

Game: 100 or more points. All trick points are multiplied by two in doubled contracts, by four in redoubled contracts. (Overtricks are scored above the line as subsequent tricks, or as bonus points when the contract is doubled or redoubled, in which case see "B2" below.)

B. BONUS POINTS (above the line)

1. For setting a contract

	NUMBER OF UNDERTRICKS			
UNDOUBLED	1	2	3	Each add'l.
Nonvulnerable declarer ...	50	100	150	50
Vulnerable declarer	100	200	300	100
DOUBLED				
Nonvulnerable declarer ...	100	300	500	200
Vulnerable declarer	200	500	800	300
REDOUBLED				
Nonvulnerable declarer ...	200	600	1000	400
Vulnerable declarer	400	1000	1600	600

2. For making a doubled or redoubled contract: 50

In addition, for each overtrick:	Doubled	Redoubled
Nonvulnerable declarer	100	200
Vulnerable declarer	200	400

3. Honors (can be scored by any player)

Four trump honors in one hand: 100
All five trump honors in one hand: 150
All four aces in one hand at notrump: 150

4. Slams bid and made

	Small slam	Grand slam
Nonvulnerable declarer	500	1000
Vulnerable declarer	750	1500

5. Rubber bonus

For winning a two-game rubber: 700
For winning a three-game rubber: 500

6. Unfinished rubber

One game: 300   Part score: 50

NOTE: A double or redouble does not increase the bonus for honors, slam, or rubber.

POINT-COUNT REMINDERS

HIGH CARDS
Ace .... 4 points
King .... 3 points
Queen .... 2 points
Jack .... 1 point

SHORT SUITS After finding a good trump suit, add—

3 points–for void in side suit
2 points–for singleton in side suit
1 point –for doubleton in side suit

LONG SUITS Add one point for every card over the fourth in any suit.

POINT RANGES TO REMEMBER
6– 9 .... minimum response
10–12 .... strong response
13–16 .... minimum opening
17–19 .... strong opening
20–21 •• .... maximum opening
22–up .... two-bid
16–18 .... 1 NT opening
22–24 .... 2 NT opening
25–27 .... 3 NT opening

MAGIC NUMBERS
Total points of partnership   *You should bid*

20–25 .... part score
26 .... game in notrump, hearts or spades
29 .... game in diamonds or clubs
33 .... small slam
37 .... grand slam